A NEED TO KNOW

A NEED TO KNOW

The Clandestine History of a CIA Family

H. L. GOODALL JR.

WALNUT CREEK, CALIFORNIA

Left Coast Press, Inc.
1630 North Main Street, #400
Walnut Creek, California 94596
www.lcoastpress.com

ISBN: 1-59874-041-5
Library of Congress Control Number 2005928675

Printed in the United States of America

The paper used in this publication meets the minimum requirements of American
National Standard for Information Sciences—Permanence of Paper for Printed
Library Materials, ANSI/NISO Z39.48—1992. ∞

05 06 07 08 5 4 3 2 1

For NICOLAS SAYLOR GOODALL *and* SANDRA GOODALL

In loving memory of HAROLD LLOYD GOODALL *and* NAOMI SAYLOR GOODALL

"Every important episode of the cold war has a clandestine history."
Thomas Powers

"All my creative life has been a slow return to the past. But the closer the writer goes to the truth of his life, the more dangerous it becomes."
Leslie Epstein

"Perhaps every story worth telling is a dare, a kind of pornography, composed of whatever we think we're not supposed to say, for fear of being drummed out, found out, pointed out."
Laurie Stone

"In the world of espionage, as elsewhere, absolute secrecy corrupts absolutely."
Frederick P. Hitz

"Toxic secrets poison our relationships with each other. . . . Key family stories remain untold and unavailable. These are secrets that take a powerful toll on relationships, disorient our identity, and disable our lives."
Evan Imber-Black

CONTENTS

PREFACE

I WROTE THIS BOOK BECAUSE I COULD NO LONGER NOT WRITE IT. I COULD no longer not write it because I didn't want to lie to my son or evade the questions my wife continued to ask me about my father. My father— H. Lloyd Goodall—the man I grew up with but never knew; the tall, slender, attractive man who always "worked for the government"; the kind man with gray-green eyes and a war-scarred body who kept deep secrets and found it hard to smile; the "old" man, the broken man, who died mysteriously at the age of fifty-three; the man who left me as the sum total of my inheritance a diary, a bible, and a copy of *The Great Gatsby*.

I had been running away from the truth—from *our* truth—forever. Or so it seemed.

In researching my father's mysterious life I also discovered my mother: Naomi May (Alexander) Saylor Goodall. I say discovered her because she, too, was a woman who kept secrets, most of them to protect my father's identity but others to guard the true story of her own life, her own identity. I grew to admire her far more than I did when she was alive, and to deeply regret and then to grieve for all that had been lost in those empty spaces and long silences between us. It was a loss also born of secrecy, both hers and my father's. And, I know now, of my own.

Writers of memoirs, if they are honest, inevitably uncover themselves. We find our part in the family drama and learn to see anew the situations in which our own complicity in the drama had been previously obscured or overlooked or merely forgotten. In a family defined by secrets, we *all* have secrets. We all learn to dwell within them. We craft our lives, our relationships, and our patterns of communication with others out of them, at least until we learn how to deeply question ourselves and become accountable for our own role in how things happened and how they turned out.

Secrets have consequences for the self. And for the stories we tell.

• •

I'd like to believe that when my father gave me my inheritance he was also giving me permission to investigate and to write about his life. But that is only what I'd *like* to believe.

I'd also like to believe that my mother wouldn't mind the disclosures I make about her own secret world. But I doubt that is true. My mother was a proud woman who, as all of us do, created an identity and managed it throughout her lifetime. Investigating her life and writing about it, even two decades after her death, feels a little like tiptoeing guiltily across her grave.

I tell myself it's a good thing that I waited so long to write this story because all of the principal characters and most of the minor ones in it are dead. It's also a good thing because the dead can't disagree with you. No doubt there are parts of the account, and of the perspective I provide, that would provoke disagreement from my mother, my father, James Jesus Angleton, Frank Rizzo, or Gilbert Hovermale. Contentious facts are part of the inevitable legacy of secrecy as much as they are the inevitable legacy of family stories.

How we live our lives, and what that means, is a matter of perspective. Stories about lives inherit perspective and use it to frame the tale. You can never *really* know the "whole truth," no matter how much you think you are entitled to know it or feel that you need to know it. The story is always defined by its framing, by the spaces between the words, by doubts about the words, by official denials by government agencies, and by a lingering suspicion that no matter how hard you've worked to get it right, no matter how much evidence you've assembled or corroboration you've sought, there probably is no one "right" to get.

But I do believe I got most of it right.

Nevertheless, it is important for readers to remember that this is a *story* of cold war history written from observation and memory. It is accompanied by evidence assembled from other histories, other scholarship, and other people's memories, but that doesn't make it any less of a story. It just makes the story seem more true. But "more true" is still likely to be contentious. Contentious or not, it is as true a story as I know how to tell about my experience growing up in a cold war family defined, and ultimately ruined, by secrecy.

Someone whose friendship I value asked me what possible good I hoped to accomplish by telling this story now. The clear implication was that there wasn't any good that would come of it. He, too, had been a cold warrior and an intelligence officer. The story I was telling was familiar to him.

The easy answer was that I wanted to tell the story because my parents deserved a better, more truthful account than I had previously assigned to them. I wanted to pass along their story to my son. But that was the easy answer. The harder answer was still buried inside of me.

Then it happened. One late afternoon in a cool Carolina November in 2002, while driving home from work and listening to a Bob Edwards interview with Pat Conroy on NPR, I heard the author speak words that opened up something buried so deeply inside of me for so long that I didn't know it was there. Conroy was talking about his troubled relationship with his own father, the man clearly depicted as a monster in his novel *The Great Santini*. He said that in the beginning he thought he was writing about his father because he hated him. But what he discovered was that by writing about him, he developed a relationship with him. That simple sentiment stunned me.

I didn't hate my father and I never had. I felt sorry for him and alienated from him. But when I heard Conroy speak, I realized that I, too, wanted to have a relationship with him and with his life as much as I wanted my son to have a story about him.

The relationship I had with my father, and with my mother, had not been enough.

The time I spent with them had not been enough.

They died before we had a fair chance to finish our conversations.

I missed my father. I missed my mother. I missed the truth of them in my life.

To get to the truth of their lives, I had to open up their secrets, the secrets that had poisoned my relationship to them but that now may heal it. And, perhaps, to help others find in my story a way to understand their own.

That is my hope. That is my exigency.

That is my reason for writing *A Need to Know*.

This book was written because of (then) unanswerable questions asked by my son, Nicolas Saylor Goodall, and at the consistent encouragement of my wife, Sandra Goodall. They felt I owed it to my parents to record their lives within the context of cold war history and culture. They also believed I owed it to myself to complete a personal story line that had been dramatically and (at the time) inexplicably interrupted by my father's mysterious death on March 12, 1976. Sandra and Nic contributed significantly to the research, writing, living, traveling, relocating, and editing that intermingled with and resulted in this story. Although neither of them could have envisioned the sort of book that emerged from our collaborative journey, I find I cannot fully thank them in any other way than to say, Here it is.

I have also been assisted in my research by a wide variety of interested parties, some of whom have asked to remain nameless, but others I readily acknowledge here: Charles (Stu) Kennedy, Clarence and Martha Bray, Lloyd Mitchell, Lonnie Athens, Art Bochner, Carolyn Ellis, Eric Eisenberg, Norman Denzin, Richard Hesston, Larry Kolb, Bob Krizek, Paaige Turner, Kathleen Farrell, Ron Pelias, Nick Trujillo, Bryan Taylor, Anita Vangelisti, Harvey Wiener, Roger Winton, Drew Thompson, Stew Auyash, Pete Kellett, Joyce Ferguson, Steve and Lindsley Smith, Carl Lovitt, Christopher Poulos, Jordan Halstad, Jess Alberts, Angela Trethewey, Kelly McDonald, Steve Corman, John Parsons, Sarah Amira de la Garza, Ben Broome, Karen Hays, Belle Edson, Michelle Brennan, Rosemary Carpenter, Mark Killpack, Warren Bills, Bill Hastings, Ansel Miller, Sara Levin, Betty Ann Adkins, Ruanna Hess, Shirley Collis, Margaret Grafeld, William P. McGlynn, Sharon Wilkinson, Kathryn I. Dyer, Kris Acheson, Chris Carey, Kristin Bervig Valentine, Gene Valentine, Tom Frentz, Chris and Alice Waagen, Mic Fenech, Robin Clair, Dr. David Goodall, Ernie Calderon, Scott Gastory, and Ellie Sugar.

I would not be publishing this book were it not for the enthusiasm shown for the original manuscript by Mitch Allen and the support his talented team (Jennifer R. Collier, Rachel Fudge, Rebecca Freed, Briar Levit, and publicist Kathleen Meyer) has offered to me throughout the publication process.

Although no book reaches print as a solo effort, and there is much love and comfort to be gained from the support of family, friends, colleagues, and the occasional kindness of relative strangers, in the end I own the sole responsibility for any errors or omissions that may be found in these pages.

Harold Lloyd Goodall Jr.
Chandler, Arizona
September 2005

MY FATHER DIED, EITHER IN VIRGINIA OR MARYLAND, AT THE AGE OF fifty-three, on the night of March 12, 1976. My mother told me that he died at home in his bed in Hagerstown, Maryland, but the Social Security Death Index indicates that he was pronounced dead in Virginia, although it doesn't say *where* in Virginia.

I had doubts, even then, that he died at home.

The reason for his death was a mystery.

My mother said that she requested an autopsy because three days before he died he had been told that he was run down due to a bad cold and just needed some bed rest. He was given "a shot of something" and sent home. A doctor he saw at the Veterans Administration hospital supposedly gave him this diagnosis and the shot, but my mother couldn't recall the name of the doctor, and the hospital records do not show that he had any appointments in March.

Nor did I ever see an autopsy report. One year later, close to the anniversary of his death, my mother told me that she had been informed—by "the government"—that he had died of multiple bleeding abscesses on both lungs. This was about the time of a news report that Legionnaires' disease was responsible for the deaths of several men in Philadelphia, all veterans, all of whom had also died of multiple bleeding abscesses on their lungs. My mother claimed that "the government" now believed that my father, too, had died of Legionnaires' disease.

That may or may not be true.

My mother never showed me the letter from "the government" that supposedly provided her with this information. She told me she had thrown it away. I have no doubt that she had done precisely that, if, in fact, there had ever been a letter in the first place. But by then, by March of 1977, I was so disillusioned with the idea of truth in relation to my father's life, much less his death, that I didn't pursue it.

He had led a secret life. And even in death, she kept his secrets.

• •

My disillusionment with the truth about my father began the day after his funeral. Gilbert Hovermale, my parents' attorney, gave me a key to a safe-deposit box and said, "Your father wanted you to have this."

My mother and I were in Hovermale's small, cramped office for the reading of my father's will. My mother was in bad shape, barely functioning in the daylight over the heavy sedation required to get her to sleep, and I worried that she might commit suicide. She had told me, repeatedly, "I just want to die."

I took the key, put it in my pocket, and didn't think any more about it. In fact, I didn't visit the bank to open the deposit box until two or three days later, and I only went then because it was on my way to the pharmacy.

I don't know what I expected to find. Papers, perhaps. Another insurance policy, maybe.

Instead I found two items. There was a diary and a dog-eared, heavily marked-up copy of F. Scott Fitzgerald's novel *The Great Gatsby*. These two items, along with the family bible at home, were what my father wanted me to have. Why?

I opened the diary and recognized my father's signature in the top right-hand corner of the first page. My father's signed name, like his life, was a carefully constructed series of perfectly composed, by-the-rules actions, angled slightly to the right. To the casual observer, his handwriting was entirely ordinary, and his penmanship, like his life, easily readable. If it's true that a man's signature reveals something about his character, then the character revealed here is that of a man who cared what people thought about his handwriting and, upon further reflection, about his life.

If I thought anything was odd about his handwriting, it was only the raw fact of it being used to keep a *diary*. I didn't know he kept one. As far as I knew, my father had never been a diarist. So the fact that he kept a diary, coupled with a well-worn copy of *The Great Gatsby*, and that these two items and the bible at home were the sum total of my personal inheritance from him—*that* was what I thought was unusual.

"Your father wanted you to have this," Hovermale had said when he handed me the key. I had asked him if he knew what was in the box. "No," he had replied.

I turned the page and began reading. What my father had given me was a story about his life. Not all of it—it was, after all, a diary and not an auto-biography—but enough of it to present me with what I would later learn to call "a relational identity crisis." He had passed along a story of a man whom I had called Dad for the past twenty-three years but who was not really my father. My father had been an ordinary government worker who had retired on full disability from the Veterans Administration. The story I read was about an extraordinary man with my father's name who worked for a clandestine organization, a man who ran illegal operations during the cold war, a case officer who communicated using codebooks.

The Great Gatsby and a Holy Bible were named as his "codebooks." The former for London, the latter, appropriately, I thought, for Rome. I held his copy of *Gatsby* in my hands. The bible was more of a mystery. I knew there was one at home among his possessions, although the days of my father being a religious man seemed distant.

There were also names laced throughout the diary: J. Bert Schroeder. Frank Wisner. Allen Dulles. James Jesus Angleton. William Colby. Clare Boothe Luce. Abbe Lane. Bill Harvey. Kim Philby. Angleton, again. Philby, again. Richard Nixon. Frank Rizzo. Angleton, yet again.

There were lists of dates and places, as well as a name given in all capi-tal letters that dominated the last few pages, something or someone called CHAOS. It sounded too much like an acronym to be anything but an acro-nym. BROOK LANE, too, but I thought I knew what those letters referred to and it wasn't an acronym at all. It was a psychiatric center located in rural Maryland. I had visited my father on that "farm" several times.

The last entry was difficult to make out. Maybe his usually fine hand-writing had deteriorated with his illness, or perhaps he was just less sure of himself toward the end. I could only make out the words "Church committee."

His diary didn't come with a note to me or with any instructions. What was I supposed to think about it, or to do with it?

I had no idea.

I confronted my mother with the diary—and "confronted" is unfortunately the right word—and she denied knowing my father kept one. When I asked her how much she knew about his other life, she said only that *of course* she knew he worked for the government. *Of course* he did things he couldn't talk about. That was the way it was when you worked for the government. "Your father was a *patriot*," she said, tearfully.

I left it at that. She was clearly agitated by my questions. Unnerved by them. And she was lying to me. I knew it and she knew it. We had a history of mistruths between us.

I offered to lend her the diary but she had no interest in reading it. "If he had wanted me to read it," she said, "he would have given it to me. But instead he gave it to *you*."

For her, that explanation was enough. For me, it wasn't.

Due to the sudden and unexpected nature of my father's death, there were now unresolved tensions that weighed heavily on me, on my soul. I had moved away from home, away from him, and away from what he thought was right, in ways that he could not have failed to read as signs of a definitive rejection.

The last time we had spoken, I had said as much. He had dutifully walked me to my car after another one of our unhappy Christmas holidays and we had shaken hands, as if that settled something, just to keep up the public appearance of family peace. I remember that he held my eyes as if he wanted to tell me something else, but in the end he couldn't manage it. Instead, his eyes teared up, and then, because it was embarrassing to both of us, he said simply, quickly, and now I realize *finally*, "I love you, goodbye."

I don't remember what I said. I wish I did.

Fathers and sons. What *is* it between us? That is an ancient question and it may never be resolved.

My father was a deep mystery to me. I was equally unfathomable to him. Or at least I believed I was. I had wanted him to end better than he had ended, but I also had wanted him to live better than he had been living.

He had once *been somebody*. I knew that.

But I had been merely a child during those seemingly halcyon days. By the time I was old enough to spell "vice consul of the United States of America" he had fallen from that high place to somewhere considerably farther down on the government totem pole. All the way down to something called an assistant contact officer for the Veterans Administration. It had been a slow, spiraling decline and seemed to me to be a tragic one. He had retired on full medical disability at forty-seven, and now was dead at fifty-three. In between, he had spent time in jail and in a mental hospital. He was addicted to heavy narcotics and drank as much as he could every day, couldn't sleep, and lived in constant pain.

Yet, for all his misery, he was always kind to me. Unfailingly polite. Generous. Apologetic about his problems. He loved my mother with all his heart. And she, in turn, loved him. They were classically codependent and badly enabling of each other's craziness.

I told myself that I felt sorry for him, sorry for my mother, sorry for their small, wasted lives. The alcoholism. His depression and her craziness. The past they longed for but could never reach. But really I felt sorry for myself because of what they had reduced themselves to, and because, at the sophomoric age of twenty-three, I thought I knew so much better.

And now this diary. This deeper story—his *true* story—that lived inside of the cover story I had lived with them. Why didn't he just tell me? Why didn't he let me in? Why didn't we *talk* about it? Why did he wait until he died to reveal himself, who he had really been, and what he had been doing all those years? I felt as if my whole life was turned inside out.

I had been betrayed by the truth.

• •

Knowing my father's secrets, even some of them, even though I didn't discover them until he died, poisoned my relationship to him. Like a lethal toxin released in memory, it killed whatever remained of my respect for him and tainted what I recalled of our shared times together.

For many years I refused to talk about it because I was deeply ashamed, not so much because of the clandestine work he did, but because he kept who he really was from *me*. Had our relationship become so fragile that it couldn't handle the truth? Had I proved unworthy of his trust? Who was I to him? Was I anyone very much at all?

• •

I never removed my father's diary from what became my mother's home—Naomi's home—although I did change its location. When I returned to my teaching job in South Carolina, I shelved it—cleverly and ironically, or so I thought at the time—in between my father's copy of John le Carré's *The Spy Who Came In from the Cold* and my own old copy of Ian Fleming's *Casino Royale*. My father had given me the Bond book a long time ago, back when we lived in what my parents referred to as "our exile" in Cheyenne, Wyoming. Recalling that memory brought back others I didn't want to think about. I left the diary on the shelf. I walked away from it and all that it represented.

The following June I moved home to live with and to care for my mother, who had become clinically, and I think psychically, depressed. I left my job at Clemson University and, to support myself, became an account executive for a local FM radio station, WWMD. The call letters stood for "Wild, Wonderful, Western Maryland," although these days, with our ongoing war on terrorism and a renewed appreciation for the power of acronyms, I read them as stammering out "W-weapons of mass destruction."

Pardon me. I display an ironic sense of humor sometimes. That is, I'm afraid, part of this story.

Anyway, for WWMD, I was a lousy salesman. Instead of booking a lot of appointments or making cold calls, I drove around town aimlessly most of the time, took in afternoon matinees, and read a lot of popular novels. I convinced myself that this move, this lifestyle and job, was only temporary. I didn't see a future in selling spots. I wanted to become a writer.

One day, cruising my mother's bookshelf for something to pass the time instead of making sales calls, I came across the diary. I got it into my head that it didn't belong there, so I placed it in an old cedar chest down in the basement that contained my father's World War II Army Air Corps uniform, his leather flying jacket, and his medals. It seemed appropriate to store them together. It was as if I was relegating the artifacts of his life to a locked-down space away from my view.

I was a fool to believe it would be that simple.

· ·

My days living back home in Hagerstown and semi-working as an account executive were thankfully brief. Jerry Terlingo, who had dated my mother during the war and with whom she had broken up just prior to meeting and marrying my father, blew into our lives like a colorful Italian carnival and made Naomi smile again. The two of them regularly went off together and lived large together for a while. They toured the country by car and by train; they enjoyed cruises throughout the Caribbean and to Mexico;

they flew to Las Vegas and San Francisco and Honolulu. One night, by long-distance phone call, my mother told me that I should get on with my life because she was certainly getting on with hers.

She was drunk but there was happy music playing in the background. Jerry was tugging her to do something. I could hear his loud voice urging her to hang up. She giggled like a young girl and told him to wait a minute. She was having a good time. I compared her life to mine. I hated Hagerstown. I was young and miserable and failing to become a writer. My job sucked. I decided to take her advice.

I quit WWMD. After a brief stint as a short-order cook, I was accepted into the doctoral program in speech communication at Penn State University. I threw myself into graduate school, blocking out my former life much as my father had before me. I was a good student and received a PhD in speech communication with a minor in creative and biographical writing in August of 1980. My first job out of the doctoral program was as an assistant professor of communication studies at the University of Alabama in Huntsville.

I doubt I ever consciously thought about my father's diary during the whole of this time. That I wrote my dissertation on "The Interpersonal Communication of Scott and Zelda Fitzgerald," or that I devoted a long chapter to the influence of their relationship on the writing of *The Great Gatsby*, well, those clues are probably evidence that something was going on in my subconscious that I had yet to fully work through.

At the time, I didn't think about it that way.

. . . .

Naomi died on December 21, 1983. She had stomach cancer and it had spread to her lymph glands by the time she finally saw a doctor. I think she knew she was ill long before that.

After a couple of good years with fun, lovable Jerry, she had returned to work as a nurse at the local hospital in Hagerstown. She was responsible for training new ER nurses and was seldom at home. She and Jerry shared her house but had little left in common. They realized they couldn't repeat the past, nor were they convinced that they could endure their future. Jerry had spent the last of his money wooing her and was now essentially penniless. Naomi told me she regretted ever asking him to move in but now felt guilty about asking him to leave. I, typically, did nothing.

She lasted six months after she received the terminal diagnosis. I traveled back and forth between Huntsville and Hagerstown many times during those last six months because I wanted to spend as much time with her as I could before she died. I wanted to have those final conversations that I had missed having with my father.

She told me a little more about her past but nothing really new about my father or their life together. Mostly, I believe it was important for to be with her. We spent a lot of time quietly holding hands. When the end came, it was blessedly quick and lacked drama.

I was the one who had to make the final call to turn off the life support. I kept the promise I had made to her only days before, when it became clear that she had only a little time left. We were told that a life-support system could prolong her life indefinitely, something Naomi didn't want.

I nodded to the nurse and to the doctor. It was an agreed-upon sign. Both of them were fighting tears. They had known Naomi as a nurse in this hospital, where she was much beloved.

I felt well prepared for her death but it didn't matter. Death is death and if it closes off the obvious suffering, it also opens up an emptiness where a life had once been. My mother had lasted with her illness exactly as long as she had wanted to. She died on the day that would have marked her and my father's thirty-sixth wedding anniversary. We buried her body in a grave next to his, and I felt the peace of their final, eternal symmetry.

• •

I was the sole inheritor of what was left of my mother's earthly possessions. It wasn't much: her small house in Hagerstown, a light yellow Ford Mustang coupe, some furniture and her clothing, some knickknacks, and a few books. There was an oil portrait of me, painted in Rome by Leonard Creo. A little money, although after her burial expenses not much.

This time I went to Hovermale's office alone. Making small talk prior to executing her will, I reminded him that the last time I was here he gave me a key to a safe-deposit box. I told him that I had found my father's diary.

"A *diary*?" he asked. "Really?"

"Yes, but I'm sure you knew that." He was my parents' attorney, my father's friend.

"No," he replied. "I *didn't* know that." He paused. "What did you do with it?"

"It's still in the house," I replied. "I left it there."

He smiled thinly and said, "Well, let's get started then."

He read Naomi's will aloud and there were no surprises. Jerry had a life estate in the house and the use of the car. The key Hovermale gave me this time was the key to her house, which was now legally my house.

Two months later, Jerry vacated the house and took up residence in the VA hospital in Martinsburg, where he promptly died. The official cause of death was "gave up the will to live," but the doctor on duty told me that Jerry had simply died of a broken heart. He told the doctor that he had always loved my mother even though he knew she never really loved him. When she died, he felt like he had no more reason to live.

I thought this final deathbed confession of his unrequited love was an appropriate, if sad, ending for the many sad lives that had been lived out in our house in Hagerstown. I immediately put it up for sale. There was no good reason to keep it and a lot of symbolic ones to let it go.

I asked Hovermale to handle the sale for me.

· ·

One day I returned to my office at the University of Alabama in Huntsville to find a message instructing me to call Mr. Gilbert Hovermale in Hagerstown, Maryland. This had to be good news, because Hovermale had promised to call the minute the house finally sold.

"I've got bad news," he began, not sounding at all like a man with bad news. He sounded more like a trial lawyer who had just won a big case and had to tell someone about it. "Damnedest thing, Bud. Someone broke into your house and took everything."

"*Everything?*" I asked, incredulously.

"Right down to the carpet," he replied. "Strangest thing I've ever seen." He of course had called the local police, who thought it had been a professional job. "Pretty easy pickings for an above-average thief. The house was for sale, no one was living in it. Your neighbor saw a truck pull out of the driveway but didn't think anything of it."

"What truck?"

"Whoever did the job had some balls. They used a moving truck. That's why your neighbor didn't think it was unusual. She figured you were getting rid of the old furniture."

The furniture had been a matter of contention. Hovermale claimed the house hadn't sold because the old furniture and knickknacks were still in it. He had asked me if he could send someone in to pack everything up. I said no. I didn't want anyone going through our belongings without me being present. He had then offered to do it himself; he'd even arrange for storage. I had resisted on the grounds that I didn't want to be bothered with moving the furniture until the end of the school year. I told him I would move everything out of the house myself in June.

I was half a month too late. It was mid-May and I had been robbed.

"What should I *do*?" I remember feeling more deflated than violated. This new development was another bad thing involving my family that I had to put up with. I didn't really care about whatever furniture or clothing or knickknacks the thieves had taken. Most of the memorabilia that had value to us had been lost or destroyed when Hurricane Carla flooded our first Maryland house back in 1972. I had already moved out of the house by then, so nothing my parents—or Naomi and Jerry—had acquired in the interim had personal significance.

I had removed a few things of my father's when I moved to Alabama, not out of any real connection to the items but because my mother insisted I keep something of his with me. So I had the war medals and a small men's jewelry box with his Foreign Service and Lions Club lapel pins, studs for his tux, collar stays, a nail clipper, some old trick bullets that concealed pills or something inside of them, and his small gold stiletto with the chipped, bloodstained blade.

I didn't take the diary with me. I thought it ought to remain in the house. I thought if I did take it, it would always remind me of all that had been lost between us. A relationship we never had. I didn't need that in my life. It was hard enough to live with the reality of it. I didn't want the damned thing.

So when Hovermale then offered to handle things for me, I was only too ready, too happy, to agree. He added, "I've got a cleaning service. I'll get them to go over there to tidy things up."

"Fine. Just send me a bill." *Just be done with it* is what I was thinking.

Before we hung up he said, "Sad as this is, now that the house is empty it should make it a lot easier to sell."

It did and it didn't. Hagerstown was, in 1984, experiencing an economic downturn and interest rates were hovering around 11 percent. Hovermale talked me into lowering the asking price twice before he found a buyer who was willing to pay even less for it. The house appraised for $89,000. It was August before I got an offer. By then, I was exasperated and in need of the money, so I let it go for a mere $36,500.

By the time I paid Hovermale for all he had "handled," including the cleanup after the break-in and other miscellaneous expenses, I had precious little to show for it. He never even shipped my oil portrait to me as he had promised to do.

But I didn't care. I had my own life and I had finally closed the book on my family.

Or so I thought.

. . . .

Where do you go when you are stripped of your family? When all you have left are the stories that comprise your history? When all that is left is your narrative inheritance?

Narrative inheritance—I use this term to describe the afterlives of the sentences used to spell out the life stories of those who came before us. The narratives we inherit from our forebears provide us with a framework for understanding our identity through theirs. It helps us see our working logic as an extension of, or a rebellion against, the way we tell the story of how they lived and thought about things. It allows us to explain to others where we come from and how we were raised in the continuing context of what it all means. We are fundamentally *homo narrans*—humans as storytellers—and a well-told story brings with it a sense of fulfillment and completion.

But we don't always inherit that sense of completion. Too often what we inherit is a family's unfinished business; when we do, those incomplete narratives are given to us to fulfill. This, too, is part of our cultural coding.

Consider President George W. Bush's war on Iraq. It is clear to me, as it was to some political commentators, that this war was, in part, the mission of a man suffering from an incomplete narrative inheritance. His father, former President George H. W. Bush, is remembered as a man who didn't quite finish the job in Iraq during the Gulf War of 1990–91. Having found himself, as a result of 9/11, with his own Middle East crisis, the son known to the world as President Bush found himself historically and narratively in a time and place, with ample motive and an available opportunity, to finish his father's story as well. Even though I disagreed with his decision, I felt a keen empathy with his quest.

An unfinished narrative is difficult to live with. The unfinished story of my father's life is not the story I ever wanted to write. It is the story I ran away from for most of my adult life, but one that I find that I *must* write now that I am a father. Now that my own son, Nicolas, has asked me direct questions. Now, as I grapple with the answers to the questions he asks about my parents, my childhood, my past.

I found myself repeating to Nic, automatically, the same cover story I grew up with—that my father worked for the government, that my mother was a nurse, and so on—until I realized I was doing to him what had been done to me as a child: I was passing along the lie by keeping secret the rest of the story. So, in one sense, this is a story I must tell because I don't want to pass the family secret, this toxin, this silent poison on to my own son. He deserves better than that. *We* deserve better than that.

. . . .

I didn't go into this research project believing that I would be able to discover "the truth" about my father's clandestine career, or even about the meaning of my family's cold war life. I hoped for something less grand. I hoped to find an adequate, even if partial, explanation for what happened to us, and why. I was curious about the sudden and dramatic change in our fortunes that occurred as a result of something that happened in my father's career in June of 1960. I had always wondered how he had fallen so quickly from clandestine grace, despite, as he always maintained, his being guilty only of having been right. I wanted to know more about the cold war and the intelligence services, about the men and women who created what many of us think of as the heyday of the CIA.

Still, I hesitated. I found excuses—good ones, too—to avoid this project. I am a personal ethnographer but I felt I needed something other than a personal motive this time. This was *his* story—my father's secret life and his reasons for keeping it secret—and it was also History. I worried that I had no right to invade his life, to spy on him and on my mother. I also feared I might not be up to the task.

But there are times when excuses, worries, and even fears of failure must be put aside because *not* to act is no longer an option. Sometimes human beings arrive at this tipping point because of a critical event in their lives or the life of their country, and sometimes we arrive at it because we can't bear to live with ourselves if we continue to do nothing more than find excuses. In my case, it was both of these things.

02

Where He Came From

December 7, 1941, and Its Aftermath

I ASKED MY FATHER IF HE REMEMBERED DECEMBER 7, 1941. HE TOLD me he had emerged from church that infamous Sunday morning and heard someone shouting something about the Japs attacking. He didn't elaborate.

His face always told the rest of the story. It was a good American face, handsome in a boyish way, and defined by a strong jaw, full lips, straight nose, a full head of dark hair, and green-gray eyes. At just over six feet in height and a slender 160 pounds, my father presented himself as a well-dressed, well-groomed, well-spoken man of the world. A man with serious work to do. A man, perhaps, with something going on that he wouldn't, or couldn't, talk about. A man of subtle mystery who always denied there was any mystery at all, which of course only served to enrich his overall attractiveness.

But if you looked carefully into that face you saw a certain tightness in the jaw muscles, the hardened visible lines around the eyes and mouth that hinted at a deeper traumatic pain. He did not complain. Whatever he felt in the daylight hours remained unspoken. If my father was good at keeping his country's secrets, he was even better at keeping his own past a secret.

I never knew my father's dreams, only his nightmares.

I've long been bothered by that raw fact. My initial objective in doing background research on his early life was to correct that error, to fill that gap. I wanted to understand the narrative place my father came from, the story of his life that was already well under way when he left home for the navy and entered history.

I also wanted to understand my father's side of our family tree. I had never been allowed to know them. I wanted to acquire a history of the Goodall clan, our genealogy as well as our stories. I wanted to know what fired the engines of his history, hopes, circumstances, and personal ambition, the narrative fuel that carried him into his life and that would define him as someone who once had hopes and ambitions, someone who had once slept well enough to enjoy his dreams.

I believed if I knew those things about him, I could better build a foundation for understanding his early life. And if I had an understanding of his early life, I could move ahead into the uneasy task of uncovering my father's carefully, officially, and deeply buried past.

· ·

My father made a point of not talking about his childhood. If asked, he deflected attention away from those years. He said only what he felt he needed to reveal. He dismissed follow-up questions with a wink or a small hand gesture, as if he were pushing the past away, ridding the present of any need for further disclosure of his memories.

He rarely talked about his own father, Oscar; only once or twice about his mother, Effie Ann; and never once about his sister, Phyllis. When I say never once, this is not an exaggeration. I didn't even know my father *had* a sister until I read her name in his obituary. By March of 1976, the mention of a sister, a faceless unstoried person named Phyllis, was so foreign to me that I assumed that she must have died a long time ago.

I asked my mother for clarification. "Who was this Phyllis person? The obituary says it was his sister."

"He hated her," my mother told me, coolly. And that was all she ever said to me about Phyllis. If I had pressed the point, perhaps I would have learned a few more small details. But my mother was still reeling from his death, so I didn't ask.

Nor did my mother volunteer anything more. I would later learn she didn't really know much more. Not about Phyllis. Not about Oscar or Effie Ann. Not very much at all about Lloyd's early life in Huntington, West Virginia. My father simply never talked to her very much about his past except to tell her he wanted to forget it.

Phyllis held an alluring narrative presence in my life. No one named Phyllis had showed up at his funeral, and because I desperately wanted to put his past far behind me, I assumed Phyllis was literally and figuratively dead.

I would later learn how wrong I was. Phyllis was very much alive when my father died. The hatred between sister and brother was mutual and deep. It had roots in how they felt about each other as children and how their parents treated them. Lloyd was the one most likely to succeed, and Phyllis was the one most likely to trade on her good looks for a hook into a rich husband.

But in the end it was a dispute about money that drove them apart. It had been Lloyd's money from his time in the service and his mother and sister had seen fit to spend it before he came home. Perhaps they didn't think he *would* come home. I don't know. But it was an explosion over money that caused my father to walk away from his mother, his sister, and his past. It was money that caused him to disappear from life as he had known it.

But I am ahead of my story.

. . . .

The story of our universe is one we have created out of the words "chaos" and "mystery." There may be a Yahweh, too, an Allah, a God Almighty. But with the aid of the Hubble telescope scientists have "seen" creation, the swirling dark implosion they tell us created matter and energy, as well as space and time. Perhaps a dark God can be found in the image of a Big Bang, but I doubt it. God is less obvious than that.

I think the same words hold true for stories of our own beginnings. We are descendants from mystery and chaos, from an incoherence as well as from a less obvious God. Despite family claims of uniqueness to the contrary, all of our ancestors date back to the same original pair of sinners. They may have inhabited a garden in Iraq or some grassy African savannah, or perhaps they rose up from clay models somewhere else on this earth. I doubt we'll ever know.

But we *believe* we know. Which is to say we attribute belief to what we claim to know, which is to say we settle for something a little less than the truth and hope it will do. Perhaps this is our original sin, the ignorance that comes from having no real knowledge of our origins. Instead, we make do with metaphors of innocence made out of our nakedness. We recite the

long list of great *begats* as if they were something more than mere speculation, and, as a result, we all end up descended from the King of Kings.

I do not claim a special or sacred knowledge of our origins.

I can tell you that my family descended along the same genetic pathways
as have all of our brothers and sisters in the human family I call *homo narrans.* I call us *homo narrans* because we are better understood as a species
defined by our use of language rather than as descendants of the upright apes
called *erectus,* or the tool makers called *habilis,* or the merely modern-bodied
sapiens, or even of the empirical "featherless bipeds" so cleverly named by
Aristotle. No. We are, as human beings, first and foremost, language makers and storytellers. As the French philosopher Georges Gusdorf beautifully
phrased it, we "call the world into being."

The story of my father's past as a member of his family is cobbled together
from the historic records of the town in which he was born and reared, and
from the memories of the few remaining relatives and friends I was able to
interview. It is a constructed past. As a scholar, I am well aware of its fragili-
ties and its limitations. As his son, I can only say it is the best I can do.

· ·

On October 17, 1922, my father, christened Harold Lloyd Goodall, was
born. He was named for the famous silent movie star Harold Lloyd. This
was his father's doing. It wouldn't have been his mother, who often found
it difficult to smile, especially at her husband's antics.

With money saved from working for his father in the family furniture
business, Oscar paid cash for a large, white, two-story clapboard house in
East Huntington. The house stood proud on a tree-shaded bank overlooking the Ohio River. It was a nice place. Today, we would call such a place,
with its five bedrooms, indoor plumbing, state-of-the-art appliances, and
long lawns overlooking the broad expanse of the Ohio River, upper middle
class. It was a testimony to the fact that Oscar was a successful, hardworking man before the Depression.

But in 1932 his father, William Clinton Goodall, who owned the furniture plant and who had built the Baptist church in East Huntington, closed
the plant down. His reason was that no one was buying furniture anymore
and without orders there was a lack of cash flow, which then became an
inability to pay his bills. He held on as long as he could, and it broke his
heart to close his business, as well as to render his son unemployed. Oscar,
like most working men in America, lost his job.

My father was ten. Phyllis was twelve. Effie Ann complained.

Oscar's fall from financial grace was a hard one. He joined the long, unhappy ranks of the newly unemployed, took odd jobs when he found them, and quickly ran through what little remained of the family's reserves. His diabetes worsened. His once jovial attitude was replaced by a meaner sense of humor, one that viewed life as a bad joke rather than a source of good humor. The man recalled by his friends as the fellow in the parlor who delighted children with wordplay—"Who's going to arrest the crook in my arm?"—became a far edgier presence.

Effie Ann took in laundry. Both children worked and contributed what meager sums they were paid to the family coffers. Bill Hastings, a childhood friend of my father's, recalled times when the Goodall family took in lodgers and when Bill's own family—only slightly better off—provided them with cornbread, molasses, and milk. During the Depression, cornbread, molasses, and milk made a meal.

Eventually Oscar found work as a janitor in the old Huntington High School that my father attended before the new East High School was completed in 1940. Many times my father assisted Oscar in his janitorial duties.

Oscar was sick a lot. His diabetes was unstable. There wasn't enough money for health care.

Effie Ann became bitter about Oscar, about how he was sick all the time. She was bitter about men in general, including her son, who she increasingly believed was engaged in too many after-school activities when he should be working, bringing in money. Effie Ann was depressed by her circumstances, her husband, and her son, and often remained in bed all day long. Phyllis took over cooking and cleaning duties in exchange for Effie Ann's unconditional support in anything she wanted to do.

. . . .

If my father seldom spoke of his parents, relatives, or upbringing, he spoke even less about growing up in Huntington. He was born there, and from his service records I know he enlisted in the navy on March 17, 1942, and left for Naval Aviation preflight training in Athens, Georgia, on May 25, 1942. In between these known dates I have nineteen years and seven months of virtual silence.

Huntington was, until the Great Depression, a thriving commercial center with broad, tree-lined main streets, and rows of prosperous mansions. Although the Depression claimed many jobs and times were as hard in

Huntington as anywhere else, this city of 100,000 people was a pleasant, if decidedly white-bread, kind of place.

He once told me that he had worked at a soda shop and then at a men's clothing store—Watts-Ritter Dry Goods & Notions. On another occasion, he mentioned that he had graduated from East High as president of the Presidential Club and editor of the yearbook, and had the leading role in school plays. I believed him and, as it has turned out, all of these tales were true. I have his 1941 East High School yearbook and the evidence is there.

He once spent a summer working as a carny in a traveling circus, where he learned how to cook "circus food" (eggs scrambled over diced potatoes fried with onions and bacon, and served with ketchup) and, in his words, "clean up elephant crap," which may or may not have been a metaphor. He also, he told me, learned what happens when "you get caught talking when you should be listening," a life lesson that was given added weight by a broken nose acquired when a summer dalliance with a well-seasoned circus performer made enough noise to attract the angry attention of her husband.

He mentioned once, and then only in a kind of melancholy way, that he had played the trumpet in the 1939 World's Fair. He added, almost as an afterthought, that on that day he played in front of the King and Queen of England.

I never believed this fanciful story. How could I? When he told it to me, when we lived way out in the wilds of old Wyoming, he was mostly gone away to that place he went to in the company of gin and memories. The distance between our life in Cheyenne and him playing for British royalty in New York City was more than could be measured on any map.

I should have believed him. I learned from Warren Bills, his high school pal, that their high school band won the 1939 state championship and their reward was a trip to the Big Apple, where, yes indeed, they played before the King and Queen of England.

Moreover, Lloyd is remembered by his surviving friends for a soulful jazz trumpet performance he gave one perfect Easter Sunday in 1941. He stood alone and proud on a giant sundial overlooking the river just behind the Kelly-Hatfield mansion and blew the horn for the assembled guests. "I can still see him plain as day in my mind," Bill Hastings recalled. "He was *beautiful*."

When I heard this story, I wondered whether my father ever dreamed of becoming a professional musician. Was that one of his ambitions, one of

JANUARY

ADKINS, JOYCE—Home Economics.

BAYS, SYBIL—Social Science; Current History; Girls Athletic Association; Art Club.

BLACK, LUCILLE—Home Economics; Home Economics Club.

BOND, CAROL—History; Dramatic Club.

BRAFFORD, JUANITA—Commerce.

BRODTRICK, JUANITA—Retail Selling; Home Economics Club; Current History; Art Club; Phi Beta Chi.

CARRIGAN, CHARLES—Mechanical Drawing.

CASEY, WILLIAM—Manual Arts.

CHAPMAN, ERMA JO—Commerce.

CHRISTIAN, LILAS MAE—Home Economics; Current History.

CORN, IDA MAE—Home Economics; Kappa Theta Kappa.

CRUM, ELIZABETH—Commerce; Class Secretary; Torch; Current History; Presidential Club.

DEATON, JAMES W.—Math; Class Treasurer; Boy Honorarian; Torch; Current History; Presidential Club; Easthi Staff.

FERGERSON, ARVILLE—History; Current History; Latin Club; Presidential Club.

FLEMING, ROSS HENRI—History.

FORTH, GERALDINE—Home Economics.

GOODALL, H. LLOYD—Science; January editor of Easthi; Glee Club; Dramatic Club; Spanish Club; Presidential Club.

GWILLIAMS, RUSSELL—Bookkeeping.

Page 20

FIGURE 2.1 H. Lloyd Goodall entry from the 1941 East High yearbook.

his hopes? I don't know. Teenagers and band members across the full range of musical talent do have those dreams. I know I did. I know my son does. The trumpet was, in my father's era, a ticket to Tommy Dorsey land, just as a guitar is a ticket to fan-filled arenas now.

If he did dream that musical dream, it was snatched from him during the war. His medical records are clear: he suffered a shattered eardrum as a result of repeated close proximity to aerial bombardment. His ear for music was destroyed, and his pitch was permanently altered. Perhaps as a result, he seldom listened to music in our house. I never saw him so much as glance at trumpets displayed in the windows of music stores.

I never heard my father play the trumpet. It was, I guess, another one of those things about his past that he walked away from.

I wonder if he knew that Warren Bills, his old band buddy, ended up a professional musician? Bills went far in the music world, producing records for Perry Como and Patti Page in addition to serving as the musical director for the *Lawrence Welk Show*. I wonder if my father saw Warren Bills's name listed on the credits and remembered their high school band days?

I'd like to think so. I'd like to believe my father had fond memories of his youth. Or if not of his entire youth, then at least of some small part of it. And if not even some small part of it, then perhaps only one or two brief shining moments in that time before the war.

• •

My grandfather Oscar, as I said, was diabetic. In 1942, at the age of forty-nine and after a prolonged sickness and personal descent, he drowned at home in his own bodily fluids. His death was, by all accounts, horrific. Odd, isn't it, that my father is also said to have died at home after a prolonged illness. I cannot help but wonder if there isn't a family pattern in that. For my own sake, I hope not. But you never know.

Oscar could have received treatment at the local hospital, which was less than a mile away, but because, as a relative told me, Effie Ann didn't want "to waste any more money on him," he died in his bed. No matter how hard I try, I cannot imagine such a coldhearted sentiment. Hearing Effie Ann's own words quoted to me by a relative only makes it colder still. I have tried to figure it out as something other than the cruel intention of a mean woman to just let the bastard die, but without much luck. Perhaps Effie Ann—who, I learned, suffered from a mental depression as well as an economic one—saw an opportunity to cut her losses. Or perhaps a doctor had told her that there was little hope for him. Still.

And what of Phyllis? She would have been twenty-two at the time, still living at home, and old enough to voice an opinion. My father told my mother that Phyllis always sided with Effie Ann, and that was part of their deal. So maybe that was all there was to it. Phyllis was not as close to Oscar as she was to Effie Ann, but what of that? How can a daughter—any daughter—stand by and allow her father to choke to death?

My father believed it was simpler than that. He believed that Phyllis viewed Oscar's dire situation as her chance to gain control over Effie Ann and what was left of her money. With Oscar out of the way, Lloyd away fighting the war, and her mother depressed, Phyllis could stake claim to the house, Oscar's pension, and whatever the government would provide in the form of a death benefit check.

It was, my father told my mother, "always about the money" with Phyllis. That Phyllis sided with her mother and allowed her own father to die a gruesome death was to him undeniable. That Phyllis *planned* it as a way to gain control over her depressed mother and to seize whatever meager amount of money might come from it is almost unbelievable, at least to me. But this coldhearted, premeditated murderous account is what my father believed was true. It was *his* story of what happened. It was how my father understood Phyllis and Effie Ann.

If it is true, these are the acts of cold, despicable people. Cold and despicable enough to cause a man to walk away from his family, and to never look back.

But that final decision, the irrevocable break between my father and his family, would occur only later, when he discovered their conspiracy against him. Which is to say when he returned home wounded after serving in the war.

. . . .

At the time of Oscar's death, my father was at the Naval Aviation Cadet School in Anacostia, Maryland. He did not make it home in time for Oscar's funeral. Oscar was buried cheaply in a pauper's grave. It was additional evidence of what was by that time obvious to other family members: Oscar's wife and daughter had even less regard for him in death than they did when he was still among the living.

My mother told me that my father had loved Oscar. He had been close to him. He had repeatedly defended him to Effie Ann and Phyllis and had worked in Oscar's place when Oscar was too sick to show up for his job. After the United States declared war on Germany and Japan, it was Oscar's signature that got my father into the navy against Effie Ann and Phyllis's objections. They thought Roosevelt's war was male folly run rampant and this would be yet another excuse for men to do stupid things. Men should be home with their families, preferably working to support them.

My father didn't agree. He was a patriotic kid. He was also wise enough, as Bill Hastings told me, to realize "that you had to sleep on the ground and get shot at in the army," which is where draftees were likely to go. By volunteering for the navy, you got better living arrangements and training. You learned to fly aircraft and enrolled in classes that received college credit. In the navy, you weren't wasting your life or your time.

My father and Bill Hastings joined the navy at the same time. Because the V-5 aviation cadet program took high school graduates (instead of the usual college graduates), it required parental signature to get in. For all Lloyd would ever know, Oscar's willingness to sign for him had cost Oscar his life. It was shortly after Lloyd entered the program that Oscar died.

When my father finally heard the news of Oscar's death, along with his mother's and sister's dark decision-making roles in it, he promptly failed his final flight test. He told everyone he had failed it because he "couldn't hear the radio operator's instructors for finding the aircraft carrier," but I doubt that was true. My father had a stellar record in primary and intermediate flight schools. He had been the highest rated cadet in his class and had over 100 hours of flight time prior to that one failed test. He loved to fly and I know for a personal fact that he was good at it.

I think he was distraught over the loss of his father. I think he was angry with his mother and sister. I know he felt betrayed by them. But I'll never know why he failed the final flight test. It is part of the incoherence of his war story.

What I do know about this turn of events in his war story is somewhat more curious.

Lloyd, who lacked only a final solo landing on an aircraft carrier to earn his wings, and who claimed he flunked the test because he couldn't hear the radio operator's instructions, found himself instead in the Army Air Corps as a radio operator on a B-17. After receiving an honorable discharge from the navy, he had been ordered to report to his local draft board. That meant the army. It meant the infantry. Sleeping on the ground and getting shot at.

Instead, probably on the advice of a senior officer in the know, my father beat feet down to Tampa, Florida, and enlisted in the Army Air Corps. He was given the rank of private first class based on his previous service, and assigned to a B-17 flight crew to train as a radio operator. He trained for a year in the United States before his crew picked up their brand-new airplane in Savannah, Georgia, and flew it to England.

He graduated first in his class.

He was promoted to the rank of staff sergeant. He was a fully trained radio operator and waist gunner. And now, with his B-17 crew, he went off to the Second World War aboard an airplane called the Flying Fortress.

He had, he figured, given the rumored statistics on B-17s, a less than even chance of returning home alive.

. . . .

My father's shooting war was, like his childhood, not a subject he talked about. I remember as a kid in Wyoming coming across his Air Corps uniform in a basement closet. It was the first time I became aware that my father had even *been* in the war. I was a budding student of history, a male child during the cold war with an interest in all things military, and so I asked him about his uniform down in the closet and what the ribbons pinned on it were for.

It would be our one and only conversation on the subject.

He led me back downstairs, opened the closet, and explained each one of the medals, the Eighth Air Force insignia, and what the wings represented. He pointed out the stripes on his sleeve and told me he had been a staff sergeant. He also showed me his leather bomber jacket—stained with his blood, although at the time I didn't know that—and laughed a little about the insignia of a bear throwing a bomb from a cloud. He turned the jacket around and pointed out the Russian phrase on the back of the jacket, translated it as "What the hell am I doing here?," and then he closed the closet door.

I asked him, "What is war like?"

He drew a deep breath. His eyes seemed to travel back in time. "War is a loud bloody nightmarish hell," he said. "You make friends and then watch them die. I got lucky. I got all shot up and they shipped me home." He paused. "Home wasn't my home anymore." He was sadder about that than he had been about the war. Even as a child I could see it. "I don't want you to *ever* have to go to war," he said.

He had never spoken to me quite that way before. Unlike older men I knew—my friends' fathers and some of my teachers—my father didn't talk about "what he did" in the war. If asked, he said only that he had been in the Air Corps in England. He preferred to let other men tell their war stories, although I could tell he didn't enjoy listening to them.

It would be years before I finally learned why.

It was November 14, 2002, when I arrived home to find my wife, Sandra, waiting for me in the kitchen. "I found him," she said.

"Who?" I knew she had been tracking down records of my father's military experience. I didn't know what progress she had made.

"Ansel Miller," she beamed. "He was the tail gunner on the plane with your father. I talked to him this afternoon. He wants you to call him."

I was stunned. I was also apprehensive. I had grown up with a story about my father's war experiences that, however fragmentary, I was comfortable with. Did I really want to disturb the past? On the other hand, how could I pass up this opportunity to learn the truth?

After a couple of hours and a stiff bourbon, I placed the call.

· ·

Ansel Miller was a great interview.

He told me my father had a nickname—"Duke"—because "he always carried himself royally." He gave me a moment-by-moment description of their last flight together. On my father's sixteenth combat mission, on August 1, 1944, their B-17 was seriously shot up over Tours, France. My father was gravely wounded. Were it not for tail gunner Ansel Miller's injections of morphine to quell the pain caused by seventeen inches of hot flak having torn through my father's back and legs, coming to its final resting place against his sciatic nerve, he would have died of shock before the bomber managed to limp home.

The plane had missed its target on the initial bombing run and the captain turned around and demanded a second run at the German airfield. "You'd think we could hit a damned airfield the first time," Ansel quipped.

The second run was a big mistake. The German flak gunners were ready for them. "They blew the hell out of our plane," Ansel recalled. "I thought we were going down. I crawled up the floor from the tail gunner position to see who was still alive and there was hardly anything left. The whole side of the plane had blown out. Your father was a bloody mess, lying there on the floor, paralyzed, going into shock. The only thing that saved him was the radio console, because it protected his upper body. Both legs were wounded and he was screaming in pain. I yanked out the morphine and got him calmed down. We barely made it back. Came in on two engines and without much in the way of a tail. The airplane was so badly damaged they junked it."

A loud bloody nightmarish hell.

My father was hospitalized for the next two months. He was sewn up and rehabilitated but the doctors decided against removing the seventeen inches of flak against his sciatic nerve. The risk to permanent paralysis was too great. He would walk again, eventually without crutches.

That was the best they could do. He would live the rest of his life in constant pain but without any real feeling in his right leg or much of his left one. The commanding officer pinned a Purple Heart on his chest and signed the orders to ship him home. My father's war was over. His buddies told him this was good news.

But his war was not over. It would never be.

He had been traumatized by the experience in ways that wouldn't show up for a year or so, when he would suddenly be seized by a recurring nightmare of being blasted out of the air. The nightmare was the work of memory being replayed, of something so clear and yet surreal that it seemed to be happening all over again. It included his body *actively* reliving the experience.

It is hard to describe accurately even though I witnessed it, and learned to fear it, and finally to cope with it, throughout my youth.

Imagine flying over enemy territory as the big guns open up below you. Imagine knowing your plane is their target. Now imagine being blasted from your seat onto the floor of a plane in flames and having your flesh ripped open by searing, burning metal. Imagine a pain so intense but being incapable of movement to get away from it, at least from the waist down. Imagine it passing out of your consciousness slowly, as the miracle of morphine moves into your blood.

Now imagine waking up on your floor years away from the war, in your bedroom, soaking wet with sweat, nauseated, and shaking violently from head to foot. Imagine realizing that what your body had just relived was only a nightmare.

Only a nightmare.

These days we call such episodes evidence of post-traumatic stress, but back in those days it was called shell shock, and the man who experienced it was labeled as just having a bad case of the nerves. There wasn't much anyone could do about it. Sleeping pills, maybe. Alcohol. Somebody sympathetic to talk to.

But nothing made the nightmares go away.

· ·

After recuperating in a field hospital and sailing home on the *Queen Mary*, Purple Heart and the other medals pinned proudly onto his uniform, Staff Sergeant H. Lloyd Goodall turned twenty-two and returned to his childhood home. He was still officially in the army and had to report for duty at the veterans hospital in Martinsburg, but he was given a two-week

FIGURE 2.2 Lloyd recovering in a British field hospital after being wounded over Tours, France.

furlough. "Go home, see your mother," he was told. "You're a hero. Everyone will want to buy you a drink."

If only it were so. Effie Ann and Phyllis were less than happy to see him alive, and not particularly sympathetic to his war wounds. They also had a secret that they didn't want to share with him. Eventually, though, he figured it out. He went to the bank and asked to make a withdrawal from his savings account. Ever since he went into the Air Corps he had been sending money home to his mother to be deposited in the bank. He lived cheaply and smiled when he thought about how much he would have saved when he got out.

He had planned to use the money to attend Marshall College. Phyllis and Effie Ann strongly disapproved, because they believed that Lloyd should find a job, any job, as soon as he was able, and continue to support them. "Never mind," he told them. "I've got enough saved to help out here while I go to college." They fell silent.

He discovered that the money he had sent home was gone. His bank account was almost empty. He limped home on his crutches and confronted Effie Ann and Phyllis. "Where's my money?" he demanded.

They didn't say a word but he figured it out. The story I heard from my mother, at the dying end of her own life and maybe laced with her own negative feelings about Phyllis, stopped there. My guess is that my father shrugged, made a dismissive hand gesture, and looked away. He knew what had happened. Maybe he had always known. His mother and sister had used the money to support themselves. In all likelihood, they didn't count on him living through the war. Everyone who read the newspapers knew that B-17 crews had high casualty rates. It's a coldhearted theory but, as he understood it, they had conspired to do coldhearted things before.

As far as I know, he never spoke to his mother or his sister again. He walked out of their lives, out of Huntington, and into a world where he could reliably claim no past.

As Bill Hastings told me, "Lloyd was very bitter about what happened to him with his mother after the war. *Very* bitter."

I don't doubt it.

· ·

Bill Hastings recalled more details about my father's early life than anyone else I talked to. He knew, for example, that after the war Lloyd had gone to work for the government. He knew that because Phyllis figured that there was some money in it, and she and Effie Ann told him they had twice hired private detectives to find Lloyd. The first time, they told Bill, they wanted to locate him to see if they couldn't "find some way to make it up to him." The second time it was Phyllis who hired a private eye to find him, believing, as she emphatically told Bill, that Lloyd ought to shoulder financial responsibility for their aging, increasingly unstable mother.

Both times the detectives failed to find him. Both times they informed his mother and sister that the government denied knowing anything about anyone named Harold Lloyd Goodall. According to "the government," this person they sought didn't exist.

Or at least that is the story Bill got from Phyllis.

I'm sure that is what Phyllis told Bill, but I find her story suspicious. For one thing, when these private detectives were hired, once in the late 1940s and again in the early 1950s, my father was living in Martinsburg, West Virginia, working at the Newton D. Baker Veterans Hospital as a contact officer. His name is listed in the city directory for the years 1947 to 1953, and his position at the hospital is still preserved on everything from pay records to a directory of employees, complete with an address on the post and a phone number. How hard would it be for any private detective, much less two of them, working in the same state, to find him?

Not very.

Unless . . . they were told not to.

I have no doubt that is exactly what happened. It would have been easy to arrange. A matter of national security would be reason enough. During the cold war, no one in America had anything to say except "yessir" after that.

. . . .

"His dreams for his life?" Warren Bills repeated back to me after I aired my question. "Well, no, I wouldn't say I knew his dreams at all. Lloyd kept things like that to himself."

I asked the same question to Bill Hastings. "No," said Bill. "I wouldn't know anything about that. Lloyd never gave up much about himself."

Bill had known my father all of his life. They had grown up a block from each other, played together, gone to school with each other, and enlisted in the navy on the same day. But never during their shared history did Bill remember my father disclosing much that was personal.

What he does recall is perhaps more revealing than whatever Lloyd's dreams may have been. Bill remembers vividly a clear, cold January day in early 1955, downtown in Huntington at the bus depot, on his routine way to work, whereupon he suddenly came upon my father. My father was leaning against the depot wall, casually smoking a cigarette, wearing a well-tailored blue suit and crisp white shirt and dark tie.

Bill shouted, "Lloyd!"

My father turned and looked at him. His expression gave away nothing.

"Lloyd? Lloyd *Goodall*! It's me, Bill Hastings!"

My father just stared at him for what Bill remembers as a "long time," then abruptly turned, tossed the butt of his cigarette into the gutter, and walked away.

"It was strange. We had been close friends and he acted like he didn't know who I was. Or maybe he didn't want me to see him there." Bill, who knew of his sister's quest to find her brother, immediately found a pay phone and called Phyllis.

Bill didn't know that Phyllis's interest in finding my father was to milk him for money, which may be why my father behaved as if he didn't know him, or at least didn't want to be seen back in town. He probably knew that Bill and Phyllis were friends. Of course Bill would call her to say he'd spotted Lloyd—the man the government had twice said didn't exist.

· ·

There is one more thing.

Well, two things actually, both involving photographs.

In interviews with family members, former friends, and coworkers, the *only* photographs of my father that survive his growing up in Huntington are contained in the 1941 East High School yearbook he edited.

Think about the chances of that happening.

I have personally examined thick family photograph albums, hundreds of loose Polaroids, and prized collections held by elderly people for whom these images contain the visual proof of their lives, their friends, their children, and their relatives. And not a single one of them contain a single image of my father.

Sandra, Nic, and I have all looked at multiple photographs of family gettogethers and Fourth of July holidays, spring picnics, Thanksgiving and Christmas celebrations. There are carefully posed photos of reunions, funerals, and revivals, as well as candid shots of every other member of his family.

But there is not one image of my father. *Anywhere*.

FIGURE 2.3 The Goodall family, circa 1938–39. Lloyd not pictured.

We wanted to know why. But nobody knew. They thought it was "strange," or "odd," or "very unusual." But nobody had an explanation for why or how it might have occurred. During these interviews it felt as if we were investigating a missing stranger rather than a blood relative. There often followed an empty, awkward silence, the kind of silence that reveals that, as awkward as it is, there is nothing else for anyone to say. Or perhaps it can be interpreted as a silence that conceals something too hard to say, something bad or just too difficult to articulate.

There must be some reasonable explanation. One is that Lloyd may have been the person behind the camera taking the pictures. After all, he worked in a dry goods store for a time, and it may have contained a dark room for developing customer photographs. He had always been interested in science—was, in fact, a science-track graduate at East High—and he was good at mastering technical things. Cameras, like radios, were high-tech items back then. Maybe his skills led him to become the designated family photographer, in the same way that his science diploma later led him to become a radio operator in the Air Corps.

It's a stretch. I know it is a stretch. Even if it were true, it wouldn't account for his absence from childhood family photographs, or baby pictures, where everyone except him is present and accounted for in the Goodall clan.

Given his later clandestine life, I can almost accept the "man who didn't exist" theory on the grounds that the government often went to extremes to protect case officers' identities. But the *kid* who didn't exist? Come on. The truth may well be stranger than anything we can make up, but there has to be a simpler explanation.

My father had a childhood in Huntington. People knew him. He had friends. He had girlfriends.

He grew up in an upper-middle-class household where pictures were as ordinary, and as everyday, as store-bought white bread and milk and creamery butter.

I come back to Phyllis. Here was a woman with at least some of her mother's unbalanced blood and a strong desire to preserve her story about what happened when Lloyd left town, when he—according to her—"abandoned" them. She hated him enough to betray him, bad-mouth him to anyone who listened, and hire private detectives to try to track him down.

Exasperated by her efforts, and too often reminded of him when she visited relatives who displayed family photographs featuring him, perhaps she asked everyone to remove photos of Lloyd from family albums. Perhaps her smoldering resentment of him for walking out of their lives led her on some kind of quest to rid his image from any recorded history, any visual representation, of their lives together. I have known divorced people to behave this way, even going so far as to scissor away halves and quarters of old photographs, as if by cutting them out the previous partner was summarily removed from any historical connection to them.

But if this were true, if this is what happened, wouldn't at least *one* family member or friend be willing to tell me about it? Phyllis is dead. How much damage could be done?

I don't know what to make of it.

And then there is the second mysterious thing. It is even more inexplicable. There is a large bound volume entitled *West Virginians Who Served in World War II* held in the reference section of the Cabell County Library.

In it are pictures of all servicemen and women, by county, who served in the war—including all those who survived, died, were killed in action, or reported missing. This volume is the official government record of military service during World War II for the state of West Virginia.

Neither my father's name nor his photograph appears in it.

Nor is this man who became my father listed under any alternative spelling of our last name: Goodal, Goodell, Goodale, or Godall.

It is as if he never existed as an aviation cadet, or an Air Corpsman, or a veteran.

What would you think?

. . . .

I inherited my father's copy of *The Great Gatsby*. He'd also used the Holy Bible to do his work during the cold war, but it was *Gatsby* he left for me to find. Though I considered myself somewhat of an expert on the novel—after all, I had written my doctoral dissertation and based scholarly articles and papers on it—I hadn't opened it in years until I began doing the research for this book. So it was that at the beginning of my quest for the truth about his life, a truth I knew was connected to this text, I turned to it for a clue—any clue—that might resolve for me the mystery of his childhood.

On the first page is a passage I feel was intended for me. It's a quotation from Nick Carraway's unnamed father, and it reads: "Whenever you feel like criticizing anyone . . . just remember that all the people in this world haven't had the advantages that you've had."

I read on. "He didn't say any more but we've always been unusually communicative in a reserved way and I understood that he meant a great deal more than that."

There was my answer. Or, if it wasn't my answer, at least it was enough of a clue to get me thinking. I had entered this project with the naive idea that I could discover what I needed to know through research. I believed I could find the truth by asking the right questions. I could ask people who knew my father what sort of young man he had been. I would be able to locate photographs, letters, and other artifacts that attested to his childhood in Huntington, West Virginia. I'm a trained interviewer, an ethnographer, a person who knows how to get people to open up to me. His relatives would surely open up to me.

WHERE HE CAME FROM **45**

I hadn't counted on the ambiguity in their language or on a nearly complete absence of photographic evidence. I hadn't figured into my questions any human calculation of what their relationship to him, to Phyllis, or to Oscar and Effie Ann had been. For all I knew, the people whom I talked to may have disliked or disapproved of him. After all, for many townspeople he was a man who turned his back on his own family and essentially walked away from them and from Huntington.

If my response to what I couldn't get from them led me to want to criticize them, I needed to remember that these were people who didn't know the man he had become. They were unaware of his role in the cold war. They had no idea of the physical, psychological, and emotional struggles he endured, nor the depth of the nightmares he suffered. The young man I was asking them about no longer existed. He had, in fact, ceased to exist as that young man when he left Huntington and entered the navy.

Perhaps, too, there was a message for me in the idea that my father was, like Nick Carraway's father, "unusually communicative in a reserved way" even in his childhood, even among his friends and family members. He had, in fact, "meant a great deal more than that." Of that, I was certain.

Later in Nick Carraway's opening soliloquy, he foreshadows the mystery, and the final chaos, I would learn to associate with my father's life. It is a famous passage, one often quoted in literary anthologies and therefore memorized by undergraduates in order to pass exams. But in my father's life, I am convinced this passage—underlined by his own hand several times and with a perfect star penned for emphasis next to it—meant much more than that.

Here is the relevant passage:

> If personality is an unbroken series of successful gestures, then there was something gorgeous about him, some heightened sensitivity to the promises of life, as if he were related to one of those intricate machines that register earthquakes ten thousand miles away. . . . [I]t was an extraordinary gift for hope, a romantic readiness such as I have never found in any other person and which it is not likely I shall ever find again. No—Gatsby turned out all right at the end; it is what preyed on Gatsby, what foul dust floated in the wake of his dreams that temporarily closed out my interest in the abortive sorrows and short-winded elations of men.

I closed the novel. For now, I didn't need to read any more. For now, I needed only to put behind me the doubts and uncertainties I had about his childhood, much as he had. I needed to move along into the evolving story line.

If there were mysteries, so be it. There would always be mysteries.

If I lacked photographs, well, there would be others.

And if I still didn't know his dreams for his life, couldn't articulate his hopes or his ambitions, at least I knew he had left a message, his "gift for hope," for me. His story for America would turn out all right at the end.

My job was to find out why he believed that end would be so.

Hidden Tales Within the
Paper Trails

April–December 1946

ON JULY 12, 1973, A FIRE SWEPT THROUGH THE NATIONAL PERSONNEL
Records Center in St. Louis, Missouri. My father's official employment files
were destroyed, along with an estimated sixteen to eighteen million others.
The St. Louis center was the central repository for archived files on government personnel in military and nonmilitary roles.

I received official notification of the fire nearly two months after I filed
my initial Freedom of Information Act request, in October 2002. The news
saddened me, but I was well aware that very little in the federal government exists in unduplicated form. My father had worked as a government
employee for over twenty-five years. I filed additional requests with the
Department of State, the Veterans Administration, and the Central Intelligence Agency. Surely, at least one of these agencies would have a record
of my father's employment.

While I waited for news, I received an invitation to present a lecture at
St. Louis University. It was a propitious moment. I agreed to do the lecture,
and in March 2003 Sandra and I traveled to St. Louis. While I made the
usual academic rounds that accompany the visit of a guest scholar, Sandra
visited the National Personnel Records Center. It was Sandra's contention
that a personal visit might be worthwhile, as government workers are more

likely to be persuaded to provide information in person that they will not, or cannot, provide in a letter.

Sure enough, Sandra returned with a photocopy of my father's personnel file. Using her considerable interpersonal skills, she had discovered that because my father had officially retired in 1969, a duplicate copy of his file had been made that year and transferred to the civilian records office. With a few keystrokes by a government worker who prefers to remain anonymous, she was able to obtain the location of the folder. Once the location was known, it didn't take long to obtain a complete photocopy of its contents.

This was *good* news!

The file consists of seventy-three pages of more or less linearly organized government documents. It begins with Lloyd's initial application for federal employment in 1946, and contains a piece of paper for every official pay raise he received throughout his career. It documents his various transfers and promotions in the Veterans Administration and the State Department. It contains a photocopy of the letter nominating him for a position in the State Department, as well as the form that granted him consular status. There are letters of commendation as well as one official letter of reprimand. The FBI investigation of him, complete with the personal signature of J. Edgar Hoover, is included. And, as he received secret and top secret clearances, more paper had been added to the file. There is a chart indicating the training he supposedly received, much of it the mundane and probably boring training required of career bureaucrats. Toward the end of the file, there are the final medical and psychiatric evaluations used to qualify him for a 100 percent medical disability retirement in Philadelphia in 1969.

Reading over these pages I felt an enormous debt of gratitude to Sandra, for without her personal touch I would never have seen these files. I hadn't thought to request them. As a scholar this oversight is embarrassing, but at the time I wasn't fully aware of the vagaries of the federal archival system.

We noticed that on several of the pages there is a handwritten notation directing someone—no doubt a secretary or other underling—to either "copy for the Dummy folder" or to "include in the Dummy file." I asked my scholarly friends who do archival work with government documents what these notations meant.

"Thank God for overworked government censors!" was the enthusiastic response. Apparently, the file I was now in possession of was a photocopy, not of my father's *official* records, but of his dummy folder.

A dummy folder confirms the cover story for a clandestine officer. Materials in it are mostly true and entirely factual. But the folder is also partial. It is the light fiction version of my father's federal employment intended for people who didn't need to know anything more about him. The story it spins is one of a rather ordinary government worker employed by the Veterans Administration. He had two overseas assignments—in the American embassies in Rome and in London—but his official dummy job from 1946 until 1969 was as a contact officer for the VA.

Armed with the knowledge that what the file contained was a documented version of the truth rather the whole truth, I began a critical reading of these materials. Documents, like photographs, tell stories. They represent a life. But documents are coded by a set of rules for interpreting them. It is much like the experience of reading a poem done as haiku.

A proper haiku contains exactly seventeen syllables organized in three unrhymed lines of five, seven, and five syllables. It is a highly evolved aesthetic that only works for a reader when, as the literary critic Kenneth Burke once expressed it, "the form *is* the appeal." In other words, you must first understand what haiku *is* before you try to appreciate what the specific haiku poem is *about*.

Government records are American haiku.

Each official government form is numbered and required information is boxed. It is designed to be filled out in a particular way. Information is organized by the rules for full disclosure as the government has ordained them. This means that "full" disclosure is never really *full* disclosure.

To appreciate the artful language required to make an intelligent, factual, but partial report requires an understanding that brevity and ambiguity are likely to work wonders when the intention is to deceive. Detailed factual responses are not a good idea. Whatever is written or typed onto the form is likely to be checked and then rechecked by someone else up the line. So, at least in the era of my father's work, *anything* that might be suspect or that might suggest he was anything but a full-time all-American patriotic heterosexual nondrinking ambitious Judeo-Christian citizen was a bad idea.

The boxes on government forms are mostly squares. There is probably a good reason for that. If your past in any way doesn't fit into those squares or accord with behavior or attitudes the authorities consider "right," it is verboten.

A government form is valuable for what it reveals. But, at the same time, it can be more valuable for clues it provides to what is being concealed.

Like haiku, the poetry often is what happens *between* the lines.

• •

Perhaps a more appropriate comparison, given my father's association with James Jesus Angleton and Angleton's fascination with the poetry of Ezra Pound, is to Pound's most famous and confounding work, *The Cantos*. The title is from the Latin *cantos* and refers to main divisions in a lengthy poem.

Think of the likely comparison this way: my father's secret intelligence career spanned over twenty-five years. The materials in his dummy file can be grouped as the main divisions in his cover life. The divisions appear to be defined by work accomplished in specific places—Martinsburg, Beckley, Rome, London, Washington, Cheyenne, and Philadelphia. Yet, as in *The Cantos*, naming those places is very much like the naming Pound does of the ancient capitals, from Constantinople to Rome.

The naming of ancient capitals is little more than an exercise to deflect attention away from what is the true business of the poem: the historical construction of a much larger aesthetic metaphor. For each individual division in Pound's poem, as for each segment in my father's dummy file, each canto holds part of the secret to the overall meaning, but none of them hold all of it.

The cantos are sophisticated word games for linguistic spies done as poems for an educated elite. For people in the know. For people who enjoy searching for clues. Angleton knew that. My father knew that, too. As in all word games, meanings are interpreted differently depending on how you understand the game itself, and, following that clue to its logical ending, what you think the secret really *is*.

• •

According to my father's initial application for federal employment, filled out by his own hand supposedly in Huntington, West Virginia, on April 23, 1946, he claims that following his release from active duty in the Army Air Corps, he had attended the Ohio State University while simultaneously being employed as a real estate salesman. The account reads:

5-8-45 to 4-20-46
Huntington, West Virginia
J. Bert Schroeder
Room 203—W. Va. Building
Listed real property for lease, rent, & sale. Sold, rented, & leased same.
Supervised preparation of sales, rental, & lease contracts; deeds & trust
deeds. Negotiated & processed mortgage loans. Prepared advertising. In
complete charge of office. Supervised preparation of all correspondence.
Performed research for titles to certain properties. Processed insurance
for transfer.

None of this information is likely to have been true. The first clue—a very
minor one—leads to more questions than answers. Why would my father
leave a relatively prosperous job selling real estate (it paid $200 a month when
he quit) to take a less prestigious job with the Veterans Administration as a
clerk-typist that paid less than $150 a month? It seems odd, unless, of course,
the job he took was simply a cover job.

The second clue is the name of his otherwise anonymous and therefore
convenient boss, Mr. J. Bert Schroeder. It is a clue of some kind because
J. Bert Schroeder was the first in a sequence of names—Wisner, Dulles,
Colby, etc.—that my father had associated in his secret diary with clandestine service. I don't know if the use of J. Bert Schroeder on his "initial"
application for government service means anything, but it might. Is the
name some kind of code intended for the person reviewing his file, perhaps
to suggest whom my father spoke to about government employment? His
recruiter, perhaps?

My father never sold real estate. I cannot find anyone who knew a J. Bert
Schroeder. He may or may not have actually existed.

This "official" file of my father's government employment is labeled
clearly as his dummy file. It is a fabricated account, a light fiction intended
as a cover story. The account provided is close enough to the truth to be
easily mistaken for the truth itself. Unless you either knew the truth—the
whole truth and nothing but—or knew my father and his careful use of the
English language, his style of composition, the way he crafted a lie, it would
pass. For a person as meticulous about language as my father was, these
seeming minor slips spoke volumes to me.

There is also some covert fun hidden behind the imprecise verbiage.

FOR FEDERAL EMPLOYMENT

Form approved.
Budget Bureau No. 50-R046.

INSTRUCTIONS.—Answer every question below ... y and completely. Typewrite or print in INK. If you are applying for a specific United ... tes Civil Service examination, read the examination announcement carefully and follow all directions. Mail this application to the office named in the announcement. Be sure to mail to the same office any other forms required by the announcement. Notify the office with which you file this application of any change in your address.

Elig: Contact Rep CAF130-7
Sirned, Place :
9/23/46

1. Name of examination, or kind of position applied for:
Contact Representative | 9258

2. Optional subject (if mentioned in examination announcement):

DO NOT WRITE IN THIS BLOCK
Date of Civil Service Commission Applicable

| | Material | Entered :
Appor. | Submitted |
Non-appor. | Returned |

3. Place of employment applied for:
Veterans Administration

Notations: | App. Review:

4. Mr. Mrs. Miss (First name) (Middle) (Maiden, if any) (Last)
HAROLD LLOYD GOODALL

Approved:

5. Street and number or R. D. number:
305 - 32ND STREET

OPTION	GRADE	EARNED RATING	PREFER-ENCE	AUGM. RATING

City or post office (including postal zone), and State:
HUNTINGTON, WEST VIRGINIA

6. Legal or voting residence (State): *WEST VIRGINIA* | 7. Office phone No.: *29316* | Home phone: *22366*

☐ 5 points (tent.)
☒ 10 points *Enter*

8. Place of birth (city and State; if born outside U.S., name city and country):
HUNTINGTON, WEST VIRGINIA

☐ Wife or Widow

9. Date of birth (month, day, year): *10-17-22* | 10. Age last birthday: *23* | 11. ☒ Male ☐ Female

☐ Disal.

12. ☒ Married ☐ Single | 13. Height without shoes: *6* feet *0* inches | Weight: *165* pounds

☐ Being investi-gated

14. Have you ever been employed by the Federal Government? ☐ Yes ☐ No
If now employed by the Federal Government, give present grade and date of last change in grade:
CAF 2 - APRIL 23 1946

INITIALS AND DATE

Indicate "Yes" or "No" answer by placing X in proper column | YES | NO

15. (a) Would you accept short-term appointment, if offered, for—
1 to 3 months? | | X
3 to 6 months? | | X
6 to 12 months? | | X

(b) Would you accept appointment, if offered—
in Washington, D. C.? | |
anywhere in the United States? | X |
outside the United States? | X |

15. (c) If you will accept appointment in certain locations ONLY, give acceptable locations:
WEST VIRGINIA

(d) What is the lowest entrance salary you will accept: $ *3397* per year.
You will not be considered for positions paying less.

(e) If you are willing to travel, specify:
☐ Occasionally ☒ Frequently ☐ Constantly

---

16. EXPERIENCE.—You are requested to furnish all information asked for below in sufficient detail to enable the Civil Service Commission and the appointing officers of agencies to determine your qualifications for the position for which you are applying. In the spaces provided below describe EVERY position you have held. Use a separate block for EACH position. You may also include any pertinent religious, civic, welfare or organizational activity which you have performed, either with or without compensation, showing the number of hours per week and weeks per year in which you were engaged in such activity. Start with your PRESENT position and work back, accounting for all periods of unemployment. Explain clearly the principal tasks which you performed in each position. Describe your experience in the Armed Services in question 17 (Military Experience).
(a) If you were ever employed in any position under a name different from that shown in Item 4 of this application, give under "Description of your work" for each position, the name used.
(b) If you have never been employed or are now unemployed, indicate that fact in the space provided below for "Present Position."

PRESENT POSITION

Dates of employment: (Month, year)
From: *4-23-46* To present time

Place of employment (city and State):
HUNTINGTON, WEST VIRGINIA

Name and address of employer (firm, organization, or person). If Federal, name department, bureau or establishment, and division:
VETERANS ADMINISTRATION

Kind of business or organization (e. g. wholesale silk, insurance agency, mfg. of locks, etc.):
GOV'T. AGENCY

Number and kind of employees supervised by you:
4 - CLERK - TYPISTS CAF-2.
1 - STENOGRAPHER CAF-3

Name and title of immediate supervisor:
JOHN T. WATSON, CHIEF
ED. & TRAINING SECTION

Reason for desiring to change employment:
ADVANCEMENT

Exact title of your present position:
CLERK - TYPIST CAF-2

Salary or earnings:
Starting, $ *1704* per *ANNUM*
Present, $ *1954* per "

Description of your work: *SUPERVISION & DELEGATION OF ALL WORK TO BE DONE. CHECK VALIDITY OF ALL INVOICES FOR TOOLS, EQUIPMENT, & SUPPLIES FOR VETERANS IN TRAINING ON-THE-JOB. SUPERVISE PREPARATION OF TRAVEL REQUESTS & VOUCHERS FOR ALL TRAINING OFFICERS. ADVISE TRAINING OFFICERS OF POLICY REGARDING PURCHASES; TRAVEL; NEW REGULATIONS CONCERNING SAME — CONT'D*

(CONTINUED ON NEXT PAGE)

FIGURE 3.1 Lloyd's initial Application for Federal Employment, 1946. From the dummy folder.

16. CONTINUED

| Dates of employment: (Month, year) From: _5-8-45_ To: _4-20-46_ | Exact title of your position: REAL ESTATE SALESMAN | Salary or earnings: Starting $ _100_ per _mo._ Final $ _200_ per _mo._ |

Place of employment (city and State): HUNTINGTON, WEST VIRGINIA

Name and address of employer (firm, organization, or person). If Federal, name department, bureau or establishment, and division: J. BERT SCHROEDER ROOM 203 - W. VA. BUILDING

Kind of business or organization (e. g., wholesale silk, insurance agency, mfg. of locks, etc.): REAL ESTATE

Number and kind of employees supervised by you: 1 - SECRETARY

Name and title of immediate supervisor: OWNER: J. BERT SCHROEDER

Reason for leaving: TO ACCEPT POSITION WITH VETERANS ADMINISTRATION

Description of your work: LISTED REAL PROPERTY FOR LEASE, RENT, + SALE. SOLD, RENTED, + LEASED SAME. SUPERVISED PREPARATION OF SALES, RENTAL, + LEASE CONTRACTS; DEEDS, + TRUST DEEDS. NEGOIATED + PROCESSED MORTGAGE LOANS. PREPARED ADVERTISING. IN COMPLETE CHARGE OF OFFICE. SUPERVISED PREPARATION OF ALL CORRESPONDENCE. PERFORMED RESEARCH FOR TITLES TO CERTAIN PROPERTIES. PROCESSED INSURANCE FOR TRANSFER.

| Dates of employment: (Month, year) From: _2-10-41_ To: _5-20-42_ | Exact title of your position: ORDER CLERK | Salary or earnings: Starting $ _60_ per _mo._ Final $ _70_ per _mo._ |

Place of employment (city and State): HUNTINGTON, WEST VIRGINIA

Name and address of employer (firm, organization, or person). If Federal, name department, bureau or establishment, and division: WATTS-RITTER + CO. HUNTINGTON, WEST VIRGINIA

Kind of business or organization (e. g., wholesale silk, insurance agency, mfg. of locks, etc.): WHOLESALE-DRY GDS. + NOTIONS

Number and kind of employees supervised by you: 1 - CLERK-SECRETARY

Name and title of immediate supervisor: C. N. PETIT, CHIEF ORDER DEPARTMENT

Reason for leaving: TO ENTER U. S. NAVY

Description of your work: WORKED AS ASSISTANT TO HEAD OF DEPARTMENT. RECEIVED, CHECKED, + POSTED ALL INCOMING ORDERS. SUPERVISED DISTRIBUTION TO VARIOUS DEPT'S. FOR FILLING. ASSEMBLED SAME UPON RETURN FROM DEPT'S. SUPERVISED GATHERING OF SAME BY GATHERERS IN ORDER TO PLACE IN LINE FOR PACKING + SHIPMENT. IN ABSENCE OF DEP'T. HEAD I ACTED IN THAT CAPACITY.

| Dates of employment: (Month, year) From: To: | Exact title of your position: | Salary or earnings: Starting $ per Final $ per |

Place of employment (city and State):

Name and address of employer (firm, organization, or person). If Federal, name department, bureau or establishment, and division:

Kind of business or organization (e. g., wholesale silk, insurance agency, mfg. of locks, etc.):

Number and kind of employees supervised by you:

Name and title of immediate supervisor:

Reason for leaving:

Description of your work:

| Dates of employment: (Month, year) From: To: | Exact title of your position: | Salary or earnings: Starting $ per Final $ per |

Place of employment (city and State):

Name and address of employer (firm, organization, or person). If Federal, name department, bureau or establishment, and division:

Kind of business or organization (e. g., wholesale silk, insurance agency, mfg. of locks, etc.):

Number and kind of employees supervised by you:

Name and title of immediate supervisor:

Reason for leaving:

Description of your work:

If more space is required, use a continuation sheet (Standard Form No. 58) or a sheet of paper the same size as this page and birth, and examination title. Attach to inside of this application.   Write on each sheet your name, address, date of

c9-16-47298-1

FIGURE 3.2 Application for Federal Employment, page 2.

Examine the language of my father's claim: "In complete charge of office." The space between "In" and "complete" perhaps should be closed. *Incomplete*, maybe, as in "not entirely there," or better, "not entirely true." Nor is the claim even a complete sentence. For a man who knew his grammar and who knew also that a man's use of grammar in an employment application was important, this offhand informality seems suspect. After all, he was supposedly a clerk-typist for the VA. Isn't proper grammar a requirement for a clerk-typist?

Of course it is. But so, too, is the ability to *type*. This application is handwritten. Perhaps this fact could be explained away easily enough as the product of quick work done on a busy day, but I think that explanation works equally as well when the whole file is understood to be a dummy job. As my father regularly said, "Never confuse the appearance of order with an absence of chaos." Then, of course, there is the bald fact that my father didn't know how to type. At least, not beyond the basic hunt-and-peck method. Supposedly a clerk-typist needed to be proficient at the level of 40 to 60 words per minute, minimum. I doubt my father could have ever managed 20 wpm, and even at that rate of speed the errors would be a clear indicator of typing illiteracy.

But of course, that is only true *if* he was actually working as a clerk-typist for the VA when he applied for this job as a contact representative. But wait a minute—hey! Isn't this file his *initial application* for government employment? It says it is on page 1. But if he worked for the VA as a clerk-typist—as this application claims—then wouldn't that mean that he had already filed an initial application in order to get that initial government job?

There is more going on here than meets the scrutiny of even a moderately critical eye. I hate to niggle over the finer details of someone's cover story, but niggling over the finer details of this cover story appears called for. It's a slack job at best, even for a dummy folder. It's not an initial application; the man who was supposedly employed as a clerk-typist couldn't type; and my father the strict grammarian would never have committed the errors evident on these pages.

Beyond these anomalies of fact, date, and language usage, I am still bothered by the facts of the background story. Why would a rookie salesman be placed in "complete charge" of a real estate office? Whoever J. Bert Schroeder may or may not have been, he would have been a very trusting soul to turn over his business to a wounded veteran with no previous experience in real estate. That fact alone just doesn't ring true.

That presumption of Schroederian trust, of course, assumes my father was, on this supposedly "official" and supposedly "initial" application for government employment, telling the truth, the whole truth, and nothing but.

Which further assumes that my father was actually living and working in Huntington during this time.

Or even further down on the list of assumptions, that he had been attending the Ohio State University following his release from military service.

. . . .

Language is always coded. The word "code" has dual meanings. According to my Microsoft Word dictionary, a code "is a system of letters, numbers, or symbols into which normal language is converted to allow information to be communicated secretly, briefly, or electronically." But it may also be "a system of accepted laws and regulations that govern procedure or behavior in particular circumstances or within a particular profession."

I think the second definition significantly modifies the first one, don't you?

After all, you have to understand "the system of laws and regulations that govern procedures or behavior . . . within a particular profession" in order to appreciate how "normal language is converted to allow information to be communicated secretly."

Which is to say, if you were my father in 1946 and you wanted to apply for federal employment, you would have to apply what you knew about the laws governing that particular institution to the information you intended to include—or exclude—from your official application.

Coded language. All you need is the codebook to read it clearly.

I am reminded of Gatsby. Early on the mystery of who this man really is dominates the story. In the third chapter, Nick Carraway and Jordan Baker attend one of Gatsby's infamous parties and come across a stout, owl-spectacled man, a drunk but an intelligent drunk, who is perusing books in the impressive library. The man explains to them that all of the books are "absolutely real—have pages and everything." He continues:

> "See!" he cried triumphantly. "It's a bona fide piece of printed matter. It fooled me. This fella's a regular Belasco. It's a triumph. What thoroughness! What realism! Knew when to stop, too—didn't cut the pages."

The implication is clear. The bespectacled drunk thought Gatsby was a fake. If he owned fake books, it would prove his case. Instead, he discovered the real thing. Not merely the real thing, but an impressive collection. By a false but logical deduction, the man concluded that Gatsby, too, was the real thing. He owned all the right books, with real pages and everything. But it didn't mean anything of the sort. Gatsby was wise enough to adapt his character to the needs and expectations of his audience. He surrounded himself with the accoutrements of wealth and learning in order to appear to have always been rich and well educated.

You must first know the rules of haiku to read the haiku *properly*.

Later on in the story, Gatsby drives over to Nick's cottage to pick him up for lunch. He says, "Look here, old sport . . . what's your opinion of me, anyhow?"

Nick, of course, is surprised by the question. He tells us, "I began the generalized evasions which that question deserves." Then the critical scene, my clue in the codebook, unfolds as Gatsby talks about his background in the "middle-west," his education at Oxford, and the death of family, upon which he came into money.

Nick knows that Gatsby is lying to him, but it is such a grand lie and so authentically delivered he goes along with it. Gatsby continues spinning an increasingly incredulous version of his life with an account of reluctant heroism in the First World War—even producing a medal for Nick to inspect—and a photograph of a somewhat younger Gatsby with a cricket bat standing among "half a dozen young men in blazers" in Trinity Quad, Oxford.

Nick concludes: "Then it was all true." Having seen the evidence and examined the artifacts, having listened to a not terribly convincing story of Gatsby's life, he nevertheless decides to believe him.

Gatsby has told Nick this story for a reason. His game, the game he has drawn Nick into, has a much larger aesthetic. He wants a favor. But Gatsby doesn't think he can ask for the favor until he has won over Nick. He must first win his confidence, his trust. Out of the stuff of relationships, the need for doing favors, and the corresponding expectation that they will be done, attains a symmetrical likelihood.

Gatsby's story—his cover story, his dummy file—is a means to an end. True to his clandestine expectation, Nick warms to him despite the errors and omissions in Gatsby's cover story. They become friends. As they enter the city, Nick says, "Anything can happen now that we've slid over this bridge . . . anything at all. . . ."

The final line of this canto reads: "Even Gatsby could happen, without any particular wonder."

Lloyd's application to become a contact representative for the Veterans Administration was formally accepted by one J. S. Snead on September 23, 1946. The number 92.5, an aptitude test score, is circled at the top of the first page, where it is duly recorded that my father also received a ten-point preference for being a 50 percent disabled American veteran.

His address is given as 305 32nd Street, Huntington, West Virginia, which was Effie Ann's address, although we know for a fact that he had broken off contact with her shortly after returning from the war. So I think we can safely assume that this wasn't his real address, at least not at that time.

But he was also selling real estate then too, right? I think he may have been selling something, but it was unlikely to be real estate. Then, again, he was also attending Ohio State University, right? He never showed me a photograph of Ohio State University. But it was a good school with a recognizable name. A step up from the smaller and more local Marshall College.

Let's continue reading.

My father's account of previous military experience is worth examining. The government's rules for anything reported in this section of the application are very clear: stick strictly to the facts. In 1946 most males my father's age were veterans. Too many men had died in the war to play loose with the truth. Besides, military records that included combat and Air Medals and Purple Hearts were coins of the realm. He had nothing to hide and no need to exaggerate.

Here is what we learn. After enlisting in the Naval Reserve at the end of spring semester at Marshall College—where he had studied mathematics—on May 25, 1942, he was initially assigned to Naval Aviation Cadet Flight School at the University of Georgia. He was there from June 23 until October 26, during which time he learned (as reported in his "initial" application for federal employment) "naval law and procedures" in addition to "aerodynamics and physics, history, and drill," and acquired an "orientation to naval procedure and life; learned to command others; [and] preparation for flight." While in school, he served as "platoon leader, company commander, and battalion commander" as well as "officer of the day."

V-5, I would learn later, was the name of the navy program that recruited high school graduates like my father with some college or a high aptitude for math and science into flight training. His rank was seaman second class.

Upon completion of his preliminary training he was transferred to the Naval Aviation Reserve base at Anacostia, Maryland, on November 3, 1942.

He remained there until February 18, 1943. During this stage of his military career, he completed "primary and intermediate flight training, served as squadron and flight commander," and, again, served as "officer of the day."

Now to the curious fact of his failed final flight test. No official explanation is given, although I think I know what happened. In interviews conducted with ex-military men serving as archivists at the National Museum of Naval Aviation in Pensacola, Florida, I was given benefit of their thoughts on the incident. Given my father's exemplary record until February 18, it is likely that he was discharged for three reasons.

First, he failed to land his airplane on the aircraft carrier on Lake Michigan, where all final flight tests for naval aviators assigned to fighter training took place. The carrier was really a converted barge with a wooden platform. Many cadets failed that part of their flight test, at least the first time they took it. No matter how good they were bringing a plane in on dry land, bringing a plane in over the water and landing on a short wooden deck was something else entirely. For personnel with exemplary records, a second or even a third test was sometimes needed before the cadet got it right. We were in a war, there was a desperate need for new pilots, and the investment the navy had made in these men thus far was not something they wanted to lose. If it took two or three tries, it took two or three tries.

My father only got one try. Despite having been rated at the top of his class, he received only one attempt at a carrier-based landing. Why?

That brings us to the second reason. My father probably pissed somebody off. That's what the guys at the museum believed to be true. Now, my father was not normally a brash young man, but on the other hand, he would not necessarily have had to be brash. He could have just been a young man. Maybe he was caught with a superior officer's girlfriend. Or perhaps he mouthed off behind someone's back. Hard to say. But certainly, in the considered view of these men, he pissed off somebody.

The third reason given was that maybe he had emotional problems. Oscar's death and his mother and sister's complicity in it would have definitely fallen under that general heading. The men I spoke with at the museum explained that of all the branches of service, naval aviators during the Second World War had the strictest regulations regarding emotional readiness for combat. Planes were expensive. Mistakes made in the sky were often fatal. If someone superior to my father thought that Oscar's death made Lloyd even the slightest bit dicey on an emotional-readiness level, he could have been dropped for that reason alone.

I suppose I'll never know. But I do believe that these three reasons made a good deal of common sense. He was, for whatever reason or reasons, honorably discharged from the navy on February 18, 1943. He was duly ordered to report immediately to his draft board. Instead of returning home to Huntington, he took a train down to Tampa, Florida, and enlisted in the Army Air Corps on March 3. One man I spoke with at the museum explained it this way: "Probably he didn't want to be drafted because that meant he would be in the army infantry. In those days, everyone knew there was going to be a big invasion of Europe and the frontline troops would be cannon fodder. A lot of guys thought their chances were better if they could enlist in another branch of service. My guess is that he went down to Tampa on the advice of someone at Anacostia. The officers in charge at bases knew where the quotas needed to be filled. Tampa, in February of 1943, just happened to have some openings for men willing to serve as B-17 crew members."

The Boeing B-17, or "Flying Fortress," was the largest long-range heavy bomber in production. It had four turboprop engines and was capable of 300 miles per hour, but with a full complement of bombs and a crew of ten men, its cruising speed was only 160 mph. This fact made the Flying Fortress one of the largest and certainly one of the slowest targets in the skies, which meant that it was destined to become known in aviation history as the airplane with the highest casualty rates in any war. By war's end, over 60 percent of the B-17 crewmen had been killed or wounded. So, undoubtedly, in 1943, there was a definite need for Air Corps volunteers willing to train for duty on the B-17.

"At least," my father joked with his friend Bill Hastings, "I won't have to sleep on the ground." But it was also true that my father didn't believe he would actually see combat. His plan was to enter the Air Corps and excel in his classes, take the officer candidate exam as soon as possible, and apply for a post in Air Administration. His record indicates that he did exactly that. He excelled in his classes, scored 88 percent on his test, but was never assigned to officer candidate training.

There was a war on. They needed B-17 crews far more than they needed air administrators. If you got shot up and couldn't return to active duty over there, you became an air administrator or some other office duty was found for you over here.

In the meantime, he learned to be a radio operator and waist gunner on a B-17. He trained in Florida, Texas, and South Dakota. His crew picked up a brand-new plane in Savannah, flew to Newfoundland, then

APPLICATION

17. MILITARY EXPERIENCE ...acquired in the Armed Services... ...on the service, write in Item (a) "No attendance..." ...of such assignment.

APPLICATION ...cements of war veterans, detailed information is needed about the training and experience they have ...or each service school you have attended. If you attended no special or technical schools while ...service schools" and indicate in Item (a) all important changes in duty assignment, showing dates

(a) First Special Service School attended:	(b) What were you taught in First Special Service School?
U.S. NAVY- UNIVERSITY OF GEORGIA PRE-FLIGHT SCHOOL	FUNDAMENTALS OF NAVAL LAW + PROCCEDURE, AIRCRAFT REC.
Location: ATHENS, GEORGIA	PHYSICS, AERO DYNAMICS, HISTORY, DRILL, MATH, ETC. PLATOON
Dates attended (months, years): From: 6-23-42 To: 10-26-42	LEADER, COMPANY COMMANDER,
Rating received at end of this training: AVIATION CADET V-5 USNR	BATALLION COMMANDER, AND OFFICER OF THE DAY.
(c) Duty assignment or rating after this training (give all important changes in duty assignment whether or not you attended a Service School): AVIATION CADET V-5	(d) What did you do during this duty assignment? ORIENTATION INTO THE NAVAL PROCCEDURE + LIFE. LEARNED
Dates of duty assignment (months, years): SAME AS ABOVE. From: To:	HOW TO COMMAND OTHERS. PREPARATION FOR FLYING.
(e) Second Special Service School attended: U.S. NAVY	(f) What were you taught in Second Special Service School?
NAVAL RESERVE AV. BASE.	NAVIGATION, AERO DYNAMICS, LAW, HISTORY, PROCCEDURE.
Location: ANNACOSTIA, D.C.	PRIMARY +INTERMEDIATE
Dates attended (months, years): From: 11-3-42 To: 2-18-43	FLIGHT TRAINING. FLEW: SQUADRON COMMANDER, FLIGHT
Rating received at end of this training: (FLYING) AVIATION CADET V-5	COMMANDER, OFFICER OF THE DAY.
(g) Duty assignment after this training: NONE	(h) What did you do during this duty assignment? NONE.
Dates of duty assignment (months, years): From: To:	

List on a separate sheet of paper any additional experience, training, service, or special duty assignments during military service or hospitalization.

18. EDUCATION.—Circle highest grade completed:
1 2 3 4 5 6 7 8 9 10 11 ⑫

Mark (x) the appropriate box to indicate satisfactory completion of:

☐ Elementary School ☐ Junior High School ☒ Senior High School

(a) Give name and location of last high school attended: HUNTINGTON EAST HUNTINGTON WEST VIRGINIA.

(b) Subjects studied in high school which apply to position desired:

(c) Name and Location of College or University	Major	Dates Attended From—	To—	Years Completed Day	Night	Degrees Conferred Title	Date	Semester Hours Credit
OHIO STATE UNIVERSITY	ECONOMICS	SEPT.'45	JAN. 1946	1/2				18+12
UNIVERSITY OF GEORGIA	NAVY	JULY 42	OCT. '42	1/4			-6	-
MARSHALL COLLEGE	MATH	JAN. '41	APR '41	1/3	✓			-

(d) List Your Chief Undergraduate College Subjects	Semester Hours	List Your Chief Graduate College Subjects	Semester Hours
BUSINESS ORGANIZATION	5		
" MANAGEMENT	1	NONE.	
ECONOMICS	5		
GEOLOGY + GEOGRAPHY	5		

(e) Other training, such as vocational, business, study courses given through the Armed Forces Institute (show name and location of school), or "in-service training" in a Federal agency: NOW TAKING 3 YEAR LAW COURSE WITH LA SALLE EXTENSION UNIV. PURSUIT: LLB

Subjects Studied	Dates Attended From—	To—	Years Completed Day	Night
LAW	PRESENT			

19. Indicate your knowledge of foreign languages:

	READING			SPEAKING			UNDERST'NG		
	Exc.	Good	Fair	Exc.	Good	Fair	Exc.	Good	Fair
SPANISH			x			x			x

(a) How was your knowledge of foreign languages acquired? 2 YEARS HIGH SCHOOL PERSONAL CONTACT

(b) If you have traveled or resided in any foreign countries, indicate (1) names of countries, (2) dates and length of time spent there and (3) reason or purpose (e. g., business, education, recreation):

20. List any special skills you possess and machines and equipment you can use, such as operation of short-wave radio, multilith, comptometer, key-punch, turret lathe, scientific or professional devices: RADIO OPERATOR 756-757
Approximate number of words per minute in typing 60, shorthand ✓

21. Are you now or have you ever been a licensed or certified member of any trade or profession (such as pilot, electrician, radio operator, teacher, lawyer, CPA, etc.)?

☒ Yes ☐ No Give kind of license and State: REAL ESTATE WEST VIRGINIA.

First license or certificate (year): 1945
Latest license or certificate (year): 1946

22. Give any special qualifications not covered elsewhere in your application such as:
(a) your more important publications (do NOT submit copies unless requested)
(b) your patents or inventions
(c) public speaking and public relations experience
(d) membership in professional or scientific societies, etc.

SEE SUPPLEMENT—17

FIGURE 3.3 Lloyd's Application for Federal Employment, page 3, with military record and education history.

to England. He arrived for the war on May 2, 1944, just a month prior to D-Day, and his formal combat training ended on May 22, 1944, just two weeks before the massive invasion began. He graduated first in his class of forty-three men.

· ·

What do you read into my father's official story line at this point? Or into his state of mind? It's clear that Harold Lloyd Goodall, or Duke as he was nicknamed, saw himself as a bright and highly motivated young man.

He saw himself, at least as his language reflects it, as a leader of men, a patriotic citizen, a responsible and honorable person, and a man possessing certain—shall we say, interesting—skill sets. These skill sets included the ability to fly a plane (even though he had flunked a flight test, he wrote "flew" on his federal application), and, under the V-5 aviation cadet program, he had completed roughly 100 hours of flight time. He knew "the law and military procedures." He knew how to operate a radio, which was then considered highly evolved technology. He could perform cryptography. He had fired pistols, rifles, and machine guns. He had seen combat and displayed "cool and calm under intense pressure," which led to an Air Medal. He had been wounded and survived, which earned him a Purple Heart. While convalescing back in the States, he rounded out his service completing office work, and knew how to interview patients, give public speeches, engage in publicity campaigns, and act in the capacity of a variety of military roles that could easily transfer into civilian, or clandestine, work.

As I say, it was an interesting set of skills he had acquired. He was a man who could pass as a lowbrow clerk-typist, a professional PR man, or perhaps even as a real estate salesman. He was a veteran. He knew how the military worked. He had excelled in every task he undertook, and in every class he had taken. He flunked one flight test, but there were probably three good reasons for that. It hardly slowed him down. He was bright and ambitious, he was skilled and had proven his mettle in war, and he was ready for something else.

Ted Gup's *The Book of Honor: Covert Lives and Classified Deaths at the CIA* provides two representative accounts of young men who joined the clandestine service after the war. Both passages remind me of my father:

> Like many, Mackiernan had joined the CIA as much out of a taste for
> adventure as a sense of patriotism. Following the war, it had been hard

for men and women like Mackiernan, accustomed to exotic places and the rush of danger, to slip back into the routine of civilian life. Some, like Mackiernan, had discovered that they felt most alive only when they were living on the edge.

Hugh Redmond . . . Like many highly decorated veterans of World War II, he was eager to continue his service to country, but he had suffered grave wounds in the war. It was doubtful that he would have been eligible for active military duty. And so, like many other casualties of war, he sought out the next closest thing—the clandestine service. In those early days the corridors of the clandestine service had more than their share of men with limps, eye patches, and other tokens of war.

. . . .

My father was also skilled in oral and written communication, where communication may be understood to be a craft of using language to make something plausible and yet also deniable, out of any and all available rhetorical resources. It is a way of thinking about yourself within the context of an evolving tale. It is the ability to tell a story from a particular point of view, manufacturing what you must while retaining enough ambiguity to encourage others to fill in their own blanks. It is a way of communicating to build relationships. To gain trust. To fit in.

Spies are great storytellers. They have to be. Their lives often depend on it. In interviews I've conducted with former CIA case officers and analysts, I have recognized in their energetic construction of scenarios and characters, in their imagination, and in their ability to meditate on the uses of language and its possible meanings the communication texture of my father's storytelling style.

But spies don't tell everything. They can't. The impression others have of them depends on keeping who they really are a secret, while they actively engage their roles. This, too, is a communication skill. It is one not made out of words, but fashioned out of silences and gestures. It is having an ability to maintain, and to carefully cultivate, *silence*—what the language theorist Roland Barthes calls "the presence of an absence"—as a source of communicative power and control in social situations.

Making sense of the documents in my father's dummy file is an exercise in interpreting the interplays of silence and absence that reside in between what is articulated and what might also be true. I am struck by the image he had of himself, and wonder I what he thought his life would be like after the war.

His first steps into his new life, or at least the first steps he records on paper, were those he took to go back to college. He had entered the war after completing a year at Marshall and he knew that the future belonged to college graduates. He had always maintained a consistent interest in higher education, at least insofar as it related to obtaining a college degree and getting a better job. That is why it comes as no surprise to me to read, on page 6 of his supposedly initial application for government employment, that following his Air Corps discharge he enrolled at Ohio State University. His major was economics, and he claims to have completed a total of thirty hours credit.

This may or may not be true. I contacted Ohio State and explained that I was working on a book about my father. I provided them with the dates of his enrollment from the file. The person I spoke with was extremely helpful. She searched in a number of places looking for any record of my father's registration or attendance. She could find nothing.

The CIA has a long habit of creating backstories for officers that includes obtaining college credits. His listed work at Ohio State included courses in business organization, business management, economics, and (for some reason, either to fulfill a general education requirement or simply because he was having a little fun filling out this form), geography and geology.

There are further anomalies.

He left Ohio State in January of 1946, supposedly to accept a CAF-2 position as a clerk-typist for the VA center in Huntington. Yet he claims on this very same form that he didn't start his VA job until April 4, 1946.

Hmmm.

He also claims that during this time at Ohio State he worked full time "in complete charge of the office" for one J. Bert Schroeder in Huntington. Fair enough, maybe. But Huntington is a far piece away from Columbus and I have to wonder how he got back and forth. He didn't drive a car. There wasn't a train. A bus, perhaps?

Hmmm.

I have no problem with the idea that he worked to put himself through school, but I do have a problem with working two full-time jobs while attending college in another state. Yet, these disparate items seem to have escaped the notice of the person checking the accuracy of this file, as well as the overworked government censor who reviewed it prior to releasing it to Sandra.

Or maybe it didn't matter.

This is a government document, an example of American haiku. The facts alleged to be true might not be entirely factual. In fact, very little if any of what is contained in his dummy file may have been *entirely* true. The important thing may not be the facts at all, but the story they suggest. It is the story of an ambitious and skilled young man who, after the war, went back to school and had to work to support himself. It was a tale that not only made him suitable for government work, but also marked him as determined to succeed.

It's not just the contradictory dates, or even the possible exaggerations that provide the tip-off to something else going on, or that signal that this official government document must be understood as a light fiction. After all, the oddities I've pointed out are small details involving dates, explanations of responsibilities, and the possible meanings of ambiguous language and fouled grammar over a brief and, for my father, intensely personal and chaotic passage of time.

He had just been in a shooting war, for God's sake. Besides, ambitious people as well as common folk routinely exaggerate their importance, or the responsibilities they've had, or their skills and abilities on job applications. Dates are forgotten, or slightly confused. Women and men I have known claim to have been serious university students when they were only taking up nap space in college classrooms.

Nor is it beyond possibility that my father saw whatever work he was then doing as a stepping-stone up the path to a grander profession. That may explain the otherwise seemingly irrelevant inclusion of knowledge associated with the legal profession on his application. My father's consistent mentioning of "the law" and his knowledge of legal issues in both the army and navy strike me as perfectly in keeping with his hopeful story line. He was then a twenty-three-year-old man who may have aspired to the law. He indicated under the heading of "Education" that he was enrolled in a three-year law program through La Salle Extension University and that this program of study would lead to the LLB degree.

Although I haven't seen a matchbook with an advertisement for a college degree program for years, I do remember that La Salle Extension University was once prominent among them. The LLB degree is not a professional lawyer's degree, per se, at least not a postbaccalaureate diploma recognized by the American Bar Association. That professional degree is the LLD or, more recently, the JD. But then again, the ABA doesn't require a professional degree to take the bar exam or to practice law. And following the war, there were many quick-completion professional programs put in place to assist veterans who had college on their minds and ready financial assistance from a grateful federal government.

None of these small, niggling details bother me. Not really.

But here again, there are ambiguities, silences, and ways of saying, or of *not* saying, things that give me interpretive pause. They also provide an opening for seeing his story in an entirely different way.

• •

The known facts of recruitment into the clandestine world have been well researched and documented. They appear in histories and in fiction, biographies and autobiographies, confessions, and testimonies before congressional committees. Here is the short version:

Following World War II, veterans, and particularly wounded veterans with solid war records, were regularly recruited out of colleges and assigned CAF-2 or CAT-2 rankings as clerk-typists. The old Office of Strategic Services (OSS), created by Bill Donovan to serve as the intelligence and covert operations arm of the presidency during the war, was dissolved on September 20, 1945, by order of President Harry S. Truman. At that time, the OSS employed over fourteen thousand people worldwide, including a sizable number of skilled operatives and analysts.

Some of the old OSS group—mostly analysts—were temporarily assigned to a Special Services office under then–Undersecretary of State Dean Acheson. No one really knew what to do with these women and men, but nobody really wanted to let them loose either. We had just won a world war, but there was the possibility that another one might be getting under way. These clandestine operatives and analysts knew too much to be let go because their skill sets might once again be needed.

Other clandestine personnel, including members of the OSS Foreign Nationals office, were reorganized under the heading of "Special Operations" for the emerging Central Intelligence Group (CIG) under OSS veteran Frank Wisner. This latter group emerged, in September of 1947, under authority of the National Security Act and the initial direction of Rear Admiral Roscoe H. Hillenkoetter, as the Central Intelligence Agency.

The explicit idea behind the creation of this new intelligence service was to provide a central clearinghouse for all intelligence, regardless of source, that could be collated, coordinated, analyzed, interpreted, and passed along to the president. Implicit in this idea of intelligence gathering was the dark secret for some, and the dark fear for others, that the true offspring of clandestine work was likely to be a covert organization capable of being used by the president to pursue personal political objectives and foreign policy through "other options."

But the other side had it and used it and didn't complain about it.

The OSS had been effective during the war, but it had to play catch-up during wartime on an international scale. Nobody wanted to play catch-up again. The stakes were too high. Our scientists had produced the A-bomb and our military had used it. The Russians were unlikely to be very far behind. If not the Russians, then the Chinese. If not the Chinese, then someone else.

We knew we couldn't trust the Communists. And we knew the Communists knew they couldn't trust us. It was a standoff of the remaining superpowers that was only too obvious in Berlin. But as long as we knew what was going on backstage we had an edge. As long as we knew what the enemy was thinking, and what the enemy was planning to do, we could turn our edge into an advantage. And as long as we had an advantage, we would stay ahead.

America needed reliable women and men on the ground in foreign countries. We needed information about leaders and factions and groups. We needed intelligence about troop movements and deployments of tanks and supply trucks. In 1946–47 it was rockets and bombs. Later, it would inevitably be nuclear missiles. We needed data on the world's economies, how the common people were living, and what the rest of the people were thinking and doing about it.

In short, we needed an organization with intelligence officers, agents, and operatives in every major country and various minor ones to supply day-to-day intelligence. We needed an organization that would also include smart analysts who could comb over reports, telegrams, cables, photocopies, and documents to supply critical information to the president.

The president was the commander-in-chief. But the commander-in-chief needed more than military might. He needed a CIA.

· ·

In the beginning, the CIA was little more than a few good men and women with grand ideas working out of a temporary building left over from the war in downtown Washington, D.C.

During this formative, if uncertain, time in the modern history of intelligence, Newton D. Baker Hospital, located in Martinsburg, West Virginia, was only seventy miles from the heart of Washington, D.C. It was a relatively new and comparatively large government outpost, modern as it could be for 1947.

As were most government facilities immediately after the war, Newton D. Baker was doing dual government duty. Named for Woodrow Wilson's secretary of war, it served as a convalescent veterans hospital for the eastern panhandle of West Virginia, the northwestern region of Virginia, and the mid-region of southern Maryland. Secondarily, it served as an intelligence-gathering post convenient to Washington for the newly arrived army of dispossessed immigrants.

In addition to being a full-service medical center with various adjoining office buildings, it also had post housing. It was a secure facility guarded by the military, off-limits to anyone who didn't have official business there. As a result, it was an ideal location for displaced persons and overflows of human traffic arriving in America after the war. It was these persons, and their knowledge of and contacts in their former native lands, that might prove useful to a nation now on the brink of a new cold war.

Contact representatives for the Veterans Administration and, later, the CIA—as well as other people using various but similarly ambiguous titles in all government agencies—interviewed veterans and their dependents, immigrants, anyone who had traveled overseas, and, of course, "foreign nationals." "Interview" is a useful word. It means to ask somebody questions, usually for a particular reason.

The purpose of these interviews was to help veterans, immigrants, and foreign nationals understand their rights, as well as the government benefits available to them. That some of these benefits were closely associated with interviewees' ability to provide strategic information about where they were stationed or about their native homelands probably seemed only fair. Many foreign nationals came from war-torn countries where the Gestapo or local gendarmes were far less polite or accommodating, and where the penalty for failing to answer questions often was imprisonment or execution.

So it was that talk between interviewers and interviewees was routinely exchanged about a wide variety of issues that went well beyond their new rights or veterans benefits: postwar politics, economic conditions, the existence in local communities of Communist groups or Socialist elements, the location of former Nazi officials, or where caches of stolen money, goods, or art treasures were hidden.

Occasionally during these interviews, the names of persons overseas or at home who should be of concern to us, or who could be contacted to support our policies, were offered. Sometimes deals were struck. Sometimes, whatever this or that "somebody else working for the government" needed or wanted to find out about an interviewee was channeled down to the local contact office. These requests to be on the lookout for someone or to learn as much as possible about something or were fishing expeditions. But you never knew when the contact officer or representative might come up with something.

You just never knew.

. . . .

Contact officers and representatives, as duly appointed officials of the government of the United States of America, were vetted before they were assigned. "Vetted" is an interesting word. It is a language product of the postwar era, a shorthand term for what the FBI calls a "background check." To be vetted means to have your life scrutinized by the government for possible illegal or immoral activities, or for political beliefs or involvements that could be considered questionable or undesirable.

Vetting candidates for government jobs has become such a widely accepted practice that we seldom think very much about it. If we did, we might question the whole idea of an American citizen's political affiliations being a problematic area for employment. We are constitutionally guaranteed our right to believe any damned political thing we want to believe. Unless, of course, we want to work for the government charged with protecting our rights.

It is more than a little ironic, isn't it?

We might also ask questions concerning the desirability of illegal or immoral activities. Intelligence work has always been about violating the laws of other nations, as well as finding ways of either breaking our own laws or finding loopholes large enough to plausibly deny that's what we were doing.

And *morality*? Whose morality would that be, exactly? As a patriotic citizen committed to upholding the Constitution and communication scholar committed to the values of free speech, I sometimes wonder whom we should have feared more—the Communists or conservative Republicans. We *knew* that the Communists wanted to overthrow our government.

Pardon me. Sometimes my politics show. I'll try to behave myself.

My father was a lifelong Republican, although he claimed not to be affiliated with any political party. That, too, was government-approved "vetting" behavior. Keep it a secret. It was—and is—better left unsaid. Don't ask, don't tell. And, until recently, never talk about religion, for Christ's sake. Better not to mention it if you want a job, if you want to keep your job, and if you want to advance your government career.

These too were part of the implicit rules. Part of the institutional surround, or what my academic colleagues who study the hegemony of institutional power term "concertive control." Part of what you needed to know in order to do the American haiku or that I need to understand to parse the meaning of my father's cantos.

Nevertheless, I know my father liked Ike and he admired Barry Goldwater. His admiration for Republicans was not, however, universal. He hated, singularly hated, Richard Nixon. I'm not sure he approved of any Democrats. I know he didn't care for the lifestyle of the Kennedys, or have much respect for the Vietnam policies of Lyndon Johnson. But it was Nixon he couldn't stand. By the time Nixon resigned and Gerald Ford became president, my father claimed to be an anarchist. I also know this couldn't have been true.

At that point in his life, a lot of his seeming lunacy turned out not to be true. It was a game he was playing with an audience in mind. He had, by that time, been marked for symbolic death, if not a real one, and his career and health had been effectively ruined.

My father knew he always had an audience. A secret government audience. He was a man who kept national security secrets as well as the secret of the "family jewels," the sexual referent used by William Colby, then director of the CIA, when he revealed the historically secret and highly illegal CIA activities before the Church Committee in 1975–76. He also knew someone else was always watching him. Domestic surveillance was, according to our Constitution, Bill of Rights, federal mandate, and the rules of common decency, illegal as well as immoral, but none of those facts mattered to the Feds. My father knew that the facts and your rights only matter as long as they don't get in the way of the greater political aesthetic, the larger political picture. He knew it only too well. He been part of the great secrecy machine.

· ·

Which brings me back to 1946, and to what a contact representative, once vetted and sworn in, actually *did* every day. In addition to serving as the initial point of contact for veterans and their dependents, recent immigrants and their dependents, foreign travelers, or foreign nationals, contact representatives also performed "other government duties." Among those other duties was to honor the implied watchdog clause in their loyalty oath, to be bound by the language strings loosely attached to the idea that all government workers are sworn to "protect and defend the Constitution of the United States."

Who or what groups, in 1946, threatened that Constitution?

According to the implicit rules and local newspapers, Communists and Socialists posed a threat. Individual Communists and groups of Communists. Individual Socialists and Socialist groups. Foreign nationals with questionable political backgrounds might do, as well. But these known and easily identified groups represented only the most obvious suspects.

It was a quick leap down the Supreme Court steps from the high plateau of known Communists or sympathizers to people who were pissed off at our government for whatever reason. They, too, might pose a threat. Included in those ranks might be people who cheated on taxes, or ex-soldiers who had wanted to remain in the military after the war but weren't needed anymore.

It might include dispossessed or displaced persons who were promised passage to New York City, where their relatives lived and where a job was waiting for them, but instead found themselves ordered to reside in Martinsburg, West Virginia, without their families or a job, for no apparent reason at all.

It included all "colored people" or "Negroes," because coloreds and Negroes knew they didn't get the same basic deal as whites. It was particularly true for coloreds and Negroes who had served in the armed forces and who had gotten it into their heads that having done so would ensure them a new standard of equality and opportunity after the war.

And there were the usual town rowdies, hard cases, moonshiners, suspected criminals, or persons who were suspectd to have contacts in what was then called the underworld.

A contact officer or representative's job was to be on the lookout for any statement or sentiment or behavior that might be construed as un-American, or potentially un-American, by any person or member of these groups. It was, of course, up to the discretion of the individual contact representative who heard or overheard or suspected something whether or not to file a report with his supervisor or with the FBI.

"Un-American" is also an interesting word.

It is an ambiguous-sounding hyphenated expression, the "un" a negation of "American," where the meaning of American is taken for granted. And yet, un-American, as ambiguous as it sounds, has an entirely *un*ambiguous meaning.

It refers to anyone at odds with the customs or traditions of those among us who got here first; grabbed the most land, water, mineral, and oil rights; wrote the laws; manned the courts and legislatures; rose in rank to be captains of industry and generals of the army; and who, therefore, armed with power, prestige, and money, called all the shots. It is no mystery who these people *were* any more than who these people *are*: elite white men (and, later, women) for whom love and marriage are heterosexual-only activities and who typically profess a Judeo-Christian belief and profound loyalty to our flag.

Code words like "un-American" were deployed strategically during the cold war to tarnish the reputation of anyone who might be different, as well as anyone who might call into question our privileged version of history or who might find irony or humor in our professed Judeo-Christian values. "Un-American" might refer to someone who publicly doubted our reasons for going to war, or for hating Communists and Socialists despite never having met any, or for the less-than-equal treatment given to women and minorities in the workplace.

By the time of the infamous McCarthy hearings in 1954, "un-American" was so well recognized as a term that it was used as the title of a House investigation committee. The House committee was officially charged with looking into Senator Joe McCarthy's bold claims about Reds in the government, Reds in Hollywood, and Reds underneath our beds, and so on. McCarthy was a serious alcoholic and habitual liar whose list of names of supposedly known Communists in the State Department was total fiction, but he was also a powerful man. The damage he did to individual lives, to careers, to the idea of freedom of speech and to freedom of association in the United States of America has never yet been fully undone. The House Un-American Activities Committee became the symbolic cold war icon for a political battle that still divides us. It was no irony of history that following 9/11 one of the first acts of our government was to detain for questioning anyone even remotely suspected of ties to terrorists, if only because their skin was darker, their religion Muslim, or their country of origin somewhere in the suspicious Middle East. In times of widespread fear, our government casts a very wide net of suspicion.

Even in 1946, the term "un-American" was not limited to suspected Reds. Or even to known Reds. It was used to refer to people who were not necessarily inclined to the radical left, or even the moderate left, of any political spectrum.

It included Jews, homosexuals, and jazz musicians.

People who drove foreign cars. Women who had never married, or women who preferred to live without husbands. Or women who didn't prefer men.

Poets. Artists. Architects. People in films.

College professors. Especially college professors who read or taught Karl Marx in a history or philosophy course.

It included the left-handed and red-haired among us. These genetic traits were thought to be visual signs of a suspect political orientation.

People with foreign-sounding names. Particularly Russian-sounding names.

Labor union members and officials. Organizers of any kind.

Pacifists.

It was up to the "discretion" of the individual government employee to decide who may or may not be un-American. Joe McCarthy's use of discretion—or his apparent lack of it—led him into the State Department and to Hollywood.

My father's use of discretion is a mystery to me. I know, because he told me, that he had a friend in the FBI who gave him a piece of advice one afternoon as they shared coffee and cigarettes together at the post canteen. The advice was to keep a separate file of anyone he suspected of being Communist or a Communist sympathizer. The man was a big man who came to the area to get away from D.C. and for fishing and hunting. He told my father that you never knew when information in one of those files might be useful. He winked at him. "Useful" was a code word and the wink was a gesture.

My father agreed to it. How many files he collected, or what he did with the information in them, I'll never know.

We are a nation of people who keep files on people. We circle names. We jot down comments. We appraise the information in them. We pass along information from those files that may be useful to our friends and colleagues. We seldom think twice about it. Our friends and colleagues may be useful to us later on, and this is just another way to build our relationship.

Viewed this way, from this common angle of office work and relational maintenance and invisible but real coercive control, it doesn't seem strange at all that my father began collecting information and making files on foreign nationals and immigrants. It was part of his job. It was his duty as a patriotic American. He had friends down the road in Washington who thought it might be useful.

· ·

Contact representatives, as well as other intelligence officers, were formally instructed to tell anyone who asked that they worked for the government. Nothing else. It was a code.

If pressed for details about their job, they were instructed to say they "pushed paper from one side of their desk to the other side," and to report who was asking the questions to their immediate superiors. Usually, they only had to do this once or twice before word got around town and they were left alone.

The "moving paper across a desk" image is a fair description of the average life of many government workers. Most of your day work was paperwork. You interviewed someone and then you filed a report. You asked your secretary to make a file, or to make a copy, or to make a phone call based on a report or a file that just came in. You signed your name to memos and letters; you authorized payments; you initiated requests for everything from office furniture and supplies to investigations of this or that.

You did, indeed, pass a lot of paper from one side of your desk to the other side. But that was expected. It was your day job. It was what you did, but it was not *all* of what you did.

· ·

My father's job was to use his communication skills to create paper trails, including his own. So I cannot ignore one additional fact of this tale inside his paper trail, this official version of his employment history. On November 18, 1946, Harold Lloyd Goodall was reassigned to the Newton D. Baker Regional Office in Martinsburg, West Virginia. His rank was listed as CAF-625-7 and his salary was $3,397.20 per year.

Of course, even this "fact" of his employment history comes with an irritating interpretive rub—the date on this official notification form is given as December 23, 1946, a month *after* he supposedly assumed his new duties. But that could be just a minor technicality. Paperwork, you know. Sometimes things just get slowed up, or temporarily misplaced. It's only a date. Nothing really important.

And as is always the case, the official record only tells part of the story—the part "they" want us to know.

But I know something else: for all its curious gaps, obvious untruths, and apparent omissions, there is another story line going on during this time. There is another way of explaining what was going on in my father's life that insists on existing, if only parallel to this generously flawed official one.

It is a story of the heart that was always left unspoken, or at least covered up, in our household during my father's lifetime. Knowing it now only deepens the mystery even though it may resolve some of my initial questions.

J. Bert Schroeder, *indeed*.

If he even existed, I bet he worked for the government. I bet his job was to push paper across his desk, too.

04

What I Didn't Know

October 1944–November 1946

HER NAME WAS EDNA MARIE CASLIN BUT SHE CALLED HERSELF 'REE, A nickname derived from the pronunciation of the last three letters of her middle name. She was, in 1945, a twenty-six-year-old raven-haired, plain-spoken beauty who had served in the Women's Army Corps (WAC).

She may have served in military intelligence, or been assigned some duty that involved working with Air Corps intelligence. Or at least I think this may have been what she did. The only photograph that survives this period of her life shows her in uniform, complete with the leather gloves that women aviators favored. The twin stripes on her left sleeve indicate the rank of corporal in the Special Services, which, according to her family's story, is the rank she held until she was accepted into officer training school.

The patch on her left sleeve identifies her as a member of the Signal Corps. Or at least that is what I now believe. It has been incredibly difficult to track down. My wife and I have perused websites devoted to insignia, interviewed personnel at military museums, and tried to identify her unit on various websites devoted to women in the military. It is still a mystery. But it is not the only one.

The Signal Corps makes sense because 'Ree knew cryptography. I believe cryptography is the key to understanding quite a bit of this mystery. She may have been my father's cryptography instructor.

FIGURE 4.1 'Ree in military uniform. Date unknown.

'Ree and Lloyd were married on December 16, 1944. The date is fixed in the memory of family members because 'Ree always said it was the first day of the Battle of the Bulge. Nobody knew how they met, or even where they met. It is possible that it was while my father was recuperating at Newton D. Baker Veterans Hospital after returning from England. But what is known is both Lloyd and 'Ree were in the service and the nation was at war. Perhaps they met when she visited a club or a mess hall on a base, and their first encounter was a chance meeting between two star-crossed souls.

I've thought that.

If 'Ree was in the service for the duration of the war, then perhaps they met when my father was still a naval aviation cadet. This would have placed them together in Athens, Georgia, or in Washington, D.C., back in 1942. Given that 'Ree was from a small town in the county just outside Baltimore, Maryland, this latter scenario is entirely plausible. However, it is equally as plausible they met at one of the bases where my father completed his Army Air Corps training—Laredo, Sioux Falls, or Tampa.

My bet is on Sioux Falls, South Dakota. My father studied code and cryptography in the Army Air Corps radio operator's school there from April 4, 1943, until September 23, 1943. 'Ree may well have been stationed there during that time. Unfortunately, the fire that destroyed the records in St. Louis in 1973 also destroyed her records. If duplicates exist, I haven't been able to locate them.

. . . .

I know they met when both were in the service and the war was still on. I know this only because it is what 'Ree confided to their daughter, Bonney, when she was old enough to ask about her biological father. And it is the story Bonney passed along to her daughter, Sara. And it is the account that Sara gave to me.

When Bonney told Sara about my father, she repeated to her the same narrative details she had received from her mother. Family stories are like that. They are often passed down word for word, as if the story itself exists only within the specific language of its telling. For those of us on the receiving end of those stories of relatives and times past, what we "know" about the people and places involved is often limited to what is contained in those words. It is a narrative inheritance and the words themselves are sacred to us. They are sacred because they contain the original text. All else is speculation, deduction, or surmise.

Here is exactly what Sara was told by Bonney, and Bonney was told by 'Ree: they met when both of them were in the service and the war was still on. They got married on December 16, 1944. They lived together in a house in 'Ree's hometown, Texas, Maryland, which wasn't more than a post office at an intersection outside of the city limits of Baltimore.

Bonney Marie Goodall was born on April 1, 1946. 'Ree and Lloyd were divorced in Baltimore a short time later. According to Sara, 'Ree had a number of reasons for the failed marriage. At one point she said my father had "other interests," which required him to travel. On other occasions, she described my father as "a crazy kid from West Virginia who had some problems after the war." Before the war, he was smart, handsome, polite, and always well spoken, but war changes people and it had changed Lloyd. 'Ree told her daughter that after the war "he had problems." Maybe the problems after the war were directly related to the betrayal by his mother and sister. Maybe she was referring to the first appearance of his nightmares, his war-induced post-traumatic stress. Having witnessed the nightmares and been frightened by them myself, I know they would scare anybody. Would the nightmares have been enough to cause 'Ree to walk away from her marriage? Or, did something happen between 'Ree and Lloyd that shook his faith in her? I'll never know.

What I do know is that after the divorce, 'Ree returned to her work in the intelligence field. From Sara, I know that she always worked in or around Baltimore or D.C. Sometime after the war, she returned to school and received her bachelor's degree from Towson State College and attended graduate school at the University of Maryland. She was a teacher (although of what, or where, she never specified). Then, for twenty years, she worked at Milton Eisenhower Library at Johns Hopkins University, in the manuscript section, as a researcher. She received personal citations by authors of various scholarly volumes, all of them centered on intelligence, the Second World War, and the cold war.

Nobody in her family knows exactly what she did. She often left Bonney with a relative and was gone for weeks at a time. She never talked about her work, except to say that she "had work to do."

Hmmm. Could mean anything. I've used those words to describe my own job.

She is as mysterious to her family as my father was to me.

Sandra believes that the divorce was not a product of my father's traumatic nightmares so much as it was due to the fact that by all accounts, 'Ree was a dedicated career woman. In those days, husbands and wives could not be employed by the same government agency. Cryptographers were highly trained and skilled professionals. For a young woman—or a young man—who grew up during the Great Depression, it was a ticket to the good life afforded by a good job with the government. It was also exciting, important work.

For many women who had stepped into jobs normally held by men during the war, stepping back out of them again was pure heartbreak. 'Ree was a woman who loved her work. After my father, she never remarried. Nor did she have additional children. She worked in the intelligence field until she retired, and after she retired she moved to Las Vegas and became a government consultant.

· ·

And then there are the photographs. If my father's childhood was hidden because of a lack of photographic evidence, then his life immediately after the war is confounded by the *presence* of photographs. They offer evidence that he was living somewhere, with someone, and doing something, during those heady post-VE days. Read in one way, he was living with 'Ree awaiting the birth of their child in Texas, Maryland. But wait, according to the dummy file, wasn't he living in Huntington, working two full-time jobs, and attending Ohio State University?

In a surviving photograph given to me by Sara, my father is wearing his Army Air Corps uniform, proudly displaying his sergeant's rank, his wings, and his war ribbons. The rank and ribbons suggest that the photograph was taken after he returned to the United States and prior to his release from service, sometime between October of 1944 and May of 1945. Clearly his Purple Heart and Air Medal had been awarded. But, of course, this photograph could have been taken anytime, for any reason, or by anyone. That it survives as a memento may only reflect the fact that it may have been the only photograph he gave to her of himself in uniform.

Hard to tell.

The man in the picture does have a sweet, boyish look about his face. He retains a hint of the earlier high school innocence in his eyes, but I remind myself that this is a posed image of my father at twenty-three. He was then a young man whose life experiences far exceeded his linear age. He had already learned how to make a secret of his past and particularly of his childhood. He had gone off to war and survived it, only to return to a home that was no longer his. He was now a new husband and soon to be a new father. He was a young man in this photograph, but he was not yet the man I knew as my father.

That man, in some ways, had yet to exist. He had yet to be officially created, or to have had a reason for someone else to create a dummy paper trail on his behalf. He had yet to have taken a job as a contact representative, or to have been assigned "other duties." That man had yet to meet and marry my mother. That man had yet to father me.

· ·

There is another photograph, a second glimpse into two lives captured by nothing more complicated than a fingertip touch on a Kodak Instamatic button. This one features the happy wife and proud husband outside of their white clapboard home in Texas, Maryland. He is holding their baby daughter. Bonney Marie must have been—what—two or three months old?

Other than being evidence of admitted paternity, this photograph also reveals a domestic angle to their relationship. It is a family life centered in a home, in a place, and at a time.

FIGURE 4.2 Lloyd in Army Air Corps uniform. Date unknown.

We know that Bonney Marie was born on April 1, 1946, in Baltimore, Maryland. That she was born on what we call April Fools' Day seems a particularly bad joke on what would become her unfortunately short life. Her life was cut short by her inheritance of some part of my father's DNA, the genetic abnormality that produces chronic diabetes. It was the genetic abnormality responsible, a generation before, for shortening Oscar's life. It was a genetic code that ran in my father's family. It did not run in the blood of Bonney's mother or her family.

The April Fools' birthday may have been a dark cosmic comment on her parents' star-crossed marriage. Astrologers would say it was alignment of the stars and planets that signaled trouble. I don't place too much faith in astrologers, but sometimes they reveal a piece of the grand design that seems inexplicable by other, seemingly more rational means. For some reason, maybe a portent made from the stars, it was shortly after Bonney's birth that 'Ree and my father were divorced.

Because my father never spoke to me about this time in his life, or this marriage, or this child, none of what surrounds this photograph or its narrative legacy was known to me. The man in this photograph, the man who became my father and who would keep secret the name of this woman, his marriage to her, and the existence of their daughter, is, therefore, a man unknown to me.

He kept secrets, including secrets about his personal life. He rarely talked about his past. But still, this unarticulated episode, this brief canto in Texas, Maryland, seems inexplicable. It is a poetic moment, because all love is poetic, but its meaning is seemingly disconnected from the poem itself.

I know it happened. I just don't know *why* it happened. Or what happened between them.

Nobody does.

But to connect the poetic moment back to the poem itself, to learn how to see this canto within the evolving context of my father's clandestine life, is still possible. It requires piecing together the fragments, the clues, one at a time. It requires the application of narrative imagination to the known historical facts. And it requires the making of a story with the language resources I've been given.

. . . .

My father used to play a word game with me.

The idea was to take a word from my weekly vocabulary list and see how many other words we could build from that root. It was a word competition and we kept score. For the word to count, we had to give its definition. I learned early on how to mimic the language of my dictionary, how to piece together plausible-sounding definitions.

At the time, I just thought it was a fun game to play with my father. I didn't know where he had learned the game, or, if he had invented it, how or where he had come up with it. I just knew I loved to play it with him.

So imagine my surprise when I discovered that Bonney had played the same game with her daughter, Sara. Bonney had learned it from her mother, although she never said where her mother might have learned it. It is intriguing to imagine that my father and 'Ree may have played the game themselves. If they did, I can imagine what might have gone on between them.

"Cryptography," 'Ree said. *She was a bit of a word bully. She played to win.*

"Cryptic," *my father replied.* "It means deliberately mysterious and seeming to have a hidden meaning."

"Cryptogram," 'Ree countered. "A cryptogram is a text or a message that is in code or cipher."

"Cryptograph," Lloyd offered. "A machine for writing or deciphering encoded messages."

"Cryptographer," 'Ree fired back. "Someone who writes, transcribes, or decodes cryptograms."

"Or who studies cryptographic methods," Lloyd responded.

"That doesn't count," 'Ree teased. "That was my word. You just added a secondary definition."

My father paused and considered the word problem at hand. The basic vocabulary of crypto- had been covered. He would have to come up with something else. "I've got it!" he said. "Cryptorchid."

'Ree frowned. "What is that? That's not a word! You are making it up."

"No, I'm not. A cryptorchid is a male human or animal with one or both testicles that have failed to descend into the scrotum." Lloyd smiled, victoriously.

'Ree laughed. "Now I wonder where you learned about that?" She raised one eyebrow, suggesting, perhaps, that he had personal experience with this medical problem.

"In science class," he said. "I was a science student in high school."

"All right, I believe you. Then my next word is cryptorchism. It is a development condition affecting humans or animals in which one or both testicles fail to descend into the scrotum." She was showing off. It was her turn to beam.

My father was undaunted. "Cryptosporidium," he said. "It is a waterborne protozoan parasite that contaminates water supplies, causing intestinal infections."

"I'm impressed," she said. "Very impressed. But you haven't won yet." She moved on. "Cryptozoic. It means belonging to a geological time in which only a few very primitive organisms existed."

"That is only one way to define cryptozoic," he replied. "It can also be used to describe invertebrates that live in dark or concealed places, such as under stones or in caves."

"Still doesn't count," she protested. "It was my word even if you supplied a different definition."

He thought for a minute. "Crytozoology," he said, finally. "It means the study of legendary creatures who lived in dark or concealed places."

'Ree smiled directly at him. She held his eyes with her own. "You mean like us?"

Of course, this conversation never really happened. But I'd like to think it could have. They were lovers during wartime, brought together out of the chaos by a language game played for a brief time. They were cryptographers. People of the code.

They were also code breakers.

They were people who got married, had a child, and then got divorced. If you lived by the usual rules, this was unusual and, in the late 1940s, highly unusual. But these two people didn't live by the conventional rules of their day.

The lived by other rules, too, the rules of a clandestine organization.

When I spoke to Sara about her take on the photographs and the story of 'Ree and Lloyd, she revealed two more important pieces of this poetic puzzle. First, and perhaps most telling, is that 'Ree knew what my father did and where he worked throughout his life. How would she possibly have known that? Methinks she may have been a spy, too. If not a case officer, then perhaps a cryptographer who rose in the company to became an analyst.

The second inherited fact was somewhat more revealing, if only in a coded sort of way. Sara remembers a story Bonney told her about the only time she ever saw her father. Sometime during the mid-1960s Bonney was walking in a park with her mother. This may have been in Baltimore. Sara wasn't sure. A well-dressed man walked past the two of them and 'Ree said, suddenly, "Hello, Lloyd. How *are* you?"

My father paused long enough to take a good look at both of them. Then he smiled, shook his head, and then gestured, as if dismissing the whole encounter. Bonney never saw him again.

I have little doubt that man was, in fact, my father.

He made twice-annual trips to Washington throughout the 1960s and Baltimore was only a short ride away on the train. He could have been there on business or he may have just wanted to see his daughter.

It is the description of what he did—the smile, the shake of the head, the gesture—that will always define him to me. I've seen him do that same thing. He would meet a person on the street, pause, smile, and then wipe the encounter away as if it never happened. I *knew* that man.

He was my father.

. . . .

I wonder now what my father's take on this canto would be?

What can we make out of his lifetime of silence about it? About 'Ree. About Bonney Marie. Perhaps he was ashamed. In those days—particularly when a child was involved—divorce was not something anyone was right-fully proud of. Shame often leads to silence.

Or if not shame, exactly, then perhaps it was a lesser embarrassment.

It could be that, once married, they realized they couldn't stand it, or couldn't stand each other. Child or no child. That could explain my father's silence as well. What could he *say*? "I married a woman who decided she couldn't live with me, even after our baby was born"? That's a little too sad. It's not the kind of thing my father would have said. He never felt sorry for himself and rarely admitted to any mistakes, even when he made them.

At the end of the day, after all these possibilities have been considered, I think the more likely answer is that he didn't tell me about it because there was no real need for me to know. He was a "need to know" kind of guy. He may have been ashamed, he may also have been embarrassed, he may have had other interests or had to travel, and for all I know 'Ree simply may not have been able to live with him. Or it may have been due to *all* of those things. But in the end, he didn't tell me about it because he didn't think I needed to know. In my father's compartmentalized life, I would never meet 'Ree or Bonney, just as I never met my grandmother or aunt. These were a part of his past, a past that, with me at least, he didn't acknowledge.

That explains why he didn't mention it to me. But it leaves open the question of how he may have felt about it. I believe he may have simply been disappointed.

When people or events disappointed my father, he walked away from them. He had walked away from Huntington. He could walk away from this situation, too.

. . . .

I think I understand my father's first marriage, and even his divorce. What I don't understand is what he was up to during the year it took place. That year—1945–46—is a time in my father's life obscured by conflicting accounts. Where was he exactly? What exactly he was doing?

Then, there is the missing artifact, which was, in the words of Sara, a "strange thing that Lloyd gave 'Ree." 'Ree would go to her locked jewelry box and take out the bullet, or at least what appeared to be a small bullet, which was, instead, a "secret hiding place." Sara remembers seeing this bullet for years.

Or was it a "hiding place for secrets"? Microdots would be my guess.

On its own, this memory of a lost artifact would have little impact on me. But I also have a jewelry box, one kept by my father, with the same kind of bullet in it. 'Ree's bullet would seem to be its secret twin.

What could *that* mean?

Was this bullet, this "hiding place," an artifact of my father's clandestine life? I think so. Visiting the CIA Museum in D.C. in November 2003, I saw one exactly like the one I have. It was one of several artifacts of the cold war on display that had been developed as ways to transfer or pass information across hostile borders. The information was contained on a microdot. It is all very *Spy vs. Spy*, isn't it?

The explanation of what the bullet—this secret hiding place—was used for during the cold war is only the uppermost pragmatic tip of a deeper, more romantic reason for keeping it. It goes to the issue of what my father hid, not so much in the bullet, but in his heart. I think he kept it with him as a memento, not of crossing hostile borders but of his time with 'Ree. She, after all, always held on to the other one. Maybe they were a perfectly matched set, separated by a higher ideal.

The question posed by this artifact is, what did it mean, or represent, in their lives? 'Ree kept her bullet in the locked jewelry box until one day shortly after she learned she had Alzheimer's. Soon after, the bullet disappeared. And why would 'Ree, late in life and long after it could have possibly mattered to anyone, have removed it—*and only it*—from her jewelry box and disposed of it? What was *that* all about?

I have often wondered whether it would have mattered if I had known about 'Ree when I was growing up. I would have wanted to meet my half sister, but beyond that curiosity, I doubt it. 'Ree had been involved in my father's life before he became my father. From a child's perspective, or perhaps just from my perspective, that man was someone I didn't know.

But then again, did I ever really know the man who was my father?

He was a man made out of flesh, blood, brains, history, and heart. He was, like all of us, flawed. I knew that. But the more I researched his early life, the more I wondered if who I wanted him to have been was getting in the way of the facts as I discovered them. I went in search of my father's dreams and found an absence of them. In their place emerged another life I knew nothing about.

I had to wonder, What kind of man walks away from his wife and new-born daughter? What kind of woman willingly lets him do it? Or, if not that, if that decision was less a question of character than of circumstance and compromise, what were the circumstances that caused these two people, once so much in love, to arrive at that particular compromise? They were young, romantic, and idealistic. They were patriotic. They were volunteers for war. Maybe they shared a sudden passion that could not sustain a married life. Maybe my father got her pregnant and stayed with her only long enough to give the child his name. Maybe my father's nightmares frightened her. Maybe their careers got in the way.

Or perhaps it was all of these things. Or none of them. I'll never know for certain.

What I do know for certain is that my father didn't tell me he had been married previously or that I had a half sister. What kind of man doesn't disclose that to his son? There is really only one answer to that question: It is a man who didn't think I needed to know.

Maybe he was ashamed. Or perhaps it was just easier not to bring it up or talk about it. When I consider the undisclosed facts of my own life in relation to my father's, I see a similar pattern emerge. I, too, have been previously married. It didn't work out. It was complicated and it got messy. I don't like to talk about it, either. That marriage produced no children. But when I walked away from it, I didn't look back.

I am my father's son.

It is a beautiful but dangerous thing to be young, romantic, and idealistic. You never feel so alive but you can so easily be disappointed. My father was disappointed with his past, and so was I. My father was disappointed in his first marriage, and so was I. My father walked away from the early disappointments in his life and entered a clandestine world that brought him purpose, meaning, new love, and me. I walked away from my early disappointments and entered an academic life that brought me purpose, meaning, new love, and Nicolas.

I am only now figuring out the deeper pattern in our lives.

What kind of man walks away from his past? I know that man.

He looks just like me.

05

Martinsburg

November 1946–September 1952

NOVEMBER 23, 1946, WAS THE FIRST DAY OF A NEW JOB AND A NEW beginning for my father. It was the day H. Lloyd Goodall reported to work as a contact representative at Newton D. Baker Regional Hospital in Martinsburg, West Virginia. Occurring when it did, just prior to the Thanksgiving holiday, seems appropriate. It was a fresh start, a new beginning at the end of what must have seemed like one holy wreck of a year.

The contact division field office was located in a small area on the first floor near the main entrance of the hospital. It consisted of two rooms, one for a secretary/receptionist and the other for the designated contact representative. The offices were sparsely furnished in standard government-issue materials. The secretary's receiving room included a gunmetal-gray desk and matching stool, three straight-backed chairs for visitors, and a pair of drab green filing cabinets. There was an absence of anything even remotely personal on display.

Lloyd's new office featured a framed print of President Harry S. Truman where not too long before hung an apparently larger one featuring the face of Franklin D. Roosevelt.

On the desk, taking up almost the whole of the desktop, was a standard government-issue calendar for the year 1946. There were two chairs and a

filing cabinet that more or less matched the color and degree of fade of the
desk. The office had a good view of the expansive front lawn and a pair of
tall oak trees.

It was just an ordinary government office with a decent view.

Throughout his career, Lloyd occupied similar offices in various Veterans Administration centers. One may have been larger where another one
had been slightly smaller, but it hadn't mattered a whit to him. An office
was an office.

He was a man who drank his coffee black.

He wore dark suits and white shirts and dark ties.

He smoked Benson & Hedges filters and lit each one with a slightly
tarnished silver Zippo lighter with the seal of the United States of America
on it. It was a lighter you could purchase at a PX on any military base or
nonmilitary post in the world.

My father was a quiet man, well dressed, self-assured, and handsome.
In his own way I suppose he was vain. He cared about his good looks. After
the fashion of the times, he used Brylcreem on his hair. *A little dab'll do ya.*
His fingernails were meticulously trimmed. His shoes—black or cordovan
wingtips—were always polished.

When I try to place myself in his first government position at Newton
D. Baker in November of 1946, I search for likely parallels. I think about
how I felt when I showed up for work on my first teaching job at Clemson
University in August of 1974. I was twenty-two, about his age. My office on
campus was ordinary and small; it was sparsely furnished but had a good
view. The desk and chair, the typing table and typewriter, were standard
state-government issue. I, too, cared about my looks. I certainly was anxious to do a good job. I was running hard from my past and saw my future
in higher education.

My father, by that time, was divorced and had a daughter. At the time
of my first job, I had a serious girlfriend but we had enjoyed the advantage
of birth control. It would take years for me to recognize the similarity of
our pattern with women, but it was already there. We were romantics who
followed our hearts.

We were idealists.

We believed in the importance of our lives in a larger aesthetic, even if
we couldn't yet define it. We were word men. We were adept at using talk to
make friends, act out roles, and influence people. We shared a professional
interest in communication. He was a former cryptographer who had bounced

radio signals across the Kennelly-Heaviside layer, and I had studied the effect of the Kennelly-Heaviside layer on radio waves. We knew some of the same things. We understood that language was coded. We believed that words were symbolic and that signs were not always what they seemed. We had read *The Great Gatsby.* We knew the importance of storytelling.

Yet, for all these similarities, our worlds were galaxies if not billions of light-years apart. He had been raised during the Great Depression and knew hunger and poverty firsthand. I had never been hungry or poor. He had been Mr. Everything in high school whereas I had hardly attended high school, and, if it hadn't been for a deal he cut on my behalf with the police commissioner of Philadelphia, I may have never graduated from high school.

He had attended college but not completed his degree. I completed one, then two, and eventually three degrees. He had volunteered for a war and I had protested one. He had been severely wounded and he suffered from nightmares that would last for the rest of his life. I never suffered from nightmares. My dreams have been mostly peaceful.

I did not volunteer for war but I consider myself deeply patriotic. Had my number been called, I would have gone. I hated the war in Vietnam but I grew up in a patriotic family. I hated the Vietnam *War*, but not the Vietnam *warriors*. I knew they were only doing their duty and that most of them would have preferred to be somewhere—and in the case of Vietnam, *anywhere*—else. I spent most of my life surrounded by Marines and members of the Air Force who had been like big brothers to me. I believe in service to our country. But my service to my country has been performed as a citizen-teacher rather than as a citizen-soldier. We make what contributions we can.

In many ways, the surfaces of my father's life were entirely ordinary. He did his duty and he worked for our government. He paid his taxes on time and voted in every election. He kept up with world affairs. He enjoyed sports and read books. He wrestled with the role of God and religion in his life. He was married twice and he was a father to two children.

But that is, of course, only one way to tell my father's story. It is the way he told it, minus the first marriage and daughter and a few other niggling details like who he really was and what he really did. But he believed he had a good reason for telling it this way. It was a partial truth that obscured the need to know the whole truth. It was the cover story for his dummy file as well as for public consumption. It was a matter of national security and all that implies. It was a story that allowed him to live his cover while he also lived another life. It was a life on an unknown trajectory, one destined to play a part in the larger aesthetic of the great game we call now the cold war.

There was, according to my mother, a steady procession of secretary/receptionists during Lloyd's first year as a contact officer. The reason for the turnover had little to do with the nature of the work or with him as a supervisor. Or perhaps, looked at a little differently, it had *everything* to do with it.

In those postwar days, it was common knowledge around the post that secretaries and nurses who went to work at Newton D. Baker did so not so much for a paycheck as to look for a husband. If you lived anywhere in the general vicinity of Martinsburg, and if you were a single woman past the age of eighteen with designs on married life, your choices for everyday man shopping were limited to the local textile mills or Newton D. Baker. Given the choices, Newton D. was the hands-down winner. It featured a steady parade of returned soldiers and wounded veterans, some of whom were genuine heroes. It also featured recently arrived immigrants, some of whom were genuinely rich. Almost all of them—the veterans, the patients, and the immigrants—processed their paperwork through the contact office.

So it would make sense that competition for the prime post of personal secretary to Mr. H. Lloyd Goodall was keen. As the story goes, it was occasionally even fierce. I am fairly certain no one knew about 'Ree. But word soon got around that Lloyd wasn't interested in women who worked for him in anything but the secretarial sense. So, the secretaries were often disappointed when their invitations for dinner or other intimacies only served to irritate their boss, rather than entice him.

Around the hospital, he was a curiosity. He was a quiet man who kept to himself, lived alone on the post, walked to work, and didn't own a car. He never talked about his past or his family. I doubt he ever mentioned his "other interests." My father was, by all accounts, a government man and decorated veteran immersed in his job.

It took seven months and five frustrated secretaries before a new woman entered my father's life. She was not a secretary, nor was she looking for a husband. Naomi May Saylor and Lloyd Goodall had a lot in common. She too had walked away from her past. She too had been married and she too was deeply scarred. She had secrets of her own.

FIGURE 5.1 Harold Lloyd Goodall in official U.S. Department of State photograph.

FIGURE 5.2 Naomi May Alexander Saylor in nurse's uniform.

Naomi May (Alexander) Saylor had turned thirty on February 12, 1947. By June she was convinced that her boyfriend, Jerry Terlingo, was never going to leave his supposedly estranged wife. She had been dating him for three years. He was an army first lieutenant, barely 5′6″ but full of energy and loaded with Italian passion.

Naomi and Jerry met at a Newton D. Baker get-together shortly after D-day. During their first year together, Jerry kept the fact that he had a wife in Philadelphia a secret from her. When he finally confessed to being still "more or less married," he claimed that his wife wouldn't divorce him because they were Catholic.

"Then convert," Naomi replied.

That hadn't happened. Nor would it have worked. Jerry's wife may not have cared for him, but she certainly relied on his income. None of Jerry's schemes to convince her to get a divorce worked, and, after three years of waiting, Naomi doubted they ever would. Although she believed Jerry loved her and that he was being honest about his wife refusing to grant him a divorce, she was tired of living this way. She wanted to be married, she wanted children, and she wanted them *now*.

She was thirty, for God's sake.

She was divorced. But that had been a long time ago, a lifetime ago, before the war and back when she was barely seventeen and wanted desperately to leave her home and her life behind. She told me that the night she graduated from high school she agreed to marry the richest, best-looking boy in Charles Town, West Virginia—Lester Alexander. The ink was barely dry on their Martinsburg High School diplomas when they tied the knot.

Les was a devoted husband. He loved Naomi and wanted her to be happy, so much so that he agreed—after five years of marriage and an absence of children—to divorce her so that she could attend nursing school in Winchester, Virginia. In those days, she told me, nursing schools didn't accept married women. So Les and Naomi divorced, but they still "dated" on the weekends. Their plan had been to remarry as soon as Naomi finished nursing school.

At the end of Naomi's first year of nursing school, Les died suddenly and unexpectedly of cancer. It was a particularly aggressive variety that attacked his heart almost without warning. He was dead within days of Naomi being notified of his illness.

She was distraught. She grieved. She considered quitting school. Her supervisor warned her that if she quit now, no matter what the reason, she would never get back in. I doubt if that was true, but it was the medicine she fed my mother to get her through. My guess is that the supervisor believed that the best cure for heartache and sorrow was hard work.

As hard as Lester's death was, things got worse. Naomi was so distraught over Lester's death and what would happen to her if she quit school, that, one evening while brushing her teeth in the nursing dormitory, she didn't notice that she was standing dangerously close to the gas radiator. The hem of her bathrobe suddenly caught on fire. The bathroom had been a place for her to be alone and cry, away from well-meaning friends and classmates. To gain some much-needed solitude, she had locked the door, which turned out to be a nearly fatal mistake. Once the robe erupted into flames, she was too frightened and upset to unlock the door and get out and her suitemates, hearing her screams, couldn't get in.

By the time she arrived in the emergency room, over 70 percent of her body was burned. She was later told that she had been as close to death as a person can be. She survived, somehow, and spent the next twelve months recovering from her burns. Skin grafts from the bottoms of her feet—one area of her body that hadn't been burned—were applied to her back and

upper thighs. Fortunately, her lovely face wasn't burned. Nor had her ambition. If anything, the fire renewed her desire to become a registered nurse.
The care and attention she received from the other nurses strengthened her
resolve. After her recovery, she returned to Winchester Memorial Nursing
School and graduated with the class of 1941.

For a long time after she returned to school, and even afterward when
she worked at Johns Hopkins Hospital in Baltimore, she refused to date.
The usual reason given to potential suitors was that she was working. It was
a lie, if a convenient one. She told herself she was still grieving over Lester.
But the real reason was her scarred body. As a woman who had always been
told she was beautiful and who had learned to count on her beauty, Naomi
was more than a little embarrassed by the body beneath her uniform. She
feared that no man would ever want her. And if they didn't want her, how
could they truly love her?

Rather than find out, she resisted all suitors. Until Jerry Terlingo
wouldn't take no for an answer.

Jerry hadn't minded her scars. Or he said he didn't.

Thirty years later I met and got to know Jerry Terlingo. He had come back
into Naomi's life a year or so after the newspapers announced the death of
my father. Jerry had never divorced. His Catholic wife, from whom he had
lived apart since the early 1940s, was dead. He was still very much the fiery
Italian, loaded with life energy no doubt fueled by the twenty cups of heavily
sugared coffee he drank every day. He was, to me, an Italian Tigger, always
bouncing, always in motion, always excited about one thing or another.

When he spoke to me about the old days in Martinsburg, back when he
was first dating my mother, his voice changed. Gone was the bravado, the
argumentativeness, the constant eruptions of laugher. In its place was a
confessional tone, an unexpected tenderness. He was, of course, remembering her as a much younger woman, brand-new to him and lovely in so
many ways. His was recalling the person she was before life induced her
craziness. But I think he was also recalling her vulnerability. "Your mother,"
he said, his voice breaking, "was the finest woman I'd ever met." Then he
smiled. There were genuine tears in his eyes and it was a sweet smile, not
his usual salesman's closing bid. "I've loved her every day of my life since
the day I met her. There has never been anyone else."

He spoke to me so openly, so vulnerably, I felt I had to believe him.
But Jerry was like that. He won friends easily and was the kind of guy
everyone loved. Yet, I suppose he, too, lived a secret life. After all, he had

been a traveling salesman for Kelvinator appliances and Pepsi Cola who spent his life mostly on the road and, by apparent choice, away from his wife and son. He had managed to hide his marriage from Naomi for over a year, and I have no doubt he hid it from other women as well. Jerry was the life of every party, despite being a teetotaler during a time when, in his profession, there was very little of that. I remember his initial surprise when he learned that my mother drank alcohol, and further discovered that she didn't hold it well. "Her lips never touched hooch the whole time I knew her," he said.

I couldn't imagine that. I had known a different woman.

I could tell he was disappointed. I also knew it wouldn't matter. In a way, it only deepened the compassion he felt for her this second time around. It was the deeper truth that comes from knowing they had shared a past. They had reveled in the same stories. They had lived through a highly charged era and it was the memory of their time together that rekindled their relationship.

I don't know if that was such a good idea. You cannot live for the past any more than you can repeat it. Yet these two tried to. In trying to repeat the past they replaced their true story with a nostalgic fiction, but it was important to complete the story of a life together that my father had interrupted years ago. And maybe that was the whole point.

As she put it, my mother had a "genuine fondness if not exactly love" for Jerry. But, she told me, my father had been the one true love of her life. One clear indication of how strongly she felt about it was her stipulation that she be buried next to my father in Sample's Manor Cemetery, and that under no circumstances whatsoever should Jerry Terlingo be buried in the same cemetery.

. . . .

My mother enjoyed telling and retelling the story about how she and my father met. It was, to her, a great American love story. It was the story of a pretty nurse who fell for a handsome war hero, and a handsome war hero who fell in love with his nurse. It was love at first sight, and they were married within six months.

That is one way to tell the story. It is, I think, the way all of us *want* to tell our love story. In America, true love is an entitlement. We are brought up believing in the myth of a romantic love that happens to us when we aren't looking for it. It surprises us, overwhelms us, and makes us weak in

the knees and elsewhere. We are virtually helpless against it. Viewed cyni-
cally, romantic love is like a sickness from which we never recover.

But I am a romantic, not a cynic. Probably I inherited those traits from
my both of my parents. Neither one of them alone can take all the credit,
nor should either one of them receive all the blame. My pattern is too
similar to theirs.

You learn this fact of true love listening to the language of it. Or—as
Zelda Fitzgerald once put it—to "the philosophies of popular songs." Or
from novels, movies, art, sitcoms, and theater. There is a great expectation
for a great love story, and the whole idea of "settling" for something less is
to admit that your life is not worthy. That what you are willing to call true
love is not true love at all, at least not by American standards.

My mother's story of true love, of meeting my father and falling in love
and then getting married, is the only story I ever heard her tell about it.
For years she omitted telling me about the role Jerry Terlingo played in it,
but my mother was adept at editing out the people and places in her life
that didn't fit the image she wanted to portray. Not that I blame her. I am
guilty of doing the same thing myself. It may even be something I inherited
narratively from her. I accept that.

But here is the story, not exactly as she told it, but as I understand it now.
Here is the unedited version, culled from what Naomi told me as well as
what I later learned about it from Jerry Terlingo. It's still a great love story,
only not the same love story I had been reared on.

· ·

Naomi was thirty and still single in an era when thirty was roundly considered entry into middle age. She was still childless. She had had enough
of waiting. Jerry was either a big liar or a big fool, and either way, she was
done with him.

She resolved to break it off. For *good*. But not tonight. Tonight she had
been called in because another girl was sick with the flu and she had agreed
to sub for her.

It was her least favorite duty floor, too. Post-op. Nothing much going
on because the patients were usually still asleep or else heavily sedated.
Nothing to do except check temperatures and blood pressures and monitor
the vitals. Maybe an injection or two, and some inevitable adjustments to a
couple of the older IV drips.

Nothing to get the blood up. Nothing at all.

Naomi clocked in at 10:59 p.m. to begin her 11–7 shift in post-op and found a gaggle of young nurses giggling around the nurse's station.

"What's happening here?" she said, smiling at them. "Why are you all so giddy?"

"Guess who checked in with tonsillitis this afternoon and is recuperating right now in Room 207?" one of them said.

"Who, Humphrey Bogart?" Naomi said, mockingly. "No? Let's see, then, Errol Flynn?"

"No, but close."

"Well, *who*?" Naomi pressed.

"Lloyd Goodall," came the reply. "You know. That *dreamboat* who runs the contact office."

"And who is *single*," someone else added, in that singsong voice that meant there was a distinct possibility that under her care he might experience a rather immediate status change.

"The dreamboat from the contact office," whoever he was, was no big deal to Naomi, who had other things, namely Jerry Terlingo, to deal with. Nevertheless, the girls were all vying for a personal assignment to this new patient's room. Of course, only one of them could be assigned to "special him," so the decision was quickly made to draw straws for it. It was a tradition on the second floor, and one that Naomi went along with, even though she personally had little interest in being assigned to anyone's room, Lloyd Goodall included.

When she drew the short straw, the other girls were envious. She would gladly have given any one of them her straw, but that wasn't how they played this game.

She just smiled, picked up his chart from the station desk, and walked back to Room 207.

Another boring night on the second floor . . . but at least there had been a little fun.

One consistent narrative told by both Lloyd and Naomi throughout their lives was that it had been love at first sight.

I have no reason to doubt them. I don't know about "first sight," given that he was anesthetized and she was probably a blur to him, but hey, who am I to say? They certainly had a quick romance, wounded by Cupid's infamous arrow in late June and married in December.

Jerry didn't take it well. He hadn't seen it coming, even though he knew she wanted marriage and children. But Jerry didn't want to believe that any woman would dump *him*, much less for another man. In those days, it was generally the other way around.

His pride was wounded. He was offended. He was deeply in love with Naomi. He vowed to kill Lloyd Goodall.

My mother laughed when he said that. Lloyd had seven inches of height and probably forty pounds on Jerry. He was younger, stronger, and a decorated veteran. He knew how to take care of himself. She wasn't worried. Besides, Jerry could always talk a good game. It was follow-through he lacked.

Of course, saying those things to Jerry only further encouraged him to want to prove himself, even against these odds. It confirmed and consolidated his hatred. If he couldn't face him man-to-man, maybe there was another way to get even and win Naomi back.

By July he was desperate. And so, for the first time in his life, Jerry got drunk. And not just drunk, but slap-ass stupid drunk. For any man who doesn't drink, taking up heavy drinking under the duress of lost love is always a big mistake. Alcohol makes good things seem much better and bad things seem much worse. Naomi, once his ideal woman, now seemed to be his original Eve. Lloyd, once his sworn enemy, was now the serpent who had slithered into his perfect garden. It was biblical. Jerry was Catholic. This sudden turn of events wouldn't do. It was his religious right, as a good Catholic, to rid the world of this obvious devil.

He had a car, a big car. It was the new Mercury with a V-8. In his drunken altered state of consciousness, he saw the Mercury with the big V-8 as the answer to his prayers. What he seemed to have forgotten was that my father didn't drive. He didn't even own a car.

Naomi owned the car. And when they went out, she was the driver.

Jerry was by then too drunk and too stupid to realize that. What he did realize was that he recognized Naomi's Studebaker leaving the post. Two people were in the car and one of them was bound to be my father.

That my father was the passenger didn't register.

Jerry took off behind them. He tried to light a cigarette, but dropped the match between his legs and almost ran off the road digging for it. He flung the still-lit cigarette out the window and breathed in the fresh air. I don't understand the chemistry of it, but it has been my experience that fresh air only makes an already-drunk person just that much more sure of himself. It does nothing to sober him up.

He apparently had it in his head that his big Mercury could push their smaller coupe off the road. He revved up the motor and got a decent running start, but ramming into the rear of Naomi's Studebaker only succeeded in cracking his radiator. It did, however, motivate the driver of the Studebaker off the road. She thought: What in the *world* had just happened?

Steam exploded from the Mercury's big engine. My father, always a man of quick action, immediately exited the Studebaker, believing he ought to render roadside assistance. Instead of an apologetic fellow motorist, he confronted a short angry man he didn't know screaming obscenities at him. He quickly figured out this "accident" was no accident. It had something to do with Naomi.

"Who *is* this guy?" he demanded.

"He was my boyfriend but I broke up with him right after I met you." Naomi was mad. She glared at Jerry and surmised that he was highly intoxicated. "Jerry, you're *drunk!*" she cried.

Jerry was drunk, but he was also miserable. Things weren't going according to plan. He spoke nonsense.

"Then what is he doing here?"

Naomi sighed. "He told me he was going to kill you."

"Is that a fact?" Lloyd looked down at the much smaller man. He was confused, and maybe even amused, by this scene.

"I'm *still* going to kill you, you big lousy son-of-a-bitch!" Jerry shouted as he took a swing at him.

The fight didn't last long. My father punched Jerry exactly once. He hit him squarely on the bridge of the nose and broke it. Blood erupted and the fight was over.

Lloyd felt bad about breaking Jerry's nose. He offered Jerry a handkerchief, and then a ride to the hospital, both of which a somewhat more sober Jerry accepted. All the way there Naomi fiercely berated Jerry, which, my father later told me, made his heart glad and pretty much sealed the marriage deal.

She had stood up for him.

It wouldn't be the last time.

· ·

In every true American love story, there is an inevitable nakedness that precedes lovemaking. It is a beautiful moment that creates both the anticipation of pleasure and a bond of extreme intimacy. If it's true love, and not just sex, you don't want to talk about it because there aren't words good enough to express that moment. You keep it private. You keep it a secret. You enclose every second of that shared experience in a sensual, bodily memory.

This is my parents' love story, which only makes it doubly secret. I am not interested in being a sexual voyeur.

But I think I know what, in that first naked moment, drew them together. In that first unveiling of who they were that ran far below the surfaces of skin, my parents recognized themselves in each other's scars. It was a nakedness of selves joined at the soul that they shared.

They were wounded people. But they were strong. They had both made mistakes but they had precious few regrets. They had both left their families, more or less for good. Where my father had a sister, my mother had a brother. Where my father had a war, my mother had a fire. They had both been married and divorced. Whether my father told my mother about his daughter, I'll never know. But I suspect he did. He told my mother the truth.

He just didn't tell her everything.

• •

The Reverend John Keesecker married Lloyd and Naomi in a small ceremony on December 21, 1947. They spent their honeymoon in a motel by the ocean at Virginia Beach.

Following their honeymoon, the newlyweds settled down to domestic life on the post at Newton D. Baker. They made an attractive couple and were well liked. They held parties where everybody drank too much and laughed about it later. They purchased a new two-tone Pontiac and took weekend trips in it. Naomi continued nursing and Lloyd continued to do his work for the government.

They immediately tried to start a family, but encountered some difficulty. Over the next four years Naomi suffered three miscarriages. They had almost given up when my mother announced she was pregnant with me. I was born on September 8, 1952. My mother was thirty-five years old. My father was a month shy of thirty. Both of them were considered "old" for parenthood by their generation's standards.

My mother insisted that I be named for my father: Harold Lloyd Goodall Jr. But, for some reason, they always called me "Buddy." It was a good thing I was born a boy. Had I been female, my name would have been Gwendolyn Gale Goodall, and they had planned to call me "Gee-Gee" for short.

Lordy.

I've often wondered what my father might have thought about me when I was born. He already had a daughter, now six years old, living not far away in Baltimore. Her name was Bonney, and, for some reason he never explained to me, I was Buddy. Actually, he once told me my nickname came from an old wartime pal of his. When I asked Ansel Miller about it, he said he never knew anyone named Buddy in their squadron. So, who knows? Maybe the "old buddy" had been 'Ree. Maybe he was thinking of Bonney.

Buddy and Bonney. Hmmm. Some correlation? Well, maybe.

The truth is that I'll never know what he thought about when I was born. He never told me. None of my relatives were prone to such memories. My mother had a difficult pregnancy and a long labor, so I wasn't surprised that her story about my birth was simply that she was glad it was over with and that I had survived. I weighed six pounds and eight ounces, which was a little on the small side.

I have a copy of the mimeographed birth announcement in the Newton D. Baker post newsletter. It is in a column labeled "Burning the Candle at Both Ends." The column title makes me laugh, although I often laugh when other people might take the same thing very seriously. But the name is such a perfect metaphor for my father and mother's lives! For our life together as a family.

Burning the candle at both ends.

Exactly. And we all know what happens when you do that.

06

Appointment to a Cold War

June 1954–August 1955

"HOW DID WE END UP IN ROME?" I ASKED.

"We were in West Virginia and then moved to Rome."

That is how my mother used to put it. When I was growing up, I learned to think of our lives during those times in those terms, exactly. "We were in West Virginia and then moved to Rome." Before I read my father's diary, this phrase, for me, carried no conflict or weirdness or mystery at all. In those days, moving from West Virginia to Rome seemed perfectly natural. Having a father whose title was vice consul in Rome, Italy, seemed normal.

I never questioned it. At least, not for *years*.

But, in fact, the route that led us to Rome was circuitous. The route my father and mother took from one place to the other was made to *appear* normal and ordinary. The route itself involved the construction of believable, if not entirely legitimate, cover stories—his bona fides—and his bona fides took years to create and cultivate. The cover story—the Veterans Affairs contact officer with a true enough work history back home—required an internal transfer from Martinsburg to the unlikely town of Beckley, West Virginia.

According to the official dummy file paperwork, H. Lloyd Goodall transferred from the VA Center in Martinsburg to the VA center in Beckley on

June 13, 1954. On Standard Form 50, Notification of Personnel Action, the reason listed for the transfer is "promotion and change [of] headquarters"; his rank improved from a GS-8 to a GS-9, and his new salary was given as $5,980, an improvement in his financial circumstances that amounted to $610 per annum. In those days, $610 was a significant increase. In the world of bona fides, it was perfectly reasonable for a career government man to seek a promotion and raise, even if it required a transfer. So, maybe the move was all about the money. But I doubt it.

In Beckley, according to our family story, we lived in a small rented house not far from the VA center. My father walked to and from work. My mother temporarily retired from nursing to stay at home with the infant me. In one surviving photograph from the era, I am pictured buck naked in our backyard, climbing out of a plastic swimming pool guarded by our large black-and-tan German shepherd named King.

Beckley isn't much now, but in those days, when coal mining was still a large part of the West Virginia economy, it was a thriving medium-sized town with a pleasant enough downtown. The VA center and hospital occupied a prominent hill overlooking the city, and my father's larger office—still there today and largely unchanged—occupied the northeast corner next to the main entrance. West Virginians are a patriotic breed, known for high per capita levels of volunteers for wars, and I have no doubt that the large VA center was located there because there was a large population of veterans in the vicinity. West Virginia was also a blue-collar labor state with a substantial number of impoverished citizens, the very heart of old Appalachia. Was heady government thinking in those days that West Virginia was ripe for Communist Party takeover? Probably. Organized labor in the United States had remarkably close ties to the Communist Party. If the Reds got into West Virginia, could Kentucky be far behind? Was that it?

I wonder what my father was actually *doing* there. On Standard Form 50 there is the same "INT" classification he had carried since 1947. "INT" refers to "intelligence," so I have to assume that the work was largely the same: domestic surveillance on veterans, foreign nationals who had served in various European armies or navies or air forces, and travelers back from visits overseas. He is listed as a "Contact Representative" although the designation "Chief" used in Martinsburg is not carried over into the new column for this position in Beckley. Yet on the form it clearly states that this transfer was due to a promotion and a change of headquarters. If a promotion means moving up, what is up from chief? Super Chief?

It is unlikely that my father worked in the contact office *for* anyone. There wasn't a corps of contact representatives to organize and lead. And it says he was sent there because it was a change of headquarters. But, I ask, the headquarters of *what*? The contact division field office? I doubt it. The field office continued operating out of Martinsburg during the same time my father was relocated to Beckley.

Given what he was doing in Rome nine months later, I have to believe that Beckley served as a training ground of some kind. Perhaps its location in the south-central region of the state is a key. But if he were doing routine CIA training, wouldn't he have been assigned to Fort Peary, Virginia? If he were doing the routine CIA prep work for an upcoming overseas assignment, wouldn't he be working at the Italian desk in Washington? Wouldn't he have lived somewhere other than *Beckley*?

I reach an intellectual and practical dead end. Neither of these possible explanations accounts for our move to Beckley. And certainly not for why he only spent nine months there. That was hardly enough time to learn a new job in a new place. Not really long enough to build enough trust in political relationships capable of producing valuable intelligence information.

Then again, I am working from documents in an official government file that is clearly labeled "dummy folder." This means I am benefiting—if you can call it that—from the apparent (and rather consistent) oversight of the anonymous government censor who reviewed these forms long ago. Allowing me, however accidentally or graciously, to see this file, or at least this portion of it, is perhaps only evidence of what those in the know *want* me to see, what they *want* me to know.

Just because you are paranoid doesn't mean there isn't a conspiracy, right? Particularly where the CIA is concerned. Maybe we weren't living in Beckley at all. Maybe my father's name and local address printed in the city directory was false.

I only know that on March 8, 1955, my father was nominated, for no known reason and without benefit of a paper trail application, by one Mr. H. V. Higley, the administrator of the Veterans Administration in Washington, D.C., to become a vice consul of the United States in Rome, Italy. He would be in charge of veterans affairs in the embassy. It was the perfect cover.

If you examine the language closely, you will find that it was composed by someone who was grammatically challenged. But beyond issues of passive voice, vague language, and inappropriate comma usage, there appear to be three distinct anomalies.

VETERANS ADMINISTRATION
WASHINGTON 25, D. C.

OFFICE OF
THE ADMINISTRATOR OF
VETERANS AFFAIRS

March 8, 1955

The Honorable
The Secretary of State
The Department of State
Washington 25, D. C.

Dear Mr. Secretary:

The Veterans Administration has been requested by the
Director, Office of Special Consular Services, to nominate a
candidate to replace Mr. Uley K. Wise, whose resignation as
Veterans Affairs Officer (FSS-8) in the American Embassy at
Rome, Italy, has been accepted by the Department of State. We
have been advised by the Department that the replacement is to
be assigned in the Foreign Service as a Reserve Officer.

I wish to submit the nomination of Mr. H. Lloyd Goodall,
for transfer to the Foreign Service as a Foreign Service Reserve
Officer, Class 5, for assignment to the vacancy in Rome, under
provisions of Public Law 724, 79th Congress, and Executive Order
9932. Mr. Goodall is now serving as Veterans Admininistration Contact Representative and is in charge of the Veterans Administration
Office at Beckley, West Virginia. It is understood that he is eligible
for transfer to the Foreign Service at a salary of $5673.00 per annum,
which most closely approximates his present salary of $5560.00 per
annum. Mr. Goodall is considered to be well qualified by education
and experience to fill the position for which he is nominated. For the
past nine years he has been performing duties for this agency which
closely approximate those that will be required of him in the American
Embassy at Rome.

There are attached Standard Form 57, Application for Federal
Employment, and DSP-34, Supplement to Standard Form 57, which have
been completed by Mr. Goodall.

Sincerely yours,

for John J. Pettinos

H. V. HIGLEY
Administrator

Encl:

FIGURE 6.1 Letter recommending the appointment of H. Lloyd Goodall to Foreign Service.

First, the salary listed for his current position in Beckley is incorrect. In fact, it is off by nearly $500, which was not an insignificant sum in those days. I also doubt that my father would have taken a cut in pay, but perhaps with the generous living allowances and other benefits provided to overseas personnel, it was not really so much of an issue for him.

Second, there is language to the effect that "Mr. Goodall is . . . in charge of the Veterans Administration Office at Beckley, West Virginia." I wonder if this is akin to his having once claimed to have been "in complete charge" of the real estate office of one J. Bert Schroeder? It reads as if the same authority-oriented person composed it. If he *were* in charge of the Beckley office, wouldn't he have retained the title of "Chief"? Or even Super Chief? What then to make of this inconsistency with the Standard Form 50?

Third, this letter claims, in the final paragraph, that Standard Form 57, Application for Federal Employment, and DSP-34, Supplement to Standard Form 57, "which have been completed by Mr. Goodall," are attached. But they *aren't* attached. They may never have been filled out. Or at least they weren't included in the official documents released by the State Department to either the Civilian Employment Office archives or even to me, in a separate release I received nearly a year later. Instead, Form DS-1032 is included, and it befuddles more than clarifies the anomalies.

Notice again the double discrepancy in salary, now reported to be $6,145, *up* considerably from the letter of nomination, which supposedly preceded it. But the discrepancy in salary is not the end of the oddities on Form 1032.

Notice toward the bottom of the page the notation "Reserve status— None" that appears to be in direct contradiction not only to the letter of nomination but also to his currently designated rank—FSR-5—which rather clearly indicates that his is a reserve officer appointment.

Hmmm.

These are anomalies, but viewed against the larger aesthetic they speak of small things really, things that could be fairly and logically explained. They could be understood as simple bureaucratic errors. Or explained as forgettable mistakes and oversights in some relatively meaningless paperwork.

In other words, they could be plausibly denied.

However, there is one implausibly undeniable section of the letter of nomination. It is the tail end of the sentence that ends the first paragraph, and the much longer one that opens the second paragraph. Both quite clearly define what would become my father's new job title as—and I quote—a "Foreign Service Reserve Officer, Class 5."

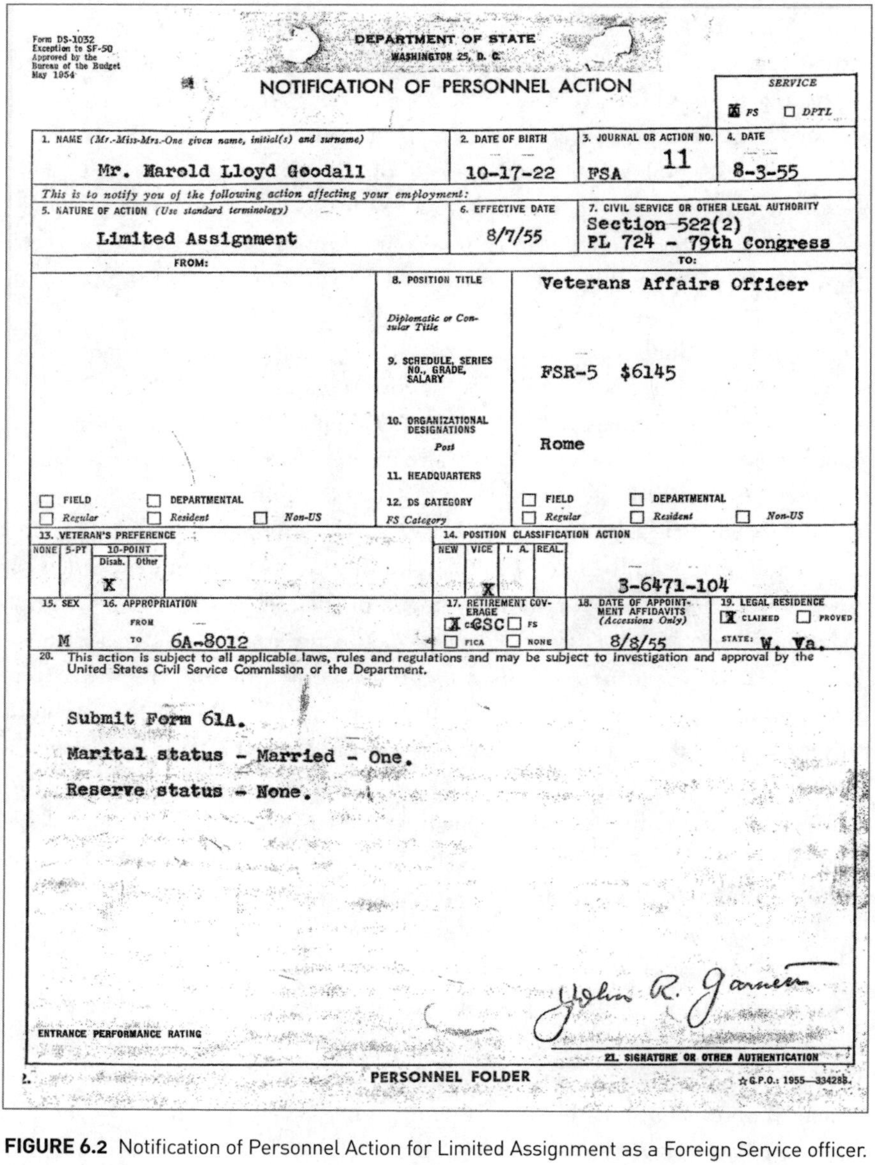

Form DS-1032
Exception to SF-50
Approved by the
Bureau of the Budget
May 1954

DEPARTMENT OF STATE
WASHINGTON 25, D. C.

NOTIFICATION OF PERSONNEL ACTION

SERVICE: [X] FS [ ] DPTL

1. NAME (Mr.-Miss-Mrs.-One given name, initial(s) and surname): Mr. Harold Lloyd Goodall
2. DATE OF BIRTH: 10-17-22
3. JOURNAL OR ACTION NO.: FSA 11
4. DATE: 8-3-55

This is to notify you of the following action affecting your employment:

5. NATURE OF ACTION (Use standard terminology): Limited Assignment
6. EFFECTIVE DATE: 8/7/55
7. CIVIL SERVICE OR OTHER LEGAL AUTHORITY: Section 522(2) PL 724 - 79th Congress

FROM: / TO:

8. POSITION TITLE: Veterans Affairs Officer
Diplomatic or Consular Title
9. SCHEDULE, SERIES NO., GRADE, SALARY: FSR-5 $6145
10. ORGANIZATIONAL DESIGNATIONS — Post: Rome
11. HEADQUARTERS
12. DS CATEGORY — FS Category: [ ] FIELD [ ] DEPARTMENTAL [ ] Regular [ ] Resident [ ] Non-US

13. VETERAN'S PREFERENCE: NONE / 5-PT / 10-POINT (Disab. X / Other)
14. POSITION CLASSIFICATION ACTION: NEW / VICE X / I. A. / REAL. — 3-6471-104
15. SEX: M
16. APPROPRIATION: FROM — TO 6A-8012
17. RETIREMENT COVERAGE: [X] CSC [ ] FS [ ] FICA [ ] NONE
18. DATE OF APPOINTMENT AFFIDAVITS (Accessions Only): 8/8/55
19. LEGAL RESIDENCE: [X] CLAIMED [ ] PROVED — STATE: W. Va.

20. This action is subject to all applicable laws, rules and regulations and may be subject to investigation and approval by the United States Civil Service Commission or the Department.

Submit Form 61A.

Marital status - Married - One.

Reserve status - None.

ENTRANCE PERFORMANCE RATING

John R. Garner

21. SIGNATURE OR OTHER AUTHENTICATION

2. PERSONNEL FOLDER ☆G.P.O.: 1955—334288

FIGURE 6.2 Notification of Personnel Action for Limited Assignment as a Foreign Service officer.

Stuart Kennedy, a fine scholar and former diplomat who created George-town University's Department of State Oral History Project, told me that designation was pure code, "a tip-off that he was CIA." It was a code, a bureaucratic linguistic device, used during the cold war to identify CIA agents operating overseas under diplomatic cover. It was used for duly authorized and trained CIA case officers and analysts—persons who had already completed the mandatory class at Fort Peary and at least nine months of prep work at the overseas assignment desk in Washington.

William Colby, who would become my father's CIA boss in Rome and later would serve as its director, includes in his memoirs the same basic story. When he initially accepted his Foreign Service reserve officer cover for Sweden, he was also asked to complete paperwork that made the new job appear to be official despite the fact that it only served as his cover story.

• •

Back to my original question: What was H. Lloyd Goodall *doing* in Beckley, West Virginia, for nine months, in 1954–55? Even if I accept as fact the language of the nomination letter about his then-current job and place of employment, I still have one pertinent question: how, in government life, do you go from working as a contact officer in a VA center in Beckley, West Virginia, to an appointment as a Foreign Service reserve officer and vice consul of the United States of America assigned to Rome, Italy, in the space of nine months? Rome in 1955 was the European centerpiece of the CIA's anti-Communist effort. It was considered vital that the 1956 elections maintain the Centrist government and not show any gains for the Socialists or the Communists.

This isn't the sort of new job that gets posted on a bulletin board.

Nor is it the sort of job that you *apply* for.

Someone has *to ask you to do it*. In this case, somebody at State, who, according to this nomination letter, put out the word that they needed a CIA case officer in Rome. Someone familiar enough with Veterans Affairs and political issues to do a day job using that cover.

No one assigned to Rome in 1955 got there by accident or by the Horatio Alger route of "luck and pluck" or marrying the boss's daughter. Colby says as much in his memoirs. Seasoned intelligence officers were recruited. Veterans' groups were key. Someone assigned responsibility for veterans' groups in Rome was entering a very high-profile office, not only on Colby's radar but also on the ambassador's. And not only on Ambassador Luce's radar, but also on Allen Dulles's and J. J. Angleton's. Perhaps even on the president's radar, if only as an occasional blip.

Our Veterans Affairs man in Rome had to be someone who knew *exactly* what he was doing. Someone who had prior experience in intelligence work, in political infiltration, and in propaganda. Someone already fully engaged in the larger ongoing cold war conversation. Someone who could keep a secret and who told believable lies. A storyteller. A person at ease with others, easy to know and to be around, who not only knew the job, but also knew a great deal about the culture, the economy, and the people.

There were other qualifications. The person chosen for this job should, preferably, be someone who spoke the language. Someone who already knew somebody over there in the citizenry, or at least who knew of people among the veterans' citizenry, who themselves had already been targeted as possible leaders, rabble-rousers, and agents. Or veterans in pro-Communist groups who could be "turned." Human beings who, for love of adventure or an idea, or fear of being found out or blackmailed, or simply for the pure love of money, might be willing to betray their professed political beliefs or their country.

Now I ask you, does *this* job description sound like one perfectly suited for an ordinary government employee from Beckley, West Virginia?

No. Of course it doesn't.

. . . .

According to my mother, the appointment to the cold war in Rome actually represented a last-minute change of plans. She remembered a late-night phone call that interrupted a party at our house on New Year's Eve. The caller—someone from State, she didn't remember who it was—asked my father if he would accept a position in Central America. She thought it might have been Panama, but perhaps not.

My father accepted it, she said, "because you never said no to the government." But, for some reason, we did not go to Panama. Nor Guatemala. Nor Paraguay. Nor Venezuela. Nor Ecuador.

Instead, we moved to Rome. We began preparing for Rome in March and arrived there in August. In between those dates my father participated in Foreign Service training in Washington, D.C.

Hmmm. I wonder what *kind* of training.

Language training, certainly. He spoke, at best, restaurant Italian. Perhaps he also received a short course in Italian politics, economics, and

CIVIL OFFICER

APPOINTMENT AFFIDAVITS

(As defined in 5 USC 21a and 21b)

I, **Harold Lloyd Goodall**   **West Virginia**
(Name in full)   (State)

do solemnly swear (or affirm) that

A. OATH OF OFFICE

I will support and defend the Constitution of the United States against all enemies, foreign and domestic; that I will bear true faith and allegiance to the same; that I take this obligation freely without any mental reservation or purpose of evasion; that I will well and faithfully discharge the duties of the office on which I am about to enter, SO HELP ME GOD.

B. AFFIDAVIT AS TO SUBVERSIVE ACTIVITY AND AFFILIATION

I am not a Communist or a Fascist. I do not advocate nor am I a member of any organization that advocates the overthrow of the Government of the United States by force or violence or other unconstitutional means, or seeking by force or violence to deny other persons their rights under the Constitution of the United States. I do further swear (or affirm) I will not so advocate, nor will I become a member of such organization during the period that I am an employee of the Federal Government.

C. AFFIDAVIT AS TO STRIKING AGAINST THE FEDERAL GOVERNMENT

I am not engaged in any strike against the Government of the United States and that I will not so engage while an employee of the Government of the United States; that I am not a member of an organization of Government employees that asserts the right to strike against the Government of the United States, and that I will not, while a Government employee, become a member of such an organization.

D. AFFIDAVIT AS TO PURCHASE AND SALE OF OFFICE

I have not, nor has anyone acting in my behalf, given, transferred, promised or paid any consideration for or in expectation or hope of receiving assistance in securing such appointment.

Harold Lloyd Goodall
(Type name of appointee)   (Signature of appointee)

Subscribed and sworn before me this ___**8th**___ day of ___**August**___, A. D. 19__**55**__,

at ___**Washington, D. C.**___
(City)   (State)

(Signature of officer)

[SEAL]

Sec. 206, Act June 26, 1943
(Title)

Department of State   **Foreign Service**   **Washington, D. C.**
(Department or agency)   (Bureau or division)   (Place of employment)

Foreign Service Reserve Officer of Class-5;
Veterans Affairs Officer   **August 7, 1955**
(Position to which appointed)   (Date of entrance on duty)

NOTE.—*If the oath is taken before a Notary Public, the date of expiration of his commission should be shown.*

16—61849-1   U. S. GOVERNMENT PRINTING OFFICE

FIGURE 6.3 Oath of Office signed by Harold Lloyd Goodall in 1955.

history. But I don't know that. Maybe some clandestine training, as well. Colby indicates they all did clandestine training, everything from the usual spy stuff of using one-time pads to making dead drops to using surveillance gear. Reserve officers received an introduction to spy psychology, supposedly useful for locating potential agents and traitors. Undoubtedly they received a primer in Communist political theory. They also learned judo and fired weapons of various calibers. Most of the reserve officers jumped at least once out of perfectly good airplanes, although I seriously doubt they talked my father into doing that. Or perhaps he was declared exempt, given his Army Air Corps training during the war. That's possible. He graduated from spy training—or whatever they called it—with his class, although, unlike other aspects of his education along the course of his career, there is no formal written account of it in his work history and no accompanying rating or ranking of his success.

All I have to document this period of time is my mother's account of it.

He took the oath of office and signed Standard Form 61a on August 8, 1955. Notice, please, that his signature is appended to a document that officially lists him to be a "Foreign Service Reserve Officer of Class-5" first and foremost. The "Veterans Affairs Officer" is entirely secondary.

I wonder if this ordering of responsibilities is important. If nothing else, it suggests that he had two jobs to do in Rome. But, of course, it is my contention that he had been doing two jobs all along.

· ·

If J. J. Angleton and Bill Colby defined the ways in which the cold war in Italy would be fought, Ambassador Extraordinary and Envoy Plenipotentiary Clare Boothe Luce was surely the engaged leader to ensure it would be fought hard and well. Her Excellency Mrs. Luce served as the ambassador to Italy as a result of having been an accomplished and successful playwright, a prominent Republican fund-raiser, and the wife of influential *Time* magazine founder and editor Henry Luce.

She was also a well-known and vehement anti-Communist, at least as much on ideological grounds as on her more recently acquired religious one as a converted Roman Catholic. Communists were atheists. They were a godless horde of Reds, unfortunate victims of an ill-conceived political revolution launched by push-button orators who had betrayed the very principles they had so loudly espoused. A madman, Stalin, who was a known liar on the world's stage and mass murderer of his own people, had led them. Now, in 1955, it appeared his assumed assassin, Beria, was leading them. But no one knew for sure.

No matter. Communism, for Ambassador Luce, was evil incarnate and had to be stopped. For her, the cold war in Italy was a crusade, a holy war, a battleground between the forces of white elite Republican Judeo-Christian Good, inflected with a deep Catholicism, against the forces of uneducated, impoverished, armed peasant darkness, the Godless Communist Evil that, doing Satan's handiwork, was capable of unleashing a nuclear holocaust.

Sound vaguely familiar? It's déjà vu, all over again. Only in our time the "crusade"—named correctly as such by President Bush in his address to the nation on September 20, 2001—is between fundamentalist versions of Protestantism and Islam.

The crusade against Communism was worldwide but Luce's particular domain was Italy, where, during her tenure, she pursued a ruthless campaign against Socialists and Communists alike. Colby provides a detailed and favorable testimony of her leadership and there is no doubt she cut an intriguing and intelligent figure in the political world. Mrs. Luce was a brilliant woman and a striking blonde, beautiful of face and body, learned, socially elite, politically lean and conservatively Republican right down to her bones. She carried out her anti-Communist duties with the able assistance, and often inspired thinking, of other members of the CIA who operated under diplomatic cover at the American embassy, including men I learned to call my "uncles": Bill Colby, Gerry Miller, and Tom Braden.

But it was this formidable force of nature who formally welcomed us to Italy when my father, my mother, and I deplaned in Rome. I ask you to imagine, for a moment, what it must have been like for us to meet, and to be greeted by, Ambassador Clare Boothe Luce in Rome in 1955. My father was a junior diplomat and nighttime spy and she was his all-knowing, all-powerful new boss. As hierarchically divided as this initial meeting was for my father, consider my mother. She was, in August of 1955, a middle-aged woman moving to an international metropolis from the Appalachian burg of Beckley, West Virginia. Her personal history included being a member of the working-class rural poor who, to seek a better life, ran away from home with the richest boy from Charles Town, whom she had then divorced in order to enter nurse's training. She had not graduated from a fine college or seen a Broadway play, much less authored one.

Imagine those differences and then try to smile graciously, as my mother did.

Trying to make polite small talk with my mother in the limousine from the airport to our new digs along the Via Grazioli, the ambassador asked her what she called her "little boy."

"We call him Buddy," my mother politely replied.

Mrs. Luce noticeably stiffened. "Is that his *Christian* name?"

"No," my mother replied. "His Christian name is Harold Lloyd Goodall Jr. He is named after his father."

"Then *by all means*, Mrs. Goodall, from now on as the wife of an official representative of the United States of America, you must use *only* his Christian name."

There was a moment of stunned silence as my mother recovered from shock. She had looked forward to meeting Clare Boothe Luce. She had been full of anticipation for this moment. She had rehearsed a little speech about herself that was now entirely unnecessary. The ambassador had silenced her, put her—and us—into our rightful place. And she had done it without so much as blinking an eye. My mother, as she later told me, never imagined that *anyone* would tell her what she was allowed to call her own son.

"Do I make myself *perfectly* clear?" the ambassador asked.

"Yes, *perfectly*," replied my mother.

Welcome to our new life in a cold war. It was to be a frosty war on a variety of fronts.

• •

There are many ways to define conflict, many ways to argue what divisiveness of any kind is really "about." My father's conflict was defined by, and as, the cold war. My mother's was equally cold but had a gendered, feminine, social class–based inflection. It was a conflict about the genetic code of hierarchical rank, the implicit pecking order of supposedly democratic and freedom-loving persons, the concertive control that cuts across all boundaries and enforces a strict discipline and command structure at all times and in all places and in all actions that derive meaning under the rules of national security in wartime.

When I think about my mother and Mrs. Luce in the backseat of the embassy's highly polished black Cadillac, and when I replay this oft-repeated conversation, I locate the origins of a deeper conflict, a personal one that is also a political one. A conflict that defined my mother's life. It is a cold war conflict rooted in the strict disciplining of warriors, and warriors' wives and children, according to social class and educational attainments, economic standing, and perceived diplomatic or clandestine worth.

But it is also a cold war conflict derived from the consciously constructed postwar narrative that our nation had to be perceived as not only "right" but also as the best at everything we did. The stakes were, and are, high. We were not only conquerors of the world; we had to demonstrate that we were so because we were ideologically superior. That our lifestyle and way of life was the best. Hence, American representatives had to appear better than anyone else.

Our enforced familial formality was a sign of our race's dominance, a dominance organized by a mannerly perfection disguised as political etiquette. Yet, our formality was also a cover story. It was a tale told to the world in well-lit rooms about who Americans were, and what we stood for, and at the same time it hid our dark undemocratic secret, the unspoken but everywhere apparent truth that despite our democratic and egalitarian vistas, we were—and are—essentially *un*equal.

Therein lies a major source of democratic conflict, and, in my experience, perhaps the primary one. If we are, as the poet Walt Whitman once wrote, a nation of contradictions, then surely it is a contradiction that enables social class and economic distinctions to separate us from each other. Believing that you are better than someone else, better than another American, is only a sin if you aren't willing to admit it. For all of our professed love of the common man and common woman, no one I've met wants to be one. Our lives are entitled to be larger, more storied, grander, and better off than whatever we perceive as average, or ordinary, or common.

My mother's conflict was one of managed appearances in everyday life among diplomatic wives and her husband's superiors. It was womanly, feminine, and mean. It was evidence of an internal power struggle that coexisted alongside of, and significantly contributed to, the managed appearances that defined the bigger power struggle for ideological control of the cold war. Women vs. women, class vs. class, spy vs. spy.

· ·

William Colby wrote that his wife, Barbara, kept him from becoming enmeshed in what would become known as the "cult of secrecy" in the CIA. It was a culture he believed derived from the double lives of officers and the need to never talk about what they really did outside of their privileged inner circle, if even then.

He pointed out that this cultural divide between spies and the rest of the world had long-term negative consequences. As was demonstrated in testimony during the 1970s Watergate, Rockefeller, and Church hearings, it created among them a belief that they were separate from, and superior to, other people. They were living lives larger than ordinary life, and because no one knew about it, and they couldn't talk about it, it was as if that "other" life, their secret life, entitled them to do things that no one else felt entitled to do, either morally or legally. It was the ego without benefit of an id.

This creation of a clandestine super class of cold warriors ultimately accomplished two goals: it prevented all-out nuclear war between the superpowers and it contributed significantly to the proliferation of a culture of fear, secrecy, dishonesty, duplicity, anxiety, and lies.

How did Barbara Colby prevent the negative effects of Bill Colby's double life from destroying their marriage? According to him, she insisted on maintaining a "normal life" outside of the CIA inner circles. She resisted the strong inducements to organize their social lives solely around the clandestine service personnel and embassy functionaries. She required him to talk to her, not only about what he was working on, but also how he felt about it. And she demanded that he spend quality time with their five children. In other words, she put their lives together ahead of the job he had to do.

But then, Barbara Colby *could* do that.

She never thought twice about it. She was a blue-blooded member of the well-educated American social elite. If all else failed, her well-connected husband would still be an Ivy League graduate and highly regarded lawyer. Among those who ruled America's clandestine services during the cold war, their own personal entitlement to a life rich with adventure, duty, and patriotic sacrifice simply didn't cost as much. Clare Booth Luce never instructed Barbara Colby what names to call her children. But it's seldom the lives of the leaders we find amid the ruins of any war.

It is the lives of those who were, and who still are, led by them.

• •

From the moment my father entered the clandestine world in Rome there ceases to be an official record of his activities, at least beyond the few pieces of paper that I include in the following chapters. All we have left is the family story, the family secrets, and the memories and names shaped by my father's diary.

From this turning point in the narrative and until our 1960 exile in Wyoming, the world I re-enter is largely, and necessarily, a historically derivative and narratively imagined one. It is made up of persons, places, conversations, and things that I have constructed out of the raw material of what I know, what I've read about, the patterns I recognize, and what I believe to be true. It is a version of the truth, not the whole truth, or maybe even the main truth. I try to be clear about that.

But it is a spy story, after all, shadowy and clandestine.

It is a story of complicated lives in interesting times. Making a coherent story out of complicated lives in interesting times is often messy work. I do not apologize for the messiness. All I can say is that the story that follows is the best I can do with the materials I've been given, culled, thought about, read about, and lived with.

07

Setup:
Angleton, Colby, and Italy

1946-1954

MY FATHER'S EUROPEAN ROLE IN THE COLD WAR BEGAN IN ITALY IN 1955.
Why Italy?

To understand what he inherited from his intelligence and diplomatic
forbears in Italy, and to appreciate why the clandestine cold war in Italy
was so important, requires recovering its history as viewed from the per-
spectives of two powerful men who shaped it: James Jesus Angleton and
William Colby.

• •

James Jesus Angleton was a Yale graduate with well-developed literary sen-
sibilities and a practiced expertise in fly-fishing. Later he would add to these
diverse talents by becoming a respected breeder of rare hybrid orchids.

Angleton was born in Boise, Idaho, on December 9, 1917, and given
his middle name, pronounced in the Spanish style, to honor his mother's
Mexican heritage. His mother, Carmen Mercedes Moreno, was a lovely,
gentle-spirited, and devoutly Catholic woman, who met his father, Hugh
Angleton, in Nogales, Arizona. As a young man in 1916, Hugh Angleton rode
as a cavalry officer with General John J. "Black Jack" Pershing in pursuit of
Pancho Villa on the Arizona-Mexico border.

Jim was their first son in what would become a family of four children. Following his service in the military, Hugh Angleton went to work for National Cash Register in Idaho, carrying the business machines on mules into mining towns. He became so successful a salesman that he was transferred to the corporate offices in Dayton, Ohio, and then, in 1933, he was sent to Europe to conduct a business survey. Hugh was offered more money to stay with NCR in Dayton, but he wanted to work for himself and instead offered to buy their fledgling Italian franchise. NCR agreed and he moved the family to Italy.

Jim became fluent in Italian and knowledgeable about the culture. He lived overseas as a well-to-do expatriate, attended Malvern College in England, and became well acquainted with British social class codes and customs. He graduated as a prefect, a corporal in the Officers' Training Corps, and a member of the Old Malvern Society. He also acquired a lifelong habit of imitating upper-class "City" dress codes and was seldom seen in anything other than a dark suit, regardless of the climate.

He returned to the United States for study at Yale. There, he demonstrated a single-mindedness about pursuing his interests—poetry, jazz, philosophy, bowling, women, current affairs, and the law—to the near absolute neglect of the rest of the curriculum. He graduated—barely—with a low-C grade-point average. Yet, despite his low marks in some subjects, he excelled in what interested him and won the attention and affection of his teachers and friends.

While at Yale, Angleton edited a literary magazine with his roommate, the poet Reed Whittemore, called *Furioso*. It was dedicated to modernist and avant-garde writing and featured new poetry by e e cummings and Ezra Pound. Jim worshipped Pound's work in particular, and used his magazine's growing influence and his Italian connections to lure the poet to Yale for a reading. Pound was duly impressed. According to Angleton's wife, Cicely, the poet described Jim Angleton as "one of the most important hopes of literary magazines in the United States."

He was already developing a reputation as a man of mystery and contradictions. Angleton was an excellent organizer, hard worker, and tireless salesman, but not much of a writer nor at all tolerant of views that contrasted with his own. At Yale, he was uncomfortable with his Chicano heritage, spoke with a slight British accent, and dropped his middle initial from his records. He was furious with a professor who once mockingly used the Jesus appellation aloud in class. According to later statements by Whittemore, he had labored for hours writing the brief two-page introduction to *Furioso*, and his other written work was, at best, "constipated." He was already a vehement anti-Communist. And it was at Yale that Angleton became known as a legendary insomniac, a condition that would afflict him for the rest of his life.

Despite his poor grades, he was accepted at Harvard Law School and entered it in the autumn of 1941. War loomed on the near horizon and, like all young men of his era, he knew his future was uncertain as long as Hitler continued his march across Europe.

On December 7, 1941, emerging from a movie house in Boston, he heard of the Japanese attack on Pearl Harbor. That evening, in a sincere attempt to get drunk at the Oyster House, he met Cicely d'Autremont, an English major at Vassar who hailed from a heavily moneyed Minnesota family. It was, according to her, "love at first sight," and they married in July of 1943.

Jim's father was already at war, serving with the newly formed Office of Strategic Services operations in Italy. With his father's connections and a recommendation from his old Yale English professor, Norman Pearson, Jim went straight into the OSS training program, and from there to their X-2 counterintelligence operation in war-torn London. At X-2, he distinguished himself as "single-minded" in his work and earned a promotion to captain and, eventually, the Legion of Merit. He also made the acquaintance of Harold Adrian "Kim" Philby, the MI6 officer who trained Jim in counter-intelligence and with whom he formed an early—and what would become a fateful—friendship.

In London, after only six months on the job, Angleton became the chief of the Italian desk for the European theater of operations. He was transferred to Italy in October 1944. At the end of the war, at age twenty-seven, he became the youngest branch chief in X-2 and the only non-British officer cleared to benefit from the intelligence gained from the cipher-breaking Ultra. He had established himself as a major figure in postwar intelligence, and now turned his attention to targeting Communist networks. He began a lifelong habit of relying on his hobbies for language useful in counter-intelligence. Using his love for orchids and of gardening in general, he deployed agents code-named with floral icons—"Bloom," "Briar," "Pansy," and "Rose."

His love of counterintelligence superseded, at least temporarily, his obligations toward his wife and his new son, James Charles, who had been born in August of 1944. He resisted any attempt by his wife to lure him home, and when he did manage a two-day visit, it was disastrous. Cicely remembered it as a time when they both seriously contemplated divorce.

Jim had no interest in anything other than his work. Yet, they remained together and in love.

In 1948 Angleton received his first CIA appointment, as an aide to Frank Wisner in the Office of Special Operations. There, he continued to run his European networks, making frequent trips abroad. In October of 1949, he was promoted to the rank of GS-15 with a salary of $10,750 a year. When Allen Dulles took over the CIA in 1953, he commissioned a study of Agency operations. Conducted under the auspices of General James Doolittle and called "The Doolittle Report," it was a critique of recent errors that recommended a serious expansion of counterintelligence operations. Angleton had Dulles's ear and his confidence; he also had an unparalleled record of accomplishment in counterintelligence. In December of 1954, James Angleton (no middle name given) became the first chief of the CIA's counterintelligence staff. It was a post he would retain until his forced retirement in 1974.

If Angleton was an accomplished counterintelligence leader, he was also a very odd man. He was a legendary paranoid, increasingly suspicious of everything and everyone, which made him perfectly suited for counterintelligence work, to a point. Just as there is a fine line between genius and madness, so too is there a similarly thin line between the ability to see hidden patterns and the inability to question what you yourself have constructed, as a result of seeing those patterns, to be true. True to the nature of the spy business, Angleton's record can be read either way.

For all of his attributed brilliance and lauded counterintelligence accomplishments, there is also the fact of his legendary failures. First, he championed defectors, including KGB Major Anatoliy Golitsyn, who flattered Angleton's fundamentalist perspective on the evil posed by the Soviets. Despite the evidence that what these defectors gave us was of little practical value and much of it was manufactured conjecture given in exchange for large sums of money, Angleton remained steadfast. Second, he refused to admit that other legitimate defectors, such as Aleksandr Cherepanov and Oleg Penkovskiy, had provided valuable intelligence information, even going to the extent of imprisoning Penkovskiy for years in the basement at the CIA headquarters in Langley, Virginia. Third, he built up a network of internal Agency loyalists who were genuinely feared because they spied on other Agency officers and provided information and innuendoes that killed careers. This network allowed Angleton to defeat many officers who opposed him, but it also hardened other officers against him, one of whom would be responsible for ending Angleton's intelligence career. Fourth, and most notably, Angleton seemed to possess an inherent inability to change his mind. It was this failure that led to his unwavering support for his friend and former mentor, Kim Philby, a double agent spying for the Soviets.

If Angleton's failures were notable and tragic, they were also made of the same stuff he used to create his achievements and success. As the chief counterspy, it was his job to find out what was being concealed and to discover and disarm all hidden conspiracies. Here, his personality and paranoia found their mark. He looked for conspiracies within otherwise ordinary relationships and found patterns of deceit within everyday language usage.

Furthermore, his job was to turn appearances of propriety upside down, to examine all the angles, and be the master of deceit capable of locating deception and impropriety. But paranoia is a tireless companion. As he rose in counterintelligence stature within the Agency, Angleton's belief that there was a Soviet mole in the Agency dominated his obsession with finding out everything he could about the people he worked with, and for. He developed personal files on Agency personnel that included many by-products of suspicions and intensive surveillance, including the dates and times Agency personnel had formal or informal contact with other Agency officers and analysts. Eventually these files were expanded to include dates and times of any friendly or professional contacts he deemed worthy of suspicion, as well as their favorite restaurants, drinking habits, pastimes, sexual preferences, and financial transactions. These categories were cross-referenced based on literally hundreds of possible links. As Angleton often said, "If you control counterintelligence, you control the intelligence service." And he was right. Control was his passion. He didn't believe that *anyone* he couldn't personally vouch for was truly above treason.

Angleton was a moderately tall man but it wasn't his height that attracted attention. He was dark in his features and had a wasted-away thin physique. Cloaked in a black hood and accessorized with a scythe, he would have passed as the Grim Reaper. He had the beady eyes that, in old cartoons, we associate with whatever is illegal or sinister. He was seldom a pleasant man, yet he could be charming and was deeply poetic. He was, by all accounts, a brilliant man, a master of puzzles, patterns, and sophisticated games.

When he died, in 1987, some of his last words to his wife Cicely were, "I have made so many mistakes." To my knowledge, there were two. One of them clearly was in underestimating Bill Colby. The other one was what he did to my father, and ultimately to our family. But I am getting ahead of the story.

· ·

William E. Colby appeared to be a typical Washington bureaucrat. He was neither tall nor short, neither handsome nor unhandsome, neither particularly friendly nor unfriendly. He blended in rather than stood out. He was easy to meet, and, if not exactly excellent conversational company, usually quite interesting and very knowledgeable. The older he got, the quieter he became. He was proud, without tending toward either vanity or hubris. He believed in a Catholic version of God, and a traditional version of honor, duty, family, and his country.

Son of a career military officer with a love of literature, the young Colby graduated from Princeton and joined the army just as World War II was getting under way. He was recruited into the OSS out of youthful frustration. Afraid that his posting as an artillery instructor and replacement officer at Fort Sill, Oklahoma, would cause him to miss the action, he volunteered for the paratroopers and wound up assigned to "Wild Bill" Donovan and the OSS. His knowledge of French and training as a paratrooper led him to clandestine activities behind enemy lines in France, and then again in Norway. He was awarded a Bronze Star, Silver Star, Croix de Guerre, and St. Olaf's Medal before returning to the States at age twenty-five, a major and a war hero. Once there, Colby married his pre-war sweetheart, a Barnard graduate and fellow Catholic named Barbara Heinzen. He returned to Columbia University and completed law school, and then took a job with "Wild Bill" Donovan's firm at Two Wall Street, where he met Frank Wisner and Allen Dulles.

During the brief pre–cold war era following the surrender of Germany and Japan, Bill Donovan and his friends lobbied hard for the creation of a permanent central intelligence service to capitalize on what they had learned during the war. President Truman was reluctant to do so and many Americans were cautious. Newspaper editorials in Washington, New York, and Chicago had already railed against it. One prominent piece in the *Washington Times-Herald* by Walter Trohan, on February 9, 1945, drew the attention of nervous politicians. It urged against it on the grounds that an "all-powerful intelligence service" would serve to spy on citizens in the United States while, at the same time, affording spies lives of "bribery and luxury" at taxpayers' expense.

Nevertheless, encouraged by the somber turn in world events, and fearing the expansion of Soviet influence in Europe, Truman signed the National Security Act on July 26, 1947. The CIA, along with the United States Air Force, was born. The president hoped to avoid an "American Gestapo" by stressing that the CIA would only deal with foreign intelligence and specifically banned domestic surveillance of any kind. Despite his cautions, the lines between "foreign" and "domestic" were often blurry, particularly during a time when so many postwar immigrants to the United States were well connected politically overseas. Did interviewing a foreign national in West Virginia constitute domestic surveillance, or the collection of foreign intelligence?

After the war, Colby, a liberal Democrat, practiced labor relations law and joined the American Civil Liberties Union and the new American Veterans Committee, a liberal alternative to the more conservative American Legion. He witnessed firsthand a meeting of the AVC in New York City where the Communists attempted to take control of the organization, bringing home the fact that the cold war was likely to be fought on domestic as well as foreign soil. By 1950 he was bored with the workaday life of a labor attorney. The outbreak of the Korean War made him an easy target for recruitment by his old European OSS commander, Gerald Miller. He was assigned to work with his former colleague from Two Wall Street, Frank Wisner, in the newly established Office of Policy Coordination, the clandestine planning and operations group within the CIA.

Colby's first posting lasted two years, from 1951 to 1953. He served as political officer in Stockholm, Sweden, under State Department cover as a Foreign Service reserve officer. His wife, Barbara, took up junior diplomatic wife status and organized women's charity, local housing, and children's play groups for the embassy.

In his 1978 memoir, *Honorable Men: My Life in the CIA*, Colby discusses his dual role of daytime diplomat and nighttime and weekend spy in ways that resonate with the experiences shared by my parents. The cover-role parallels are clear, as are the clandestine activities Colby engaged in while in Scandinavia. Colby's political work included establishing resistance networks and recruiting foreign agents who would supply information in exchange for money or favors, as well as attending embassy meetings with various political envoys and showing up for embassy functions. Chief among his successes was the recruitment of "gray men," the ordinary, invisible, plainly dressed, and unlikely outside officers and foreign agents necessary to gather intelligence information. Using his training in psychology and political theory—training he admits was of much better quality at Princeton than was provided by the CIA—he learned to meet contacts away from their offices, and to use trust and friendship to build relationships. It was Tradecraft 101 in practice and Colby excelled at it.

His success as the political officer in the American embassy in Stockholm led to a new posting in sunny and splendid Rome. There, under State Department cover as a Foreign Service reserve officer, Colby worked closely with Gerald Miller, the CIA's chief of station in Rome. Colby, Miller, Ambassador Luce, and my father were instrumental in shaping the outcomes of Italian elections, as well as using officers and agents to infiltrate various political, religious, and artistic groups.

. . . .

In 1947 the Communists thought they would win the elections if they could prevent voters from believing any of the scare propaganda that the Christian Democrats—and, of course, the Agency—were placing in the local papers. So, in a desperate if enlightened moment, the Communists bought up all the newsprint in the country.

Postwar bureaucracy complicated the story. At the time of the newsprint fiasco, James Forrestal was being installed as the U.S.'s first Secretary of Defense. It was a brand-new office and he didn't yet have the funds to provide help to the CIA, so he asked Allen Dulles to seek donations from his friends at his golf and fishing club. Angleton needed money or the Communists would win. It was that simple. Dulles held a dinner party and literally passed around a bronze church collection plate.

Within days, Angleton had enough lire in a leather satchel to turn the election our way. The CIA effectively bypassed the Communists with direct payoffs and threats to any opinion leader whose vote could be bought, and had some of our local friends set fire to the storage facility where the Communists stored their supply of newsprint.

Meanwhile, Angleton used Forrestal's clout to truck down a supply of newsprint from an American military base in Germany, which in turn allowed Angleton to keep up the good inflammatory printed propaganda that was the key to counterintelligence in postwar Italy.

Of course, the Italian Communists promised revenge.

Revenge came years later. During my father's early assignment in Rome he helped uncover an ingenious plot by the Communists to poison Ambassador Luce. The plot involved the removal of old paint from the elaborately decorated ceiling in the ambassador's bedroom. The poisonous agent was cyanide. A weak solution of sodium cyanide was often used by knowledgeable practitioners to remove gold or silver. So it was nothing unusual when the workers used hydrocyanic acid to remove the old silver and gold ornamental work from the ceiling. What was unusual was that they left just enough of it behind to be toxic.

The intended instrument of the ambassador's demise was ordinary nighttime breathing. Slowly, while the ambassador was sleeping peacefully, the cyanide released its deadly toxins into the bedroom. Had the plan worked, it would have taken weeks for the level of toxicity caused by her steady inhaling of the air in the room to poison her blood. Initially, she would have felt nothing. Within a week or so she would complain of symptoms that resembled a cold; the cold would progress into symptoms doctors routinely associate with the flu. By that time no antidote could reverse the poisoning.

The ambassador's death by cyanide poisoning would have been interpreted as either a tragic accident or an assassination. The Italian Communist Party would have denied any involvement, of course. Such a tragedy. So lovely a woman. Who could *do* such a thing?

It was, after all, only politics. Moscow would be proud. The plan was probably approved in Moscow because the Italian Communists didn't have access to the advanced technology required to lace the new paint without dissipating the toxins.

This assertion of Soviet guidance could never be proven, of course.

Even if it could've been proven, it wouldn't have been announced. To do so would seem to be a slap in the face of Italians for not being technologically advanced enough to pull it off on their own. It would also be perceived among members of the intelligence community as an unnecessary compliment to Russian scientists. There were those in the community as well as outside of it who believed that the Russians were way ahead of us, at least in technology. Had this plot worked, Ambassador Luce's death would have been a major victory for Italian Communists.

Eventually the truth would leak out, but by then a thousand other things would have occurred to capture public attention, a hundred other heinous plots would have been reported, dozens of notable deaths would have been duly noted, and perhaps even a nuclear war would have been threatened. Ambassador Luce's unfortunate death would have been the sweetest kind of political revenge, the cold, deniable kind served without any obvious clues and discovered only after it no longer is useful news.

In the cold war this was how it was.

• •

The name of the counterintelligence game is propaganda. During the cold war, information provided by ex-Nazi war criminals and other foreign nationals was used to create a massive coordinated program of disinformation to rival, if not grandly exceed, the efforts already in use in Europe by the Soviets. Central to this spread of propaganda was the appropriation and penetration of communication media of popular culture. The CIA under Wisner and Dulles were unparalleled in their day in their use of the radio, magazines, films, and, later, television, to combat what Joe McCarthy coined "the Communist menace."

The appropriation of media required the establishment of front organizations. For example, under Dulles's guidance, the National Committee for Free Europe, Inc. was established as a government-sponsored program in 1949, Dulles serving as its "chairman." The idea was to recruit prominent Americans to use their business and social contacts with exiled leaders for propagandistic purposes. The goal was to persuade these contacts to speak to their fellow citizens in Europe by radio, through letters, and using articles placed in popular magazines. By repeating the essential message that democracy offered the only viable alternative for those seeking freedom, and by aligning this message with the needs, hopes, and fears of citizens who often now resided in displaced persons camps, or some godforsaken somewhere behind the Iron Curtain, or to anyone who opposed Communism anywhere in the world, this "National Committee" adopted the known power of mass communication to further the propaganda and disinformation purposes of the CIA. By far, the most effective outreach program sponsored by this group was Radio Free Europe.

Home base for Radio Free Europe was in Munich, Germany, where a 135,000-watt medium-wave transmitter was launched into service. By 1952, cheered by early success, Dulles, Wisner, and Angleton had several "Radios" operating under various names, each one supposedly sponsored and funded with contributions from a host of made-up organizations with patriotic names, including the American Committee for the Liberation of Russia, the Free Asia Committee, Radio Liberty, and the Council Against Communist Aggression. These patriotic organizations were fronts for CIA operations, and their funding came either from the rapidly dwindling but still available millions in impounded Nazi money or from undisclosed government accounts laundered through the Carnegie, Rockefeller, and Ford charities. In an ill-advised attempt to be thorough in its coverage of Europe, there was even a Radio Free Albania for a while, at least until CIA field officers discovered that there were very few radios in Albania because there was little electricity and no batteries, and the radio was transferred elsewhere.

Frank Wisner, as deputy director of operations, used these Radios to block the local reception of competing Soviet propaganda by using a constant piping of organ tones into the airwaves that he later referred to as "The Mighty Wurlitzer." Eventually, Radio Free Europe would broadcast eleven and a half hours a day in twenty-nine languages and dialects. They featured popular music banned by Communist governments—jazz, blues, "race" music, and eventually rock and roll—sprinkled liberally with impassioned denunciations of Communists by supposedly local informants. In some cases, radio programs operated as what today would pass as right-wing fanatical talk radio, complete with scripted discussions of important issues of the day that were thinly disguised excuses for regular infusions of inflammatory diatribes, provocative answers to questions, and outright lies.

All is fair in love, war, and counterintelligence.

My father's work in Italy was deceptively straightforward. He was, in his guise as Veterans Affairs officer in the U.S. embassy, to infiltrate local Italian veterans' groups and gain whatever information money could buy or threats could encourage. He also recruited and developed agents within those groups to broaden the scope of the information from corollary labor union, cultural, and religious organizations. Thus, the tasks of intelligence gathering within Colby and Miller's network and the distribution or dissemination of counterintelligence information throughout the network were effectively joined.

. . . .

By 1958, Colby had served in Rome for five years and the elections he was sent over to influence had been won. He was asked to serve as a CIA advisor for political intelligence operations in Southeast Asia, based in Saigon, and later became chief of station and director of Far East operations, where he spearheaded a community-based self-defense and self-improvement campaign in South Vietnam. In 1967, Lyndon Baines Johnson appointed him as personal ambassador to Vietnam. It was the first time a spy had risen to such lofty heights in the diplomatic corps and prompted some humor from his Agency colleagues. Later, his authoritative knowledge of Southeast Asia gained during the Vietnam War led to his appointment as director of central intelligence in 1973. He reportedly was surprised by the appointment and not entirely pleased.

I've read that William Egan Colby was a decent and honest man who simply knew too much. In 1975, in response to a formal request for information from President Gerald R. Ford, he revealed the "family jewels," or the deep secrets in the Agency's covert past. These secrets included the many intelligence and counterintelligence escapades involving paramilitary groups; plots to assassinate Fidel Castro by exploding cigars and poison; the real as well as the attempted overthrow of foreign governments; the clear violation of the laws of our country through domestic surveillance; and the clear pattern of violating the laws and sovereignty of other nations while fighting the good fight against the twin evils of Communism and Socialism worldwide.

Colby himself has written that when he began releasing this information he was asked by Vice President Nelson Rockefeller, "Do you really have to present all this information to us?" Henry Kissinger mused, "Bill, do you know what you do when you go up to the Hill? You go to confession." Colby's willingness to testify openly and honestly about covert operations stunned everyone, including the American public. His revelations led to House and Senate Select Committees. The Senate Select Committee became known as the Church Committee hearings, and the Church Committee hearings changed American history. They also changed the Agency and forever sealed the fate of my family.

My father had planned to testify before the Church Committee.

Time lines do not have to limit story lines, but they often prove useful in showing personal trajectories that look, at the other end of things, to be either serendipity or destiny. This is surely true when I think about the relationship of William Colby and J. J. Angleton to H. Lloyd Goodall. Viewed from the end of things, their connection to the CIA and to Rome creates a narrative exigency that arcs toward Washington, D.C. in 1975.

. . . .

Throughout their clandestine service history, Colby and Angleton neither liked nor approved of each other.

Angleton believed that Colby's support of the Christian Democrats in Italy was proof of his known leftist leanings and demonstrated a total disregard for the effectiveness of counterintelligence. This latter view would later be confirmed—at least for Angleton—by Colby's alleged ignorance of, and inability to penetrate, the extensive Communist espionage network in Southeast Asia.

Colby, for his part, was always wary of Angleton. He respected the man's mind but knew Angleton used his position to bully career officers. He heard the internal stories of forced submission, early retirement, and perhaps even suicide, the products of Angleton's "suspicions" about their loyalty or allegations that they were weak on Communism.

Nor did Colby believe Angleton was effective in his longtime role as director of counterintelligence. By the time of Colby's appointment as director of central intelligence, he was acutely aware that Angleton had never once in his long career so much as located a single foreign agent operating within the Agency. In fact, Angleton had, on two important occasions, delayed approval for the bona fides of defectors, thus reducing the probable value their then-current information could have had on clandestine operations.

Colby also had another doubt about Angleton. He harbored the suspicion that Angleton himself could be the long-suspected "highly placed Soviet mole" in Washington. Angleton, of course, harbored the same suspicions about Colby. After the release of the "family jewels," Angleton said as much, arguing that no one but a Soviet mole would have released such damaging information to the Senate.

Did Angleton seal his fate with that sentiment? I don't know. What I do know is that it wouldn't be long before Colby would ask for and accept Angleton's resignation.

* *

The genesis of CIA operations in Italy and the resulting conflict between Colby and Angleton is, as I've said, superbly chronicled in a variety of histories of the Agency. There are many ways to tell this story, depending on how you interpret the motives of your favorite characters or what your political perspective on influencing elections in sovereign nations might be. There is no "pure" account. This is a political story, a human story, defined by conflict and tempered by an ideological war.

Regardless of which way you tell the resulting story, one thing is perfectly clear: Italy was a prime location for post–World War II CIA activities.

Success in Rome was vital not only to our national security interests but also to the careers of the women and men who served there.

Why Italy? As the Iron Curtain descended in Europe and Communist influence spread, the fear in Washington was that the Italian government would go Red, thus providing the Soviets with an important political satellite as well as a formidable foothold in southern Europe. To stop the spread of Communism in Italy was a pragmatic as well as a political decision, and it carried with it ominous nuclear undertones.

NATO military defenses in the region could not afford to be compromised by a takeover by the *Partito Communista Italiano*, nor could the United States' intermediate-range ballistic missile-defense systems aimed at the Soviet bloc afford to be exposed. That we had implanted nuclear missiles in northern Italy over the objections of Alcide de Gasperi and his Vatican-supported Christian Democrats was a matter of record. But given our economic support for the rebuilding of his country and our political support for his centrist government, there was little Gasperi could do, as long as the elections remained tightly in centrist control.

Following the Second World War, Italy had been in ruin. The economy—if you could call it that—featured staggering unemployment and inflation, and its currency had been so devalued as to be almost worthless. The CIA used money and propaganda to influence the outcomes of the Italian elections in the late 1940s and to establish strategic control over its political leadership throughout the 1950s. The strategy was one of helping our friends by establishing among them, with conviction, the idea that democratic rule was the superior option. This meant channeling money into various cultural and political groups and organizations as well as cultivating a political connection between Western interests and the Vatican.

Our intelligence and diplomatic efforts were premised on the notion that by building support among our friends, we could prevent in Italy the path the popular front had taken to seize control of Czechoslovakia and other Eastern European nations. The CIA estimated that the Soviets were pouring roughly $50 million a year into Italy. The money supported the PCI and other political groups and Communist front organizations. It also fueled their decidedly low-tech but occasionally very effective propaganda campaigns consisting of the widespread distribution and public display of inflammatory posters and slogans used to smear opposition politicians and local leaders of cultural, veterans', and religious groups opposed to them.

Italy, and especially Rome, was pulling itself out of military defeat through a cultural embrace of a *dolce vita* attitude, aesthetic, and lifestyle. It was a seemingly carefree atmosphere and it permeated the Italian upper crust as well as shaped the imaginations and fantasies of ordinary citizens and visitors from other countries. The lavish lifestyles, the splendid parties, and romantic images of the good life filtered down to the general population through a revived popular culture and film industry.

As good as the *dolce vita* spirit was for Romans with money in their pockets, it was at least as productive for the Communists and Socialists, who presented viable options for a government that was dedicated to lessening the distance between those who did well and those who didn't. Those differences were often pronounced, particularly among laborers and the rural poor, and it kept alive the ideal of a workers' paradise in which all people could enjoy the new postwar prosperity. There was also a lot of sympathy for leftist ideas of social justice, equality, fairness, and a brotherhood of man among the artistic and literary crowd.

It would require covert political action to combat the surface appeal of Communism on all of these fronts, as well as a substantial budget to counter the anti-American, anticapitalist campaigns. But the mandate given to the CIA was clear: Build support for democracy and capitalism, prop up the centrist government, and prevent the Communists and Socialists from winning the upcoming 1958 elections.

The CIA's success in halting the Communist influence in Italy—however mediocre the 1958 election outcomes and however short-lived the hoped-for longer-term political effects might have been—was largely responsible for establishing the agency's new power and professional credibility within the European intelligence community. Our common ideological and political foe was firmly entrenched, clever, and formidable, and the Agency's covert efforts against the relentless campaign of the Communists is crucial to understanding not only the rise of the CIA as world intelligence power, but also the politics and culture of Italy during this era.

Yet, having said that, history is too easily represented as the battle of opposing forces and ideas rather than the personal engagements, hard work, and sacrifice of women and men. Nowhere is that sentiment truer than it is in the intelligence underworld of clandestine activities. Armies gain control of countries by mass force, superior technology, and armed occupation. But spies and diplomats gain control of countries with words, relationships, lies, more lies, and money. Their work is conducted privately and their success is won by personal initiative, skilled conversation, imagination, and luck.

• •

My father's Italian story began before he ever saw Rome. Like all personal stories, this one reaches back into the lives of other people, is shaped by the trajectories of larger historical forces, and becomes recognized as part and parcel of the story line only in retrospect. So it was that, with the appointment, in 1946, of James Angleton as counterintelligence station chief in Rome, my father's clandestine story in Italy begins.

In 1947–48, the newly formed Special Procedures Group of the CIA was used to funnel tens of millions of dollars, as Burton Hersh describes it, to, "influence local elections, finance splinter groups, pay bribes and engage in propaganda." The money itself can be traced even further back, to what the CIA referred to as "the Exchange Stabilization Fund." This fund consisted of seized money and frozen assets the Americans had appropriated from the Nazis following the war, and which, of course, the Nazis had originally stolen, mostly from the European Jews. Under Angleton's singular guidance, aided by the current availability of almost unlimited funds, the CIA wielded influence over the Italian elections by sending large shipments of food along with undisguised threats to Italian politicians that the supplies would be cut off if they supported the Communists.

In the States, Wisner, Dulles, and Angleton used intelligence officers in a variety of government agencies to contact Italian Americans and recently imported foreign nationals who maintained ties with their home country. The purpose of this contact, as well as the subsequent dynamics of peruasion we can only imagine during these "personal interviews," were unusually effective: Italian Americans were to write letters to relatives in Italy, telling them in no uncertain terms exactly how to vote and pleading with them to fight against the threat of Communism.

Additionally, Hollywood movie stars with Italian surnames recorded radio messages that were broadcast in Italy in an attempt to use their American star status to influence votes. With all of this food, money, radio propaganda, and an effective letter-writing campaign, Angleton's personal war on the 1948 Italian elections worked wonders. In what otherwise could have been—and probably would have been—a *very* different outcome, Italy went centrist by 58 percent, largely as a result of Angleton's clandestine propaganda machine, arm-twisting, gunrunning, food threats, and illegal payoffs. American influence, this experiment in re-engineering a society torn between opposing ideologies into one safe for democracy and capitalism, had worked.

But the Great Game was only afoot, not over.

It was no secret that from 1947 to 1953 Italian politics and intrigue made the Italian desk one of the favorites in the Agency. It was also one of the most active and the most, shall we say, experimental. It was here that Agency officers came up with new and better (usually more intrusive and personal) ways to influence attitudes, values, beliefs, and—most important—behaviors. The laws of nations were routinely bypassed or simply ignored, and the Italian peninsula afforded ample opportunities to try out various covert strategies for influencing outcomes.

For example, the CIA infiltrated and co-opted the Italian security services by helping with college tuition for senior officials' children. It also poured large sums of money and leftover captured or war-surplus arms into an assortment of anti-Communist cultural and veterans' groups as well as political factions. Some of these groups openly flaunted their CIA/American connection to the local authorities, mention of which often successfully silenced opposition.

But this was Rome and no political action was complete without the blessing of the Pope. The *Actione Catholica* movement was organized as a lobbying organization with an estimated forty thousand members and was used by the Agency to stir up anti-Communist sentiment, distribute anti-Communist posters, and to get out enough votes to frustrate the Reds at the polls.

Anything that could be conceived as a way to maintain centrist control of the country, as well as anything that could be thought of to help nudge public sentiment toward democracy and capitalism, was carried out in a nation still reeling from the devastation of the war, large-scale unemployment, and the almost daily street chaos created by various competing ideologies working through action groups and marching as political parties. In these conditions, perfect for the conduct of experimental covert plots and activities, nothing that could be bought, wheedled, coerced, threatened, or bribed was left unexplored. The CIA even made inroads to the Pope—and, by extension, to a nation of Roman Catholics—by regularly providing sound trucks for Vatican religious broadcasts.

In 1953, our second key man enters the Italian scene. William Colby, hard-working intelligence officer, was appointed chief of political operations in Rome. He worked out of an office in the embassy and continued the CIA's involvement in influencing Italian elections, internal politics, and policies.

Colby and Gerald Miller were also responsible for creating intelligence inroads to a variety of groups, parties, and Communist front organizations. To accomplish this task, they imported Agency personnel from the States (and elsewhere) with already-established cover stories and bona fide credentials. For example, labor union officials from the AFL-CIO maintained contacts within the pro-Communist Italian Labor Party. Similarly, veterans' groups were a major source for recruiting resistance leaders and excellent places to acquire information about political sympathies and activities within those groups. Journalists were regularly recruited because they had access to locals who wouldn't discuss anything with embassy employees. And businesspeople with legitimate dealings in the country routinely provided information to the CIA, or were recruited to be on specially created boards of directors for CIA-fronted organizations in the country. Scholars, artists, poets, movie producers, actors, and actresses were involved in intelligence gathering whenever possible.

Even students were recruited. Colby, in his memoirs, fondly recalled one night on the streets of Rome, when, desperate to provide last-minute support for the Christian Democrats, with the help of a graduate student he personally distributed millions of lire to Italian partisans from the backseat of his Fiat. He remembered well the use of his diplomatic immunity to smuggle information, radio transmitters, and a few defectors across borders.

By day, Colby operated as all case officers did, doing junior diplomatic duties under the cover of a State Department appointment. By night and on the weekends, he used his diplomatic immunities and privileges to carry out a series of successful covert action campaigns. As a result, Italy remained a little less Socialist, and far less Communist, than it otherwise might have been.

Colby believed that the long-term future of Italian politics not becoming Communist would rest with a gradual campaign to build the popularity of the Christian Democratic Party. Their leaders often had a pro-Socialist agenda, but for Colby, they represented the broadest base of Italians. Angleton, back in Washington, was irate over Colby's encouragement of the Christian Democrats. For a man paid to see into the gray areas, Angleton was very much a black-and-white guy when it came to political parties. A leftist or pro-Socialist agenda was not much different from a pro-Communist one, in his opinion, Colby was dooming the future of Rome.

No doubt Angleton and Colby deserve major credit for the successes of the CIA in Italy. But their differing views on how to handle the political situation there also fueled the growing animosity between them. Splinter factions and loyalists for both men ran throughout the diplomatic and clandestine corps. In the glory days before CIA and State Department men and women claimed neutrality on issues of internal politics, hitching your career wagon to Colby or to Angleton meant making far-reaching friends and acquiring unseen enemies.

But there were other men and women also involved in these not-so-covert operations. Other men and women who actually did much of the skunk work that Angleton and Colby conceived and organized. Other men and women who were part of that far-reaching web of unknown friends and enemies.

One of those men was my father.

08

Rome

1956–1958

DESPITE HER INITIAL AND RATHER STARTLING INTRODUCTION TO OUR lives in Rome, my mother loved her new life abroad. It was a foreign fulfillment of her out-of-state dreams. It was exotic and exuberant and exciting. It was populated by colorful, often famous people who arrived in Rome after having seen and done the most amazing things—ridden camels and elephants, shot tigers, started revolutions, smuggled jewels, conducted secret affairs with deposed princes, and worshipped Buddha.

My mother spoke of Rome as a romantic speaks of love, as if the word itself contains all that is vital to life in the world. The Eternal City was less a place on a map than the location of the *dolce vita* spirit. It was a divine spirit that she believed defined her new life abroad and that would last forever.

She got half of it right.

As the wife of a junior diplomat, her job was not a secret. Her constant preoccupation and her all-encompassing profession was to support my father's vice consul cover story at all times. In other words, she was always "on." She had to look and act the part of an intelligent, attractive, engaging, and lighthearted American woman equally at ease with children and kings. She had to strike an appropriate social balance between being "in the know" and "not in the know," a mistress of both practical knowledge of sunlit things and a delightful and entertaining deniability of whatever might lurk within the shadows.

She cultivated her own sources of useful information. Among wives and children, secrets were often shared about the movements and moods of official men. She was privy to intelligence of a private and even intimate variety, and was instructed to pass along whatever she acquired that might be useful to someone at the embassy. Affairs, deceits, cautions, weaknesses, illnesses, and even vaguely expressed concerns—these were the stuff of talk that could be collected for files and refashioned into material in support of ongoing covert activities. The more she knew, the more she revealed, the better for my father.

It was all part of the larger aesthetic. She was an unpaid employee of the federal government, an agent on the ground in Italy. She worked hard at it. It was all very patriotic and grand. For a woman who had been to her share of romantic movies, it was the embodiment of the scripted life performed impromptu everyday. She told me she loved every half-minute of it, but worried how well she was doing during every other half.

In that second half, she never questioned what she was doing, but she did question who she was. She was astute enough to know that doing her job well, being the perfect diplomatic wife, didn't erase where she'd come from. She wondered if Naomi May Saylor (Alexander) Goodall was as good as anyone else. She had doubts about that. So, she did what any good spy would do: she began to cultivate her own legend, tweaking the truth until it fit the circumstances she found herself in.

A legend is a story. It is a story about who you are, where you came from, and what you are doing that is close enough to the truth to be lived believably. A legend always contains kernels of the truth, because you never know when someone might check a fact or go in search of an inconsistency.

For my mother, this legend consisted of a series of small alterations that deflected attention away from her humble origins. It was delivered as a rehearsed speech among people at diplomatic parties who were inclined to think of humble origins as inversions of what they considered to be right. For them, poverty was seen as pathetic rather than as evidence of the hard work required to rise above a rough life.

For my mother, this meant dropping "West" as a modifier to Virginia. Rather than describing her family as small rural farmers, they were "in agriculture." And, when she spoke of her time at Johns Hopkins, she talked about it with the breathless enthusiasm of a coed, waxing poetic about the "campus" and the "mixers," conveniently omitting her nursing duties.

These were only minor alterations to the surfaces of social talk but they carried with them a significance that subverted her own sense of worth and identity. Over time, these alterations devalued what was true about her life, rendering her life experiences close to worthless and her true identity almost shameful, at least to herself. More important, her legend came with a high price. She lived in constant fear of being exposed as a fraud.

She calculated that her chances were slim of ever running into anyone who knew her as a child. Nor did she believe she would find herself chatting at an embassy function with someone she had gone to school with in Winchester. But it was entirely possible she would meet someone who recognized her from her days in Baltimore, or from her life as a wife on the post at Newton D. Baker. But it was a gamble she was willing to take. Or, perhaps, that she felt she *had* to take.

Her job, after all, was to support my father.

It was her sacred duty on behalf of the man she loved. But it was also her patriotic duty as an American. She had to be willing to sacrifice herself—who she was, as well as the story of who she had been—for her husband and for her country. It is the way things were in the diplomatic corps during the cold war.

. . . .

One of my mother's favorite songs from the early 1960s was the hit "Never on a Sunday." I'm sure it held some personal meaning for her. The lyrics speak of a popular woman's mostly happy burden to be always available, and in particular how that sauciness spices the requests made for her company by men. The title is taken from the chorus, wherein the singer's readiness to engage in these relationships every other day of the week is balanced with her refusal to do it on a Sunday, "for that's my day of rest."

I know my mother identified with that line, if not with the rest of the song. For her, it was an apt metaphor.

My mother needed a rest, too. While my father was busy with whatever it was he was doing, my mother—like all State Department wives—was also serving a term as an unpaid emissary of the United States government.

Naomi S. Goodall, as the vice consul's wife, had a schedule of duties and cultural performances to complete daily. She always had to be, if not available, then at least attractive, intelligent, informed, and poised. Sunday was the exception. Ambassador Luce, following from her Catholicism, expected everyone—spouses and children included—to attend church services on Sunday. One way or another my mother usually found excuses to avoid church, although we spent a fair share of Sundays on our way to churches dressed as if we fully expected to enter them. More often than not, my mother would find a park or a bench with a good view of the city where we would pass an hour or two in harmony with nature or the secular rather than the strictly sacred. It was a small act of personal resistance to the domination of the State Department in our lives, and Naomi was positively reverent about it.

My father, by contrast, seldom had Sundays off. Nights and weekends were generally reserved for his second job, his reserve officer work. The rest of the time—the weekdays—was for performing whatever embassy duties accounted for his cover story in Veterans Affairs.

As a child I remember a father hardly ever at home. He was always working.

This ambiguous explanation helped me understand why I spent Sundays in the company of my mother. To make up for my father's absence, my mother treated every Sunday as a holiday. We slept in late and then lounged at home as Alfoncina—our beloved cook and housekeeper—prepared breakfast. Then we headed out into the city for sightseeing or adventures that placed us in a park or a gallery or a fine piazza during the afternoon. My father sometimes joined us for dinner. If he was through for the day, we would all take a cab ride back to our apartment. If not, he would arrange for someone to escort us home while he returned to whatever it was that he wasn't through with.

. . . .

Another reason my mother was fond of Sundays was that she wasn't required to attend the daily cocktail gathering held at an embassy or an ambassador's residence. It wasn't that she didn't enjoy meeting the often-colorful souls who attended them—artists, educators, important business people, celebrities, and diplomats. Nor was it that she didn't get along well enough—at least publicly—with the other embassy wives or their husbands. It was, she told me, "a lot more complicated than that."

"Complicated" was another code word in our family. When I was younger, I thought it meant a multiple layering of issues or parts, and, to some degree, I suppose it did. But nowadays I think of it a bit differently. For my mother, "complicated" issues were issues of identity. She didn't use the word to describe conflicts in her schedule or the inevitable balancing of her wifely duties with her more formal or embassy-prescribed ones. She used it when what was at stake was *who she was supposed to be*. When she was "gone" on Sundays, she was free to be who she was. But the rest of the week, particularly during the time spent at cocktail gatherings and official functions, things for her became "complicated."

Embassy social gatherings were an American cultural performance. They relied heavily on appearances and the careful cultivation of approved patterns of perceptions. My mother was given detailed instruction on appropriate behavior at social functions during a State Department orientation session for spouses. She learned about the art of giving and receiving handshakes and greeting kisses. In the case of handshakes, she had been warned against using too firm a grip with the men and too insincere a grip with the women. Kisses were airbrushes against the facial cheeks, only, and she was to *receive* them, never to publicly give them, no matter how well she and the other person were acquainted.

She also had been coached on conversation. She knew how to appear interested in a topic when she was uninterested in it; how to deflect talk when confronted with an unwanted question or merely something tedious or dull; how to appear happy and energetic when she felt tired and unhappy; and how to appear helpless or clueless to get out of trouble if the case required it.

She received detailed instructions on how to dress for social and political success at diplomatic gatherings. Her clothes were of fashion-show quality and the body beneath them had to remain imperially thin and well tended. Her hair was constantly redone, so as not to wear out any one look. So were her nails. She adorned herself with pearls, diamonds, sapphires, and emeralds, and, given our salary situation, this meant she was often reduced to borrowing jewelry from someone else. "Every day was a costume party," she added, "and costume parties can be hard work."

She had to stay up on everything, unless she wanted to risk playing the role, as she put it, of "some dumb Dora." This meant she read the newspapers daily as well as whatever the Book-of-the-Month Club sent her. She knew whose artwork was being featured at which gallery and whom to contact to get in. She remembered the names and nationalities of the persons whose company she kept and acted with the focused interest of a doctoral candidate in anthropology when they talked about their beloved culture's capital, geography, history, politics, customs, traditions, religions, food, and holidays.

She had to carry on intelligent but light conversations with everyone, regardless of her interest in what they wanted to talk about. She had to impress men and women alike, even if most of the men were obviously admiring only her breasts and many of the women talked badly about her behind her back. She had put up with bodily touching of various alien sorts, including many "friendly" slaps on the bottom used by irascible men to test her tolerance for them.

From 4 in the afternoon until around 8 most evenings, she was expected to hold a practiced smile. "And *brighten it*, dear, because remember, you are representing the American people," Ambassador Luce had urged. *"There's a good girl."*

In the presence of Ambassador Luce my mother often felt, she said, like "a prize poodle being required to sit up and shake a paw." She told me that she fully expected one day to have someone pat her head. As the wife of a vice consul of the United States, my mother was taught how to be a woman in ways she had never known before.

But then the embassy in Rome was a long, long way from West Virginia.

There were times when she knew that she was in *way* over her head.

Here she was, a girl from Dargan, Maryland, a.k.a. Frog Hollow, who was expected to be intelligent and entertaining for the world's kings and princes. It was like waking every day and having to be Cinderella. Or better: it was *The Wizard of Oz* as narrated by the Wicked Witch of the West, who also happened to be an American ambassador and her husband's boss.

Here, in the City of Eternal Light and later in the Court of St. James, she shared champagne toasts in the afternoons surrounded by sparkling women who had graduated from Radcliffe, Smith, Vassar, and Mount Holyoke, and whose husbands knew the ins and outs of Yale, Harvard, Brown, Dartmouth, and Princeton. These were people who had learned all there was to know about Europe while they were still teenagers, and could speak authoritatively and from personal experience about the opera season in Vienna as effortlessly as they named the Pakistani dress maker in Piccadilly Square or discussed the quality of the parquet floor beneath the *Mona Lisa* in the Louvre.

That Naomi May (Alexander) Saylor Goodall was—or at least had once been—a registered nurse who graduated from Winchester Memorial Hospital in Virginia and, who had never been any farther away from home than she was now, made her seem very small, even to herself.

Despite all of that, she was determined to do well. Here, in Rome, she was Naomi S. Goodall, the vice consul's lovely and charming wife. This was our family's big chance, our one shot to transcend our circumstances and to live large. My father's job here would lead to an even more important one elsewhere, and then to an even better one after that. Her role was to help ensure that it happened.

So if the political officer from the German Democratic Republic kissed her a little too long, or the British cultural attaché used the supposedly friendly bottom slap to fondle her cheeks for a brief moment or two, well, so what? That was part of her job, too.

It could be a lot worse than this. She could be back living on the VA post in Beckley, or Martinsburg. That thought always brought back the smile, the diplomatically correct bright smile. It worked every time she thought about being exploited, was bored witless, or felt particularly blue. Yes, indeed, it could be *a lot* worse than this.

Her bright smile was for appearances' sake. It was her cover for the real work she was performing. Her bright diplomatically correct smile really meant, "Like hell will I *ever* go back to living anywhere like that."

For my mother, things in Rome were "complicated." But a complicated life was better than a simple rural life in West Virginia.

. . . .

So the small weekly freedom that Sunday provided was important to my mother. It meant a brief and needed respite from the watchers. The rest of the week, "they" were watching her, and she well knew it. We were *always* being watched. If not by guards or persons from our side, then by whoever happened to be assigned that duty on the other side. We were told we were being watched for our own good as well as for the good of our country. We were told that it was important to be watched because my father worked in a sensitive position, and people in these positions had to be carefully observed, as well as their families and friends and associates, because you just never knew who might be spilling what to whom.

Not unless you watched them. Not unless you listened.

Not unless you subjected your own seemingly good citizens to the same sort of treatment you reserved for people from other nations who might be in a position to cause trouble. Or to pass along information. Or to sell secrets. Or to betray their country.

For this reason, couples lived in apartments or houses already fitted with listening devices and learned early on in their assignments that if they wanted a private conversation, the best place for it was the bathroom with the water running. Even sex lives were subject to being listened to, which seriously dampened the enthusiasm of some wives, although it apparently enlivened the vocal performances of others.

There was no real escape from the need to keep up appearances. But on Sunday, at least, there were no official duties or responsibilities.

It was my mother's day of rest. No wonder she loved that song.

. . . .

It was on a Sunday afternoon that Abbe Lane, one of the colorful glitterati living in Rome, entered our lives. The opening line of our much-repeated family narrative goes: "Abbe Lane discovered you."

She allegedly discovered me in a public park one Sunday afternoon as I lazed alongside my delighted mother. I was four, maybe five years old. According to an entirely suspicious account published in the *Rome Daily American*, the actress was so taken with me ("Oh, what a *beautiful* boy he is!") that she personally commissioned a portrait by the popular British portrait painter Leonard Creo, who was also in residence in Rome at that time.

The newspaper story was just that, a *story*. Bill Colby used the *Rome Daily American* like it was his private organ, playing whatever song fit his needs or moods. Of course it had some elements of factual reporting in it and all of our names were spelled correctly, but the story was placed there for a reason. Perhaps it was to establish a relationship between the actress and my family, or between my family and Mr. Creo. Or perhaps it was to establish a relationship between Mr. Creo and Ms. Lane. Or perhaps it was a story that within its celebrity sentences carried another message to an agent or contact. I have no idea.

All I have for certain are some deep childhood fragments of a park, a beautiful woman, my mother, and a few afternoons spent sitting in a red velvet chair holding my little stuffed Scottie dog. I also have a picture of my mother and me (during my ugly Buddy Holly period when we were living in Cheyenne) with the portrait visible in the background.

In the portrait, a dark oil painting embellished by an ornate frame, I am positioned in a relaxed posture on a huge chair, and I am holding a small black Scottie dog. According to the published account, the artist "guided my hand" while I painted the dog. I think I actually remember doing it.

In keeping with Creo's style during this period—one heavily influenced by an Italian High Renaissance tradition of rendering elite patrons' children as inherently noble, or as the given sons of Christ—my head is

FIGURE 8.1 Naomi Goodall and H. L. Goodall Jr. in front of Leonard Creo painting, circa 1963.

larger than normal and my flesh tones appear to be immaculately conceived. My eyes are oversized and oval. As a result, I appear to be either decadent or innocent. I can't decide. Perhaps that was Creo's intention: a child of the risen Christ, yes, but also a child of a failed Eden. Either way, I have my father's eyes.

The outfit I am wearing—a white cotton dress shirt and dark blue shorts with dark belt, socks, and dress shoes—reflects a desire for realism, I suppose. It was a ridiculous costume I wore to my Italian kindergarten each day, and I hated it. It serves artistically to embody the idea that as a schoolboy, I am learning how the world works. Given my relaxed, suggestive posture and innocent/decadent facial expression, I am depicted as a child ready for whatever comes next, but already somewhat saddened by it.

That's what I see in the painting, anyway.

But what I see in it is not really important. It, too, is a still life, a mere if memorable image. What is important is the *fact* of the portrait combined with the family story about how it came into our lives.

The story is a little bit baffling. I am as vain as the next man, but the idea that a lovely actress in the prime of her career would suddenly be so taken with my face as to commission a portrait of me is absurd. That she accidentally discovered me in a public park on a Sunday afternoon is equally suspect. This story, this family story, as silly and outright laughable as it is, nevertheless begs for a little analytical unpacking.

· ·

Abbe Lane was born Abigail Francine Lassman, December 14, 1932, in Brooklyn, New York. Her mother wanted her to be a star. By fifteen, she had already blossomed into the fullness of her beauty, which led to an early career doing commercials for Vita-Phone. But it was clear, with her looks, her drive, her talent, she was destined for bigger things.

The former announcer became a dancer, then a singer married to the bandleader Xavier Cugat, and then an actress. She was banned from Italian television in 1954 because her redheaded beauty and striking vivacity had inspired men in a public place to riot. Her lean, curvaceous, photogenic body was truly one of the twentieth century's inspiring ones; it beckoned sexually to men much as the Sirens' call beckoned to Ulysses. In a rare interview with Frank Thistle published in *Adam* magazine in 1963 she said, "Jayne Mansfield may turn the boys into men, but I take them from there."

Dazzled by her beauty, her body, and her sultry voice, you may not have noticed that she was also smart. She was serious about acting, about building her career. But was there more to Abbe Lane?

· ·

Espionage has always been a profession for both women and men. As Elizabeth McIntosh's excellent history, *Sisterhood of Spies*, reveals, women—particularly attractive women—have served in operations more during wartime than in times of relative peace. Following the Second World War, successful intelligence officers with extensive operational experience in the field—such as herself, but also many others—left the OSS for good because there were so few opportunities for advancement within the new CIA. A taste of the fieldwork action did not translate into happiness behind a secretary's or even an analyst's desk in the male-dominated Agency.

Although McIntosh later returned to work at the Agency at Allen Dulles's urging, she admits that spying was sexist business during the cold war. In fact, it wasn't until the mid-1990s that a class-action lawsuit brought by women in the CIA against the organization permanently changed things. Stalled at GS-11 or GS-12 mid-level ranks and barred from further promotion due to a lack of operational experience, women sought a legal remedy that was resolved internally. Today, the CIA is roughly 40 percent female, with women enjoying work as highly placed officers, heads of station, and field agents.

But in Rome, in the late 1950s, gender issues weren't quite so evolved. There were women—Ambassador Luce, for example—and men like Bill Colby who championed women in intelligence service. But in counter-espionage, where the operational task was to infiltrate dissident groups and splinter factions, the service was nearly male-only.

Women had a distinct advantage in some realms. Whereas government men could gain admittance and acceptance in a wide range of businesses—from the ambiguous import-export firms that often provided legitimate cover for illegal activities to the vast bureaucracies that made both sides of their operations possible, if not inevitable—they often had difficulty gaining much of anything from those persons who lived and breathed as "lefty" artists, as members of the avant-garde, or as rebels with or without causes.

Members of the artistic classes distrusted anyone not already known. Because they thrived on the fringes of everyday society, they often came into contact with those whose politics were extreme. In those days, in Rome, the saying was "If you want to find a bomb-throwing Communist, go see the new pictures at some out-of-the-ordinary art exhibit, or attend the showing of a political film, or spend your late evenings in a smoky jazz club." Artists and radicals mixed. Gray men and radicals didn't.

The obvious solution was to recruit agents from the artistic underworld. But this was far more complicated that it appeared. There was a simpler answer. A better one: we could gain information from artists simply by *befriending* them.

There are several published accounts of well-known artists and celebrities who in one way or another served as agents of intercultural information in the intelligence community. The usual recruit—the friend—was already an actor, such as Noël Coward and many others; or a poet, such as Frank Wisner's friend Stephen Spender and many others; or a novelist, such as the Nabokovs and many others; or well-placed journalists, such as Joseph and Stewart Alsop as well as many others; or filmmakers—hell, the CIA in

Rome owned a production company called Imperial Films run by ex-OSS officer Michael Burke, himself well known for his skill in organizing resistance groups. Even Julia Child, already a famous chef, had more than once proven useful. In terms of information from the artistic community, the Agency was well fed, well versed, hip, and even occasionally thorough, but I don't want to convey the wrong impression.

Many of these afternoons in the park admiring etchings and evenings at the club with artists and actors and others of their ilk were born of genuine friendships. Just as many informants who happened to be actors or artists willingly and gladly provided whatever information they could provide. Some of them did it out of a sense of patriotism and duty; others did it because they just loved being involved in the intrigue. It was another stage to act upon, another canvas upon which to create an impression, another image or story to circulate. It was a wrapping of truth within something novel and packaging it as "fiction," or "surrealist," or "avant-garde," and it all occurred within a world where those labels afforded plausible deniability and yet at the same time fed the public's insatiable imagination for making the lie and the truth seem increasingly interchangeable. It was the birth of the postmodern and the death of belief in any grand historical narrative, but scholars have largely failed to see how the intelligence community was implicated in it.

My mother knew that my father's work at times meant him sitting at a desk analyzing information. At other times it was more of "something else." But isn't this true of any desk-bound profession? Saying that there is "something else" at other times really doesn't help.

If she knew he was gone off somewhere to be a "spy," she never said so. When I asked her, even as a child, where my father was, she replied that he was "out of town doing his job for the government." If I pressed for details, she only ever said, "I don't know. It's complicated." This was the other use she had for the word "complicated." Voiced this way, it meant we weren't going to discuss it.

So I grew up with no understanding of what my father's work really was. Overseas, he worked for the State Department. In the U.S., he worked for the Veterans Administration. By the time I was old enough to ask more pertinent questions, I had received the same unsatisfying answers for so long that I simply didn't ask them anymore. I never thought of him as a spy. The image of a spy was owned by James Bond and seemed so far from my image of my father as to be untenable. But I was wrong.

These days I think of being a spy as a slow-gathering evolution toward some unseen but defining event and then a gradual decline and dissolve away from it. It is composed of what we see in photographs, and what we get from a close reading of documents, but only as those artifacts help us understand the trajectory of a life, the unfolding of a spy's story.

I am at home with that processual explanation. It frames the background in the pictures I see, the documents I read, when I think of my father. Viewed this way, early success in collecting useful clandestine information, maybe the information exchanged over drinks one night in the Suez, might expand a man's sense of himself, of his job, of his role in the cold war, perhaps even in history.

· ·

You can call the sudden summer "friendship" between a dazzling American actress and that Veterans Affairs officer and his wife just a coincidence. They both lived in Rome at the time. They were Americans. They knew a lot of the same people. They knew Len Creo.

She was an actress with a wide circle of friends and she was used to playing a variety of screen roles: doctor, thief, secretary, bad girl. All of that is *true*.

But none of those explanations account for the oil painting, do they? Not if we accept the official account in the newspaper, probably written by Colby, as anything other than a fictional story line.

Nor do they help us to understand what my supposedly sudden discovery as a "beautiful boy" in a park on Sunday afternoon means to our tale. Or what *any* of this had to do with the American portrait painter Leonard Creo.

I was only five years old, so what could I have known? My mother dressed me in that silly school costume and escorted me to a small artist's studio. There was an open window and the air was thick with the smell of oils. I sat in a red velvet chair while the grown-ups talked. I don't remember paying any attention to what they talked about. I sat still and held on to my black dog.

· ·

I always wondered how, or even if, Abbe Lane was connected to Leonard Creo. Was my portrait relationship to them part of the larger aesthetic?

Creo was—and is—an interesting and accomplished man. He was born in New York in 1923 and served in the U.S. Army during World War II. He suffered shrapnel wounds and was left for dead on a battlefield in France. But he survived, returned to New York, and began studying at the Art Students League. From there, he moved to Mexico, where he studied painting. After that, he moved to Rome and spent a year apprenticing to Pietro Annigoni. His work over the years has appeared in many museums and collections, and still adorns a variety of mural walls in Rome. He has been honored with one-man shows in Montreal, New York, London, Los Angeles, and Rome. He lives in England and is known there as an accomplished sculptor and painter as well as a world-champion racewalker.

I know quite a bit about the surfaces of Len Creo's life but not enough to understand his deeper connection to my father, the connection that may lie outside the framework of my portrait. I believe, but I do not know for sure, that he may have known a fellow artist and prominent London art dealer named Tommy Harris, who was a close friend of Kim Philby. Tommy Harris and his wife, Hilda, owned the Spanish Art Galleries and a beautiful house called Garden Lodge in Logan Place off Earls Court Road.

Tommy Harris and his wife loved to entertain. They also loved to entertain artists along with MI5 and British Secret Intelligence Service (SIS) officers, so much so that, according to Phillip Knightley, their grand home often resembled "an off-duty drinking club" for spies. Guy Burgess, Anthony Blunt, Dick Brooman-White, and Kim Philby were regulars. My guess is that Creo and Harris and Philby had at one time or another hung out together. There was no reason not to have done so. Philby cherished such gatherings and was well known in artistic circles.

I think maybe the key to understanding this portrait episode in our story is Creo's relationship to the art world, not Abbe Lane's relationship to, or with, my father. Only then does Abbe Lane's link in this chain of information handling or gossip exchange make any sense. She may have been the celebrity medium, and an unwitting one, not the clandestine message. The question is always the same: what did they know about my painting, and how did their names in our family story figure into my father's diary?

In 2004 I wrote several times to Mr. Creo and asked him about my painting, about Abbe Lane, and about my father. I received no reply. Then, in a last effort to help me clean up details regarding this part of the story, Sandra tried him again. This time he replied. Here is the text of his reply:

Dear Mrs Goodall: I am sorry but my memory of this period is not good. I did many portraits at that time and with very little discipline did not keep a Studio Book and don't remember the circumstance of this commission. . . . However, I do remember the boy's portrait and his mother, as there was a Cocktail Party in their home for the hanging of the Portrait. (Which then remained in their possession . . . don't you have it now?) . . . and I also went there on another occasion.

I don't think there was a black dog in the picture . . . nor did I ever even meet Abbe Lane, who I don't think was resident in Rome at that time . . . however some commissions came through Gloria Swanson who was resident. . . . Also commissions came from Canon Shrieve from St Paul's, The American Episcopalian Church.

But there is one thing that may be helpful. . . . Last month I was searching the boxes (that I call my files), at the request of the Smithsonian's Archives of American Art. . . . I found a lot of very old business cards and among them was a business card serving as an invitation . . . that stayed in my memory. When I received your email . . . I started to look for it. After a long frustrating search (I thought that I had possibly sent it to the Archives, but knew there was no reason to have done so) I have found that card. . . .

An amazing coincidence. I don't remember the people mentioned but do remember that the residence was in the Pariole section of Rome. . . . I have attached it. . . . If you have trouble opening it (I'm new to scanning) let me have an address and I will air-mail it.

I'm sorry I can't tell you more but hope this is some help.

Regards . . . . Leonard Creo

There are mysteries within mysteries, are there not? Not Abbe Lane, but perhaps Gloria Swanson! She was the famous actress from one of my favorite classic films, *Sunset Boulevard*. My mother clearly knew the difference between Ms. Lane and Ms. Swanson, and there was the published story that mentioned Ms. Lane as the person responsible for the commission.

The business card Mr. Creo attached to the e-mail identified my father as Harold Lloyd Goodall, Veterans Affairs Officer, the Embassy of the United States of America. In my father's familiar hand was written the rest of the invitation, including our address. This scanned card was precious to me. Yet it too raised questions that I hoped Mr. Creo could help me answer.

I e-mailed him and provided more of the context. I explained that the dog in the portrait was not a real dog, but a small stuffed animal. I asked if he had any more specific information about my mother and the general tenor of the times within the artistic and diplomatic community in Rome. I also told him what I think happened to the portrait when it "disappeared" with the rest of my inherited belongings following my mother's death.

Mr. Creo did not recall much more than he had included in his original e-mail, but he kindly supplied me with one additional piece of information: the American community in Rome used the *Rome Daily American* as a way of communicating with each other because, as he put it, "everyone read it." The *Rome Daily American* was, moreover, definitively linked to the CIA, which supplied 40 percent of its funding.

· ·

I had contacted Abbe Lane earlier in my quest for information about her link to my portrait and to my parents. She was alive and well and living in Los Angeles. She didn't reply personally, but communicated with me via her personal secretary. I was told that Ms. Lane couldn't recall my father and didn't remember the painting. She wished me good luck with my book. That was it.

Was this a case of "deny everything, admit nothing, and send your questioner away"? If so, it would be stock in trade for an actress who reportedly rarely gives interviews, but so too would it be stock in trade for any decent spy. "Good luck with the book" indeed. But I don't know that Abbe Lane had any information value for those engaged in espionage; there's certainly no evidence that she was ever a spy nor, now, that she ever *knew* my father and mother. Given Len Creo's account, she may not even have been involved in the commissioning of the portrait.

Yet my mother always told this story the same way, with the name of Abbe Lane figuring prominently in it. My father never objected to the way my mother told it. And there was that article in the *Rome Daily American* my mother forced me to read and reread that also contained her name. So if the story were true, why would she deny it?

I suppose there could be a lot of reasons for that.

I never heard either of my parents talk about Gloria Swanson or Canon Shrieve. So I am left with more questions, and the mystery of the portrait, and of what really transpired on that Sunday afternoon, endures.

· ·

In *The Great Gatsby* Nick Carraway is an information agent, a spy if you will. He invites Daisy to tea but his real intention is to deliver her to Gatsby.

That deception is a slight one, done for love, but it is still a deception. It is a small lie that prefigures the larger one on their horizon. It is romantic love as noble ideology pitted against whatever you might call her merely legal marriage to Tom Buchanan.

Daisy is complicit with the lie. She is, in fact, delighted by it. It offers a lift out of the ordinary, an unexpected inflection of true love in this life, a cause for the heartfelt celebration of a passionate late-summer intrigue. Enjoining the lie, she pledges undying affection for Nick, yet she inexplicably abandons him just as she abandons Gatsby.

Not so much as a word of goodbye.

Not so much as a card at Christmas.

No photographs survive.

I wonder if, in later life, Daisy would recall Nick at all. She would remember Gatsby; she would have to. But not necessarily Nick. Having ceased communication with him and having had no contact for so many years, his role in her summer romance and the unspeakable murder of Myrtle would easily be forgotten. If she remembered him at all, it would be only as her distant cousin who may have once visited her and her husband Tom a long time ago. Or was that someone else?

Books are written about Gatsbys and Daisies, about the Colbys and the Philbys, about the Luces and the Lanes. Minor characters are easily forgotten, as expendable as ex-wives or the people we once called our friends. Nick Carraway's name survives today only because he is the narrator of the Gatsby story, but even as fiction often mirrors life, if he were real and his story of Gatsby and Daisy were true, his small role that summer wouldn't make him any more of a *person* in their lives. Do you remember the name of that fellow who rented the house across the bay from you?

The same explanation could be true of my parents' "friend" from that remembered Sunday in the park, Abbe Lane. In her life, we were akin to the fellow in the rented house so many years ago. What *was* his name?

Beneath that metaphor for lost memories are some important questions about friendship, at least as it was defined in our family.

Friends hang out with each other, don't they? I don't recall that Abbe Lane *ever* hung out with my parents. Friends appear in photographs kept in family albums, don't they? There are no photographs of them together. And friends—real friends—don't abandon friends, do they? After that summer, once the paint had dried on the canvas, she became absent from our family's story.

It is as if Abbe Lane appeared on our stage in Rome, performed her role, and then disappeared back into her own magnificent life.

Is that how friends behave?

Some do, admittedly. But most don't. In this case, between "some do" and "most don't" lies a world of difference. And in this case, of mystery.

· ·

Was Ms. Lane's alleged connection to my family and Mr. Creo's association with the art community in Rome and London part of this, or merely part of what confounds this story? Was Kim Philby the basis for the information they shared? Maybe not. And then again, *maybe*.

If there was a connection, it would have been an important discovery for a man, for a particular man who was my father, who was interested in Philby. Perhaps it was only a surmise. Or even just a suspicion.

I know that my father's next diplomatic posting was to London. I know that while he was in London he worked against the Soviets. That, too, is a fact. For a man who had risen in the intelligence community based on his knowledge of, and contacts within, veterans' groups and the Italian Communist movement, this change of venue and alteration of focus had to be based on *something*.

It's not like my father spoke fluent Russian. Or, as far as I know, that he even knew any Russians.

Someone supposedly working in Rome in 1957 tipped the Agency off to the strong possibility that Philby had been, and still was, operating as a Soviet mole. This, too, is a fact.

Was that person my *father*?

I don't know. But I am left with a lot of ways to think about it. It is still a mystery. I am also left with Ms. Lane's suggestive words in her interview with Frank Thistle about her time in Italy:

> "In Italy they had no preconceived idea of what I was like in the United States," she said. "I did a variety of roles, among them a doctor, a thief, a secretary and a bad girl." We asked Abbe if living in Italy had changed her very much.
>
> "Yes, it's made me think differently," she said.

Me, too, Ms. Lane. Me too.

09

Philby

FOR AS LONG AS I CAN REMEMBER, MY FATHER KEPT A KNIFE IN HIS pocket. It was a short stiletto, four inches long, with a gilded edge circling a narrowing tapered blade.

I'm not certain where he acquired it.

I've always associated the stiletto with Rome, although my reasons for doing so are purely subjective. A *stiletto* is a known Italian blade, so my association of it with Italy is a matter of language rather than a known fact. But my father did own it in Rome. That much I do know.

What is a stiletto for? Why would my father carry one?

I've puzzled over these questions and come up with other associations that lead to more questions. For example, so far as I know, my father didn't use the knife for anything at all, yet he always kept it with him. He didn't whittle. He didn't play mumblety-peg. He wasn't coarse enough to trim his fingernails with it. Nor did he use it as a letter opener or as a tool for turning screws or cutting through ropes. Yet he must have used it for something.

It still has a bloodstain.

Perhaps he nicked himself. But I doubt it. I never saw my father nick himself with a blade of any kind. He had a way with knives. He knew how to care for them, was careful with them, and never left one lying around. When

I was a Boy Scout in Wyoming, he taught me how to use a whetstone. In our house, he was the designated carver of meats and the slicer of vegetables.

My father knew knives.

Yet I never saw him use his stiletto.

Perhaps he kept it on his person for protection. But a stiletto is a small dagger, not a defensive weapon at all. It is favored by silent assassins who know precisely where to stick it or street toughs who want to show off. My father never showed off. Never.

Which leads me to believe it was part of his clandestine life.

When I think about his stiletto in that context, other images and memories from our life reappear. My father used to make a throat-slitting gesture across his neck. It was a single stroke, delivered with a quick stab with his thumb into the jugular vein and then dragged across the windpipe. Very precise. When he used the gesture, he wasn't kidding around. In our family, he reserved it for those few times when he was serious about shutting us up.

But a lot of people use that gesture. It's commonplace, a recognition signal for instant silence.

Here's the other memory. My father hated Richard Nixon. As vice-president, Nixon visited the embassy in London and gave my father a service award. My father often talked about the incident as one in which he should have "cut the throat of the son of a bitch when I had the chance." He wasn't kidding, either. Whatever personal slight Nixon performed in his presence, or however noxious Nixon's politics may have been to him, or even if it were something as simple and uncomplicated as Nixon's mere existence on the planet, it was one that in his mind deserved the ultimate censure.

· ·

For some reason, unspecified in any document I possess, my father's official consular title wasn't granted until nearly a year after his initial appointment as a reserve officer in Rome. Perhaps it was a promotion of sorts. While it did not carry any increase in salary, it did afford him better diplomatic cover.

Apparently his work in Rome required it. Or, given the unfolding events in the Suez, perhaps his anticipated assignment in Egypt required it. I'll never know.

It is, however, an interesting appointment to contemplate, particularly given its timing. For one thing, it reveals the speed and efficiency possible

Form DS-1032
Exception to SF-50
Approved by the
Bureau of the Budget
May 1954

DEPARTMENT OF STATE
WASHINGTON 25, D. C.

NOTIFICATION OF PERSONNEL ACTION

	SERVICE
	☒ FS ☐ DPTL

1. NAME (Mr.-Miss-Mrs.-One given name, initial(s) and surname)	2. DATE OF BIRTH	3. JOURNAL OR ACTION NO.	4. DATE:
Mr. Harold Lloyd Goodall	10-17-22	FS 141	7-27-56

This is to notify you of the following action affecting your employment:

5. NATURE OF ACTION (Use standard terminology)	6. EFFECTIVE DATE	7. CIVIL SERVICE OR OTHER LEGAL AUTHORITY
Granting of Consular Title	7-21-56	

FROM:	8. POSITION TITLE	TO:
Veterans Affairs Officer		Veternas Affairs Officer
	Diplomatic or Consular Title	Vice Consul
	9. SCHEDULE, SERIES NO., GRADE, SALARY	FSR-5 $6,145
	10. ORGANIZATIONAL DESIGNATIONS	
	Post	Rome
	11. HEADQUARTERS	

		12. DS CATEGORY		
☐ FIELD	☐ DEPARTMENTAL		☐ FIELD	☐ DEPARTMENTAL
☐ Regular	☐ Resident	☐ Non-US	☐ Regular	☐ Resident	☐ Non-US
		FS Category		

13. VETERAN'S PREFERENCE			14. POSITION CLASSIFICATION ACTION			
NONE	5-PT	10-POINT	NEW	VICE	I. A.	REAL.
		Disab.	Other			
		X			X	3-6471-104	

15. SEX	16. APPROPRIATION	17. RETIREMENT COVERAGE	18. DATE OF APPOINTMENT AFFIDAVITS (Accessions Only)	19. LEGAL RESIDENCE
	FROM	☐ CSC ☐ FS	☐ CLAIMED ☐ PROVED	
	TO	☐ FICA-C ☐ NONE		STATE: W. Va.

20. This action is subject to all applicable laws, rules and regulations and may be subject to investigation and approval by the United States Civil Service Commission or the Department.

Nominated: 7-17-56.
Confirmed: 7-21-56.
Attested : 7-21-56.

Execute SF-61a in accordance with 1 FSM IV 124 as Vice Consul of the USA.

PERSONNEL FILES
1956 AUG 2
OFFICE OF PERSONNEL RECEIVED

ENTRANCE PERFORMANCE RATING

21. SIGNATURE OR OTHER AUTHENTICATION

PERSONNEL FOLDER

☆ G.P.O.: 1955—334288

FIGURE 9.1 Notification of Personnel Action granting consular title to Harold Lloyd Goodall, 1956.

within the federal bureaucracy when circumstances require it. Notice the dates of nomination (7-17-56), confirmation (7-21-56), and attestation (7-21-56)—a mere four days from the official request to the execution of an order to make a man, a seemingly ordinary man from Huntington, West Virginia, serving as a "Veterans Affairs Officer," into a vice consul of the United States of America. Yet it was a year late in coming to him.

It is interesting to think about the office itself, to ponder the raw authority, power, and arrogance of it. The *language* of it.

When a person is appointed to this rank, an official plaque is issued that spells out the privileges of the office. The one we have in our possession is a lovely artifact, larger than a college diploma and done in a fancy Edwardian script. It reads:

The President of the United States of America

To all who shall see these presents, Greetings:

Know ye, that reposing special trust and confidence in the abilities and integrity of Harold Lloyd Goodall, a Vice Consul of the United States of America, I do assign him as Vice Consul of the United States of America at Rome, Italy, for Rome and its prescribed district and do authorize and empower him to have and to hold the said office and exercise and enjoy all of the rights, privileges, and immunities thereunto appertaining during the pleasure of the President of the United States; and I do hereby enjoin all Captains, Masters, and Commanders of ships and other vessels armed or unarmed, sailing under the flag of the United States, as well as all other of their citizens to acknowledge and consider him the said Harold Lloyd Goodall accordingly; and I do hereby pray and request the Government of Italy, its Governors and Officers to permit the said Harold Lloyd Goodall fully and peaceably to enjoy and exercise the said office, without giving or suffering to be given unto him, any molestation or trouble, but on the contrary to afford him all proper countenance and assistance. I, offering to do the same for all those who shall, in like manner, be recommended to me by the said Government.

In testimony whereof, I have caused these Letters to be made Patent, and the Seal of the United States to be hereunto affixed.

Done at the City of Washington this twenty-first day of July, in the year of our Lord one thousand nine hundred and fifty-six, and of the Independence of the United States of America the one hundred and eighty-first.

By the President: Dwight D. Eisenhower

John Foster Dulles

Secretary of State

According to this finely articulated document, as a vice consul my father now enjoyed diplomatic immunity from arrest or prosecution of any kind. He also had the capacity to commandeer any vessel flying an American flag—including warships at sea. Our family, already watched by "them," was now afforded at all times the full protection of the United States Marines.

As a vice consul, my father had the power to secure the cooperation of any official person in Italy (or, presumably, elsewhere) he deemed necessary to complete his assignments and duties. A vice consul has the power to get people out of jail free and to carry any arsenal of deadly weapons as well as dispense any sum of federal money. Such a person is free to negotiate formal and informal contracts on behalf of our government and to invoke the name and authority of the President of the United States, as well as—in this case—the President of Italy, to support whatever he wanted to do or to order done.

It all seems far more *On Her Majesty's Secret Service* than *Organization Man*. And you may wonder, as I do, what on earth a man serving as a Veterans Affairs officer would need with all that power, authority, and possibility?

You may notice, as I do, that his rank on Personnel Form DS-1032 is still given as an FSR-5. The "R" means that he was still serving as a reserve officer. Examining his newly granted immunity, authority, powers, and licenses—even what became known in popular James Bond parlance as "a license to kill"—it would seem that his day job was very much playing second fiddle to his night and weekend work.

It had to be. Otherwise, why all the fuss?

His initial appointment as Veterans Affairs officer carried no such power, authority, or assurances. Collecting information or infiltrating veterans' groups was part of his job. If he *were* just doing his job—doing *that* job—he wouldn't need or particularly benefit from a consular title. But things changed as the situation in the Middle East heated up. There was no increase in his pay, only a change in his diplomatic labeling. But this is a business of labeling, where language is political as well as rhetorical.

The language itself raises larger questions about meanings. What are its literal referents? What does the label represent?

Veterans Affairs representative.

Foreign Service reserve officer.

Vice consul.

Spy.

My father met Harold Adrian Russell "Kim" Philby in the Suez.

Philby, son of the famous Arabist scholar Harry St. John Philby, was living in Lebanon at the time, posing as a freelance journalist. He was also
collecting intelligence in the region for both MI5 and the Soviets, although
neither the British nor the Soviets admitted it at the time.

Philby was one of the infamous Cambridge spies, four or possibly five
young men recruited into the Russian intelligence service in the early 1930s
by their Trinity College economics lecturer, Maurice Dobb. The known
four of them—Philby, Maclean, Burgess, and Blunt—rose to positions of
authority within British intelligence or the Foreign Office and all of them
eventually defected to the Soviet Union or committed suicide. The hypoth-
esized fifth man is still unknown, but there remains some rude speculation
that it may have been Sir Roger Hollis, who served as director general of
MI5 from 1956 to 1965. If this suspicion is true, then Hollis gets the prize
for the highest-ranking penetration agent for the Soviets during the cold
war; if not, that prize remains Philby's.

Philby had one of the most interesting résumés in all of cold war spydom.
Following graduation from Cambridge and seized with idealism wrapped up
in the new Communist ideology, he went to Vienna and married a spirited
fellow traveler, Litzi Friedman, to save her from arrest. The marriage didn't
last long, although Philby didn't complete the divorce paperwork until after
the Second World War, and by then he had been living with his second
wife, Aileen, long enough to have fathered three children.

Between marriages, Philby posed as a pro-fascist in Franco's Spain
(where he was personally decorated by the dictator for bravery under fire).
This early success led to his gaining the bona fides needed to win a strategic appointment—through fellow Cambridge alum and active Soviet agent
Guy Burgess—in Section D of the secret service (SIS). It was ironic that
Guy Burgess worked for section D. The "D" stood for "destruction," and it
was the job of this section to use sabotage to build up resistance forces in
Europe. In many ways, being a spy for Russia serving in Great Britain was
the ultimate sabotage.

During the war, Philby quickly rose through the ranks of the SIS. He
authored the paper that laid out the design of a training school for espionage agents, served as an instructor in it (one of his students was none
other than James Jesus Angleton), and monitored all incoming intelligence,
siphoning off the most applicable parts to his Russian handler. He learned

that the Allies intended to support the pro-Communist resistance groups operating against the Nazis until the war ended, at which point they would turn against them. This information, passed on by Philby through his Russian handler, was vital to Stalin's ability to prepare for meetings with Roosevelt and Churchill as well as to steel him against placing too much trust in their promises for a postwar peace.

Following the war, Philby managed to worm his way into a job in Valentine Vivian's counterespionage group in SIS. While there, he continued to pass along information to his Russian handler. The information he passed has been linked to the deaths of dozens of agents who served in Eastern Europe and the Baltic states. While he was betraying his country and friends, he was, by all accounts, a rising star within the department being groomed for the top job—"C"—or chief of the SIS. He was named first secretary and assigned to Washington as the SIS liaison to the CIA in 1948, where, once again, he was teamed up with his former student Jim Angleton.

They became—insofar as it was possible—"friends."

All would probably have gone according to the Russian covert plan had the Korean War not broken out. When that happened, in 1950, Burgess was posted to Washington and moved in with Kim and Aileen Philby. Unfortunately for Philby, Burgess, a serious alcoholic and a homosexual, made it a mission to offend almost everyone. Despite his repeated attempts, Philby could not get his American colleagues to like Burgess as much as Philby did. According to an account published in Burton Hersh's *The Old Boys*, one drunken evening at a party in CIA agent Bill Harvey's home, Burgess, a gifted caricature artist, was asked to do a drawing of Harvey's wife, Libby. He dashed off a mean caricature of her with, "legs spread, dress hiked up above her waist, and crotch bared." Harvey was incensed, and even though Philby intervened and cooled him off, the incident cemented Burgess's fate.

Meanwhile, a third member of the Cambridge Five, Donald Maclean, was stirring up trouble of his own. He, too, was an alcoholic. When he was stationed in Cairo, he destroyed the apartment of an American secretary, and was placed on a six-month leave. Back in London with nothing to do, his drinking took over, and in November of 1950, he confessed to "working for Uncle Joe [Stalin]" at a dinner party. When Philby learned of the error, he convinced Burgess to return to England to help straighten out the situation.

Some accounts attribute to Philby the tip-off to Maclean that he was about to be interrogated as a spy. Before that interview, Burgess spirited Maclean off to Southampton in late May of 1951. Both of them boarded the *Falaise,* a cross-Channel steamer, which took them to France, where they then disappeared. They eventually defected to Moscow, where they appeared before the press together in 1956.

Once Philby learned of their escape, he realized that he, too, was in trouble. According to his own account of the affair, he returned home, collected his clandestine accessories—copying camera, etc.—and buried them next to a tree by the Potomac River. He knew his friendship with Burgess and Maclean would damn him with the Home Office. He was recalled to London, and shared a last drink in the airport bar with none other than his CIA pal Jim Angleton.

With a supreme show of pluck, when Philby was questioned about the defection, he offered his resignation to Dick White, the senior officer in MI5. Phillip Knightley has recorded the offer as it supposedly occurred: "I'm no good to you now, and I never will be again. I'll put in my resignation. I think you'd better let me go."

They did let him go, although he was officially cleared of criminal wrongdoing and remained on the SIS books for years. He was granted a £4,000 dispensation in lieu of a pension. In 1955, after being cleared once again of being the "third man" in the Burgess and Maclean case, he took up his journalism cover-job career and moved at the request of the SIS to Beirut. His job there, for both the Soviets (for whom he had never stopped working) and for the British, with whom he was once again working, was to monitor political events in the Middle East. At a salary of £500 per year, plus 30 shillings per hundred published words, on the weekdays he became a stringer for the *Economist* and the *Observer.* Nights and weekends he pursued his "other job."

He abandoned his wife, Aileen, and their children. She had figured out that he was, indeed, "the third man." This realization of what she told friends was his "treachery," of the secret he kept from her their entire married life, led her into a death spiral fueled by an already-weakened heart and copious amounts of alcohol. She died in December of 1957 at the age of forty-seven.

By then Philby was already deeply in love with Eleanor Brewer, who was married to Sam Pope Brewer, the *New York Times* chief correspondent in the Middle East. Sam Brewer realized what was going on between them and granted Eleanor a Mexican divorce. When Philby told him he planned to marry her immediately, Brewer's response was, "That sounds like the best solution. What do you make of the situation in Iraq?"

That odd conversation occurred in late 1958.

• •

But in 1956, when Philby was still in Beirut practicing journalism, the news reports from the Middle East focused on the crisis over the Suez Canal. It was a time of high international drama.

It is, frankly, not a drama I knew very much about until I began to research it. As a result, the story I've pieced together is drawn from a variety of published sources reassembled here into a much briefer narrative format. I do this not to draw attention to my father's work there (his role was quite small), but instead to provide a historical context for readers who may be as unfamiliar as I was with the profound importance of this occurrence during the cold war.

What became known as the Suez crisis began as most crises in the Middle East still do: with an attack and a reprisal that in turn affected the price or supply of oil. In response to David Ben-Gurion–led Israeli attacks against Palestinian civilians in the Gaza Strip (which was itself a response to Egyptian fedayeen incursions into Israeli territories), Egyptian president Gamal Abdel Nasser nationalized the canal, effectively cutting off the significantly shorter route to Asia and to Middle Eastern oil for Britain and France. This move also threatened banks and businesses in Great Britain, which had a 44 percent stake in canal holdings and revenues, and effectively prevented the Soviet naval fleet from leaving the Black Sea.

Nasser was young, impatient, and desperate. Despite promises made by the United States to maintain neutrality in the Middle East, the Israelis were our known allies and were already well armed and technologically advanced. As tensions soared during the summer months, and reprisals for attacks on both sides escalated, Nasser turned to the Soviet Union for support. He was adamant about securing new armaments, even though he was acutely aware that this move would be read negatively by the West. Soon after his request, Soviet MiGs and Ilyushin bombers began populating Egyptian airfields and the French moved Mystère IVs into Israel.

The British and the French, in a last desperate attempt to maintain colonial control in the Middle East and to protect their shortcut, formed a secret alliance with Israel for the purpose of taking over Egypt. The Israelis were not interested in oil or in keeping open a faster route between the East and the West; they wanted to end what they perceived as the Arab threat to their dominance in the region.

The French, led by Premier Guy Mollet, balked at the broad sweep of the Israelis' proposal and the British refused to consider it. By the end of these heated negotiations, Ben-Gurion believed that the British and French could be counted on to protect only their own interests in the Middle East, and while a partnership with them could be formed in light of the present situation, in the end, Israel would have to rely on its own forces to carry out its plans for expansion.

Attacks and reprisals in the region continued.

Meanwhile, Dwight Eisenhower was in the final week of campaigning for his second term as president. Richard Nixon, his vice president, was urging him to become more active in the Middle East. Nixon, an avowed anti-Communist, wanted to go against the French, British, and Israeli positions to protect Nasser from becoming more closely aligned with the Soviets. Eisenhower reminded him that we shared too much history and civilization with the French and British to ever go against them, although he hoped that cooler heads in London and Paris would prevail. Nevertheless, Eisenhower's own CIA, under Dulles and Wisner, was, at that very time, planning to stage a coup in Syria in an attempt to stabilize pro-Western sentiment in the region.

Events elsewhere in the world quickly worsened. In response to anti-Communist protests in Poland and Hungary, Soviet tanks crossed the Hungarian border and opened fire. For years, CIA-sponsored Radio Free Europe broadcasts had urged popular uprisings and promised United States backing when it happened. Yet, in the midst of a major Middle East crisis over the Suez and ongoing diplomatic negotiations aimed at preventing war, nothing was done. According to published reports, two hundred thousand refugees fled Hungary, forty thousand lost their homes, and twenty-five thousand were slaughtered.

In the midst of this diplomatic nightmare, U.S. Secretary of State John Foster Dulles was hospitalized for stomach cancer. Ariel Sharon, then a commando in charge of Israeli border forces, charged, without provocation, into Egypt. Soviet Premier Nikolai Bulganin fired off angry letters to the British, French, and Israelis threatening nuclear war if they continued hostilities. The letter to Ben-Gurion suggested that Israel would be erased from the earth, saying "the very existence of it as a state" was in question. In an ironic twist perhaps unparalleled in recent diplomatic history, the Americans and Russians entered into negotiations *to work together* to prevent the British, the Israelis, and French *or* Nasser from seizing control of the canal. In the meantime, Bulganin recalled the Soviet ambassador to Israel.

In the first few days of November 1956, the world came as close as it could come—as perhaps it has *ever* come save the Cuban missile crisis—to nuclear war. Back in the United States, most citizens were unaware of the ominous course of events in the Suez. They were concentrating on the upcoming presidential election. They were also enjoying life. Unemployment was at a low 3.7 percent, interest rates hovered at 1 percent, and the good suburban life with a new house and new car in the driveway beckoned.

The link between Middle Eastern oil and what, in a preamble to war in the Persian Gulf in 1991, President George H. W. Bush would call "threats to the American way of life" was not well understood by the average American. Our new interstate highway system, Detroit's new cars with gas-guzzling engines, our petroleum-dependent factories, and our thirsty new jets seemed impervious to whatever exotic events were then unfolding half a world away. In hindsight, historians now look at the Suez Canal crisis of November 1956 as the true beginning of American involvement in the politics of the Middle East. But at the time, few people either understood or appreciated the strategic importance of alliances—much less enemies—made in this region.

Then, on November 6, war erupted. According to Donald Neff's excellent account, *Warriors at Suez*:

> The rising sun disclosed an astonishing sight off the tranquil shores of Egypt. There, spread out in battle array, was the mightiest European invasion force assembled since World War II. Floating gently on the blue waters of the Mediterranean were more than two hundred British and French warships, aircraft carriers and heavy cruisers, a battleship—France's formidable Jean Bart—scores of destroyers and frigates, freighters and tankers, and hundreds of tiny landing craft crammed with thousands of soldiers in battle gear. Guns of the powerful ships boomed, their smoke snaking lazily into the clear sky where it obscured the roaring flights of jets and helicopters. In the distance, on the palm-fringed beaches around the Suez Canal, there arose black clouds and the angry flashes and thumps of explosions.

This attack—the U.S.'s first Middle East war—lasted only eighteen hours. I say "only," but for the combatants—and particularly the civilians who lost their lives, their homes, and their businesses, the children who lost their parents, and the many women who were reportedly raped—it was a full season of horror in a loud stinking bloody hell. It seems too small and insignificant a concession to say that it could have been much worse.

But it *could* have been much worse. It could have gone nuclear.

In one of the first postwar displays of the power of money to control the fate of nations, the cause of the war's end was not the control of land or the movement of troops or even the dropping of hydrogen bombs, but the failure of the British pound on world financial markets. Gold reserves had dropped £100 million in the week leading up to the war and Washington withheld a much-needed loan of $1.5 billion until Prime Minister Anthony Eden agreed to a cease-fire in the Suez.

With the application of such powerful economic pressure to the achievement of diplomatic ends, the United States became a major political force in the Middle East. The Soviet Union also proved that its entry into the situation there would not be at all temporary. Within a short period of time Soviet influence led to the collapse of pro-Western leadership in Iraq and Lebanon. As a result of their failure in the Suez, the British and French were suddenly relegated to lesser status on the political stage, effectively replaced in the region by the interests of the Soviets and Americans.

Hungary and Poland still burned. Vietnam loomed on the near horizon.

But it was the crisis in the Suez Canal that set into motion the forces of a new world history. It would be a history written in oil as well as in blood.

It would establish the continuing conflict between Israel and the Arab world as one impossible to settle peacefully. It would inspire a generation of terrorists, and religious fundamentalists, on both sides.

And it would lead to more wars, more political and cultural divisiveness, and the horrific terrorist actions such as the attacks on the World Trade Center on September 11, 2001, that are still very much with us.

But by the end of November in 1956, this was a world history as yet to unfold and as yet largely unimaginable.

• •

Prior to the crisis, my father had been assigned to "handle things," including the evacuation of American expatriates, workers, veterans, and other American passport holders then living in Egypt. Working as a liaison officer to coordinate efforts among the CIA, local authorities, diplomats, and the United States Sixth Fleet, he was partly responsible for organizing the transport of 2,086 Americans to safety.

The operation was deemed successful two days in advance of the invasion. After that, the ships of the Sixth Fleet turned their attention to a possible shooting war, although, as Admiral Arleigh Burke, chief of naval operations, later recalled, in the conflicting midst of crossed diplomatic efforts, "I didn't know who the damned enemy was."

Philby knew. For the Soviet agent, the enemy was the alliance of British, French, and Israelis, but the more interesting question was whose side the Americans were likely to weigh in on. Philby, acting in his role as a freelance reporter for the *Observer*, supposedly interviewed my father about the likely American response to the then-circulating rumor that the British, French, and Israelis planned to seize control of the canal.

Although Philby had published an earlier piece in the *Observer*, on September 30, called "Western Oil Threat by Lebanon," to my knowledge he never published anything derived from this interview with my father. Who knows what Philby's real reasons were, or what my father may have told him.

But the important issue, at least as far as my family story is concerned, is that the two of them struck up a conversation that led to an evening of Scotch-swilling at local watering holes. "L-L-Lloyd," Philby famously told him at night's end, "I f-f-fear I may have g-gotten you b-bloody drunk."

To which my father replied, "F-fear not, Philby, you Red bastard, just buy me another b-bloody drink!"

I don't know what Philby's response to my father's taunt was, or even that this often-repeated conversation ever really took place. I don't know what else they may have said to each other. Nor do I know why my father, a vice consul for the United States of America, operating in a time of crisis in the Middle East, ever consented to be interviewed by a man whose reputation and questionable loyalties were still the topic of conversations at embassy parties.

Looked at differently, perhaps this conversation was fated. Perhaps it was just another step my father took on his journey to exile. Or maybe it was simply an exaggeration, a partial falsehood made up out of a romantic's fond remembrance couched in a drunken boast that begins in its utterance to mark another pattern in our family's mysteriously evolving life canto.

Or it could be true. It is interesting to contemplate but impossible to verify.

It was a tale performed by my father much later in his life, at Brook Lane Psychiatric Hospital, while he was in group therapy, long after Philby had finally been driven to defect and had been declared by the Presidium in Moscow "a citizen and hero of the Soviet Union."

· ·

When I was growing up, my father was gone quite a bit of the time. "Gone" was a code word in the Goodall family. It meant that my secretive, stiletto-carrying dad was away from home "working for the government." Later its meaning would morph into something else entirely, a state of mind called "blotto." But in Rome it meant that he was "gone" somewhere else that always remained unnamed, doing something always undefined and probably deeply classified.

I requested materials about my father's Agency activities for the years 1955 to 1960. It took the CIA eighteen months and two different case officers to respond. The result of this time and effort was a one-page, single-spaced letter. The letter said that, by law, any covert action he may or may not have been involved in would never be released. Not to me, or to anyone else. They were willing to admit a "voluntary relationship" existed between my father and the Agency, but that was it.

Hmmmm. What would you think?

Veterans Affairs representative.

Foreign Service reserve officer.

Vice consul.

Spy.

It doesn't matter what they admit. What does matter is that when I was a child my father was often inexplicably gone. There were times as a child when I imagined him entering a nether world, sometimes underground, sometimes up in the clouds, a world I called "Gone." I only saw him *enter* this imagined world. I never knew what he did there.

When he left us for these periods of time, my mother and I continued on as if nothing was different. We went through our routines. We looked forward to Sundays, although I know now we looked forward to Sundays for different reasons. Sundays were my mother's "other" world. Her Gone.

I know she worried a lot about him. She told me, near the end of her life, that she had to learn to accept the idea that on any of these trips he might not come back. That was part of her job. She, too, I suppose, had a "voluntary relationship" to uphold.

· ·

"*Spy?*" My good friend Richard spat the word out as if it disagreed with him. He looked at me and asked, "And what *is* a *spy?*"

Richard has, shall we say, an interesting personal history. At least the part of his personal history I know, which is, of course, only the part that he chooses to tell me.

The part I am familiar with includes his growing up in Bulgaria, where his father—an ex-SS fighter pilot—was a wine grower and well-respected man in their community. When the Communists rolled in, Richard's father was given a simple choice illustrated with a drawn weapon: join us or be shot.

It was a choice he well understood.

He "chose" to join the Communists. Because of his standing in the town, he had influence with the party. But, as Richard recalls fondly, his father was no Communist. He used to hang a framed picture of Lenin on a dead tree in the orchard, and they used it for target practice. Each head shot was awarded a chocolate.

It's an amusing story, wouldn't you agree?

Richard was an exceptional student and sportsman, and, with a rather insistent nudge from his father, he entered the Russian Naval Academy. He graduated at the top of his class and was immediately recruited into the KGB. He became one of the youngest men in the KGB to attain the rank of major.

He had, shall we say, many youthful adventures.

But he retained a lifelong fondness for chocolate.

He grew increasingly dissatisfied with his life as a faux Communist and doing the cold war bidding of Moscow. He saw and wanted what the West had. Intellectually, he understood that a capitalist pig was little better than a Communist pig, but at least capitalism was a more promising and productive ideology. It encouraged people to work hard to get ahead; it offered freedom, or a kind of freedom, that he craved. Richard sees himself as an enlightened Bulgarian patriot, a gentleman, a man of honor, and a naval officer, a trader in information, perhaps, but certainly not a *spy*. Nevertheless, when an opportunity arose to attempt an overthrow of the corrupt Bulgarian government in the late 1970s, Richard seized it.

It was an attempt that unfortunately failed.

But that is, of course, to look at the event only as an attempted political coup.

You could also tell the story as a tale of Richard's risky bid for freedom. In that respect, it worked beautifully. His participation in the attempted coup opened new doors or perhaps only completed previous agreements. Either way, it allowed him to defect to the United States.

He arrived as a foreign national in the New York City harbor, armed with only a pair of khaki shorts, some cheap sandals, and a Yankees T-shirt. He also had a new first name, Richard, chosen only because he admired the British actor Richard Burton and would himself be acting in a new American role, and a new last name that he prefers I don't release because, as he says, he wishes to live "anonymously." He was also issued a new birth date (to confuse anyone looking for him and using official records) and a new legend.

I think about Richard's history as I search for an intelligent way to answer his question. "A *spy*? And what *is* a *spy*?"

"All right," I reply. "Let's just say a person who deals in the international market for useful information."

Richard considers it. "Yes," he says. He smiles. "That is *much* better."

• •

When I try to imagine my father as a spy, or—as Richard prefers I describe him—as a man who dealt in the international market for useful information, I become acutely aware of two conflicting images and story lines. It is, as my mother—who was certainly complicit enough with his work to have described it as their work—would say, *complicated*. One is the image and story line we all have of a spy, based on characters like Ian Fleming's handsome, dashing, surprisingly intelligent, charming, sexist, and lethal character, James Bond. In real life, this image is closer to that of Kim Philby or even the legendary two-fisted, hard-drinking, gun-toting, and fearless American intelligence officer Bill Harvey. But it is a rare person who can live up to that constructed image.

The other image I carry inside me has been formed from years of reading about the intelligence community. In this version, a spy also refers to an information merchant, in that people who are not field officers are workaday information analysts; they are easily less charming or surprisingly intelligent than they are merely dedicated to their jobs, hardworking, and often saturated with bureaucracy more than bravery. William Colby called them "gray men." They are rather organizationally bland in the way that government workers in Washington usually appear organizationally bland regardless of what they do. Colby fit his own definition, although he grew into the image after having lived a more dashing and handsome life. Richard Helms certainly fit it.

Robert Hansen did, too. Aldrich Ames, ditto.

My father, or at least the image I have of my father, lies somewhere between these two conflicting images and accompanying mythic story lines.

He was, at least during this prime-time spy time, handsome and dashing and intelligent, "the fair-haired boy" as my mother recalled this oft-repeated social metaphor for him. In my experience, he could be charming, although I wouldn't describe him that way. He was quieter than that, more subtle than charming. In my teenage years he more closely fit Colby's description of a "gray man."

But by then, by the time I had grown up enough to begin to observe him, he had fallen hard from any exalted status in the Agency he may have once enjoyed. He was outwardly bland and inwardly bitter. He felt he had been betrayed by the truth and by the country he had sworn to defend. We were living in exile. The price of his oath of secrecy, and our lives, was his eternal and deeply conflicted silence.

• •

I've always wondered what "useful information" my father may have had, or acquired, during his tenure in Rome. What was it that made him valuable?

The response I received from the CIA mirrored one given to John H. Richardson, himself a cold war son of the clandestine service, when he asked for operational details related to his father's service: "Not only no, but *hell* no."

Aside from the fragments I attempt to piece together from my own memories of conversations, stories, and published accounts, there is a missing piece of the puzzle that defines the subject of the puzzle itself. What did my father know, and when and how did he come to know it? What recommended this seemingly ordinary man, who was clearly not a son of the moneyed, landed leadership or educated classes, for this vital assignment? Once there, what work did he do that was important enough to win a transfer to the most coveted location of the cold war?

Were we transferred to London so that H. Lloyd Goodall could further his personal investigations of Philby? I seriously doubt it. Angleton, in no mood to consider an already-sore subject, wouldn't have allowed it. Wisner had far more important things on his mind, including the ominous situation in Hungary. Allen Dulles was likely preoccupied with his brother's terminal illness, and besides, I doubt in any case he would have been much interested in the routine transfer of a Veterans Affairs representative doing clandestine work under State Department cover.

No, it was more likely that the hunt for the truth about Philby was something my father tucked into his own clandestine agenda. He had suspicions, not proof. He would remain alert, but not preoccupied. He had other work to do, whatever it was. And whatever it was, apparently it was useful enough to those who mattered to get him to London.

So why London? Why the plum job at the height of the cold war in Europe? Our transfer to the Court of St. James can more easily be explained as a simple political reward for a job in Rome his superiors in Washington felt was well done.

My mother and my father's mutual sacrifices were paying off.

They had no idea what was coming.

10

Fragments: London

1958–1960

WHY LONDON?

It seems logical that if Philby were the target, the Agency would have sent my father to Beirut. Lebanon is where Philby was living in 1958. Wouldn't it make sense to place the tellers of two tales on the same stage to see how they run?

I am sure that if the reason my father was transferred to London had something to do with Philby, "they" considered it. But my father did not speak Lebanese, or any of the Arabic languages. Learning rudimentary Italian had been difficult. Besides, placing him in Beirut may have tipped off Philby and that would have ruined the play.

London and Berlin were the centers of cold war operations in Europe. London was an important post because it was the nerve center of diplomatic relations on the continent, because England was our most powerful ally, and because our embassy there had developed a specialty in Soviet counterintelligence second to none. To paraphrase Samuel Johnson, if an intelligence man was tired of London, then he was tired of intelligence.

My father embraced the idea of London as a poet embraces metaphor or a musician embraces sound. It was his medium and his surround.

It was his whole world.

. . . .

Nevertheless, for my mother, arriving in early February from sunny Rome and experiencing firsthand the constant cold, gray rain, London seemed less like a reward for good service than a turn of Fortune's wheel in the opposite direction.

Our small rented two-story brick house in Golders Green, suitable for a middle-class Briton working in a bank and therefore perfect cover for an American intelligence officer working at the embassy, had only a temperamental coal stove on the lower level for heat. Our new next-door neighbors, Arthur and Mary Liddington, provided instruction on precisely where to strike the ball-peen hammer on the piping connected to the tiny water heater to encourage the flow from our popping, ticking, gurgling unit. They also taught us how to remove hot coals from the stove before bedtime, place them carefully into a rectangular metal box, and tuck the box under the covers at the foot of our beds to keep warm. Still, I often wore a wool sweater and thick socks to bed.

My mother was never warm enough in London.

My father and Mr. Liddington walked to work unless rain prevented it. When it rained too heavily for comfort, they still walked together, but only to the bus stop. It was a strange pairing. The two men appeared to have almost nothing in common except the war and their neighborhood, but apparently it was enough. Weekday mornings they departed from their respective front doors—each man wearing a suitable dark suit, raincoat, hat, and carrying the ubiquitous British brolly—at precisely 7:30 a.m. They greeted each other briefly—"Hello, Mr. Liddington" followed by "Hello, Mr. Goodall"—and then headed off in a kind of reserved silence to catch the bus or to their respective places of employment.

Mr. Liddington told us he worked for the Chancellery of the Exchequer as a securities manager. My father told the Liddingtons that he worked in Veterans Affairs for the American embassy. Mrs. Liddington worked in the home as a housewife, as did my mother, although in those prefeminist days "worked in the home as a housewife" was not in common usage. They described themselves, happily and simply, as "wives" and it was understood that this term defined a range of household duties that were seldom, if ever, performed by men. My mother, still missing her beloved nursing profession and the excitement of an emergency room, was a little less happy about calling herself "a wife" than Mrs. Liddington apparently was.

Both women kept busy. Mrs. Liddington had her garden club and charity work to occupy any free time, and my mother had embassy functions almost every afternoon or evening. Mrs. Liddington, who loved children and adored me, volunteered to keep me occupied at her house until either my mother or father picked me up in the evening. It was an offer my parents graciously and gladly accepted and that I thoroughly looked forward to. The Liddingtons were terrific sitters.

Little did I know . . . indeed, little did I *know*.

Occasionally Mr. Liddington and my father journeyed home together, but not often. More often than not my parents arrived at the Liddingtons' together following one of their embassy functions. When they didn't arrive together, my mother came home alone in a cab to retrieve me from the Liddingtons' floor, where had I set up toy soldiers and, using Mr. Liddington's historical expertise, we re-created the great British military battles and variously defeated either the French or the Huns. My father, as I clearly recall, often worked long hours at the embassy; apparently Veterans Affairs was quite a going concern in London.

· ·

What little we supposedly knew about Arthur Liddington was told to us one night during a shared spaghetti dinner in our tiny dining room. Mr. Liddington was born to farm life in the Cotswolds and had enlisted in the army to escape it. He was wounded at Dunkirk before being stationed at intelligence headquarters at Blenheim Palace. Blenheim, just six miles north of Oxford, had been Winston Churchill's childhood home, although at the time it belonged to his uncle—the Duke of Marlborough—and to his grandparents. The three-hundred-year-old grand estate had been a gift from the queen to the first duke after he defeated the French at the Battle of Blenheim in Bavaria during the War of Spanish Succession.

During the Second World War, Blenheim had been appropriated for military use and became the center for secret intelligence operations against the Nazis. Well, "secret" perhaps to some people, but apparently well known enough by the locals, as the story was told to us on a visit there how the bus driver announced the stop as "Blenheim Palace, please exit now all military intelligence officers, supposed diplomats, secret agents, gentleman and ladies of duplicity, and spies." Hitler was even fond of Blenheim. He had determined that Blenheim would serve as the seat of his occupational government when the Germans triumphed over England. Hitler had ordered his Luftwaffe not to release bombs in the immediate area, which explained why it and neighboring Oxford were still in perfect condition.

After the war and following the tax reforms that made it virtually impossible for wealthy and titled British upper-class citizens to keep up their castles and estates, Blenheim, in all of its Cotswold limestone majesty, was deeded back to the British people through the National Trust. It served thereafter as a national historical site.

It became a favorite tourist spot, with its huge oaken doors and great hall that holds five hundred people and the fine furnishings and painted tapestries featuring scenes from the great battle. Blenheim also contained various original historical documents, including the victory note penned by the first duke's hand and delivered by horse courier to the queen, the note itself written on the back of a French restaurant menu. Outdoors were the Pleasure Gardens, containing the world's second-largest maze, huge checkerboards and chess games for children, a putting green, and a butterfly house. The grounds themselves featured a grand, finely mown expanse of greenery leading to the Temple of Diana, once the private walking and riding domain of the Marlboroughs and their guests, but available now to anyone who had a couple of quid for admission. The present Duke and Duchess of Marlborough lived far more moderately in apartments overlooking the original courtyard, freed from their tax burden but also keenly aware of what the will and sacrifice of the commoners after two world worlds had required of them and others of their class.

Mr. Liddington's official duties at Blenheim weren't discussed. "State secrets, old boy," he jollied to my father. My father smiled and dismissed the comment with his characteristic hand gesture.

After the war, Mr. Liddington left the military, attended the London School of Economics, met and wed Mary, and took a job at the Chancellery. I asked him what he did there, and he replied: "It's all quite dull. There are times when I sincerely wish I had gone into another line of work."

That is a statement I now find humorous. Had I been a little older and more alert to conversational ploys, I might have noticed that Mr. Liddington diverted his personal history into a discussion of the history of Blenheim Palace. But then again, he was British.

· ·

Tradecraft. It is an interesting term, isn't it? Its root is drawn from the working-class penchant for developing a skill set known as a "trade" combined with the artisan's ability to "craft" something finer, more textured, or meaningful out of it. The first time I saw the word used to describe the work spies do was years ago in a John le Carré novel, *Smiley's People*. It was new to me at the time, but for those particular craftsmen practicing their trade in the world, it was just another case of literature drawing upon the known resources of clandestine life.

• •

I'm not sure when, or for that matter, *why* my father first picked up a copy of *The Great Gatsby*. Scribner's had issued a new college edition in 1957, capitalizing on the revival of Fitzgerald's work occurring in literary circles during that time. It was the buzz on campuses and, interestingly, was alive in the talk of late-afternoon cocktail parties in various American embassies worldwide.

It is strange for me to think that my father walked into Blackstone's and bought it, although he may have. It is equally difficult for me to imagine him up on what was hip. But there were many aspects of my father's life that were perfectly normal for him, at least for the character he played in this larger story.

I'd like to think I remember seeing the cover of the book in his brown leather briefcase, but I don't. I never knew what he kept in his briefcase, and, truthfully, I never really cared.

I don't recall seeing him read the novel, either.

Yet he must have read it. Given how marked up his copy was when I received it, he must have read it a thousand times. He must have known it inside and out, both as story and as plot. He must have reflected on the meaning of the secret lives of Jay Gatsby and Daisy Buchanan. Of Gatsby's tale of being in the war, of his being wounded not by bullets or flak but by lost love. Of Daisy, the corrupted innocence of her, of the idea of her, and of the story of her that Gatsby told himself despite the abundance of evidence to the contrary.

My father must have hated Tom Buchanan, as we all learn to hate him, for being the rich, arrogant American blue-blooded bastard he is. For the raw unfair fact that all that wealth and privilege—certainly not love—is what won Daisy's fealty, if not exactly her heart.

What could he have thought about Jordan Baker, the tennis player who concealed so well her true self? Or about Myrtle, the unrequited lover whose tragic and pitiful death led to Gatsby's taking the blame for something he didn't do in order to protect Daisy? Jordan and Myrtle were bit players whose bits figured largely into the destination of the overall plot, although I wonder if my father would have read them that way.

And what about Myrtle's feckless husband, George Wilson, the poor mechanic who knew what was going on between his wife and Tom Buchanan but was willing to pretend he didn't in exchange for a good price on a fancy car? In my father's clandestine world, this was the perfect analogue for an agent, a traitor, any person willing to give up his country in exchange for money, or for what money could buy them.

Then there is the not so small matter of the great billboard overlooking the valley of ashes, the advertisement featuring the huge blue eyes and the "enormous yellow spectacles which pass over a nonexistent nose" of Dr. T. J. Eckleburg. Did my father read into the eyeglasses an omniscient source of a central intelligence, the awesome presence of someone to watch over us but not to interfere? Or maybe to remind us that the interferences have already occurred, and they are deeply and irrevocably already written into this story, in ways that we only later learn about, then fear, and then blame?

Could those gigantic blue eyes, with "retinas one yard high" be a sign of an ignored forewarning, a symbol of our need to see things differently? I wonder if my father recognized Fitzgerald's telltale error, that it was not the "retinas" that were so large, but either the irises or pupils?

These are the general questions I have about Lloyd's supposedly close reading of the novel. But I have another question, a more personal one. And for me, a more important one.

How did this novel figure so prominently into his work in London? Was it merely a matter of convenience, or did its selection have a point? Was it something he used in staged brief encounters, or something else?

· ·

In the recorded history of coded messages, novels figure prominently into the spy story. They have served officers ably as places to hide instructions and to exchange secret information. They are codebooks that teach agents how to read what lies beneath their storied surfaces.

It is an ancient technique. The oldest recorded use of coded messages is found in the oldest recorded language artifacts we have—Egyptian cuneiform symbols. The symbols appear to record food stores and supplies, but when read with the aid of a codebook, they provide secret instructions about the location and strength of an opposing army.

The most well-known artifact of coded messages from the ancient world is the Rosetta stone. Here again, the rock appears to be a relic recording the existence of a lost language, but it is actually a symbolic template used to construct any number of secrets. How many secrets were hidden among its seemingly innocent poems and songs is unknown.

Coded messages increased in their sophistication with the available science of the times. Leonardo da Vinci created a carved puzzle codex and Galileo made secret writing that would only appear when light or heat passed over the paper. These technological innovations were useful to patrons and princes, who used them to conceal secrets from husbands, kings, and warriors. Once again, the true story was hidden inside the letters.

With the advent of the printing press, the ancient technique of concealing coded messages experienced a renaissance. The same book or pamphlet could be used by a number of people simultaneously to share and yet conceal a common secret. At first, the King James version of the Bible was a popular resource because it was common to most households and could be found in every kingdom, but when the novel grew in popularity in the late eighteenth century, the old ways found a new medium.

At first, secrets were decoded in a way that would have seemed familiar to an Egyptian: the story contained within the story could be read with a codebook that explained which letters—among all the available ones—should be recombined, or reordered, or renumbered to reveal the secret message.

The Vigenère system evolved from this standard. It consisted of a table based on a 26-by-26 pattern. On a particular day, codes could be constructed based on any starting place in the alphabet. This system had the added advantage of being changeable at will. If we begin today's coded message with the letter "C," we can begin tomorrow's with the letter "X" (see Figure 10.1).

The coding itself—the fashioning of an intelligible pattern for secret communications—required diligence, patience, intelligence, and cunning.

When the typewriter was invented, the new technology was transferred immediately into the clandestine world. Machines replaced handwritten notes or printed pages. In fact, the most famous coding machine—the German Enigma—is little more than an elaborate typewriter set up on a complex and changing alphanumeric code. So effective was this method of passing coded messages during World War II that British intelligence devoted an entire building—Bletchley Park—and a considerable budget to figuring it out. Once broken, it provided access to information that literally shortened the war for the Allies and saved countless lives.

My father lived and worked in the historical era after Enigma and prior to electronic computers. It was an interesting time for coded messages, a

A	b	c	d	e	f	g	h	i	j	k	l	m	n	o	p	q	r	s	t	u	v	w	x	y	z
B	c	d	e	f	g	h	i	j	k	l	m	n	o	p	q	r	s	t	u	v	w	x	y	z	a
C	d	e	f	g	h	i	j	k	l	m	n	o	p	q	r	s	t	u	v	w	x	y	z	a	b
D	e	f	g	h	i	j	k	l	m	n	o	p	q	r	s	t	u	v	w	x	y	z	a	b	c
E	f	g	h	i	j	k	l	m	n	o	p	q	r	s	t	u	v	w	x	y	z	a	b	c	d
F	g	h	i	j	k	l	m	n	o	p	q	r	s	t	u	v	w	x	y	z	a	b	c	d	e
G	h	i	j	k	l	m	n	o	p	q	r	s	t	u	v	w	x	y	z	a	b	c	d	e	f
H	i	j	k	l	m	n	o	p	q	r	s	t	u	v	w	x	y	z	a	b	c	d	e	f	g
I	j	k	l	m	n	o	p	q	r	s	t	u	v	w	x	y	z	a	b	c	d	e	f	g	h
J	k	l	m	n	o	p	q	r	s	t	u	v	w	x	y	z	a	b	c	d	e	f	g	h	i
K	l	m	n	o	p	q	r	s	t	u	v	w	x	y	z	a	b	c	d	e	f	g	h	i	j
L	m	n	o	p	q	r	s	t	u	v	w	x	y	z	a	b	c	d	e	f	g	h	i	j	k
M	n	o	p	q	r	s	t	u	v	w	x	y	z	a	b	c	d	e	f	g	h	i	j	k	l
N	o	p	q	r	s	t	u	v	w	x	y	z	a	b	c	d	e	f	g	h	i	j	k	l	m
O	p	q	r	s	t	u	v	w	x	y	z	a	b	c	d	e	f	g	h	i	j	k	l	m	n
P	q	r	s	t	u	v	w	x	y	z	a	b	c	d	e	f	g	h	i	j	k	l	m	n	o
Q	r	s	t	u	v	w	x	y	z	a	b	c	d	e	f	g	h	i	j	k	l	m	n	o	p
R	s	t	u	v	w	x	y	z	a	b	c	d	e	f	g	h	i	j	k	l	m	n	o	p	q
S	t	u	v	w	x	y	z	a	b	c	d	e	f	g	h	i	j	k	l	m	n	o	p	q	r
T	u	v	w	x	y	z	a	b	c	d	e	f	g	h	i	j	k	l	m	n	o	p	q	r	s
U	v	w	x	y	z	a	b	c	d	e	f	g	h	i	j	k	l	m	n	o	p	q	r	s	t
V	w	x	y	z	a	b	c	d	e	f	g	h	i	j	k	l	m	n	o	p	q	r	s	t	u
W	x	y	z	a	b	c	d	e	f	g	h	i	j	k	l	m	n	o	p	q	r	s	t	u	v
X	y	z	a	b	c	d	e	f	g	h	i	j	k	l	m	n	o	p	q	r	s	t	u	v	w
Y	z	a	b	c	d	e	f	g	h	i	j	k	l	m	n	o	p	q	r	s	t	u	v	w	x
Z	a	b	c	d	e	f	g	h	i	j	k	l	m	n	o	p	q	r	s	t	u	v	w	x	y

FIGURE 10.1 Vigenère system of coding.

nuclear age when the need for secrecy was supreme among a class of persons, some of whom considered themselves clever as well as literary.

Many officers were college educated, and of those quite a few had been English majors. Wisner was devoted to the crafting of language and was an avid reader of popular and literary novels. Angleton was known around the Agency as "the poet" because of his lifelong affinity for verse, particularly experimental verse. Angleton still devoted hours each day to reading and often dropped literary phrases—usually in the form of elliptical allusions—into his talk at the Agency. It was this combination of cultural factors that led to an entirely new way of using novels, poems, and even the literary essay as resources for giving instructions and sharing information via coded messages.

Perhaps the use of novels was yet another way of being anti-Communist, too. Whereas the Soviets relied on numerical coding devices, maybe "our side" chose coding that relied upon words. One of the great espionage breakthroughs of World War II had been the accidental discovery of the burnt remnants of a Russian codebook found on a battlefield in Finland. But there was enough of it salvaged that a group of American cryptanalysts were able to figure out the bases for the Russian cipher system. It was a system of "super-encipherment" that relied on the addition of random numerical values to already-established five-digit code groups. In David C. Martin's *Wilderness of Mirrors*, that process is elaborated:

> The code book might reveal, for instance, that the five-digit group for the word *agent* was 17056, but it would not reveal that the "additive," as it was called, was 05555. With the additive the word agent would appear in the enciphered message as 22611 (17056 plus 05555), which the codebook would list as the five-digit group for a word or phrase with an entirely different meaning. Only someone in possession of both the codebook and the additive would know to subtract 05555 from 22611 and arrive at 17056 and the word *agent*. Since each code group used a different additive, the effect was an infinity of codes.

The "infinity of codes" was virtually impossible to break without the complete codebook, despite the concerted efforts of British and American cryptographers. Furthermore, the Russians figured out that we had salvaged part of a codebook, so they changed the additives in 1947.

Our cryptographers were stymied, reduced to guesswork and tedious calculations based on hunches derived from interceptions of coded messages that could be traced back to known empirical events, such as the movement of Soviet troops or the installation of a radio transmitter atop a building in Berlin. It is no small accident that the British intelligence officer assigned to the special group working on the problem was none other than Philby. Nor that his American counterpart was Angleton.

The important thing to remember at this juncture in our tale is that the fierce competition between the Russians and the Americans for world dominance meant that anything the Communists stood for, developed, or used had to be countered by something Western, capitalist, and *better*. Americans would eventually triumph in the international competition over superior espionage technology, particularly missile and computer technologies that would establish the National Security Agency (NSA) as the premier electronic surveillance organization on planet Earth. But during this historical period, following the Second World War and prior to the Cuban missile crisis, a simpler, *better* solution was believed to be in language, in the way we combine letters to form representations of thoughts, actions, and passions.

How my father may have used them is still a mystery to me. Was my father trying to send me a coded message? I think he was. Was part of that message the idea that there is something in the story line of *Gatsby* that I needed to know? That I needed to find out about him? I think so. I also think that although my father was certainly no Jay Gatsby, there were elements of Gatsby's character and story that mirrored his own, right up to the very end of the novel.

Nick wonders aloud, toward the novel's fateful end, "What foul dust settled in his wake?"

This is an American novel, and his was an American life, all about unanswerable questions born from a character's loss of illusions.

• •

In London my mother had a black dog named Troubles.

It was a female Labrador retriever puppy, maybe six or eight months old, a flea-bitten stray she had taken in, cleaned up, and named. It was her plan for the dog to be *my* pet. But the dog never bonded with me or I with the dog. It was always my mother's pet, at least for the short time we cared for her.

My mother loved Troubles. I think she identified with her. My mother used to say she was a "mutt who had been taken into high places." She loved that little black dog. Unfortunately, Troubles developed the disease called canine distemper and had to be destroyed.

I remember seeing a glimpse of the wild-eyed dog foaming at the mouth. I remember hearing my mother scream for me to keep away from her, and I remember being routed for safekeeping into the Liddingtons' house.

I never saw Troubles again. I never received much of an explanation of what happened to her.

My mother cried for days over our loss.

But my mother cried a lot in London. She cried, she told me, because she was worried about my father. No doubt this statement was true. Since we arrived in England, he was hardly ever at home. He was always "gone." It was "complicated." He would be absent for a week or two at a time and

FIGURE 10.2 Bud and Naomi in London, circa 1958–59.

my mother would only know that he was away "working for the government," although she didn't know where he was or when he would return.

As I say, Veterans Affairs must have been big business in London.

He returned from his trips exhausted and sometimes angry. But for me he acted as if he had never been away. He emerged from the fog cold-cheeked and smelling of Old Spice and cigarettes, put his briefcase down on the chair, and kissed my mother. He always brought me a toy, but aside from that small gesture, he never discussed where he had been or what he had been doing. He must have confided some details to my mother, but whatever he told her only served to make her more nervous the next time he left without explanation or was "gone" for any period of time.

As my mother said, it was "complicated."

• •

Meanwhile, I attended primary school. I was initially enrolled at St. Dunstan's Church of England Primary School, a private British academy run in a Christian militarist fashion, as if it were the HMS *Dunstan*. The school itself resembled a dark fortress. It had been some minor lord's home, complete with a great hall used for assemblies and meals, and a large library stocked floor to ceiling with classics. Visitors were no doubt impressed with its prim and proper exterior. I remember austere lecturers in black gowns who provided instruction and a small concrete courtyard around back that was our hard playground. It was all very Harry Potter without any of the magic. My knees were always skinned from playing soccer on such an unwelcoming surface. We were taught Latin and Greek from a battered old textbook and recited tired passages from Homer and Virgil by rote. We wore uniforms.

At Christmas, the headmaster called us into the great hall for his annual speech. The speech began with something close to the following words: "Christmas, children, is not a time for jollifications. No. It is a solemn time to remember the birth of our savior and Lord Jesus Christ and to remember what wretched sinners we are. . . ."

I am sure he repeated these words to every group of students prior to the Christmas break. St. Dunstan's was, for me, neither a joyous place nor was it a self-esteem-enhancing environment. It was school and I learned only to hate it.

My parents were alarmed when the first written evaluations of my work and character were sent home. I was apparently a bit of a problem child who couldn't remember to remove his school cap when entering the building and who faked recitations during oral group activities. I had at best a mediocre intellect and showed no particular aptitude for sports. Remedial tutoring was strongly recommended.

My parents were shocked and disappointed. This wasn't how their son, their only son, was supposed to turn out. St. Dunstan's was a good school, and an expensive one. How could I have let them down? Didn't I understand what this could mean for my father's career? For our lives here, and afterwards?

I have no idea what I said in reply to these questions. I only remember feeling very small. It wasn't my intention to let my parents down. I was sorry I was so stupid.

My father immediately arranged for a tutor recommended by someone at the embassy. The tutor examined my skills and my attitude in some detail prior to commencing our daily exercises together. He explained to my father and mother that although I was a slow reader, that wasn't the cause of any deficiency in intellect or a learning problem. In his professional opinion, my problem stemmed from being an American assigned to a British private school. It was a problem of acculturation, "a bad fit of child to school." I

FIGURE 10.2 Bud, in American School of London photograph, circa 1959–60.

would be better off and my grades would surely improve if I transferred to the American School in London.

At that time, the American School was housed in an old multistory brick building overlooking a corner of a large park. My teachers didn't wear black cloaks and there was no uniform. The classrooms, if old, were airy and bright, benefiting from the large windows. Recesses were spent in the park, and there were no more required concrete soccer games. I happily went to school there, relieved to be away from St. Dunstan's, and immediately applied myself with a never-before-found enthusiasm for the subject matter.

I wanted my parents to be proud of me again.

My tutor discovered that my reading skills improved dramatically when I was given comic books and was no longer expected to recite Latin or Greek from a textbook. My father, acting on this good pedagogical advice, made sure that every Saturday he was in town we visited "the store"—a mini-military-style PX—in the basement of the embassy, where he purchased for me two or three American comic books, a Mr. Goodbar, and large chocolate milkshake. He disappeared upstairs and I got high on sugar while enjoying the adventures of *Sad Sack*, *Beetle Bailey*, and *Sergeant Rock*.

I looked forward to Saturdays.

I liked my new school. I made friends. I became the teacher's pet. I excelled in history and language arts. I earned straight A's on my report card and took pride in being called a good student. I was selected by my classmates to lead the Pledge of Allegiance to the American flag.

My transformation from a sullen, stupid sort into a happier and brighter boy occurred at about the same time that my mother became more agitated and ill at ease. As I would later learn, this was the period when she also became dependent upon white pills to get through the nights and yellow ones to "perk up her smile" during the days. My mother kept her anxieties about my father from me, but in a way that ensured I always knew something was wrong.

It wasn't solely a concern for my father's welfare that haunted her. Naomi was getting older. She had entered her fortieth year and resented the cultural and social implications of having arrived at that particular age. She found new gray hairs that brought tears, and she complained constantly about her weight. However, no matter what was going on inside her head or within her body, she was determined to keep up outward appearances.

If my mother were like any character from *Gatsby*, it unfortunately would be Myrtle. Good-looking, a risk taker, determined to improve her lot in this life. Instead of her tragic end being the result of an affair with a careless rich man, my mother's was in a loving marriage to my father. Not that it was a bad marriage, because it wasn't bad at all. But because by marrying him she got exactly what she had wished for—a handsome husband, love, commitment, a child, and a ticket to a fairy-tale life lived in the diplomatic corps among all of the best people and visiting all the best places in Europe.

Be careful what you wish for. Isn't that an old Yiddish expression? Or perhaps it's Chinese.

Or perhaps it is just common sense. The sort of common sense that comes from seeing what happens when wishes do turn into horses that beggars can ride. In any case, success is what afflicted my mother, getting her ticket to the big leagues, which was exactly what she had wished for. By getting it she realized just how far away from home she was, a distance that could only be measured internally because it was experienced in her mind and body every day. She was mentally caught within the webs of her personal *in*significance, spun into it and held there by the intricate netting of the life story she lived by, the one that she had used so successfully to gain entrance, the one that had built and supported her deepest sense of self.

She rarely talked about it. It was "complicated."

But the poor little girl from the small West Virginia farm who, by luck and pluck, became a registered nurse and doting mother was not a story line that worked to any advantage here. It didn't matter if she omitted some of the details—such as her first marriage, or having flat feet—or altered some others—such as being "from Virginia" and having parents who were "in agriculture." These minor conversational disguises were applied like make-up in a vain attempt to cover up a self-perceived flaw. They were gestures suggesting a personality that she hoped created a good impression, like Gatsby's casual remark about having been "at Oxford." But among those who knew the reality, these gestures were politely received, but the person uttering them was instantly doubted.

Nor did her oversights and exaggerations work very well for her. These fictional story lines by which she had invented a better self did not erase her true life. The evidence was inscribed on her body, written into the deepening creases that lined her mouth and the now ever-present darkness around her once bright and beautiful eyes. She thought it was her age that was the cause of her new anxieties, but I don't think it was her age. It was her lack of confidence about the person she had talked herself into becoming, a story that was thin to begin with, but was now showing distinct signs of being worn out, of being threadbare.

Foreign Service reserve officers and their wives were the social cannon fodder of the diplomatic corps. They were invited to embassy functions, but, unless they could add value to the conversational mix, they were often denied full acceptance once arriving there. My mother worked very hard to be up on the latest things and was no more averse to dropping a famous name than the next wife, but when the talk around the grand piano or the open bar turned personal, she became noticeably silent.

There was too much hidden.

She couldn't risk being who she really was, not in the company of the charming Ambassador Jock Whitney and his lovely, educated wife Betsy. If Clare Boothe Luce had been a rude introduction to the American system of social class, then the Whitneys represented a decidedly higher tier, a tier of old money rather than new. Jock's life story, told offhand and with a modesty so genuine it defied even so much as a question, was that he happened to be a direct descendant of the American inventor Eli Whitney. Ambassador Whitney hardly ever mentioned it, but his family endowed their own museum. Reared in wealth and privilege, he had attained all of the champion ribbons of youth, which became the great medals of war, which he only added to a drawer already stuffed full of honors and prizes.

Betsy Whitney was equal to her husband's legend. Hearing her talk about her childhood was like listening to a best-selling author read aloud from an accomplished work destined to become an American classic. Theirs was a perfect marriage made in very American heaven. And it was a heaven so high above anything West Virginian that it required copious infusions of amphetamines and alcohol for my mother to deal with it.

Nor did my mother's life story work in polite cocktail conversation with the State Department's guests of honor. Imagine it as my mother lived it, each day another social performance with luminaries such as George Kennan, Kay and Phil Graham, Richard Nixon, Dick Bissell, or Chip Bohlen.

Or with celebrities and stars such Elizabeth Taylor, Rock Hudson, Cary Grant, Lauren Bacall, or Katharine Hepburn.

Or with world leaders, the list of whose names was long, if not always as historically or culturally distinguished.

Or the merely wealthy hoping for influence, and they were legion, but mentioning their names here would be no better than listing the names of characters who attended Gatsby's parties.

My point is that there was nothing dazzling my mother could offer them except her hourglass figure, her dark, smoldering eyes, some gossip she might have picked up in Rome, and that well-practiced, well-rehearsed bright smile.

Naomi May (Alexander) Saylor Goodall was a remarkable woman in her own right, but she didn't quite believe it. She believed her real story was not quite good enough for diplomatic company. She had survived an impoverished childhood and raised herself up in the world to become a nurse, a wife, and a mother, and yet none of these positive attributes seemed to her worthy enough to be *sayable*. That she had been divorced, or that she had suffered burns to 70 percent of her body, or that she had only gone to school long enough to become an RN instead of graduating from some fine college in New England—these were the facts she perceived to be fatal flaws in her story line. She feared that others would believe these facts of her life reflected deeper flaws in her character. That she had helped save lives in hospital emergency rooms, or volunteered for duty with the terminally ill, well, none of these really mattered here.

Not in London. Not at formal embassy functions.

My mother came, if not exactly to hate herself, then surely to distrust the dignity of her own identity. She came to hate where she had come from and what she hadn't done. She learned to distrust who she really was beneath her skin. She was undone in London by a build-up of self-loathing that now, when I think about it, brings a heavy sorrow into my heart and tears to my eyes. These details were part of my mother's secret story that I didn't know until near the end of her life, when impending death freed her up enough to talk openly about it. Had I known all this when I was growing up, I'd like to think it might have changed things between us. But that is hindsight. And hubris. And bullshit that doesn't matter in the end.

What makes it so much worse is that my father also didn't know of her deep despair. She hid herself and her cares from him as well as she hid it from the rest of the world. He would tell me, much later, when I had criticized some small thing she had said to me, "Your mother is a saint." He was shaking visibly, a little intoxicated, and near tears at the time. But I think he had finally figured it out.

He was too late to this recognition. But by then, it was already too late for all of us.

. . . .

You don't have to be a good woman ashamed of your lower-class past in a new life among the rich to live your life as a lie. You can also be a self-satisfied and smug man of privilege. If my poor mother was guilty of having invented a self to pass off in polite company, then Kim Philby was guilty, too.

Ideologies aside, what is truest about us always comes down to identity, doesn't it?

It comes down to who you think you have to be *now* measured against whom you know yourself *to have been*. To measure up to the appropriate level, we find language capable of sustaining the *now* against the constant scrutiny of the *then*. We adapt our known history to one that is available to us. We neither confirm nor deny the facts of our true but covert identities, because to do so would place us in jeopardy of being discovered, and once discovered, *exposed*.

We cannot allow that to happen. None of us.

We keep our true self (if there is such a thing) a secret and present to the world a plausible story. We blend a selective account of what actually happened with a perspective—a point of view—that provides a suitable framework for the tale.

We may include in that tale what my mother called "little white lies" designed to gain some perceived advantage. We may become even bolder in our presentations of self for others, by creating whole cloth an imagined past to pass off as the whole truth and nothing but. That is far riskier and, in a clandestine world prone to checking facts for traces of true identities, it is far less effective. It is much better to use bare facts shaped into a life by crafting a plausible perspective, a believable and credible legend, than to tell barefaced lies. It is better to enable others to construct one way, or multiple ways, of interpreting the meaning of our story, of reading "our motives as shorthand terms for situations," as Kenneth Burke puts it. Motives are the soul of our selves, however clandestine.

So it is that all of us—soldiers, Saylors, spies, sons, daughters, traitors, patriots, and betrayers—acquire the necessary conversational skills to carry our characters into the world. We develop a story of the self for ourselves, one that we practice on myriad audiences, each time gauging the responses we receive from others, using those responses to make modifications on our story line.

We adjust the specific words and phrases we speak to gain maximum effectiveness and efficiency in social interactions. We monitor what we reveal and what we conceal, and to whom we have said what, and why. We are keen to the events that work for us as well as those better left unsaid or omitted or forgotten. We learn to smile, brightly. We practice looking at ourselves in mirrors to see what others see when we say this or do that. We laugh at ourselves and pass off whatever threatens to cause harm to our identity as only a misunderstanding. Blaming, of course, and rightly so, only ourselves. Which is to say, blaming the whole thing on what is *lacking* in our selves, which are all of the elements of our story line that have been gradually lost, changed, or stripped away from years of practicing personal tradecraft in polite, competitive company. This is, of course, only one way of understanding what happens to the truth.

Our truth.

11

London, Berlin, Washington

1960

SOMETIME DURING THE LATE SUMMER OF 1959 WE MOVED FROM OUR little brick house in Golders Green to a brand-new and much grander apartment building in St. John's Wood. It was a much tonier area and our apartment was far more modern, but I missed seeing the Liddingtons. I don't remember seeing either of them again. The Liddingtons were friends, like Abbe Lane, who just one day disappeared from our family story.

I wonder *why* we moved.

It wasn't convenience. My father no longer walked to the embassy. I had a longer bus ride to the American School. My mother complained that she had to endure more of the maddening midtown traffic to pick up groceries or take me to the park on weekends. So it wasn't a move that made our lives more convenient. It was something else entirely.

Even as a child I thought it odd that my parents spent time together talking to each other in the bathroom, always with the door closed and water running in the shower or tub. It was years before I stumbled across an explanation for this behavior. Within the intelligence community it was common knowledge that our phones were tapped; that surveillance was conducted on our movements, bank accounts, and friendships; and that our homes were bugged. Angleton was big on keeping tabs on anyone who was supposedly keeping secrets. It was normal to be observed by unseen others. It was normal to see my parents close the bathroom door and turn on water. With the water running, bugs were less able to capture voices.

I grew up being cautioned by my parents about what I said aloud in our apartment. In retrospect, I am fairly certain we moved into the new apartment because it had been fully equipped with the latest in electronic surveillance technology. Technology was a way of keeping tabs on those keeping secrets. Probably for this reason, my parents led strictly quiet lives. But it was my mother who was also quietly leading a life of increasing desperation.

Here is one memory I have of her that I think is telling.

When I recall that last year in London, I always remember that one day in the park. At the park, my mother and I walked in slow circles around a duck pond. This activity, for us, wasn't unusual. It wasn't fun but it was what we did together. We didn't talk. I fed the ducks crusts from day-old bread that we carried with us in a paper bag, and then we tossed the rest of the bread on the sidewalk for the already well-fed pigeons. But that one day drizzle became light rain. Light rain became a downpour. The pigeons fled.

I was cold and wet and after a few minutes I asked to go home. My mother, who, again in retrospect because at the time I didn't suspect that she was behaving oddly or that she lived mostly inside her own head, smiled her too-bright junior diplomat's wife smile and promptly put up our wide black umbrella. "Silly," she said. "Why didn't you tell me it was *raining* out here?"

. . . .

My father continued his work at the embassy. Tensions between the superpowers grew more ominous. As a child I had already acquired a rudimentary grammar for it involving words such as "superpowers" and "nuclear" and "war." I knew that the Americans, the French, and the British were strong allies; the Soviets and the Chinese and the North Koreans were mortal enemies; and Germany was divided. I could identify weapons of mass destruction as easily as I could identify military ranks by insignia on uniforms.

I couldn't yet understand the reasons for the cold war but I was sure our side was good and the other side was evil. I'm equally sure that children growing up on the other side of the Iron Curtain felt the same way, only in reverse. You fight for the side you are born on, and that side is *always* the right side.

When I played with my male friends—all of us kids from the embassy or sons of the military or defense contractors—we always played war. Killing each other and imagined others was our favorite pastime. Only when we were with girls did we pull out polite turn-taking games like Monopoly or Scrabble or agree to a round of tiddledywinks. But as boys, we played war games. The only turns we took were turns launching invasions, and if we could seize even a slight cheater's advantage on when to begin, we took it. We were merciless. We invented newer and better weapons, fashioned largely from our imaginations and aided by our naturally occurring environment. Balloons filled with water made bombs. The bigger the balloon, the larger the bomb; the wider the dispersion of water and the louder the screams of our victims, the better.

We divided ourselves into officers and enlisted men with the understanding that enlisted men died first. Who, under these rules of engagement, would volunteer to be an enlisted man? All of us did. We thrilled to the idea of battle. We worked ourselves into warrior frenzies and charged across fields, hid behind trees, made forts, and readily tossed toy grenades and fired toy rifles and pistols at passersby, at public buses, at random apartment buildings, and at each other. We were only eight or nine or ten years old and we were already prepared to give our lives for our country.

Children who grow up in war zones are always ready to fight. As children, we learn the language of warfare. We are fearless and proud. We don't question orders. We live for glorious victories or, failing that and if we find ourselves with no option other than to blow ourselves up to save our men, to save our country, to save the free world, well, then we just do it. That's what it means to be a soldier in a war. That's what it means to die with honor.

I remember my youthful war games when I watch the horror explode in the streets of Baghdad, or Fallujah, or Jerusalem, or amid the war-ruined burned-out tribal villages in Afghanistan and Iraq. I know firsthand how children acquire the grammar, and the logic, of war. It is a natural response to any fearful and dangerous environment, a natural part of learning how to be a young man among fighting men or a woman brave enough to sacrifice herself for a cause. I am not surprised that there are thousands of otherwise reasonable adolescents who, often uneducated and unemployed and surrounded by religious hatred, volunteer for this radical Islamic jihad and who then become terrorists and suicide bombers.

How could I be surprised? I, too, grew up in a war zone. But our war was a cold war, not the hotter war on terror, and my playmates were not living hand to mouth without hope or much of a future in an occupied country beholden to religious fanatics. I doubt the magical presidential words "freedom" and "democracy" have much diplomatic impact on these kids, except to strengthen their resolve against us and further fuel their acts of resistance. When we kill—for whatever reason—their mothers and fathers, brothers, sisters, aunts, uncles, and cousins, it only gets worse. It doesn't matter that we believe we are "right." As I said, when you grow up in a war zone, you fight for the side you were born on.

"Right" has nothing to do with it. Which is truly unfortunate, because in this war the children are already learning how to fight against us.

• •

One of the documents in my father's personnel file is labeled "Extension of Limited Assignment." Its effective date is August 7, 1959, probably about the time of our move into the apartment. It authorizes Mr. Harold L. Goodall (notice the slight change in his name) to extend his time in London until the following August 6, which the document claims is the "maximum period of time for a reserve appointment." I suppose his work—at least his work involving a reserve appointment—required an extension.

Reading over the document, I am pleased to see that he received a raise—to $7,810—although his rank remained stable at FSR-6. I find it curious that the date of the authorization is blacked out. Of all of the clues to my father's work for the United States government in London—his FSR rank, the terminology used to define "a reserve appointment"—the fact that a censor would have chosen the *date* to mark out seems somewhat odd.

But perhaps the date is important in some other way. Not as the date of a personnel action so much as a date that would appear incongruous with something else in the file, or with recorded history. But I can find nothing out of the ordinary that happened that particular day in history. So perhaps the real explanation is simpler. Perhaps the paperwork was late.

I don't know. But I do know that reserve appointments were typically for two years, so another oddity in this record is that my father's appointment to the Court of St. James had been in effect only since February 8, 1958, about seventeen months. It seems unusual, but probably not unheard of, that he would have been transferred to London for so short a period of time.

Two available explanations occur to me. First, my father may have been *temporarily* assigned to the embassy in London, although that isn't what his official transfer papers indicate. Still, it could be. The papers wouldn't have to indicate that it was a temporary posting. It could have been some sort of tryout to see if he would fit in, or perhaps if he were really needed.

DEPARTMENT OF STATE
WASHINGTON 25, D. C.

NOTIFICATION OF PERSONNEL ACTION

SERVICE
☒ FS ☐ DPTL

41790

1. NAME (Mr.-Miss-Mrs.-One given name, initial(s) and surname)	2. DATE OF BIRTH	3. JOURNAL OR ACTION NO.	4. DATE
Mr. Harold L. Goodall	10-17-22	FS 44	8-7-59

This is to notify you of the following action affecting your employment:

5. NATURE OF ACTION (Use standard terminology)	6. EFFECTIVE DATE	7. CIVIL SERVICE OR OTHER LEGAL AUTHORITY
Extension of Limited Assignment	8-7-59	

FROM: | TO:

8. POSITION TITLE	Veterans Affairs Officer
Diplomatic or Consular Title	Vice Consul
9. SCHEDULE, SERIES NO., GRADE, SALARY	FSR-6 $7810
10. ORGANIZATIONAL DESIGNATIONS Post	London
11. HEADQUARTERS	

12. DS CATEGORY
☐ FIELD ☐ DEPARTMENTAL ☐ Non-US
☐ Regular ☐ Resident
FS Category
☐ FIELD ☐ DEPARTMENTAL ☐ Non-US
☐ Regular ☐ Resident

13. VETERAN'S PREFERENCE
NONE 5-PT 10-POINT Disab. Other

14. POSITION CLASSIFICATION ACTION
NEW VICE I. A. REAL.
3-6471-427

15. SEX   M

16. APPROPRIATION
FROM
TO   OA-4012

17. RETIREMENT COVERAGE
☒ CSC ☐ FS
☐ FICA ☐ NONE

18. DATE OF APPOINTMENT AFFIDAVITS (Accessions Only)

19. LEGAL RESIDENCE
☐ CLAIMED ☐ PROVED
STATE:

20. This action is subject to all applicable laws, rules and regulations and may be subject to investigation and approval by the United States Civil Service Commission or the Department.

Limited Assignment effective 8-7-55 is hereby extended not to exceed 8-6-60, the legal maximum period of time for reserve appointments.

ENTRANCE PERFORMANCE RATING

21. SIGNATURE OR OTHER AUTHENTICATION

2.   PERSONNEL FOLDER

FIGURE 11.1 Extension of Lloyd's limited assignment in London, 1959.

Which brings me to the second possible explanation. Perhaps the lead he claimed to have had on Philby panned out. My guess is that by August 7, 1959, it had. But that is mere surmise. What I did know was that during our last year in London, my father traveled often to Berlin to work with Bill Harvey. Harvey himself had large doubts about Philby and I cannot believe they didn't discuss what they knew, and what they conjectured, with each other.

• •

Berlin, in 1960, was a divided city and tensions were high. If London was the nerve center of the anti-Soviet campaign, then Berlin was the front line proper. Here our troops patrolled along the barbed-wire fences and mined corridors, and guarded the infamous wall twenty-four hours a day, seven days a week. They carried fully armed weapons but had strict orders not to fire unless fired upon. There were 30- and 50-caliber machine-gun emplacements, mobile rocket launchers in plain view, and Sherman tanks awaiting what the enlisted men feared was inevitable and more than several generals secretly hoped would finally come—a full-scale invasion from the East, which is to say, from Russia through East Germany and right across Checkpoint Charlie.

There were tactical nuclear weapons in West Berlin. These were small handheld or shoulder-mounted devices resembling bazookas whose load was a small one- to two-megaton nuclear warhead. They were perfect for neutralizing the enemy at short range, which really meant vaporizing them and leaving behind enough radiation in the air to prevent any human being, however well protected or armored, from reentering the zone. These weapons of mass destruction were only to be used if necessary, although there was no doubt that it would be necessary if the invasion from the East started.

Pity the poor bastard firing one. In a museum in Huntsville, Alabama, I saw one of these tactical relics—unarmed, of course—and did the math. One conclusion was clear. Its effective blast and radiation range ensured the man firing it couldn't reach safety. He—or, these days, maybe she—would have been roughly equivalent to a suicide bomber on a nuclear scale.

The brutal fact of the actual existence of such a poorly designed tactical battlefield weapon as well as detailed instructions on how to deploy it provides further evidence of the insane state of military tensions between the superpowers at that time. That, practically speaking, such a weapon would be designed and built and distributed to military personnel in Europe without first being field tested is even further evidence of the extreme mental imbalance that defines the cold war nuclear age. But then again, the fact that during this same period of time megaton nuclear weaponry was quickly overshadowed by kiloton nuclear warheads that were then superseded by multiple warhead intercontinental ballistic missiles capable of wiping out life on planet Earth tens of thousands of times over is probably cultural evidence enough of nuclear warfare insanity.

In our present time such a state of mind is often difficult to imagine or even to recall. We have, as a culture, a short nuclear attention span. Since the Berlin Wall came down it has grown frightfully shorter. Most Americans have no idea how many nuclear weapons were constructed, how many are still stored, or how many are still unaccounted for.

Bryan Taylor, a preeminent cultural studies scholar and former president of the Rocky Flats Nuclear Museum in Colorado, writes eloquently about the untold human fallout from the nuclear age. He explains that leakage alone from nuclear sites has poisoned land, air, and water as well as human beings in virtually every storage facility and surrounding areas, and that the numbers of radiation-associated cancers, infant mortality, and other fatal diseases continue to rise as awareness of the intimate relationship between nuclear testing and long-term health consequences are established.

That women and men on both sides of the cold war built and deployed these weapons of mass destruction knowing their casings would deteriorate within as little as seven years and without a plan for containing the waste is part of the untold fallout story that lives within us all. But, of course, back then, in the cold war days, we more or less counted on the inevitability of using those weapons *before* they would deteriorate. The tragic irony is that even though we didn't use them, it doesn't make them, or us, safe. We live contaminated by weapons of our own mutually assured destruction.

Behind the front lines and throughout Europe there were secret nuclear missile sites containing intermediate-range ballistic missiles (IRBMs) that were only to be launched if an all-out military invasion in Berlin began. However, the presence of our nukes in Europe heightened the alarm most Europeans felt and, by late 1959, had become problematic for the political futures of some of our closest allies. In top-secret documents available in the Dwight D. Eisenhower Memorial Library, evidence of resistance at the highest levels to American nuclear power is clear. For example, Prime Minister Charles de Gaulle called us "selfish" in regard to decisions about the placement of nuclear weapons and used this position to leverage other concerns about our leadership of NATO and the strong presence of our military forces throughout the continent. Throughout the spring of 1960, our closest ally, British Prime Minister Harold Macmillan, tried to get President Eisenhower to find an alternative location for our Polaris nuclear submarines due to growing protest in the UK over American nuclear weapons being housed on their shores. We wanted to use the dock facility at Clyde to house the Polaris fleet, but Macmillan feared that placing nuclear submarines in a facility so close to Glasgow was unwise. Only after we agreed not to launch a Polaris-based nuclear strike within a hundred miles of the UK coastline did Macmillan agree to it.

Similarly, the Italian government—with far less success—balked at our proposal to place IRBMs along its northern borders back in 1956, but we placed them there anyway. In the Dulles archives, housed in the Seeley G. Mudd Manuscript Library at Princeton University, are microfilm accounts of the daily intelligence briefings given by Secretary of State John Foster Dulles to President Eisenhower that reveal how futile the Italian objections were. "The President of Italy objects in the most stringent terms to the placement of IRBMs in his country," one report begins. "Duly noted," is the dry response. The missiles were, in fact, already in place.

In 1960 Europe was ready for an atomic showdown with the Soviets. Everyone knew where it would happen: Berlin. The only remaining question was when, and how, it would begin. The only thing standing between us and losing a balls-out thermonuclear world war was the success of intelligence gathering on the ground and through new electronic surveillance devices at the front.

· ·

Bill Harvey was the CIA chief of station in Berlin. He was by all accounts a squat, fat, pistol-toting former FBI man from Indiana with an insatiable appetite for women, double martinis, and hands-on espionage. He would later in his career be introduced to President John F. Kennedy as "the American James Bond" and, partially as a result of that iconic reference, he would be asked to organize the assassination of Fidel Castro. It was a plan that failed miserably, dragging Harvey's reputation for success and his career ambitions down with it.

But in the Berlin winter of 1959–60, Bill Harvey's reputation was still the genuine stuff of legend. He was one of the most experienced field officers in the Agency, a veteran at ferreting out spies and coordinating intelligence-gathering efforts. But his reputation had been stamped in gold in Berlin. He had been credited as the mastermind behind the infamous Berlin tunnel.

The tunnel—dubbed "Harvey's Hole" by Allen Dulles—was a technical marvel. With a then-unprecedented $25-to-30-million price tag, it had served as an intelligence listening post for us for eleven months in 1955–56. It was expensive and it was illegal—it did, after all, violate the sanctity of the East Berlin border in ways that made President Eisenhower very unhappy when it was discovered. But it served Allied interests during the months of its operation and was considered by insiders *the* source of major intelligence for future penetrations of the Soviet espionage network. The tunnel may have also prevented a nuclear war, in that it provided the first-ever information that suggested a massive Soviet attack along the Berlin divide was unfeasible because the railway lines required to transport troops, tanks, and supplies—lines severely damaged by Allied bombing during the war—were not yet capable of sustaining heavy traffic. It also provided details of Soviet troop movements that were then matched against previously recorded cipher codes, which in turn led to our ability to decipher the Soviet codes for the first time since 1947.

For the eleven months of its operation it provided us with what we believed at the time was an unprecedented advantage in intelligence gathering. Harvey's Hole was our secret. But then the tunnel was "discovered" one morning by the acting commandant of East Berlin, Colonel Ivan A. Kotsyuba, on April 21, 1956. Seizing the propaganda opportunity for a worldwide audience to witness America's illegal surveillance on the free and peace-loving people of East Germany, the good colonel invited the whole of the Berlin press corps to tour the site. He explained, calmly and with good humor, that if they followed the line of the tunnel west, they would find themselves housed in an American military building with a recently installed radio transmitter on the roof.

Our official response to the exposure was a testy if stony silence. But if the Soviets intended to show the world how devious we were, the plan seriously backfired. The tunnel became a source of pride in the West for the inventiveness of Americans and of the superiority of our technological know-how. It became a major tourist attraction and a snack bar was even installed. Today, visitors can see a replica of it in the International Spy Museum in Washington, D.C.

Harvey's Hole also represented an early victory for those in the Agency and Congress who saw electronic surveillance as the future of espionage. The days of extreme black budgets for field operations were being replaced by even more extreme black budgets to support research and development of new technologies. Harvey's Hole was touted as a victory for our side in the cold war, as well as the pudding proof of electronic surveillance in a nuclear age, but had the operation really been the success story we believed it to be?

It depended on whom you believed, for how long you believed them, and on how you told the end of the story. Even when the tunnel was supposedly discovered, there were some in the intelligence community who doubted that the Soviets hadn't already known about it. After all, it was an "acting commandant" from the Soviet Union who had "accidentally" happened upon it that barely sunny April morning. The real East German commandant was—shall we say conveniently—out of town. If the Russians already knew about the tunnel, perhaps it had been "discovered" simply because the new man hadn't been thoroughly briefed.

Or perhaps because he *had* been briefed. If the Russians knew about the tunnel but had decided that it no longer suited their best interest to pretend they didn't know, perhaps they had temporarily assigned Colonel Kotsyuba to the zone so that *he* would be the one to make the discovery, thus protecting the supposed innocence of the real commandant, and, by extension, the "integrity" of the Soviets' deepest secret, which was that *they already knew*. If that possibility existed, it meant that the Soviet Union was using the existence of the listening post to pass along their own misinformation.

These deductions, guesses, and hypotheses, are, of course, the product of speculation and hindsight. But it is hindsight that may be justified. In 1961, we learned that the tunnel operation had been blown by the Soviets almost as soon as it had been given approval in Washington. George Blake, a British intelligence officer privy to the details of every major CIA operation in Europe since the early 1950s, confessed it to Ferguson Smith, of MI5. Blake's confession was devastating to intelligence services on both sides of the Atlantic, because it meant that all of our supposed victories and breakthroughs had, in fact, been done with the full knowledge and probable support of the Soviets.

His confession, his story, turned the CIA and MI5 upside down. It gave an incoherence to the ongoing narrative of the Great Game. It messed up the story line. It fouled up the symbolic order in the nature of intelligence things.

The penalty for these violations was harsh. Blake was convicted as a British traitor and handed a forty-two-year sentence for espionage. How-

ever, after eight years in captivity, Blake escaped from Wormwood Scrubs
Prison by jumping out of a window with the aid of a man he had befriended
in prison—Sean Bourke. Blake lay low for a while in Bourke's flat not five
minutes from the prison proper. He then easily, if somewhat nervously,
crossed the Channel on the Dover-to-Ostende ferry, walked into East Berlin, and was promptly escorted to Moscow. There, George Blake, former
British subject and senior intelligence officer, formally defected and was
awarded the Order of Lenin in a public ceremony.

But even that august betrayal was not necessarily the end of this intricate spy vs. spy story. Blake may have been fed the details of his own
confession by his Soviet handler in London to further bolster the fear in
Western intelligence circles that their supposedly trusted networks were, in
fact, well-known in Moscow. What better coup! Take what you *don't* know,
feed it back as a fact, and wait to see what happens.

Regardless of whether or not there was Soviet knowledge of the tunnel
during its season of operation, this ingenious counterplan worked. If the
Soviets had, in fact, known about it, Blake was providing evidence of Soviet
superiority in intelligence matters via his confession. If the Soviets did not
know about it, not only would there be the same net result, but it would pay
dividends worldwide. Formerly secret agents and contacts behind the Iron
Curtain reading about the confession believed that they were already being
played. Fearing imminent exposure, they took unnecessary risks, made mistakes, and thus made their exposure and capture far more likely.

Or worse. If caught they could be offered one and only one option: to
be turned against their own agencies and governments. If the subject were
already operating in this risky role as a double, then no doubt they would be
offered a chance to turn again, this time serving as a triple. As my ex-KGB
friend Richard once explained it to me, "You never know what you truly
believe, or what you will actually do, until we put a gun to your head."

Failing that test, the poor son of a bitch would simply be eliminated.

This, too, was how the Great Game was played.

. . . .

Why did my father make those trips to Berlin?

Bill Harvey, in addition to being the mastermind behind the Berlin tunnel, had also been the man inside the Agency who authored the top-secret
memo raising suspicions about Philby back in 1951. Harvey had arrived
at his intuitive conclusions while stalled at a Washington traffic light,

shortly after learning about the defections of Burgess and Maclean. As he later told friends, it was at this traffic light that all of the dirty pieces of this particular puzzle fell clearly into place, and each connecting piece had Philby's name on it:

1. Philby had been in charge of the Volkov defection fiasco in Istanbul.

2. Philby had known both Burgess and Maclean since their Trinity College days at Cambridge, and Philby was the one man perfectly placed to know *beforehand* about the allegations raised about them and to tip off both of them about the impending investigation.

3. Philby's "above suspicion" status as a member of the English upper class only further supported any espionage allegations made against him. While still in the FBI, Harvey had worked on the Alger Hiss and Elizabeth Bentley cases, and he knew that wealth had its privileges, but that one of them should never be that the privileged are above suspicion.

Harvey's deductions, amplified by his distrust of privilege, led to one inescapable conclusion: Philby was a Red. He wrote his memo and bad-mouthed Philby around town.

Harvey and Angleton clashed mightily over his conclusions.

Angleton wrote his own top-secret memo clearing his friend. Angleton had few friends throughout his lifetime in the clandestine world and Philby was one of them. Angleton never liked big, bad Bill Harvey, and this allegation against Philby, this public insult to his judgment, was one that he would never forget nor forgive.

Angleton, you recall, until the end of his life believed that he had *never* once been wrong.

My father's final visit to Harvey's domain in Berlin in 1960 could be understood as any one of a number of operational things, but I believe it was all about Kim Philby. Or rather, it was really all about fitting together the pieces of a larger puzzle involving my father, Philby, and the beliefs Harvey held about Philby, and the beliefs that Angleton held about them all.

Whatever transpired during that last visit to Berlin, it sealed my father's fate with Angleton. Perhaps Angleton resented my father's continuing allegations about Philby and saw the alliance between my father and Harvey as something that threatened his position within the Agency. Men and women were—and still are—ruined for less in many organizations. Or perhaps Angleton simply seized the opportunity to bury my father on purely bureaucratic grounds: he had reached the end of his "extended limited assignment." That, too, is often given as reason enough to reassign a problem employee out of town, particularly if the problem employee works for the government. Or perhaps it was something else.

Whatever Angleton's reason, suddenly transferring a seasoned intelligence officer from a strategic cold war location to a pitiful one-horse town in the middle of nowhere is beyond suspect. It reeks of ulterior motive.

It was, as my mother put it, "complicated."

. . . .

Our dramatic change of circumstances occurred without warning. I remember still being in school, which is why I know our hasty departure from London did not occur in August. It was earlier, perhaps late May or early June.

An embassy car arrived for me at the American School and, instead of driving me home to our apartment, took me to Heathrow Airport. There, waiting for me, were my mother and father. I've tried to recall their faces but it's no use trying. The swirl and confusion of the day is all I recall. I'm not sure we even had baggage.

My mother explained that we were going home.

The next thing I knew we landed in Washington, D.C.

. . . .

My father's official termination papers as a Veterans Affairs officer for the State Department were filed on a date that has been scratched out by the censor. The date that is officially given—August 25, 1960—is inaccurate as far as I know. It doesn't correspond to our arrival back in the States nor does it match up with our physical departure from the Washington, D.C., area. It may have been the date used to settle State Department records and financial accounts, or it may have been a date selected for some unknown clandestine reason by the censor. I'll never know.

I find it interesting that the filing authority is given as one "J. J. Jova." Was this an alias for James Jesus Angleton? Angleton was a wordsmith with a wry sense of humor. The J. J. certainly corresponds to his first and middle initials, and the "Jova" could be short for "Jehovah." He was the Lord and Master to his flock.

The language of the reason given is also rhetorically telling. "Expiration of limited assignment." Had my father remained in Angleton's good graces, my bet is the language would have read "Completion." Not expiration. Expiration is a passive final action. It is a way to signal the end of a career without further elaboration.

Persona non grata. The words aren't on this termination paper, but they were recorded in my father's personal diary. At the time I first saw the words, I had no idea what they meant. I only know they were on the same page with the word "Angleton."

I have to believe that the government censor could have done a much better job of covering up the factual inaccuracies. If the person filling out this form had only checked the original paperwork, she or he would have known that my father was scheduled to remain in London until August 6, 1960. The person responsible for filling out this termination form could have made an effort to align this form with the officially recorded dates.

Or have bothered to check his reported salary. Where did this raise in pay come from? There is no supporting paperwork. I would have thought at least the government file clerk and/or the later censor would have done that. Or corrected the juvenile spelling of "Vetrans."

But no. I suppose there was no real need. On paper it was probably enough to indicate that his limited assignment had expired. That "all leave [was to be] transferred to the VA upon receipt of 1960 leave card" strikes me as peculiarly bureaucratic. My father had, until recently, been able to commandeer naval vessels in the Suez as well as seats for his family at the captain's table with Walt Disney, carry large sums of illegal monies on behalf of the President of the United States, and, if necessary, commit murder. Yet now he was reduced in status to someone so ordinary as to have to formally account for his annual leave.

With this final paperwork, my father simply ceased to exist for the State Department. Officially, he had been dumped back to the Veterans Administration from whence he supposedly came. The forwarding address given—Route 4, Martinsburg, West Virginia—doesn't even contain the courtesy of a box number, making it highly unlikely that any mail from Washington would ever find him along that heavily wooded rural lane. For the record, it was the address of the highway that ran along a road adjacent to my grandparents' farm. It is their route number and Martinsburg was, at that time, within the general mailing vicinity.

DEPARTMENT OF STATE
WASHINGTON 25, D. C.

NOTIFICATION OF PERSONNEL ACTION

SERVICE
☐ FS   ☐ DPTL

41790

1. NAME (Mr.-Miss-Mrs.-One given name, initial(s) and surname)	2. DATE OF BIRTH	3. JOURNAL OR ACTION NO.	4. DATE
(Category C) Mr. Harold L. Goodall	10-17-22	FS-28	8-25-60 ~~XXXXXXX~~

This is to notify you of the following action affecting your employment:

5. NATURE OF ACTION (Use standard terminology)	6. EFFECTIVE DATE	7. CIVIL SERVICE OR OTHER LEGAL AUTHORITY
Termination of Limited Assignment	CO 8-6-60	

FROM:		TO:
Vetrans Affairs Officer 3-6471-427 Vice Consul	**8. POSITION TITLE** Diplomatic or Consular Title	
FSR-6 $8655	**9. SCHEDULE, SERIES NO., GRADE, SALARY**	
	10. ORGANIZATIONAL DESIGNATIONS Post	
London - 232	**11. HEADQUARTERS**	
☐ FIELD ☐ DEPARTMENTAL ☐ Regular ☐ Resident ☐ Non-US	**12. DS CATEGORY** FS Category	☐ FIELD ☐ DEPARTMENTAL ☐ Regular ☐ Resident ☐ Non-US

13. VETERAN'S PREFERENCE			14. POSITION CLASSIFICATION ACTION			
NONE 5-PT	10-POINT Disab. Other		NEW	VICE	I. A.	REAL.

15. SEX	16. APPROPRIATION	17. RETIREMENT COVERAGE	18. DATE OF APPOINTMENT AFFIDAVITS (Accessions Only)	19. LEGAL RESIDENCE
M	FROM 1A-4026 - 2337 TO	☒ CSC ☐ FS ☐ FICA ☐ NONE	☐ CLAIMED ☐ PROVED STATE:

20. This action is subject to all applicable laws, rules and regulations and may be subject to investigation and approval by the United States Civil Service Commission or the Department.

Reason: Expiration of Limited Assignment.

All leave transferred to the V.A. upon receipt of 1960 leave card.

Address: Route no. 4
Martinsburg, West Virginia.

ENTRANCE PERFORMANCE RATING	21. SIGNATURE OR OTHER AUTHENTICATION
	★ U. S. GOVERNMENT PRINTING OFFICE: 1959—499499

PERSONNEL FOLDER

FIGURE 11.2 Termination of Lloyd's Foreign Service assignment, August 1960.

The lack of even a mailing address was a sign that he was finished and he probably read it as such. But he was determined not to let it defeat him.

We did not move back to the farm in Martinsburg during his transition, but instead we were housed in a temporary apartment serving the needs of military officers and other government agency workers in Fairfax, Virginia. It was not a good time for us.

It was summer in Washington. It was hot and humid. There was no air-conditioning in our rental unit. Our furniture and belongings were in transit and then in storage. Someone had packed up our apartment for us.

My mother, by then desperately worried about my father as well as anxious about our future and fretful over her "English addictions," became so nervous that it was all she could do to prop me in front of the television set in the morning with a bowl of Cheerios and return to her bedroom. She closed the door and I remember hearing her cry.

My father didn't return to our rental unit. He was "gone." My mother didn't know exactly where he was, but I suppose she had gotten used to that. I suppose I had gotten used to it, too. I don't remember being frightened by his absence, only aware of it as a more or less constant in our ever-changing lives.

Later I would learn that my father went into Washington and knocked on a lot of doors. He called on old friends but received in return only their commiserations. It was a time of change. There was a lot of talk about the fall elections and the possibility of a Kennedy win. People at State maintained that if Kennedy were elected, he would clean house and people at the Agency had already prepared for it.

But the change that was taking place in America was larger than that. It was the end of an era. The cold war would last another thirty-one years, but the election in 1960 marked the end of the beginning of it. It had been a beginning defined by good old-fashioned human intelligence gathering and analysis. It had been the iconic era of spy vs. spy. It had been a high time. for the old boys of Dulles, Wisner, and Angleton's literary crowd, for moderate Republicanism in foreign policy, and for a postwar economic boom (and with it, a higher standard of living, home ownership in the suburbs, more educational and social programs, and better cars and highways) that settled for the vast majority of Americans the threat that Communism posed to our American Way of Life. The Red Menace, after a relentless domestic campaign to win the hearts and minds of the public, had been effectively tagged and would be forever demonized. Only one task remained: removing that Communist threat from the face of the earth, before, as the poet Allen Ginsberg once put it, "them Russians, them Russians, them Chinamen, and them Russians" removed *us* from the face of the earth.

Technology was the answer. Intelligence gathering was becoming more SIGINT than HUMINT and budgets were being adjusted accordingly. Seasoned field officers were being retired or reassigned. New women and men, college educated in science, mathematics, statistics, and computational engineering, replaced English and history majors in the recruitment pools.

Technology, or the practical application of scientific solutions to human problems as well as to the cold war, was the new hope of a new generation. In 1955 Jacques Ellul characterized the blossoming modern technological society by the pervasive presence of what he termed *la technique*, "the totality of methods rationally arrived at and having absolute efficiency (for a given stage of development) in every field of human activity." *La technique* was not so much a new way of solving problems—scientific methods had spawned new technologies since the dawn of the Industrial Age—as it was a new way of organizing society for the production of technologies capable of reducing the dependence of those societies on the labor and the fallibilities of humans.

By 1960, with increasing nuclear tensions and the fate of competing ideologies as well as the earth at stake, anything that removed the possibility of human error from the drama of everyday life was considered not only a sign of "progress" but moreover an inevitable movement forward in humankind's relentless pursuit of a perfectible state. In this way, technological superiority was equated not only with better intelligence but with better national security. We were investing in our *safety*, not just in fancy surveillance machines and robots and missiles.

But this proved to be a somewhat flawed premise. As we learned from the 9/11 Commission Report, there is no substitute for ongoing intelligence collection on the ground in foreign countries. Satellites capture images, but human beings capture nuances and subtleties of language, culture, and religion. *La technique* should augment but never replace human intelligence gathering.

· ·

I cannot know for sure what transpired when my father met Angleton in Washington. The diary was not much help.

I only know that my father firmly believed that whatever he claimed to know about Philby was the reason he was condemned to a long exile in

Wyoming. I also know that by piecing together the evidence from events prior to that turn in our family's affairs and by the evidence emerging from the events after it—particularly those of July 1963—this belief seems a plausible explanation.

I have a theory. But that is all I have. My theory is based on years of night reading about James Jesus Angleton, spies, intelligence agencies, politics, and the cold war that occurred while I was performing my day job as a college professor doing ethnographic fieldwork and analyzing communication in organizations. I found myself seeing parallels between the Angleton I came to know in memoirs and novels and the other rare men of genius and madness who exercised power over others in high-tech organizations and government agencies.

There is a familiar pattern in this sort of organizational behavior. The men I witnessed (and they were all men) were brilliant and manipulative while being singularly interested in the essential centrality of themselves. They framed and therefore understood the ongoing action from their own center-stage perspective and believed themselves to be vital to the unfolding drama of everyday organizational life. These men defined their leadership role by their ability to influence, if not control, the destinies of others and the organization they ran within a broader community, a profession, and, in one or two notable cases, a worldwide market. Taken only so far, these leadership traits, habits, and skills characterize many successful people who, while a little self-obsessed, nevertheless use their authority to shape positive outcomes for their organizations and the people around them.

Taken a little bit further, these same character traits define a dangerous ego-obsessed mentality. What we see is a classic Machiavellian control freak, often a noxious but effective political game player thoroughly skilled, more than willing, and easily capable of using others as pawns in order to achieve his own interests, goals, pleasures, and stature.

Taken to the full extreme, we find an Angleton. We find a brilliant, manipulative, ego-obsessed, highly effective, political game player interested in controlling destinies who becomes, for whatever reason, terribly paranoid. Reading the work of criminologist Lonnie Athens I have learned that these men, if exposed to a violent early life and if they then find themselves rewarded for acts of violence against others, often become cold-blooded killers.

In my experience as an ethnographic observer in organizations, this criminal pathology can also be turned into what Kenneth Burke calls "the symbolic kill." For men like Angleton, steeped in the natural entitlements spawned by upper-class values and already poetically inclined, the Great Game of espionage was largely one of manipulating others to do the necessary dirty work while maintaining control over the narrative of the whole world. For anyone caught threatening the coherence of their own beautiful lie, there is only one outcome: the kill, or the symbolic kill. It is probably further evidence of my narrative inheritance that I have written about the performance-appraisal interview as a form of a symbolic kill.

But I also read this pivotal moment in my family's history in relation to the larger coherence of the Agency's narrative, and particularly Angleton's personal narrative. By 1960 Angleton had control over the narrative of the Great Game that my father's allegations threatened. If my father was right and Philby was Red, and worse, if Philby was still working for the Soviets, Angleton would have been wrong. For a paranoid, that is bad enough. But for Angleton, and for men like him, the complexity and integrity of the self become intricately intertwined with the necessity of achieving coherence in the everyday narrative story line. There is no admitting they were wrong. Or even that they have made a mistake.

Philby spying for the Soviets would be, for Angleton, an act of personal betrayal as well as a flaw in the progression of his personal narrative. Admitting he was wrong would prove he had been duped, played as a fool. He would lose authority if not his official position in the Agency. He would be second-guessed, effectively forever, and with this admission of his own fallibility, he would forfeit narrative control over the game. For Angleton, for the man he had talked himself into becoming, that could not be allowed to happen.

What no doubt made it worse was that my father was not even of his social class or Agency pedigree. How could a man like my father be allowed to bring him down? No. It could *not* be allowed to happen. Furthermore, my father's insistence that J. J. Jova—er, pardon me, Angleton—was wrong about Philby was probably perceived as an act of personal as well as hierarchical betrayal. Angleton had cultivated my father, brought him along, trained him, and promoted him from a pawn to a knight. How dare he challenge him!

I believe Angleton could stand no further penetration into his professional affairs. No more editorial intrusions into his way of telling—and of cultivating—the story. No more questions about how he brought his characters along.

There was only one thing to do. Rather than terminate him—symbolically or in fact—Angleton would simply allow my father's appointment to the cold war to "expire." It was passive, it was aggressive, and it communicated a clear and present message: my father's clandestine role in James Jesus Angleton's clandestine story was *over*.

So Angleton did what Angletons everywhere do. It is what I've witnessed other men who are infected with power and who have an unreasonable need for control, and who are also in charge of departments, sections, units, and companies, do. He removed the threat symbolically. He performed rhetorical last rites, this symbolic kill, in his office in Washington on a day sometime at the end of August in 1960. It was easy. Neat. And perfectly within his rights, given the legitimate authority he held over the whole of counterintelligence at the CIA.

He allowed my father's appointment to expire. He then denied my father's request for another overseas posting—a posting that would have furthered my father's counternarrative about Philby—and instead of firing him he exiled him, exiled the whole of my family, to the nether regions of the world known as Cheyenne, Wyoming. Out there in the American Siberia, away from the center stage, Angleton could watch over him, manipulate him, taunt him, laugh at him, and ultimately maintain control over his story.

Angleton's bespectacled eyes were, for my father, those of Dr. T. J. Eckleburg. Our valley of ashes was instead a godforsaken windswept prairie.

It was Angleton, and only Angleton, who declared my father *persona non grata*.

• •

My father's State Department career under cover as a vice consul was over. Any hopes he may have had for advancement within the clandestine service were over as well. He would still be doing Agency work, but he wouldn't like it. He was *persona non grata* in Washington, too.

My father's last words to Angleton were not recorded in his diary. I wish they were. I think I can imagine what they might have been: "*Ugadat, ugodit, utselet.*" It's Russian for "Pay attention, ingratiate, survive."

What other choice would he have had? He was, as he later put it in group, "hung out on the spy line." His new job was to pay attention, ingratiate himself, and just find a way to survive.

• •

J. J. Angleton grew rare orchids in his private garden. He also created his own hybrids, flowers that had never before existed in nature but that through his careful cultivation achieved their bloom.

Orchids are particularly poetic flowers, with petals so delicate to the touch that they feel almost like human skin. Angleton believed that orchids possess unique characters or souls. He once said that just as the characters in any good story often took years to mature, so too did these fine orchids often require years of patient handling before they would grace us with a bloom.

He said that the bloom of a rare orchid is an exquisite thing, but, for the gardener, cultivating that eventual bloom is far more rewarding. It is how the flower is coaxed into exposing itself that is the true source of its intoxicating beauty.

Perhaps Angleton saw the orchid as a fitting expression of his own life. Of his own work, of his unique calling. He was a man who knew all there was to know about making orchids bloom, a man who appreciated the longer story, or the full life cycle of a particular flower, something that required years of study just to understand.

12

Wyoming

1960–1961

WE DROVE TO CHEYENNE IN LATE JULY OR EARLY AUGUST. THE WEATHER was extraordinarily hot and humid. Of course, for a family who had just spent the last two years in London, anything over 70 degrees was extraordinarily hot. Perhaps it wasn't uncomfortable by local standards. Perhaps our complaints about the weather were merely signs of a more general malaise.

I remember feeling trapped in the backseat of our Opel for long days that seemed like long years as we crossed a vast expanse of open land. Years later, reading Kafka's *Amerika*, I laughed aloud when I realized that for K., Oklahoma was located just outside New York City. It mirrored what I thought as a child before making that trip: I thought Wyoming was just outside Washington, D.C.

I had no idea how far away from everything I had known the state of Wyoming really was.

. . . .

We arrived in Cheyenne on a Saturday. Or at least I think it was Saturday because there was no traffic. It could have been Sunday.

My father insisted on seeing the "city," which, as I recall, took about fifteen minutes. Cheyenne is the capital of Wyoming, but in 1960 the town proper stretched barely three miles in length. The population was thirty thousand.

"*Shit*," my father said when we reached the western end of the city limits. What else could he have said? Having spent the past five years living in Rome and London, this unlovely cow of a town on the prairie must have seemed beneath him, an insult even at eye level. I think that was the first time he fully accepted what being *persona non grata* meant for any future unfolding of the story of his life.

We located an efficiency motel in what passed for downtown Cheyenne. The motel was old and run-down, a squat pueblo structure mostly inhabited by traveling salesmen and refinery workers who had been temporarily assigned to the huge outlying Frontier oil facility. We didn't remain in the motel very long. My parents arranged for the immediate purchase of a small ranch house, but I can still remember Cheyenne as it appeared from the door of that efficiency hotel.

I had never seen anything like it.

I was in the American West. The spaces were wide and open, the splendid colorful sunsets spread out across five hundred miles of available horizon. The air was noticeably cleaner and considerably thinner. Breathing was harder, my father told us, because of the high altitude. But the quality of air was better, he said, lighting a cigarette.

While in temporary quarters at the motel, we ate dinner in the Frontier Hotel, which looked a lot like Kitty's saloon on *Gunsmoke*. There was a store called the Hitching Post on the main street that actually had hitching posts outside for horses, if you cared to ride into town on one. I wondered if people did. In the evenings, I heard my first South of the Border music played on one of the two local radio stations. The other one featured static and sports, and when we arrived there were nightly games of scratchy baseball on the air. I had never heard of baseball. I didn't understand the rules. I didn't recognize the names of Stan "The Man" Musial, or Mickey Mantle, or Whitey Ford, or Willie Mays.

My soccer ball in the car seemed strangely out of place. But our foreign car seemed out of place, too.

We seemed out of place.

I saw men in cowboy hats and boots walking around as if it were perfectly normal to walk around wearing cowboy hats and boots. It would take time for me to realize that in Wyoming it *was* perfectly normal to dress like that. But then, it would take all three of us some time to realize what we needed to adapt to in order to fit in with the local culture. Although we spoke the same language, this would prove more challenging than fitting into the culture and customs in Rome or London.

I entered Wyoming public school speaking with a British accent. I had on my school clothes from London. I dressed like a proper young English gentleman, which seemed to the locals very odd indeed. It didn't take long for them to ask my mother to have me "say something in English" to them.

I was recognized as an American citizen everywhere else in the world, just not yet in my new American home. In Wyoming, I would have to learn how to be an American. But that was okay. I had once wanted to be a cowboy. Now I lived in a state where a cowboy on a bucking bronco replaced the DPL on our license plates.

• •

"Containment." It means "action taken to restrict the spread of something hostile such as an enemy, or something undesirable such as a disease." It was also a cold war term first advanced by George Kennan and later adopted as a principle of American foreign policy that defined our approach to stopping the spread of Communism. By containing Communism, we could control it.

When I think of that definition, I think of our family exiled in Wyoming. Which were we—the enemy or a disease? Or were we all suffering from the same dis-ease? Either way, Angleton contained my father and controlled the destiny of my family.

• •

My father worked at the VA center on East Pershing Boulevard. Or at least at the time I believed that was where his work was done. It would be years before I connected the dots and saw clearly the relationship between my father's "work" for the VA and the VA's relationship to the Francis E. Warren Air Force Base. Or understood what the Francis E. Warren Air Force Base had to do with the ongoing conduct of the cold war. Or thought about the incongruities between the skill sets that my father had developed as an Agency officer and those that he supposedly needed to perform as a contact officer for the VA.

Among the papers contained in his dummy folder are two Xerox copies supposedly summarizing the "training" my father had during his career with the Veterans Administration. One of the oddities of these documents is that virtually all of his training took place from October of 1960 to October of 1966, or, put differently, during the time we were reassigned to Cheyenne, Wyoming. Given that he had supposedly been working as a Veterans Affairs representative in Europe, and that he had a background in contact office duties in Martinsburg and Beckley prior to that, I find it unusual that he was required to receive training in even the most basic elements of a contact officer's job, including "refresher" courses designed to explain to him what the job actually was.

More peculiar still are the titles of some of the courses he was required to complete: "telephone techniques," "plain letters," and "fire safety procedures." I imagine my father in those classes and don't know whether to cry or laugh. He still carried his golden stiletto. I have no doubt there were days in classes like these when he seriously wanted to slit his own throat.

I note that most of the courses were completed during his first year in Cheyenne. That could mean one of two things. Either this reassignment back to the VA was real and that he had duties and responsibilities as a contact officer for which he needed to be retrained, or that these two Xeroxed pages are part of his legend, the imaginative manufacture of a dull afternoon on East Pershing Boulevard.

I can see him perusing a list of in-house seminars and finding those items most likely relevant to the life of an ordinary contact officer. I can imagine him using those items to make up a list such as this one.

The conundrum represented by these two photocopies remains. I lean toward accepting the evidence of them as factual. Even if they form part of my father's cover story, the courses may well have been required of him. Trying to imagine him in these training courses gives me a large clue as to why he felt punished in Wyoming. For a proud man in midcareer who very recently had far greater duties and responsibilities, who had run agents in Europe using codebooks, and who had interactions with some of the world's most celebrated people, being forced to complete courses in "telephone courtesies" or "the in-basket exercise" must have been a singularly depressing letdown.

But these emotional considerations of his state of mind and appreciation of his frustrated perspective came to me much later. When he reported for work—whatever his "work" was—I knew only that my father entered the building known as the Veterans Administration Regional Center in Cheyenne, Wyoming. He had a large office on the main floor and a nice secretary named Eleanor.

CUMULATIVE RECORD OF TRAINING AND DEVELOPMENT

1. NAME OF EMPLOYEE					2. DATE OF ENTRY IN GOVT. SERVICE	
GOODALL, Harold L.					4-22-1946	

3. TITLE OF COURSE OR ACTIVITY	4. TRAINING FACILITY OR SERVICE	5. NON-GOVT. (PL 85-507)	6. OTHER	7. HOURS OF TRAINING	8. DATE COMPLETED
Refresher Training Program for Contact Representative	3015		X	28	12-13-51
Position Classification for Supervisors	6187		X	2	?
Integrated Hearing and Appeal Procedure	"		X	1-1/2	?
Budget Seminar	4042		X	8	10-27-60
Contact Representatives Refresher Training Course	"		X	16	11-29-60
Better Group Meetings, and Effective Two-Way Communications	"		X	10-1/2	1-19-61
Training and Telephone Techniques	"		X	1	3-20-61
Training in Systematic Review	"		X	2	3-30-61
Contact Representative Refresher Training Course	"		X	16	5-16-61
Safety and Fire Protection Training	"		X	4	5-12-61
Work Simplification Training	"		X	5	5-25-61
Training on Preparation of FM 20-6566	"		X	1	9-21-61
Health Benefits "Open Season" Training	"		X	1	9-28-61
Contact Representative Refresher Training Course	"		X	16	11-17-61
Administrative Lecture Program on Work Measurement and the Development of Work Standards	"		X	4	12-11-61
Job Instruction Training	"		X	7-1/2	11-16-61
Telephone Courtesies	"		X	1	3- 9-62
The In-Basket Exercise	"		X	3	2-15-62
Managing Your Work and The Role of the Supervisor in Effective Personnel Management	"		X	18	4-15-62
"Why!" (Chicago School Fire)	"		X	1/2	10-19-62
Training on II 5-169 on "Acceptable Level of Competence" and Performance Ratings	"		X	1	10-31-62
Contact Representative Refresher Training Course	"		X	32	12-13-62
Educational Briefing on Equipment Replacement Program	"		X	1	3-13-63
Refresher Training on Performance Rating Procedures	"		X	1	4-30-63
Administrative Lecture Program	"		X	1-1/2	5-23-63
Annual Fire Training	"		X	1/2	10-23-63
Medicine, Law, and Justice!	"		X	4	1-15-64
Employee-Management Cooperation			X	6	3-18-64

(Continue on reverse)

A FORM NOV 1962 5-4627

☆ GPO : 1962 O - 652180 (126)

FIGURE 12.1 Lloyd's Cumulative Record of Training and Development, date unknown.

I wonder what my mother thought about it. I mean then, as opposed to later, when I asked her about it. I wish I knew. In hindsight, my mother remembered very little about living in Wyoming. By the time I finally talked openly with her about it, her narrative about that period omitted anything before 1963. I knew why. It broke my heart.

But there are doors to our past that cannot be opened. I suppose her actions during that time did provide clues to her sense of things, but certainly not her words. To me, she was my beloved mother. I worshipped her as only a child can. She was my steady anchor against the impending chaos, the move to the prairie, the unknown future. She took me to the park and made me Swiss-cheese sandwiches on rye bread with just a dab of mustard for good luck. I had no idea how hard she worked every day just to keep it together for all of us.

Like most wives and mothers whose marriages meant keeping secrets, she kept her feelings to herself. Like most wives who didn't really know what their husbands did every day, and who weren't supposed to ask, she didn't know and she didn't ask. And like most women who were wives of men who "worked for the government," her job was to keep a clean home, to cook economical and nutritious meals for her family, and, of course, to raise her child. Beyond maintaining appearances of these known parameters of a so-called normal life, she was free to think whatever she wanted to think, and to feel however she may have felt about it, just so long as she didn't tell anyone what she was really thinking or feeling.

That is the way it was. Every responsible woman in a classified family did it.

I am struck, when reading biographical accounts of spy life, how similar it was for the women who were married to intelligence officers and agents on both sides. Philby's women, for example. He was married four times during his career, three of the four occurring prior to his official defection in 1963. His first marriage, to Litzi, was short-lived, but she had no idea he was a spy. His relationship with his second wife, Aileen, lasted nearly twenty years and produced four children. There is little evidence that he spent much time with any of his kids. But we know that when Aileen discovered that Kim was, in fact, the "Third Man" and had willfully betrayed their country and lied to her for two decades about it, the realization drove her over the brink and was a major contributor to her early death. She had had no idea he was a spy. Eleanor, his third wife and the one he appropriated from Sam Brewer while still ostensibly married to Aileen, also had no clue about his political loyalties. She says so in her memoir. When he defected, she thought the whole story was made up to discredit him.

J. J. Angleton remained married to the same woman—Cicely—throughout his clandestine career. He once claimed that she thought he worked for the post office, but he claimed this fiction in angry response to a *Washington Post* story that identified him as the director of counterintelligence. I doubt Cicely believed he did any such thing. Nor do I know for certain what she did believe. Probably that he "worked for the government" and that he "moved paper from one side of his desk to the other." Their children remain anonymous.

Wives and children were common emotional cannon fodder during the cold war. We were entrusted with nothing beyond what the officers and agents thought we needed to know about them and about their work. When I interviewed Lloyd Mitchell, a career intelligence officer with the CIA from this same era, he admitted it, saying: "I lied about myself to everyone. I lied to my family and to my friends. I lied to our relatives. I even lied to people I probably didn't need to lie to. But it was part of the job." Mitchell went on to explain that one good reason for keeping the truth secret from family members was that knowing too much could jeopardize their situation. No doubt that is true. But was it not also true that *not* knowing the truth had negative effects?

It is certainly a fair representation of how I grew up. For my part, I was an only child in a nuclear family that, as a rule, didn't talk about what my father did or what my mother thought or felt. My job in our family was to be a good boy. I was expected to be a good student, to obey my parents, to always be presentable, never to be disagreeable, and to involve myself in sports. Later, I would be expected to join the Boy Scouts. When I did join the Scouts, this was my pledge: "On my honor I will do my best to do my duty to God and my country. To obey the Scout law, and to keep myself physically fit, mentally awake, and morally straight."

I was expected to be: "trustworthy, loyal, helpful, friendly, courteous, kind, obedient, cheerful, thrifty, brave, clean, and reverent."

As a boy, I *was* a lot like that. At least I was like that in the great State of Wyoming.

Later, after our lives in Wyoming turned into our lives in Philadelphia and our lives in Philadelphia turned into our lives in Hagerstown, I misplaced the "obedient" part of the pledge. It was in Hagerstown that I learned I had been expected to follow in my father's government footsteps, and it was in Hagerstown that I was first interviewed about a life in the Agency. But by then I had learned how to keep my own secrets and think my own thoughts. I saw what happened to my father and mother. As a result I did not follow in my father's footsteps.

I suppose I am making good on that family expectation now. I am following my father's footsteps, if not exactly *in* them.

· ·

My parents and I moved into a small, white, two-bedroom, one-bath rancher just a few blocks down from the large U-shaped VA center on East Pershing Boulevard. Our new address was 2817 Henderson Drive; our zip code was to become (when zip codes were issued nationally) 82001. The price of the house was $12,500 and my father paid for it in cash. He sold it in 1967 for exactly the same sum, plus one copper penny. He made a point of the extra penny. I think he was determined to show some sort of profit for our time in Wyoming.

I didn't think it was unusual to have paid cash for a house. My father paid cash for everything. He collected US Savings Bonds and placed two $100 certificates every pay period into a fireproof safe in their bedroom closet. When he wanted to make a major purchase, he cashed in bonds that had "fully matured." If he didn't have the money, he didn't make the purchase. He didn't believe in credit cards or in loans of any kind. I remember that he carried a single American Express card in his wallet, but he told me that was strictly for "business travel."

I wish I asked him what his "business" really was. Or what the purpose of all that travel might have been. What did he do when he was "gone"? Why did he make all those business trips to San Francisco, and Chicago, and St. Louis, and to Washington, D.C.? But of course, I didn't ask him. I was a good boy.

Good boys didn't ask embarrassing questions. We didn't pry into our parents' affairs. We understood the bond of family secrecy extended down to us.

· ·

We moved into our Henderson Drive house in time for me to begin school. The plainly named Henderson Elementary School was located directly across the street from our house.

It was a modern single-story brick structure with a large playground that included a baseball field and a basketball court. Classrooms were brightly lit in the popular prison manner with humming fluorescent tubes. Each room contained exactly twenty-five seats, each with its own attached writing surface and storage space. There was one wooden desk for the teacher centered at the front of the room, a chalkboard that ran the length of the front wall, and an intercom system that had been installed as a civil defense preparedness device in case of nuclear war, but served well enough for daily school announcements.

In retrospect, I guess "they" wanted the children to have advance warning when a nuclear warhead was on course to obliterate us. Knowing our death was imminent would certainly be a comfort. We had enough nuclear safety drills that must have been based on that principle. No one really believed that removing our eyeglasses, getting underneath our desks, and covering our heads would do anything more than provide a moment for final prayers.

But I didn't think about it then. I was a child. I was a good boy. My father worked for the government. My mother "stayed home." I went to school across the street from our house. Its brightly painted green front doors seemed welcoming and friendly to me. The skies were Wyoming blue and there were no missiles making arcs in the air over our heads.

I looked forward to meeting new kids. To getting along with them. To making friends. To losing my British accent.

I wanted to learn how to play baseball. I wanted to know who Stan "The Man" Musial was. And Mickey Mantle. And Willie Mays.

I wanted to learn about Cheyenne, Wyoming. I wanted to figure out what we were *doing* here. I was eight years old but I knew that we were sent here for some reason that had to do with my father's new job.

I thought I might learn about that in school.

School was where you learned about important things, right?

. . . .

The true story of why we were in Wyoming was not one I learned in Henderson Elementary School. Nor did I learn it at Carey Junior High, nor at Roxborough High School in Philadelphia nor South High in Hagerstown. It is not a story whose truths were revealed to me at Shepherd College, or at the University of North Carolina at Chapel Hill, or at Pennsylvania State University. You could say figuring out the story of what we were doing there has been the product of lifelong learning.

It is a story that begins with a place and a name for that place. The place is marked by its name: Francis E. Warren Air Force Base. The place still exists on the western edge of Cheyenne, Wyoming.

The story is *not* about the fact of the base itself, so much as the facts concerning what the base was for. The appropriate question to begin this investigation is: what was Francis E. Warren Air Force Base *for* in Cheyenne, Wyoming?

To answer it requires reviewing Wyoming history, which itself is a story that must be told in a particular way. I don't claim that it is the only way to understand the city or any of its people. But I do believe that telling our story this way is the only way to understand what my father, and my family, was doing there.

. . . .

In 1949, Francis E. Warren Air Force Base was established on what had once been a US Cavalry outpost in the old Dakota Territory—Fort D. A. Russell.

Fort Russell had been created in 1867 to protect white settlers, cowboys, and Union Pacific railroad workers from the Cheyenne, the Shoshone, and the Arapahoe, but mostly from the Sioux. The Sioux were great warriors who were finally forced to surrender their lands—and their freedom—after slaughtering Lt. Col. Custer and what remained of his Seventh Cavalry at Little Big Horn in 1876.

The base that had been Fort Russell was renamed to honor a legendary figure in Wyoming history: Francis E. Warren. That's a man whose history we need to explore. Understanding him is a key to appreciating a trajectory of persons, places, and histories that bring us to Cheyenne in 1960.

Francis E. Warren was born in Hinsdale, Massachusetts, on June 18, 1844. He won the Congressional Medal of Honor at nineteen while serving as a corporal during a Civil War battle in 1863. After the war, he tried farming but, like many heroic men after a war, Frank Warren yearned for something more adventuresome, someplace more exciting, where perhaps a fortune could be made.

He moved to the wild new town of Cheyenne, an unmade place for white settlers out on the wide-open spaces whose economic future was being enabled by the construction of the transcontinental railroad. He got to Cheyenne by horseback, riding nearly 1,500 miles from Hinsdale. To call Cheyenne a town when he arrived in it is a bit of stretch. Cheyenne, in 1867, was little more than a collection of military and railroad tents set up along Crow Creek. It was wild and it was dangerous and it suited Frank Warren perfectly.

It appealed to him because in addition to being brand-new, it was also "the West," which for Warren meant it was dedicated to a true "democratic spirit," one in which—as he often put it in speeches—"fraternity, equality, and opportunity" were intricately linked.

In 1869, Wyoming became the first territory to grant women the right to vote and would become (sharing the honor with Texas) the first state to elect a female governor (Nellie Tayloe Ross, 1925–1927). If men migrated on their own to Wyoming, women often were imported. In 1871, Frank Warren married a fine adventuresome woman from back home—Helen—and brought her to Wyoming.

Warren quickly became a successful and prosperous man, a leader in the community. He tried his hand at several business ventures, including real estate, ranching, and selling dry goods, but his talent was getting people to work together to get things bought, built, financed, and done. Today we would call him an entrepreneur who became a venture capitalist, and who then used the money he made and the influence he generated to become a major political figure.

As a successful young man about town with a few dollars in his pocket and a fine new wife, Frank Warren may have developed an honest civic conscience and may have wanted to enter politics because he felt he could make things better. Or perhaps he simply saw the economic advantages that were possible for a man in a position of political leadership and influence in the blooming chaos that was young Cheyenne. Either way, with Helen's support, he was elected as a member of the Cheyenne City Council in 1873–74 and later served as mayor in 1885. That year, 1885, President Chester A. Arthur also appointed Warren to the powerful post of territorial governor.

Territorial governors in the Old West were the rough domestic equivalent of foreign ambassadors. They had all the rights, privileges, powers, and immunities that were enjoyed by high government officials worldwide, but with a good bit more leverage. They could virtually make their own laws and find the men—good and bad—needed to enforce them. They could appropriate money given to them by the United States Treasury for whatever reason they thought warranted it, which usually meant they could create a stable of hired guns and influential citizens willing to support them in whatever they wanted to do. They could appoint judges, sheriffs, and deputies, and call on the services of the United States Marshals and the United States Cavalry. They could ask for favors and had the power to commute prison sentences. It was not uncommon to commute the sentences of outlaws in return for "certain considerations or favors," which often meant large sums of gold. They could, in coordination with the military, engage in open warfare against tribes of Indians or striking Chinese railroad workers. They could load the dice one way or the other with their signature on a piece of ordinary foolscap. They could determine whether the sheepherders or the cattlemen prevailed. And they could use their office to build a war chest of seized land, property (including herds of sheep and cattle), currency, and gold.

If they were wise, they rewarded their friends, punished their enemies, and grew richer on the job. If they were wise and thoughtful, they also used their position to create business opportunities for *other* people, opportunities that brought into their domain new revenues and citizens. And if they were wise and thoughtful and politically ambitious, they could do what Frank Warren did, which was to lobby the United States Congress for Wyoming statehood. The only office more lucrative than territorial governor was likely to be one with an office in Washington, and that is where Warren saw his future.

In 1890 Wyoming was admitted to the Union as the forty-fourth state, and Warren had a large hand in writing the state constitution. It was no surprise he was selected by his many friends to serve as the founding governor, a grand undertaking that he graciously accepted and whose duties he performed diligently for a total of six weeks. Then the state legislature, using the new special powers of appointment they inherited under the newly declared Wyoming constitution, had the wherewithal to vote their newly elected governor into office as Wyoming's first United States senator. He and Helen once again graciously accepted the honor. He resigned as governor and the couple moved to their new home in Washington.

So it was that Francis E. Warren, able son of Hinsdale, Massachusetts, Civil War hero and frontiersman, proud pitchman for the new state of Wyoming, rounded out a distinguished political career by serving ably in the United States Senate as a Republican for the next thirty-seven years. Or, told differently, until death parted his hands from the Senate rostrum, in 1929.

In 1930, as a tribute to his dedicated public service, and at the behest of the Republican president and friend of Frank, Herbert Hoover, Fort D. A. Russell was reborn as Fort Francis E. Warren.

Twenty years later, using the powers contained in the same act that created both the United States Air Force and the CIA, the base would again be transformed. This time, its transformation would not be "in name only" but in mission. It was a mission that defined an important canto in the history of the cold war, a canto all about the command and deployment of nuclear missiles during the cold war.

But that is not the end of this story, nor even our version of this story, about Francis E. Warren and his narrative influence over the city of Cheyenne, and over my family as well.

· ·

Frank and Helen had one daughter. Frances was a strong, lovely, and vital Wyoming woman who, in 1905, after a proper courtship and the approval of her parents, married an army captain and ex-Sioux fighter from Missouri named John J. "Black Jack" Pershing.

You remember Mr. Pershing, don't you? He was the man Hugh Angleton rode with chasing Pancho Villa. Hugh Angleton, father of James Jesus. James Jesus, nemesis of H. Lloyd Goodall. Lloyd Goodall, now in Wyoming at work on East Pershing Boulevard. History has a strange personal trajectory sometimes. Coincidence? Fate? I don't know.

Black Jack Pershing was one hell of a man and, no matter how you tell it, his life was nothing less than one truly amazing American story. Pershing, an "Indian fighter" who then served with distinction in the assault on Santiago de Cuba with Teddy Roosevelt and who would later command U.S. forces in World War I, was the only man ever to be promoted from captain to brigadier general on the order of a United States president. That president was Teddy Roosevelt. Pershing was eventually promoted to general of the armies, a title only once before ever bestowed on anyone, and that anyone was George Washington.

Pershing was a military leader who served with great distinction. He *defined* the image of a military leader, and military leadership, for his time. He also embodied what it meant to put God and country above all else, including family. This doesn't mean that he didn't love his wife and children, or that he didn't always carry their tragic, untimely deaths due to a fire in the military headquarters of the Presidio with him as a hollowness in his heart. It means that he, like many other men, saw his life's work in terms that may seem alien to many of us today. He was a man, a government man, who put duty, honor, and allegiance to the flag above any personal concerns. He was a patriot.

In 1921, Frances Warren Pershing Memorial Hospital opened in Cheyenne. It was named for General Pershing's deceased wife, the daughter of the Senator and Mrs. Francis E. Warren. The main boulevard in the new section of Cheyenne was named in Black Jack's honor—Pershing Boulevard—and it was along the outermost rim of the eastern section of this highway that the new Veterans Administration center and hospital was constructed.

Later, after the general's death and after Fort Francis E. Warren was transformed into an air force installation with a special mission, the name "Pershing" would be attached to a new missile. It was a new missile that was designed to carry a nuclear warhead.

To appreciate a nuclear warhead atop a missile named for a dead general who also happened to be married to the only daughter of Frank and Helen Warren requires coming at the story of Cheyenne in yet another manner. It is to look at Cheyenne, Wyoming, as a place rich in the historical trajectory of a cold war story aimed at total annihilation of our Soviet enemies.

• •

The original Fort Russell had been strategically located near Crow Creek to serve as a military outpost at the geographic midway point between Canada and Mexico. On July 4, 1867, according to local lore, the first tents were pitched along the creek in what grew into the city of Cheyenne. The name of the city was drawn from the Sioux word "Shyenne," which itself was a term the Sioux used for a group of nomadic Indians who roamed the area and were known as the "Dzitsistes." Cheyenne, in Sioux, means "aliens or people of a foreign language."

The first residents of Cheyenne were Union Pacific Railroad workers, vagabonds, Civil War refugees, pitchmen, whores, outlaws, trappers, cowboys, miners, and soldiers. Given the proclivities of this distinctively male culture, Cheyenne quickly acquired a reputation as a Wild West haven. There were five variety theaters featuring naughty nightly burlesque shows along the main street, where every other building that wasn't already a whorehouse was a saloon with rentable back rooms. That colorful image of the town flourished until the mid-1880s, by which time over five thousand people lived and worked there. Cheyenne prospered because of its fun stopover status for travelers on their way to San Francisco, St. Louis, or Chicago, and because of the local development of purebred Hereford cattle.

The Wyoming Hereford Ranch changed the image of this Crow Creek camp town into a center for cultural and social amenities on the plains. Interest in the Hereford breed brought European gentry and big money, and with them came the construction of the famous Cheyenne Club, built on the model of a private English gentleman's retreat, with a large dining room, billiards room, card rooms, reading room, wide veranda, and a lounge the likes of which had never before graced the region. By the time the Cheyenne Club was celebrating the success of the good life on the frontier, the old Wild West and all that Cheyenne had been was already fading into memory.

The Wyoming state motto, prominently displayed on the state seal and adopted in 1893, was *Cedant Arma Toga*, or "let arms yield to the grown," locally interpreted as "force must yield to law." Indeed, it had. Gone were the dramas of midday gunfights, Saturday-night saloon brawls, the danger and slaughter that defined the Indian wars. In its own way, Cheyenne had become civilized and respectable, a mostly cleaned-up and well-lit source of local pride. By 1893 it had erected a new capitol building and was the most populated city on the plains north of Denver.

The last cavalry unit withdrew horses, ponies, mustangs, and mules from Fort Russell in 1927. By then, the fort had already begun its next evolution as an outpost for the new frontier of the sky, defined by the technological innovations of the Wright brothers at Kitty Hawk and by military necessities learned firsthand during the first world war over Europe.

During World War II, Fort Warren expanded in size and a prisoner-of-war camp was constructed on its premises. In 1949, eighty years after its creation as a cavalry fort to protect white settlers and to annihilate any Indians that threatened them, Fort Warren officially became an air force installation with a mission to prepare for the defense of the continental United States and the annihilation of the Soviet Union. There is a linearity of purpose that can be read into this story, but it doesn't stop with the articulation of a "special mission" for the base in 1949.

In 1958 Fort Warren joined the Strategic Air Command and served as the nation's first site dedicated solely to intercontinental ballistic missile operations. On July 1, 1963, the Ninetieth Strategic Missile Wing became the command headquarters for two hundred Minuteman I missiles located over 12,600 square miles in Wyoming, Colorado, and Nebraska. From 1963 until 1967, Warren Air Force Base was the home of the largest ICBM unit in the free world, and perhaps the largest one on planet Earth.

I say that "perhaps" Warren was the largest ICBM unit in the free world because it is likely that the Soviets maintained a similarly sized facility, although they denied it. Besides, in all things nuclear, it's not the size of the facility that matters, is it? Whether you have one Boeing Minuteman I ICBM with a twenty-megaton nuclear warhead headed for your home at 15,000 miles per hour, or two hundred of them with megakiloton warheads, is probably only intriguing if you are a war-games simulator.

Whether or not it was the largest nuclear site, Warren Air Force Base, and all it suggests about the highly nervous and well-armed state of our crazy world during the height of the cold war, seemed poised to complete its military destiny when we moved there in the summer of 1960.

. . . .

My father, a veteran cold war warrior reassigned from service in Europe to Cheyenne, was placed in Wyoming to do a job. Was that job to serve primarily as the contact officer interviewing dependents about their health benefits for the VA center on East Pershing Boulevard? I don't think so.

Was his job rather to investigate—to use his well-developed Agency skill set—any person or persons who might pose a threat to the safety and security of the United States of America in and around Cheyenne, Wyoming? Which is to say in and around the site of the largest ICBM installation and command center in the free world? My guess is that it was.

Actually, it is considerably more than a guess.

Surveillance on United States citizens was an ongoing project of the American government. The FBI had been doing it routinely since the era of J. Edgar Hoover. The CIA was formally forbidden from doing it. Nevertheless, the CIA engaged in a lot of forbidden activities. But is it possible that spying on United States citizens, or anyone else who may have been even in the broadest sense capable of posing a threat to the United States of America, was an Agency operation in Cheyenne, Wyoming?

Apparently, it was. The official history has already been outlined, if not directly stated. It became official in the disclosures of William Colby to the Senate Select Committee chaired by Senator Frank Church in 1975–76, but its genesis was an infamous and inflammatory article in the *New York Times* by investigative reporter Seymour Hersh on December 22, 1974. It was Hersh's report on domestic spying on American antiwar protestors during the Nixon era that triggered a series of serious credibility problems for the CIA in general, and internal political problems for Angleton specifically. Although Colby claimed that the report had nothing whatsoever to do with his asking for Angleton's resignation, it is highly likely that it had quite a bit to do with leveraging his ability to force the issue.

Colby, again. Angleton, again.

My father, again.

My father died on March 12, 1976. Another way to put it is that my father died during the final stages of the Church Committee hearings. Still another way to put it might be that my father died *because* of the Church Committee hearings, but that may be going too far. I'm not in a position to confirm or deny it. We do know that our house in Hagerstown was broken into some time later by men in a moving van who removed everything in it, including my father's personal diary.

This same basic pattern of sudden death and stolen property exists elsewhere. Bill Harvey died on June 7, 1976. The Church Committee had publicly revealed his defining role in the attempted assassination of Fidel Castro and various previous clandestine activities. His house was broken into—twice—immediately following his death. I don't know that there is any connection; it is hard to say. But his wife said that the break-ins were by people who had been after his papers. She was proud of the fact that she had already burned them.

My father planned to testify before the Church Committee. He had long been in the Agency business of domestic surveillance. Much longer, in fact, than the Church Committee would uncover. So it may have been, and probably was, for at least a partially clandestine reason that had to do with domestic surveillance that my father was placed into exile in Cheyenne, Wyoming. He was officially reassigned to the VA center on East Pershing Boulevard, even though he spent a considerable amount of time either on Warren Air Force Base or away on so-called business trips to San Francisco, Chicago, St. Louis, and Washington, D.C.

He may have been placed in this Wyoming exile as a *persona non grata* who had fallen out of favor with certain powers in the Agency, but that didn't mean they would let a man with his skill set walk away. There were other ways to punish a man but still make proper use of his professional talents. This job at the contact office at the VA center was, once again, a convenient cover as well as sufficient organizational punishment. "Hey, Lloyd, there's a course in telephone courtesies you ought to sign up for . . ."

But of course I didn't know that at the time.

Another way of saying these things, of telling this story, is that the home of the largest command installation of nuclear missiles on the face of the earth was located exactly 5.1 miles from our little nuclear family. From our two-bedroom, one-bath ranch house and where our phone number, like a final countdown during those cold war years, was, quite literally 654-3210.

. . . .

"What *is* a spy?" Richard's question still reverberates. In my dictionary there is a definition that may have relevance here: "somebody who is employed by a government to obtain secret information, particularly regarding military matters about other hostile countries." A secondary definition is given as "somebody who watches other people in secret."

When I talk about my father's CIA history and his work in Cheyenne with older ex-military men, missile intelligence men and women from a previous generation of warriors, they suggest another way of thinking about what he might have been doing. Clarence Bray, ex-command sergeant major of the Redstone Arsenal and former senior missile intelligence civilian employee, believes the work may have involved my father's background in cryptography. Perhaps he had been asked to once again resume his role as a "listener."

In those days, military posts made use of "listening vehicles," lightly armored trucks with multiple antennae and a variety of recording devices. They wore civilian camouflage in suburban neighborhoods and military camouflage on post. Their mission was to quietly roam through a base or a neighborhood to "overhear" the conversations of personnel and their families. Or to overhear anything that might sound suspicious. Talk among men and women on street corners. What teachers were telling students in classrooms. What employees of contractors thought was a funny joke. Or who was doing this or that on the job when they should have been working. My mother had warned me that "they" were always watching us, always listening to us, and, as it turns out, she wasn't being paranoid nor was she exaggerating the facts of our life. Ours was a classified family. Being recorded was always part of the bargain.

If this hypothesis about my father's clandestine work in Cheyenne is true, then I have no doubt that my father's exile was considered by him, and by my mother, to be a major source of punishment. For him, sitting in an assigned seat wearing earphones for hours at a time was hardly what he would call "interesting work." In the spook world, it would have been roughly equivalent to having been busted back to Pfc. It may have reminded him of washing out of the Naval Aviation Cadet program and having had to find a way down to Tampa to enlist in the Army Air Corps. In a very clear and certain way, he had risen and soared so far in his career only to find himself back at square one. Only this time, he landed on his feet back at a literal ground zero in the cold war.

I knew my father was disappointed. I didn't know why. But if Mr. Bray's deductions are correct, then he would have considered "listening" to be not only an insulting demotion in rank and responsibilities but also a demeaning way to spend his time. It also gives a whole new meaning to some of his training courses, his "refresher" seminars. Telephone courtesies, *indeed*.

No wonder he began to drink heavily.

No wonder they both did.

13

Breakdown

1962–1963

A LIFE OF SECRECY BEGINS WITH THE FIRST SECRET.

October 1962. I didn't know what a "straight jacket" was, and the word wasn't in my Thorndike and Barnhart *Student Dictionary*. I couldn't ask my father because then he would know that I knew and that would be the end of my nocturnal spying.

Finally, out of frustration and believing that teachers were both kind and the legitimate repositories of all knowledge, I asked Mr. Finkelstein. Finkelstein was a small, thin, immaculate man who wore a permanent smile above his red bow tie and who taught music by waving a baton while making us imitate the dancing ball that prompted the people at home on Saturday nights to *Sing Along with Mitch*. He was also responsible for taking our fourth-grade class on a special field trip to the Francis E. Warren Air Force Base. We were escorted by armed military men into a fully functioning ICBM silo, and Mr. Finkelstein encouraged us to "go ahead and touch the missile, boys and girls, it's the *most powerful thing on earth.*" The look in his eyes was one of pure love. Even at ten I knew there was something wrong with that. Nevertheless, Finkelstein was the one I asked.

His smile evaporated on the word "jacket."

"Where did you hear the term?" he demanded.

Sensing danger, I automatically shrugged and lied, "On TV."

"You're lying," he said. It was a fact. The ends of his lips curled into a menacing grimace. "Come on, Buddy, tell me." He quickly searched the hallways with his green eyes and then turned back to face me. "It's just you and me here. I won't *tell* anyone." He paused. "Who is *wearing* this strait-jacket?" He sneered.

Did he *know*? Did he know about my *mother*? Why was he treating me this way? All I did was ask a question about words. Maybe "straight jacket" was a bad word, like the "F-word," which had gotten Mark Wingo and Charley Rowley into so much trouble last week. But "straight jacket" didn't sound like a bad word at all. It sounded like clothing.

I refused to tell him. I stood in the main hall of Henderson Elementary and stared past Mr. Finkelstein and his red bow tie.

I kept my silence. And my first secret.

. . . .

I never asked my parents why we left London or why we moved to Wyoming. Or at least I don't remember doing so. In my fictional reality, or the reality that we lived as if it were a fiction, I was an only child and my father worked for the government and my mother used to be a nurse. That was the story. That was simply the way it was.

I didn't question it and my parents didn't offer any details.

I was too young to think it odd that our two-bedroom rancher was loaded with European finery, including the ornate Italian marble coffee table that seemed to have conquered our small living room. Or that the gilt-framed oil painting of me as a child posed in a red velvet chair and done in the Italian High Renaissance tradition by the British portraitist Leonard Creo was in any way unusual. Or that the Opel Rekord that was our family car was, in fact, a make and a model that had never before been seen in this state. Or that it was just *my* father who kept a collection of hand-carved African mahogany nudes in his bedroom. Or that the bronze bust of Winston Churchill that graced our bright yellow-and-black art deco kitchen table was somehow out of cultural step with current Wyoming decorating fashion, which consisted of red-and-white wagon wheels as yard art, colorful Indian blankets as wall hangings, and imaginative household uses for empty bottles of tequila or rusty spurs.

Slowly, as I grew into preadolescent material consciousness, these things and what they represented about my family, and about my family's stark differences from this prairie surround, deepened and annoyed me. I realized that something must have happened because why else, dear God, would we be *here*, in Cheyenne, Wyoming, so far away from the persons, places, and things—from *life* as I, as we—had known it?

Something must have happened.

Something *bad*. But good boys didn't talk about bad things.

· ·

My mother was a natural beauty, but she also had a beauty secret. She had discovered these little yellow pills in London that, as she put, really "did the trick." All of the best women secretly used them. Over there, amphetamines were readily available without prescription as over-the-counter diet pills, and they were in demand in my mother's crowd because the State Department encouraged the wives of diplomats, even faux diplomats, to be picture-perfect. We were Americans, after all. We had to not only be the best at everything but also look our very best if we were to continue to inspire the world's lesser peoples against the evils of Communism.

Communism was *ugly*. It was the opposite aesthetic in every way.

My mother had continued her thin existence, and no doubt also elevated her mood, in godforsaken Cheyenne on whatever stockpile of pills she had managed to smuggle in under diplomatic cover when we returned to the States. Once they ran out she didn't want to admit to her amphetamine addiction—it would have been bad for my father's career—so she toughed it out on her own, secretly going cold turkey during the spring of 1962. She resolved to keep her Daisy May figure perfect by simply not eating whenever possible and when it wasn't, by doing what the other middle-aged housewives were secretly doing those days, swallowing laxatives.

In June of 1962, my forty-five-year-old mother keeled over in the Safeway and cracked her head open on the linoleum floor. This "accident," as I was told to call it, was no doubt the result of going off her diet plan, not eating properly, not being able to talk freely about this miserable Wyoming exile.

This "accident," which I didn't witness and which nobody would tell me about, may or may not have happened the way I was told it did. If she had "cracked her head open" wouldn't there have been a scar?

There was no scar.

I don't think that is what happened.

I think my mother just finally lost it that morning while shopping for self-help along the laxative aisle in the Safeway. Something indeed may have "cracked her head open," but only if we understand that phrase and its covert ambiguity as a covering metaphor, a way of covering up what really happened by stating what could easily be interpreted as a statement of fact. I don't think she "cracked her head open" so much as *something finally cracked in her head*. What opened up had less to do with spilling her blood than it did with her already having been bled dry.

My mother couldn't take Wyoming anymore. Not this damned life, not these damned people, not this goddamned windswept merciless prairie. Having worked so long and so hard to control herself, her body, and her behavior for the singular purpose of obtaining her out-of-state dreams, she finally came undone in the pharmacy aisle of a grocery store. The ambulance boys found her face down on the linoleum, writhing, screaming, and completely out of control.

Cracked her head open? Well, yes, that is one way of putting it. Another way is to say that she suffered a complete nervous breakdown.

· ·

Of course that is not what my father told me at the time. She had just had "an accident in the supermarket." She was "in the hospital" for five and a half months before they released her. The "doctors wanted to make sure she was okay."

While she was in the hospital, DePaul Hospital—which was located at the top of the hill just behind our house—I was not allowed to see her. My father continued to go to work at the VA, or drive around town in a listening truck. As the estimated time for her recovery lengthened and my father supposedly enrolled in a few more refresher courses, my mother's parents were finally imported from Martinsburg to care for me. The presence of Granny and Popeye only served to fuel my fearful imagination about what was wrong with my mother, although my imagination had precious few ideas to work with. The only people I had known who stayed in the hospital went there to die.

How long does it take to fix a cracked head?

Nobody seemed to know anything. Or at least nobody would tell me. Now I was the one starving on an enforced diet of secrets and I became desperately hungry for any information.

So at night throughout the summer of 1962 I'd sneak out of my room wearing my stupid Wyoming cowboy pajamas to spy on my father and my grandparents. They camped out in our living room and spoke in whispers, but I had stealth and presumed innocence on my side. I suspected that they knew what was happening to my mother up there at DePaul. I developed a whole new vocabulary, one made out of shorthand terms for mental illness and its treatment, by listening to their night whispers during her forced internment.

That is when I first heard the word "straitjacket." But I heard it as two words, not one. Naomi Saylor Goodall, my mother, was in something called a "straight jacket," the sight of which had made Nellie Grimm Saylor cry so much and for so long that the doctors gave *her* a shot to calm her down.

. . . .

A week or so after my encounter with Mr. Finkelstein, I was on home patrol again and overheard my father say that my mother "wasn't responding to treatment."

There was a loud silence in the living room after that.

No matter how I tried to parse it, it couldn't be reduced to something good.

This phrase had made my grandparents, old and vulnerable as they were already, ever more agitated and sad. I don't know what it did to my father because not long after they arrived, he was "traveling." He always returned a little tired but brought some kind of gift for me. Thus conditioned, I learned to associate his absence with an eventual present. This time I hoped the present would be some good news about Mom.

I wasn't concerned about him not being at home with us during this time of crisis. He *had* to go to work. It was just the way things were. I had no idea how to reach him because he never told us where he was going or where he had been. It was just his job. He worked for the government. And no matter what, and no matter what was going on at home, he had to do his job.

I remained at home with my grandparents and they remained stoically imprisoned in our small house. These old people I loved were West Virginians who, like their daughter, until this time had never crossed the Mississippi, much less experienced the vast emptiness of the western skies, nor the raw constant wind that defined every day. My grandfather was a natural born roamer in the daytime. He did not adapt well to sitting indoors in front of the television, so mostly he slept. My grandmother cooked, cleaned, dozed, and quilted. She worried aloud about her garden back home—who was tending it and what vegetables or fruits were due in—and she watched the weather reports to track any storms that threatened her vicinity of the East Coast. Once a week, on Sundays, she called her son and daughter-in-law back in Martinsburg; it was the only time I saw her like her old self during her extended visit with us.

There wasn't much to be happy about in Cheyenne that summer. Over the Independence Day holiday my father drove all four of us down to Estes Park, Colorado. My grandfather was amazed at the mountains and my grandmother was pleased to be out of the house. I had seen the Rockies quite a bit, having by the age of ten already hiked into the adjoining range on the other side of Laramie with my Scout troop.

Going into the mountains was no big deal for me. But it was a big deal for Popeye. His amazement at the loveliness of the summer Rockies tipped in snow became even more pronounced the farther up the mountain we drove. Finally, he could no longer stand being cooped up inside the car. He ordered my father to stop and he got out, walked over to a still-white pile of snow, and made a snowball. I joined him. So did my father and grandmother. Soon, we were throwing snowballs and laughing. My grandmother snapped a photograph of Popeye in the snow in July that she proudly displayed for years on her mantel back home. It was the only fun I remember having that summer. It was probably the only fun they had.

I tried not to think about my mother in DePaul Hospital. I pretended she wasn't there and that everything was fine. When school started again in September and she still wasn't well, I pretended, while in school, that nothing was wrong at home. I pretended at home that nothing was wrong in school. This was a lie but it was also my part of the web of family secrecy I found myself wound up within.

It took a strange emotional toll on me. Although I was a good boy and an excellent student—I wasn't allowed to be anything *but*—over the summer I had somehow forgotten how to subtract in columns that had three-digit numbers. Over the years, I've wondered about that. It was a small madness of my mind's own invention. Perhaps it was a call for help. If we were still living in London, the State Department would have hired a tutor for me until my memory worked again, or my madness retreated, but out here in Wyoming, I had to help myself.

I was too embarrassed by life right now to ask anyone else for help.

Mr. Finkelstein was my teacher. He thought I was pulling some sort of prank. He hadn't had any sympathy for me since our encounter in the hallway and my current failure in basic arithmetic seemed to him a furtherance of my resistance to him.

"How can you be so *stupid*?" he asked me, incredulously, in front of the whole class at the blackboard unable to subtract. He then pointed at me and repeated his favorite taunt: "Idiot! *Idiot!*" Saying it, he used his hands as if he were conducting us in song.

Behind him I saw my pals Mark and Charlie imitating him, which was a sign they were supporting me, which only made me smile. He fumed and paced and waved his hands up and down, as if in this concert of actions some math miracle might occur. Then he gave up. He told me take my seat and on my way back there he hissed, "What is *wrong with you*, Buddy?"

I stared beyond him and into my life once again. There were windows at the edge of this classroom, then a long expanse of the school's front lawn, then my street, and my house was just over *there*. Turn the other way and go up the hill and there, somewhere, was my mother.

I knew when my mother came home I would be able to subtract again. I refused to think otherwise.

. . . .

Well into the fall, I spent hours walking through our neighborhood, making up elaborate ten-year-old plans for rescuing my mother from the hospital and escaping with her into a better life, one without words like "straight jackets" or "treatments." Or three-digit subtraction problems.

Before I had to abandon the familiar darkness and go back inside among the adults, I pulled myself up atop the large concrete incinerator at the edge of our backyard, looked up and over the hill toward DePaul Hospital, and tried to figure out which one of the rooms, which one of those little square windows with dull lights, held her.

I wondered what she was doing. What she was thinking. Whether she missed me.

Every night when I ran out of wondering I kissed the air in the hope that it would reach her.

. . . .

Since the Bay of Pigs fiasco in 1961 I had gotten accustomed to regular nuclear war drills. Students all across America became seasoned in the fine art of dying in a straight line, heads tucked silently against our chests and arms folded over our heads in the hallway, or with our bodies firmly planted underneath wooden desks in our homerooms.

No one believed either drill would shield us from radiation or a firestorm. Instead, we were comforted with information provided by Mr. Finkelstein about what our missiles were capable of doing to the Russkies. He called them "Russkies," which I suppose in his mind linguistically transformed the Soviet Union into something that sounded far less threatening. He tested us on our knowledge of the missiles—like the ones we had seen and touched in the silos at Francis E. Warren—and it is a lesson in factual accuracy I have never forgotten but that I have lately amended a bit. To wit:

A Boeing LGM-30A Minuteman I intercontinental ballistic missile, also known as the SM-80, was 55 feet 9 inches tall, weighed 65,000 pounds, and cost $1,315,000. The Minuteman I reflected a classic, functional, and masculine orientation to missile design. Its various megaton nuclear warhead capped a long stiff shaft filled with solid rocket propellant, and the most powerful of its three rockets formed its six-foot-wide base. A single-vein fuel line ran along the outside of the shaft. Upon launch, it throbbed with propellant. It was designed for a single use only, one bright flash of a climax worthy of all that expenditure.

The Minuteman I was housed in hardened underground silos. Upon being given the final launch order, it was released almost instantaneously. Once in the air it followed a preprogrammed trajectory and could not be recalled. Once in the air and following its deadly trajectory, we were irrevocably at war. A nuclear war. In 1962–63, that meant that any one particular Minuteman I would be joined in its campaign to end life on the planet Earth by two hundred other Minuteman Is, to say nothing of the still-deployed, if outdated, Atlas and Titan nuclear missiles. And those missiles, of course, were only *ours*. The Soviet Union—them damned Russkies—had at least as many as we did, or so we were told. What wasn't said, what was kept secret in the silences but most of us clearly took to bed with us every night, was that in the event that this endgame scenario played itself out, it was pretty much all over but the flash, the dying, and, if anyone was around to do it, the crying.

The Minuteman I was marketed by the Boeing Aerospace Company as easy to maintain, and this was true. It was easier, surely, than the liquid-fueled Atlas or Titan it eventually replaced. And in the colorful brochure for the product, the Minuteman I was said to be "reliable," if "reliable," even in quotation marks, is a fair term to use to describe a nuclear missile.

The Minuteman I was capable of traveling over 15,000 miles per hour over a range of 6,300 statute miles at an altitude of 700 statute miles. This means that a properly targeted and dutifully launched Minuteman I could traverse the 5,514 statute miles between Cheyenne and Moscow in thirty-six minutes.

Thirty-six minutes.

The Minuteman I missiles at Francis E. Warren were not aimed at Moscow. Instead, they were aimed at the known missile launch sites and production facilities that had been identified by our U-2 spy planes. This information was regularly upgraded and dialed into the preprogrammed missile trajectories. The general feeling at the Pentagon was that the Minuteman program was a first-strike project, not a reactive one. Meaning, I suppose, that the reason they were targeted at missile silos in Russia was to reinforce the idea that, if we chose to, we could launch a pre-emptive first strike on all of their missile bases, and therefore not only prevent them from launching theirs but also wipe out a considerable number of their people as well. People were always a secondary nuclear consideration. At least at the Pentagon, where the word itself was absent from briefings: "Millions may be lost." Millions of *what* was never articulated.

By contrast, we now know from records open to researchers since the end of the cold war that the Soviet Union had far less nuclear capability than the CIA or the NSA said it had. Moreover, many of their missiles probably didn't work. Quite a few were placed into silos without being completed. Others couldn't get off the launch pad. Those that could leave the launch pad often contained targeting systems so poorly designed that tests had frequently indicated they posed as much danger to the citizens of the Soviet Union as they did to Americans. But we didn't know that then. Or maybe we did. It is often hard to tell what is true and what is false in information released by the Agency—particularly information used to support increases in budget.

Nevertheless, in 1962, most Americans believed that nuclear war was likely if not inevitable. We believed that the Russkies had nuclear capabilities equal to or exceeding our own. While the CIA, NSA, various military intelligence groups, and the war game planners at the Pentagon worked on the mathematics of extinction, children were drilled in nuclear alerts to remain calm, walk single file into school hallways, remove any eyeglasses or sharp objects from our persons, and assume the position.

We all knew only too well how to assume the war position. The only instruction absent when we assumed it in our oh-so-straight lines was the unspoken but well enough understood final one: *Kiss your ass goodbye!*

"The hell with *that*," my father said when I explained our safety drill to him. "When you hear the alarm siren you *run* home. Understand?" I said I did and he made me promise I would. It was an easy promise to make. We lived directly across the street from the school. Having said that and having made me promise to run home, my father realized we still had some work to do.

So it was that in September of 1962 my father and I constructed a state-of-the-art fallout shelter in our basement. We filled sandbags and placed them in the window wells. We stockpiled canned goods, bottled water, laxatives, candy bars, and gin. We built reinforced walls inside of the cement walls that marked what my mother later called "our home tomb."

We placed a first-aid kit and a year's supply of toothpaste and deodorant on the shelf alongside my *Boy Scout Handbook* and the Holy Bible. I don't think there was a copy of *The Great Gatsby* at that time, but I could be wrong. I brought along some old comic books to read while the world burned and my father had a fancy radio with an extra hundred batteries he planned to tune in to hear whomever was left standing.

My father also brought home surplus gas masks and one-size-fits-all biological/chemical warfare hazard suits, just in case. These were not commonly available consumer items in 1962, so I have to believe that he was given them on the base because he was somehow considered vital personnel. I wonder now who, in the immediate aftermath of a nuclear holocaust, he might have been assigned to listen to then? Or what vehicle he might have used. Probably a newly glowing one.

Pardon me. That bad old humor thing again.

Granny and Popeye accepted theirs with a resigned look at my father, hoping, I suppose, that if the end came they wouldn't be stuck in this dark basement in Cheyenne, Wyoming.

We also stored two decks of cards and various board games—Monopoly, Yahtzee, and Stratego—in case we got the itch to play during the downtimes of a long nuclear winter. That is a fact I find hilarious now. It just seemed reasonable back then. And the distance between those two sentiments tells me a lot about where we were as Americans in 1962.

By the end of September our shelter was complete. All it lacked was a war. My father and I ran a few practice war drills to get used to it, which included barring and duct-taping the air passages around the basement door, after which time we mostly sat quietly in the darkness for a few minutes until my father poured himself a stiff one, called "Drill over," and we emerged into ordinary life again.

Granny and Popeye didn't participate in the drills.

They remained upstairs in the living room. Granny declared that if the big bomb fell, she hoped the good Lord saw fit to have it land directly on her head, because she didn't want to be around after that. Popeye, always the optimist, didn't believe in the idea of a nuclear war. I'm not sure he believed in Russians any more than he believed in anything else that for him existed only on television. He believed that whatever God intended to happen was going to happen, regardless of anything we or anybody else did. He was a man who had been to the top of the Rocky Mountains and thrown snowballs in July. That is what interested my grandfather. Snowballs were real.

In the meantime, he wondered aloud what was for dinner.

. . . .

On October 16, 1962, the CIA reported to President Kennedy that the Soviets had transported fourteen medium-range nuclear missiles into Cuba. The president was shown U-2 surveillance photographs that had been shot two days prior and then analyzed in great detail by an assortment of government agencies.

The photographs revealed very little that the untrained eye could tell was a missile. Bobby Kennedy, the president's brother and the US Attorney General, later recalled, "I for one had to take their word for it. . . . I examined the pictures carefully and what I saw appeared to be no more than the clearing of a field for a farm or the basement of a house." Despite Bobby or John's inability to construct what they saw as clear evidence of a nuclear threat, the analysts were not only able to confirm that what they saw were missiles but also to estimate each missile's relative degree of readiness. That estimate indicated that at best we had about thirty-six hours to do something about it.

The backstory of what became known as the Cuban missile crisis was, as my mother would have put it, "complicated." At precisely the time the CIA was informing the president and his brother of the presence of medium-range nuclear warheads ninety miles off the coast of the United States, plans were already well under way to assassinate Fidel Castro. A team of eight Special Forces commandos had set sail from Summer Land Key for Cuba, but had been spotted by a Cuban military patrol when they landed.

Six men made it back to the boat, where they awaited reinforcements and further instructions.

Bill Harvey ordered ten additional teams of commandos to assist them, but by then the president had gone on national television to explain to the American people that the Cubans, aided by the evil Russians, had nuclear missiles and that he was ordering an embargo. Furthermore, all ships entering Cuban waters would be stopped and searched, by any means necessary. The United States would not tolerate nuclear weapons in Cuba. In effect, the president was challenging the Soviet Union to a mediated duel, the outcome of which would determine the fate of the earth.

It was a showdown. So when the attorney general learned of Harvey's ordering the commandos into action, he was furious. As he would later recall, not only had he learned of the go order "by accident," but he saw the order as a sacred trespass—only the president could order military action against a foreign power. The Kennedys were already fed up with the CIA's inept handling of their standing order to assassinate Castro, and they were willing to hold Bill Harvey personally responsible for it. Harvey's ill-timed cowboy actions during the crisis ended his career.

The CIA's National Board of Estimates had, only a month before the crisis, authored a report claiming the Soviet Union would not attempt to place nuclear weapons in Cuba because it would "represent a sharp departure from Soviet practice." Their reasoning assumed that because Russia had not placed nukes in any of its satellites in Eastern Europe, it was highly unlikely they would risk the ire of the United States by placing them in Cuba. The director of the CIA, John McCone, didn't believe the report but submitted it to the president at a routine intelligence briefing. McCone then went on his honeymoon with his new second wife to the French Riviera. But on October 19, everyone who heard President Kennedy's speech didn't know or care about the CIA's flawed report. We believed that with missiles in Cuba, we were on the brink of all-out nuclear war.

I was ten years old. My mother was in the hospital suffering from a nervous breakdown and my father was doing whatever was required of him either while "traveling" or "at the VA" or out "at the base." My grandparents, probably trying very hard not to frighten me, pretended that nothing bad was really happening.

As history has it, the crisis passed when Soviet Premier Nikita Khrushchev agreed to remove the missiles in exchange for the United States ending its embargo of the island of Cuba. But that is only one way to record history, as the agreement between leaders of the two superpowers who tested each other's nuclear mettle in the month of October and agreed to back off. It is a true story, but not the only true story.

It is also true that everyone who lived through it has a personal history of the Cuban missile crisis. It is true that some of us have secrets about what really went on during those seven days when the world stood still. Bill Harvey certainly did. One of his secrets was that he had been plotting the assassination of Castro for over a year and had had two top-secret, "for your eyes only" failures. If Castro was aware of these attempts, and evidence now suggests he was, perhaps the Cuban missile crisis should be understood as only one incident in a much longer and more complex story.

If someone attempted to assassinate you, would you simply let it go?

If you knew the President of the United States wanted to take you out, that he personally had given the order to do so, and that he personally expected it to be carried out, wouldn't you consider the idea that perhaps it was the President of the United States who should be taken out? Would you believe that you might be able to save yourself by eliminating him?

But that is mere surmise. And we are a year away from November 22, 1963.

The lesson for *our* nuclear family that emerged from those tense days and nights in October 1962 was simpler: the end hadn't come.

I went back to Henderson Elementary School and resumed the position of student. My father went back to work as he always did. My grandmother cooked, cleaned, dozed, and quilted. My grandfather slept in front of the television and maybe dreamed of snowballs and mountaintops in July.

The important news was that my mother was "improving."

. . . .

After the missile crisis, I used our basement shelter and all it suggested as an incubator for my new imagined identity as an American fighter pilot—an ace, of course—during World War II. One day, having successfully shot down countless German planes but unfortunately having my P-51 Mustang take a hit that caused me to have to parachute into enemy territory, I crawled through the bomb shelter (enemy house) and over to the other side of the basement (Allied territory). It was the side of the basement my parents used for storage and a side I had never found any use for at all.

I snuck around unpacked boxes still bearing shipping labels from London and used my trusty invisible sidearm to kill a few dozen Nazi soldiers. I came upon a cedar chest that would make a perfect getaway car and opened it. I don't know why I opened it, as I planned to sit on top of it not inside of it, but I do remember opening it. Just curious, I guess. I remember that the lid was very heavy. It was a sign I should have read as a symbol, but I didn't know that then.

The smell of mothballs filled my nostrils and I backed away, but not before spying what appeared to be a military uniform. I moved closer and picked it up carefully. I recognized it as an army uniform. A sergeant's uniform. There were wings on it, and two rows of ribbons. On the sleeve was a blue and gold Eighth Air Force patch. I knew my father had been in World War II and I knew he had been in a B-17 heavy bomber because he told me that much while helping me glue a model of one.

What *else* was in this box?

I dug deeper. I found a cracked leather bomber jacket with an emblem of a bear behind a cloud throwing a bomb. There was writing on the back of the jacket in a language that I couldn't make out. The jacket was stained, too, as if someone had spilled something dark and permanent against the inside front and side of it. I remembered that my father had been wounded in the war. Maybe this stain was his blood?

I tried it on. It was too big, but not by very much.

The final items were matching blue boxes with the seal of the United States of America on them. I opened them and found medals. There was an Air Medal and a Purple Heart.

I held the medals in my hand for few minutes and felt their historical weight. These were my *father's* medals. And they were *real*. He had never mentioned them. In fact, he hadn't talked at all about his war experiences. Not to me. The only evidence I had of them was his unfortunate habit of screaming out in the night. My mother told me he did that because he "carried things inside him from the war" that caused nightmares.

That was "all I needed to know." She said.

So I never asked for any details.

I put everything back into the trunk exactly as I had found it. I closed the heavy lid and did not play there again. I went back to the nuclear side of the basement but found I had little energy left for being a fighter pilot during World War II.

I had discovered another secret about my father.

He was a *hero*. A real one. He had the medals to prove it.

14

Recovery, Vindication, and the Night Road to Ruin

November 1962–July 1963

IN EARLY NOVEMBER, MY MOTHER UNDERWENT "SHOCK TREATMENTS." It was a term I heard while squatted down in the hallway, cupping my ear to better catch the sound of it. Although I had no idea what they meant, I knew these words were powerful.

Their factual utterance left nothing alive in the air after that.

The house was still and I remained in the darkness, imagining unnameable things.

I got back into bed. Pulled the crisp white sheet and thin blue blanket over my head. And I lay there quietly, so afraid of what I didn't know that I could not move. So trapped in my own misery by secrets I couldn't even cry.

The next morning the talk at the breakfast table seemed hopeful, cheerful even. There had been a phone call from the hospital. The good news was that my mother might be coming home. I decided "shock treatment"—whatever it was—must have been a "miracle cure," which was a term used on TV all the time.

I sat down to my bowl of Cheerios and imagined seeing my mother again. If this were a miracle cure, then maybe when she came back everyone would be *happier*.

She returned to us, just before Thanksgiving, a very different person.

Mostly I remember that she was blank.

She had lost her girlish flirtiness, her little giggle, and her bright diplomatic smile. Her hair had been cut short; it looked like the rough work of a nervous barber working with a bowl and a pair of scissors. Her face was grim and worn out, as if she had awakened to a life she would prefer not to be living but was uncertain what she should do about it. She would try to smile at me but it was forced and unnatural, as if her face had forgotten how to do it. She gained weight and didn't seem to care. She didn't seem to care about her clothing, either. Or the cleanliness of our house.

This woman was not the mother I had known.

Shock therapy. When I was in college I learned that it is a radical form of treatment for a variety of psychiatric problems. It involves strapping the patient to an operating table, attaching electrodes to the body, and passing a series of electrical charges through the brain. During this procedure the patient's body reacts violently to the voltage, which is why the heavy straps are required. From the patient's point of view, the treatments are intense but generally not recalled afterward. The brain, even a clinically depressed or neurotic or psychotic brain, realizes that some memories of pain should be permanently quarantined.

One side effect of shock therapy is a more generalized memory loss. Another is the onset of a neutral affect, or an inability to feel emotion. When both side effects are present, the patient becomes very much like my mother became following her "miracle cure." The electrical current effectively fried her brain, or at least those regions of her memory and affect that held the secrets of the self. Yet, having then done "all they could do for her," the doctors pronounced her "well again." She was released back into the world without benefit of fully knowing who she was, where she had been, who she knew, or being able to feel one way or the other about it, or about most other things.

I got the impression that how my mother was following this advanced psychiatric treatment was "normal." After all, she had been "cured." Given the more generalized nuclear madness that defined everyday life during the cold war, perhaps the inability to feel one way or the other about most things and to have very little memory was considered appropriate medical science. If so, then it was a state of being for the nuclear age that rendered the self as dispassionate, enabled to function by the absence of an emotional connection to any personal pronoun. For my mother, or for the blank person who lived in my mother's body, "I" was only a word and there was no "me" anymore. "Me" requires affect and it requires memory.

These "side effects" can be short term or long term and there is no way of accurately predicting their duration. The self is still not well enough understood. There is evidence of an active rebuilding process in some persons, an urgency to make a new life out of what is left over from the old one. For other people, whatever is inside of us directing the action seems content to observe life rather than fully reengage it. But for most people who undergo shock therapy, there is a middle way characterized by a longer process of healing and recovery, a trajectory of what we might call "the only okay" that defines life in the everyday. It is a new life without spikes, without peaks or valleys, without strong feelings one way or the other.

Today, we achieve this therapeutic state of perceived normalcy through pharmacological solutions, and millions of citizens report feeling much better because of it. There is no shame and no blame. In my mother's day, however, having undergone shock therapy to realign the biochemical processes in her brain with what society deemed acceptable public behavior was an admission of weakness, or worse: evidence of madness that ran in the blood. Nobody talked about it.

Granny and Popeye stayed through Thanksgiving, an artificial measure of something to do with "seeing how Naomi did." Every day was numb. Nevertheless, a week passed and we finally saw them off at the Union Pacific depot the following Saturday. Everyone hugged, and, except for my mother, cried.

I cannot imagine what we looked like.

The last thing we said was that we would visit them the following summer.

. . . .

William M. Tuttle Jr. is an American historian. In addition to a brilliant book called *Daddy's Gone to War* he is also the author of a striking essay, "America's Children in an Era of War: Hot and Cold," that explores the ways in which children of the era absorbed the horrific images of the mass destruction of the Holocaust and the dropping of the atomic bomb, and learned to process them through continual exposure to the recurrent themes of imminent death in popular culture throughout the cold war. He compares the prevalence of these images and stories with other sociological data: the dramatic decrease in the average number of children born into postwar American families, the rise of self-help child-rearing texts—particularly those authored by Dr. Benjamin Spock—that emphasized permissiveness, and the new culture of affluence precipitated by the postwar economic boom. He asserts that the "basic contradiction" between permissive child-rearing and imminent death resulted in "a prescription if not for schizophrenia, then at least for a deep ambivalence about life and the future."

I suppose I resemble that last line in more ways than I am comfortable admitting. I have never been able to conceive of a long life, something Sandra occasionally accosts me about. For her, "growing old together" is a good thing, a positive image. I have never thought I would "grow old." I love my life but have always been ambivalent about aging. I suspect there are many children of the cold war who share my feelings but have never known why.

The cumulative effects of living in a culture of fear poised on the brink of nuclear annihilation no doubt also took a hefty toll on adults. If the declining birth rate can be partially attributed to the widespread availability of the birth-control pill, there can also be little doubt that the media's fascination with violent images contributed to what communication scholar George Gerbner calls the cultivation of a pervasive perception that we lived in a "mean world." We became not only more fearful but also more prone to believing that we weren't safe in our neighborhoods, our homes, and our communities.

My mother's mental illness cannot be solely attributed to any single cause. But I do believe that it can be attributed to the culturally induced responses she made to those causes. It was an illness based on her emotional unease in diplomatic circles, her fear of failing my father in his career aspirations, her dedication to protecting me from secret knowledge she had about our clandestine and disrupted life, and whatever biochemical toll years of amphetamine and laxative abuse took on her system. These internal causes were augmented by the cold war decisions made by our government about the primacy of secrecy—at the expense of openness and honesty—in the lives of clandestine families, which in turn was cultivated and amplified by violent images in popular culture, by the increasing nuclear tensions reported on the nightly news, and ultimately by the well-intentioned physicians who determined the course of her shock treatments.

Yes, it is clear to me that there was a psychological toll for waging the cold war. My mother's breakdown only signaled for my family the *beginnings* of it.

I became, over that long, cold Wyoming winter, a child of many secrets.

For most of the Christmas holidays, my mother sat in a chair in our living room and stared vacantly out of the picture window, refusing my suggestions to go outside. She didn't want to "see anybody," she said. So she just sat.

Before, the woman who had been my mother, who had been in that body, was always moving. In retrospect it may have been the influence of a constant diet of amphetamines, but I didn't know that then. All I knew was the woman who lived inside my mother's body now was *not* my mother.

I had no idea what I could do about that.

So, mostly, I did chores around the house. A life full of activity is often a substitute for dealing with reality. I cleaned the basement at least twice a week. I told my friends that I was busy because I was afraid to tell them the truth, which was that I was afraid to leave my mother alone in the house. I didn't know what might happen. I couldn't trust her to be in charge of anything. At least, not for a while. Not until the woman who had been my mother returned to her body.

My father, for his part in our family drama, went to work in the morning and came home at night. Maybe he listened to other people's private conversations. Maybe he took refresher courses. Maybe he passed the time moving paper from one side of his desk to the other. I didn't ask. He came home at night and joined her sitting in the living room by the picture window. Both of them remained there late into the night. I figured I was off-duty on the mom patrol when he arrived home. Although we never discussed it, he seemed to implicitly agree with me about that.

She didn't cook. We ate Swanson TV dinners on TV trays in the living room. We watched television while we ate and rarely spoke to each other. I remember that dinner hour was news hour and Walter Cronkite was the newsman. After dinner I collected the aluminum dinner plates and discarded them, washed the glasses and silverware in the kitchen sink, and either went into my bedroom and closed the door and read or crossed the street to shoot basketball on the outdoor court, where my actions were illuminated by a streetlight. In either place I imagined my life as it might be lived elsewhere. *Any* elsewhere.

This way of life continued for the rest of the winter and well into spring.

My mother wasn't allowed to drive. At first this bothered me, because we always had a good time in the car together. Before her "accident," we would sing popular songs along with the radio and she would tell me about movie stars and politicians and artists and the places we'd been and the times we'd had.

All that was past was gone.

Now, this woman who came to live in my mother's body and who didn't cook and who wasn't allowed to drive had to be reminded of the most basic maintenance habits (like brushing her teeth), what brand of cigarette she preferred (she had forgotten that she smoked), and where she left her house key.

She never sang the same way again.

She didn't respond to names out of her past until it became clear to her that this was a problem, at which time she simply nodded her agreement with whatever was being said about persons she could no longer recall. She had also apparently forgotten where my father had worked before we moved to Cheyenne, so one day she asked me to write out a list for her. And, she added, to "make a note" of where I had gone to school.

Of course I obeyed. Silently. I never told my father about her request. It was another secret kept just between us.

Years later, when my mother, at age sixty-six, lay in another hospital room and in another town dying of stomach cancer caused, or at least aggravated, by years of laxative and amphetamine abuse, she admitted to me that she had lost about four or five years of memory, covering the time we had been living in Rome and London until just before she was released from the hospital. Over the years she thought she had recovered bits and pieces of it, but never enough to make the memories full again, and never enough to fill the major gaps in her life story about those times. Cruelly, these were the years everyone told her had been some of the happiest in her life.

No wonder her identity issues were described as "complicated."

. . . .

Summer in 1963. June. My mother was not yet herself, much less up to functioning as my mother, but she was *better*. Or she said she felt better, anyway. I'm not sure that was entirely true. She had memorized a few essential facts that allowed her to negotiate everyday conversations without embarrassing herself. But how she *felt* about those parts of her life that were lost to anything other than simply naming them, she never said.

My father worried about her but tried not to show it.

It seemed to me that he wanted to believe she would wake up one fine morning and just be her old self again. He said we needed to be patient. My father loved my mother, or at least who my mother had been, and her return into our lives as a changed person didn't change his love for her.

I suppose he accepted her new lesser self in much the same way as he accepted the downturn in his clandestine luck that brought us here. But I am sure that as a man, as a husband, he wanted *more*. Their routine evenings together over the winter had regularized into a comfortable pattern of avoiding the past that by springtime had become a kind of mutually seated aggravated silence.

It was a loud silence. It was a silence that caused them to fill their empty spaces with drinks. The more they drank, the louder the silence became and the more ambivalent they became about it. They were heading downhill fast.

Finally, my father couldn't take it any longer. He decided that the thing to do to cheer her up would be to buy her a new car.

"But Dad," I said, quietly but firmly in my nearly eleven-year-old voice, "she can't *drive*."

"Not yet, maybe," he replied. "But she will. She taught me how to drive, you know." He smiled at a fond memory.

I knew the story. My father hadn't learned how to drive until he met my mother at the VA hospital in Martinsburg, a fact I found odd. He didn't tell me what I wouldn't learn until much later, which was that it had been much odder for him as a Naval Aviation Cadet. In 1942 he was the only man in his class who learned how to fly an airplane despite having never learned how to drive a car.

In early 1963 we still owned the Opel and it still worked well enough. My father was not a big car enthusiast nor did he believe in wasting money. Cars were a means of transportation. It was from my mother, not my father, that I inherited a lifelong fascination for them. When he traveled—which was often—he used a government vehicle. Usually it was a Ford. Perhaps that is what motivated him to finally buy one.

He arrived home one Saturday afternoon in June with a brand-new red-and-white Ford Falcon Futura. Even the name—Futura—pointed away from the past. It was a beautiful little car and my mother absolutely loved it. It was a *lot* flashier than I expected. The government Ford my father used was typically plain.

For the first time since she returned home my mother's eyes sparkled. She smiled. And it was her old, genuine, impish smile. She slid into the bucket seat and adjusted it, just like she used to do. Dad and I watched, a little amazed. Still grinning, she said, simply, "Keys."

He handed them to her. I started to say something but didn't. He walked around the front of the car and got in on the passenger side. "Are you coming?" he asked.

"No, you two go ahead," I said. "I'll stay here and guard the house." My eyes were saucers. By not going with them I thought I might be guarding my *own* life.

She started the engine, found reverse, backed out of the driveway, found first, and they were gone. I watched the car as long as I could, then went back inside. I had no idea how to make sense of what I had just seen. Maybe my father's therapeutic insight had been right. All she needed to jump-start her personality was a new car. But the fact of it was unbelievable to me. And the fact that she was *driving* it—that I had seen her drive away with my own two eyes—seemed even more unbelievable.

I was excited but unnerved by this new sensory information.

While they were gone, time passed slowly. I worried about them. I worried that something bad might have happened. "Gone" this time might mean they weren't coming back. More time passed and I became convinced something bad had happened. I sat by the phone waiting for the call that I figured would come. I was not entirely unhappy about it. Or at least I didn't allow myself to be unhappy about it.

They finally returned about three hours later, both wearing big smiles. I was greatly relieved. In the time they had been gone I had entertained the first episode of my "what if they never came back" self-televised fantasies. I imagined myself still living here at 2817 Henderson Drive, mowing the yard and doing chores, eating TV dinners, and becoming better at sports. Gone would be the anxieties and uncertainties I was still too young to name.

Even then I recognized this fear-induced wish to be a selfish one. Crazy-selfish, in fact. But then again, I was an only child and one of the hidden lessons of having learned to take care of myself was that I *could* take care of myself. I knew how to do adult things. I shopped for groceries and knew how to cook; I knew how to run a washing machine and dryer; I knew where the checkbook was and how to write a check. I knew how to mow a yard, grow vegetables, and burn trash in the incinerator. I couldn't drive yet, but I could walk and ride my bike. As a result of my training in the Scouts, I had merit badges attesting to my skills in first aid, ropes and knots, fire prevention, archery, boating, fishing, and hiking. I knew how to use small tools and could pitch a tent. I could purify water from a lake. I could make friends. I could take care of a dog.

Since my mother returned to us, I had put my feelings on hold. I didn't allow them to interfere with what needed to be done. Feelings made me vulnerable and I couldn't afford feeling vulnerable. I had duties. Responsibilities. Schoolwork. Yard work. Basement work. I couldn't waste my time with feelings. Things might get worse, and then what good would my feelings have been?

I thought about all of these things waiting for my parents to return. I reorganized the shelves in my room. I lined up model airplanes and cars. These dark thoughts were my way of dealing with the anxiety caused by my realization that my parents might not return, but of course I didn't know that then. I only knew that thinking about what I had to do freed me from my deepest fears. By taking a mental inventory of what I knew and what I could do in times of personal crisis, I was learning how to become a *survivor*. I've never outgrown it.

Nonetheless, I was greatly relieved to see my parents return safely. They were my family. Their well-being was part of my workload. Besides, I wasn't yet eleven years old, so what would I do to support myself if they were gone? I ran to the garage to greet them.

They got out of the car and immediately announced that we were leaving at the end of the month for a trip to Martinsburg. "Best way to break in a new car," my father said. "A drive across the country." He hugged Naomi and me. "Besides," he continued, "we told Nellie and Will we'd visit them. I have to go to Washington anyway."

My mother kissed me. She hadn't done that since coming home. There was beer on her breath and a certain new sauciness in her attitude. I thought my heart would explode. That night she cooked for the first time since coming home from the hospital. It was my favorite meal—Swiss steak right out of the *Betty Crocker Cookbook*—and she got it exactly right.

Later, in my room, helping me to get ready for bed, she said, "Your father says we are going to a family reunion. You know how forgetful I've been lately. I want you to make a list of all of our relatives for me. Okay?"

I nodded.

"And don't say a *word* about this to your father."

I didn't. But I also knew that it was going to take more than a Ford Falcon Futura to return my mother to us. I made the list the next morning, drawn as a family tree to help her make the necessary blood connections, and left it on the kitchen table for her.

. . . .

I sometimes recall that trip to Martinsburg as one of the happiest we ever made, although to be fair about it, how could it have been? We had gone through a horrific year and we were only halfway through the further horror that would forever define for us the year 1963. But we didn't know that yet.

Maybe it was the new hope for my mother's mental health that made the trip so pleasant. If so, we didn't mention it. Maybe it was the music we listened to, state after state, on the Falcon's AM radio. We did talk about that. I clearly remember us singing Nat King Cole's "Ramblin' Rose" and "Those Lazy, Hazy, Crazy Days of Summer"; I remember Ray Charles's "Hit the Road Jack," and "Sugar Shack" by Jimmy Gilmer and the Fireballs.

I remember we all sang along. Even my mother, although I could tell she was learning the words of each song as if for the first time.

My place in the family car was in the backseat. In 1963 there weren't seatbelts in cars, so I was free to lie down across the whole of it and watch the sky float by while the radio played. There were no radial tires or disc brakes either, so when it rained we slowed down and then tried to make up the time when the sun reappeared. Nor was there air-conditioning, at least not in our car. So we drove through the heat with the windows rolled down and the fresh air in our hair.

Our day began early—my father was determined to be on the road "at the crack of dawn"—and it ended around four or five, depending on how close we were to some prescribed destination on the map. My parents always stayed at a motel where there was a swimming pool and a color television, which, in those days, were advertised prominently on signs. The swimming pool was my treat. I swam until the pool closed and then returned to the room, where my parents sat smoking and drinking beer from a red-and-white Coleman cooler while watching television. On the road we ate lunch at roadside picnic tables, little sandwich lunches packed by my mother and kept in the Coleman along with beer and sodas. It would have been idyllic except for the ever-present bluebottle flies and the overripe smell of various discarded rotten things in the open roadside trashcans. American roadside picnic areas were often foul prior to the raising of our collective green consciousness about polluting the environment.

Still, I enjoyed those roadside picnics. I think we all did. My parents were happy, the car performed perfectly, and the weather was quite accommodating. In the mornings we ate stacks of pancakes or eggs and bacon at booths in what we now refer to as classic American diners. People we met were always interested in where we came from and where we were going. Somewhere east of St. Louis, the fact that we were from Cheyenne, Wyoming, became strangely exotic for the new people we met. Evenings we ate at places where my father could order a drink, or two drinks, sometimes a few more than that. My mother had embarked on a self-improvement program and resolved to lose weight, so she ate lightly and only drank a beer or two back in the room.

We arrived in Martinsburg five days after leaving Cheyenne, no worse for the trip but happy to be out of the car. My grandparents no longer lived on a farm. They had built their "retirement house" at 403 Van Metre Avenue on a hill overlooking the city. It was an ordinary house in the city's suburbs—if you can call that area of Martinsburg a suburb—but it lacked the mystery of their farm. At least it did for me. For them, their new house was a dream house. Everything in it was new except the furniture. They had purchased a double lot, so there was plenty of room for a garden, although not the same size garden that Granny had back on their farm. But she was then sixty-six years old and I'm sure the reduced size of her new garden was fine with her.

When we drove into their driveway, everyone assembled there oohed and aahed over the Falcon. In 1963, getting a new model of flashy car was a big deal. I remember a steady stream of neighbors, friends, and relatives arriving just to look at it, admire it, sit in it, and, in most cases, take a ride. I remember men in felt hats or baseball caps lifting the hood, kicking tires, running rough workingmen's hands along the smooth finished surfaces, and admiring the brightness of the red-and-white paint. While the men remained outside talking cars and jobs and politics, the women went inside talking about life "way out there in Wyoming."

I wandered around the yard and through the garden imagining, I don't know, maybe Eden. All was well while we were in Martinsburg. Summer was in full bloom and the sun was warm all the way down to somewhere beneath my skin. I could smell good country cooking on the stove. There was laughter. I lay down in the sweet green grass and named the persons and things around me. I took in a deep breath and held it—as if I were holding the feeling of that moment—for a long time. For as long as I could, anyway. Then, later, as the sundown spread its dark evening shadows across the luxuriant green grass and supper was called, I went somewhat reluctantly back into the house.

At the dinner table, I picked up on the fact that nobody truly knew the extent of what had happened to my mother. The "cracked her head in the grocery store" version of the story had made the local gossip rounds. Granny and Popeye never mentioned the straitjacket or the shock treatments. They omitted from their story any mention of her losing her mind. Or of the drug addiction that contributed to it. Or the laxatives. They either didn't know or didn't want to admit to anyone that she had emerged from DePaul Hospital with a blank stare and a full set of memories electro-burned from her brain.

Hidden within its innocent language, what would become our family cliché, was the story of "having slipped in the grocery store and cracked her head wide open." Within that metaphor was room enough for a little family humor. Her brother Jim told her she ought to be more careful where she walked, and my cousin Pete—always the biggest joker—suggested that she ought not go out shopping until she was fully awake. My mother left it at that and was content to do so, smiling benignly. Perhaps it was easier for her to act as if all that had really happened was that she had foolishly slipped on a wet linoleum floor. Or perhaps it was something else that lurked behind that wry smile, something even simpler.

Perhaps she didn't know what happened to her. Perhaps that memory, too, had vanished.

Either way, her secret—at least what I knew of it—was safe with me.

· ·

Every year my father made two official trips to Washington, D.C. I never knew why. Nor did he ever say.

I used to think Washington was a house or a place of business because whenever my father went there he had nothing much to say about it. He used the same language—"I've got to go to D.C."—with no additional embellishment or contextual clues than he would have used to describe a trip up the street to Bob Fagiani's house or over to DT's Liquor Store. He would leave, be gone for a while, then he would return. He never talked about what went on while he was "gone," never discussed whatever was discussed or the people he discussed it with, never reported to us the events of these particular days.

I now think it was because Washington was not a house, nor a place, but a convenient metaphor for the agency of government that required his presence and his reports. But in the summer of 1963 I didn't know that.

I still don't know what, if anything, my mother knew about those trips. She accepted them in much the same way as we mortals accept the weather. There isn't anything to be done about it, so we adapt. We do what we must do.

She said he "worked for the government." It was "his job."

This year, though, it was different. I hadn't ever seen my father enthusiastic about going to D.C. Usually he announced his trip as a plain statement of fact, something inevitable, as if it were a small thing. But not in July of 1963. After he saw the evening news on July 3, he was genuinely looking forward to this trip.

My father had become uncommonly excited about his trip near the end of the news broadcast. The last story was about a British citizen by the name of Harold Adrian Russell Philby who had defected to the Soviet Union. Philby—whose nickname was Kim—had been a "high-level member of the British intelligence service" at one time and had been living in Beirut, Lebanon, prior to his defection. He had been a spy. On July 3, 1963, Kim Philby was awarded citizenship and named a hero of the Soviet Union.

I understand now why my father was so excited. But at the time, I had no idea. None whatsoever.

• •

Let's suppose for a moment that my father's daytime VA job was every bit as boring and soul deadening as I have to imagine it was for him. Let's further imagine that he harbored the belief that if his allegations about Philby were ever proven, he would be vindicated. And let's finally suppose that if he were vindicated, our Wyoming exile would come to an abrupt ending. His conclusion would be that he would be reinstated in the Foreign Service, welcomed again into an Agency top job, and given another overseas posting.

For my father, vindication was *everything*.

And no wonder! In going through his dummy folder I found an award supposedly given to him for having composed the "Outstanding Letter" in January of 1962. The award—granted by the ominous-sounding Correspondence Review Committee—was for "a choice between a pen, a desk set, or a dictionary not to exceed $15.00 in value." My father apparently chose the dictionary, as the letter indicates that it had already been ordered for him. His selection of a dictionary doesn't surprise me.

I include the award letter here as physical evidence of his probable state of mind. Or, if not exactly evidence of his probable state of mind, then surely as evidence of how dull his day job was. For a man like my father, receiving a letter such as this one—and a $15 prize—must have summed up how far his career had actually fallen.

No wonder he hated James Jesus Angleton.

And no wonder he was excited about his trip to Washington, given what had been announced on the CBS evening news.

• •

I stayed with my grandparents while both of my parents went to Washington on July 5. We had spent the previous day at the river with our relatives celebrating Independence Day. The whole of the good-natured Saylor clan gathered on the banks of the Potomac to grill hot dogs and hamburgers, eat potato salad, and finish off the evening with homemade ice cream and illegal firecrackers. I remember swinging off a rope into the water with my cousins and having a grand time. It was a wonderful day.

My father was unusually animated. He told everyone that he expected to return from Washington with a new assignment that would get us "the *hell* out of Wyoming." My relatives were glad to hear it. Or perhaps they were simply happy to see us happy, given what we had been through this year.

After they left, I worked in the garden with Granny, pulling weeds and watering corn and field peas, and harvesting the tomatoes. For the duration of this visit, I slept down in the cool, damp basement in an old iron bed with Popeye, who had been banished years ago from his wife's bed for reasons he preferred not to speak about and she never mentioned.

I think I learned that summer what one reason may have been.

Popeye had the habit of awakening in the night as if poked in the eye with a sharp stick, whereupon he jumped immediately out of bed and pissed with some great urgency into a nearby tin bucket. He grunted rhythmically getting the last few squirts out and then proceeded to the basement door, where he tossed the bucket's contents into the backyard. Then he climbed back into bed and fell promptly back to sleep.

I had never witnessed such a thing. I had never known anyone to piss in a bucket or throw its contents out of a door. I didn't know whether I should be frightened by it, or think it was funny, or just chalk it up as another strange thing that West Virginian men did.

February 9, 1962

4042-A-118

Mr. Harold L. Goodall
c/o Contact Division
Veterans Administration Center
Cheyenne, Wyoming

Dear Mr. Goodall:

The Correspondence Review Committee has recommended that you
receive an award for superior performance for having been nominated
as the composer of an "Outstanding Letter" written during the month
of January 1962.

The Employee Awards Committee has agreed with the Correspondence
Review Committee and is pleased to inform you that they have voted
that you receive an award for this accomplishment. You were given
the choice between a pen, a desk set, or a dictionary not to exceed
$15.00 in value, and you selected the dictionary. This will be
ordered immediately and appropriately inscribed and delivered to
you as soon as possible.

You have obviously made a very conscientious effort while composing
your correspondence to comply with the 4-S principles, which is encouraged in the Veterans Administration. Letters such as yours leave an
excellent impression on those who receive them. The clearness and
conciseness of your letter leave no doubt in the mind of the reader
the message which you desire to convey.

May I congratulate you on behalf of the Management of this Center, as
well as the Employee Awards Committee, for having received this award.
A copy of this letter is being placed in your Official Personnel Folder.

Sincerely yours,

DUDLEY S. DEAN
Chairman, Employee Awards
Committee

FIGURE 14.1 Award for "Outstanding Letter," received by Lloyd in January 1962.

The next morning I asked him about it over breakfast. When I came upstairs from their basement into the kitchen he was already seated at the table in his overalls, pouring milky coffee from his cup into the saucer. He then dipped buttered bread into it. This was another thing I had never seen anyone do. "Granddaddy," I began, "why did you get up in the night and pee into a bucket?"

He looked up from his saucer and laughed. "Bud," he said, "when you get to be my age you never know when the good Lord is going to call on you to make water."

Undaunted, I then asked him, "Did the good Lord tell you to toss it out into the backyard too?"

He seemed to consider it. "Well, no, that was my idea. Water's good for Nellie's garden." He winked at me conspiratorially. "But don't you go telling Nellie I said that."

So many secrets marked our everyday interactions.

· ·

When my parents didn't return from Washington by the following Friday, I knew better than to ask about it.

I had overheard the hushed phone calls.

I had already imagined the worst.

I spent two or three days in episode two of what became the continuing saga of "What if they never come back?" In it, I starred as myself, or how I saw myself, I should say—as an earnest young man who had unfortunately suffered the loss of both parents under mysterious circumstances. In this latest episode I no longer lived in our ranch home in Cheyenne but instead—and without transition—now resided in the black tar-paper shack in the woods below the corn-row edge of Granny and Popeye's garden. I was sort of a semicultured West Virginian version of Huckleberry Finn. I lived barefoot on food from Granny's garden while otherwise continuing with my adventurous boy's life.

The adventurous boy's life I imagined mostly involved getting away with pranks at school and being a famous baseball player, an amazing pitcher who regularly threw no-hitters and hit game-winning home runs. There were girls and boys in this colorful episode, mostly cheering me on, and those who weren't served as convenient foils for various tests of my superior intelligence, ball-playing ability, and strength.

I scripted these daytime dramas as I went along, using the wild outdoors around my grandparents' house as staging areas for the action. I worked at them, earnest as an evangelist. Their great lawn was my own green stadium, and the tall colorful rows of corn, pole beans, and tomatoes were my dedicated fans. School was the dark garage, where I would sit inside Popeye's 1954 Studebaker Champion and plan new ways to sabotage math tests. Afternoons when it rained I reclined and dreamed aloud in Granny's rocker on the breezeway, the rhythms of my rocking pure music, the sound of my own voice a never-ending song.

I imagined myself a hero in so many ways.

My parents remained "gone."

· ·

I was fast rounding third base on my way toward home base, which was a ripe, striped watermelon I had secretly rolled out of the garden earlier that morning, when my parents finally returned.

Two unfamiliar car doors slammed. Where was *our* new car?

I ran to the corner of the house just in time to hear my mother's anger. "He was *drunk!*" she said, her fist clenched. I heard it and was frightened but was more frightened by how she appeared. My mother's head was covered in white bandages and she walked with a decided limp. Nellie had her arm and led her, slowly, step by cautious step, from the car to a cane chair.

Nellie's face was set in a way I hadn't seen before. At first I thought her face didn't know whether to be mad, sad, or relieved. But that wasn't so. Even then I knew that her face bore the telltale signs of something else. Then, standing in my safe place behind the corner of the house, I read it as Nellie's grief for the obvious pain of her daughter.

But I was wrong. It was a sign, but not of that.

I could not then name it, but hers was the face, the suddenly gone stolid, irrevocably reconciled face, of every one of us who finds ourselves caught, emotionally trapped, in a necessary family silence.

My father, guiltily hiding his swollen eyes behind sunglasses and nervously fingering a pack of Benson & Hedges, said nothing. He didn't have to.

I did not move from my safe place until the adults went inside. I did not want to be in the house with them. At least, I did not want to be in there with them *now*.

I knew too well their silences. The depth and crush of them.

I could foresee the tiptoeing strategies of avoidance and already feel the aching, draining presence of the unacknowledged but known failures and unspeakable but heavily underscored secrets that my family readily performed for each other, a sad and tragic pantomime to the corresponding heroic comedy I performed for myself in the garden. When I heard the screen door close and the storm door behind it, I chose to return to the watermelon I named home plate and to reenter my own imaginative and far less threatening narrative.

I knew only that something had happened. Something *bad*.

. . . .

My father disappeared the next morning before I got up. My grandfather told me, over cereal, that he had gone to "see about the car." He didn't know when Lloyd would be back.

My mother slept in. Eventually she emerged, with Nellie's help, from the guest bedroom and more or less faced me. Her face was still bandaged but I could see her eyes and when she spoke there was part of a mouth, just enough to allow the half-truth she was about to tell me.

"We had an accident," she began. The word "accident," intoned as if the word itself was desperately seeking a signifier, had a sudden parallel resonance for me, sliding firmly into place alongside her "accident" in the Safeway earlier this year.

"What happened?" I asked, simply. I held her hand and felt it tremble slightly.

There was a long pause. I don't know what she was thinking about but I'd like to believe that she was at least considering telling me the truth. That is not exactly what emerged on the other side of it, but it was close.

"We were driving back from Washington late at night and your father fell asleep at the wheel." So far, so good. "He was . . . *tired*," she decided. "The car ran off the road and hit a porch." Another pause. "I went through the windshield." She touched the bandages that covered her face gently. "Just two cuts and a few bad scratches." She tried to smile but it was forced. Her hand trembled again.

"What about Dad?"

She blinked. "Oh, *he's* all right," she said, dismissing him with her hand as if she was annoyed by his lack of injury. "He's got a black eye from hitting the dashboard and some bruised ribs." Clearly there was little sympathy here. "The car's a *mess*, though," she added. "They don't know when it will be fixed."

I wondered who "they" were. I wondered if we were ever going home again.

Granny started to object but thought better of it. I could tell she was spitting mad. "Y'all can stay here as long as it takes. But Lloyd should have known better and that is *all* I am going to say about it." She left the room apparently to prevent herself from saying any more and headed for the sanctity, the known earned boundaries, of her own kitchen. From the front room we could hear her muttering to herself.

Granny, too, had a safe place to speak the truth in.

. . . .

My father returned later that week with a repaired Falcon and some bad news.

He closed the door behind my mother and there were tense words between them. I couldn't hear what was being said from my listening post on the basement stairs. They were in there a long time and there had been a lot of silence before the door reopened.

Both of them looked empty and white, their faces drained of life, as if they had been damned. What could this mean? Even then, not quite eleven years old and barely reflective, I knew it could be only one thing.

We weren't going to a new future in Europe.

We were going back to Cheyenne. Our personal state of hell.

There had been a rumor of not doing that, back when this trip in our new car included the happy anticipation of my father going to Washington. He was "due for a new assignment" and "had friends to see." We "might be eating a lot of pasta soon," or maybe "trading campfire beans for French fries." My parents thought I was only sleeping those traveling nights in the motel room while they sat up late drinking Schlitz and exchanging hope through ambiguities and talking food as metaphor. But I wasn't sleeping.

The promises they had made to each other in those rooms grew into a whole new dimension after that broadcast on the evening news. My father was certain that we were leaving Wyoming after that. My mother was already making plans to sell the house and arrange a move. Now I knew none of those dreams, none of their plans to leave Wyoming, were true. I also knew it was worse than that. It was so much worse that nobody was willing to talk about it. It was an ominous silence descending into our family again.

We wouldn't speak of important things. We would "hedge around the truth." We would talk about lesser matters.

"The car's fixed," Mom said, forcing a brief uncertain smile.

"We'll head back . . . tomorrow," my father announced. He couldn't bring himself to say "to Cheyenne" or even the vaguer "Wyoming." We all knew what he meant and what was implied by what he wasn't saying. Things in Washington hadn't worked out.

"Okay," I said.

"Okay," Popeye said.

"Okay," Granny said.

And no one said anything else. On cue, as if following a closely edited family script, we turned away from each other and achieved routine. My mother packed. My father took the car up to the Esso station to fill the tank and check the oil. Popeye went down in the basement, where I knew he kept a small bottle of lime gin and a pack of Old Gold filters hidden behind the canned tomatoes. "For emergencies," he said. Granny started supper.

I don't remember what I did, but I do remember giving up on being an imaginary baseball hero. There was no future in it, and besides, hadn't I won both an imaginary World Series and the batting crown? The story line had played out and drained me of the fantasy.

But I also knew the deeper truth. I was no hero.

I was just a boy. This was my family. This was real life.

And in real life we were returning to Cheyenne.

ON THE WAY BACK TO CHEYENNE, MY FATHER WAS DEEPLY SILENT. FOR five days he sat in the passenger seat and stared at America as if it were the long, straight highway to hell and he alone was on it. But he wasn't alone.

We were all with him.

. . . .

My father had gone to Washington "to see people." When I was younger, well, you can imagine how funny I thought that sentence was. After all, couldn't my father "see people" here? Years later I would see a film called *The Sixth Sense* that contained the line "I see dead people." I thought that line was hilarious. I wasn't thinking about the film, but instead about my father, about his claim to be going to Washington to "see people." I knew by then that for all the good those calls did him, he might as well have been seeing dead people.

He was certainly dead to them.

But my father didn't actually go to *Washington*. He hadn't gone to Washington to "see people" for the past two years. Not since the CIA moved its headquarters to northern Virginia. Washington, our nation's capital, no longer stood for the pen or the sword. It was just something he said, something he was used to saying. It was a familiar story that he told without thinking about it. If he thought about it, I'd like to believe he would have recognized it as no longer true.

His true destination was Langley.

But in the summer of 1963 I didn't know that.

I don't know what my mother thought about this "Washington" trip. In the summer of 1963 she repeated my father's accomplishments as if it were a mantra that, if repeatedly uttered, had the power to change nature. She had memorized the entries, of course. If she remembered them at all—really remembered them—they were locked inside a simple grammar I had supplied to her, a grammar made less out of knowing than out of naming facts, persons, and places. "Lloyd was in the war, you know. He flew in a B-17. He was wounded. Paralyzed for a time, told he would never walk again. Came home. He learned to walk and went to work for the government. President Eisenhower sent him to Rome as vice consul for the State Department and then over to London. Vice President Nixon personally gave him an award."

That is where my mother's story of my father ended. It was a career path that revealed an arrested development, a sudden break—a full stop—that came after the list of laudable assignments and accomplishments and that silenced any mention of Cheyenne, Wyoming. I hadn't written Cheyenne down.

That may have been my fault.

But if it was my fault, then it was also my contribution to the family story line. In omitting the present from my mother's memorized list of known things, I also condemned her to a desire to repeat the past, even if her memory of it was limited to the words themselves. My father went to "Washington" to "see people" who, in her mind, could turn back time. They could reverse the course of nature. They could return our family to its real life, its storied life, a *dolce vita* life lived in Europe or anywhere else overseas.

To want to repeat the past may have been her failure, but it was such a human one. You *cannot* repeat the past. But for some reason we humans want to. For some people it is a high school romance and for others it was life in war. In my mother's case, had she then truly remembered what that past did to her in real life—the dressed-up cocktail parties where she never felt good enough, or the worry she expended over my father's absences, or the toll that altering her life story had taken on her sense of self—I cannot believe she truly would have wanted to go back to it.

But she didn't know that at the time, and I didn't either. I only knew that my mother found in the progression of words I had written for her a rhythmic progression of a powerful past life spell. It was magical because when it was cast out in casual conversation it made other people impressed, or envious, or proud. It covered up a nonremembered life with the fairy dust of words. It was a magic rendered out of rhetoric, as all spells are.

The origin of her mantra was also a carefully guarded secret between us. It could be understood only if you possessed our relational codebook. It was a codebook kept under tight security at all times and in all places—so tight, in fact, that its entire interpretive system was hidden in an absence, in a blank mind behind the brainwashed walls of unrecoverable memories.

Mother, my own dear mother, how did you *ever* live like that?

· ·

The July 1963 trip to Washington that was really a journey to Langley was also different for another reason. My parents left on this trip together. My mother told me that she was "going with him" and that they would be "back by the end of the week."

I seriously doubt that my mother wanted to "see people." She probably wouldn't have remembered them. Nor was she accompanying my father to his meetings. The world of Langley didn't work that way.

So I can only suppose two or three possible things. Perhaps she wanted to do some shopping. That would make sense because she complained about not being able to find clothes in Cheyenne. She refused "Western wear." Or, secondly, perhaps my parents wanted a little adult time, which would have made sense. Washington was replete with good restaurants and movies that never made it to Cheyenne. They could enjoy each other's company, go out on the town, and then do what people do when they share a hotel room. Or, third and finally, my mother could have asked my father to take her along so she wouldn't have to remain in Martinsburg. It was not her favorite place even before she lost her memories, and no doubt she would have found herself in situations that betrayed her surface recovery. If asked for details about this or that, she wouldn't know. That would be embarrassing.

That fear may well have been her best reason.

As I say, we had spent the previous day—the 4th—at the Potomac River down by the C&O Canal National Park. It must have been unusual for Popeye, who had worked for twenty years on that canal, to revisit it now as a national park. His own history had become part of our nation's history. I wonder what he thought about that.

Our relatives and their children had flocked about my mother, most of whom she probably felt, in 1963 at least, like she had never known before. Throughout the afternoon she would take me aside and ask for information about them. "So, Ruanna is the *eldest* daughter, right? The one I like?" Or "My brother says I once owned a pet pig. This can't be true, can it?"

I told my mother that Ruanna was Jim and Katherine's eldest daughter, and that yes, she was also my mother's favorite among their six children. I explained to her that yes, the way I had heard it, she once owned a pet pig who won some prize in a 4-H fair in high school.

She was visibly aghast. "A *pig*?" Her eyes were wild. "Who the hell *was* I? What was I *thinking*?"

I told her what she had told me about it. I repeated the words she had put to the story of her life before that story had been so cruelly interrupted. "You said you were a good ol' country girl from Frog Hollow and that pig sure looked good in a pink skirt.'"

She staggered away from me like I had slapped her. She nervously lit a cigarette. I watched her eyes, which I had learned were the windows to her soul long before that phrase ever entered my vocabulary. She eyed the assembled Saylor crowd. I have no idea what she was thinking. My guess is that she was desperately trying to reconcile what she did remember about her life—which was primarily that she had been a nurse, she had married my father, and I was her only child—with the buzzing historical reality that now chaotically surrounded her.

I had witnessed her do a similar thing some months ago when regarding her own body in a full-length mirror. She had asked my father why her back was scarred and what the incision near her belly meant. Had her hair always been this dark shade of brunette?

I had been walking down the hallway of our house toward my bedroom at the time and didn't dare enter their room. I knew she was naked because the bedroom door was closed. But I stood there mesmerized by what I was overhearing.

My father was tender with her. He explained her scars and incisions, hair coloring, and even the size of her breasts with short stories that I am sure she immediately committed to memory. Her own body was a stranger to her.

Now her relatives and her past were strangers. That my mother once doted on a pet pig in a pink dress must have seemed inconceivable to her. It was *not* something that a woman who had lived as a consular wife in Rome and London would have done, or should have done. I wonder if she understood, in that poignant realization, all that had gone wrong for her there. I doubt it. From her reaction, my guess is that she was already deeply into pig denial. Or pig alteration. It would be years before we spoke about her pet pig again, and by then she had convinced herself that the pig had really belonged to her brother and that she had only dressed it up once for the fair.

There were other family stories that surprised her on that particular Independence Day. Popeye told us about his days working on the C&O Canal, including the maybe true story about his meeting the President of the United States. "He got his buggy stuck in the mud," or so the story went, and my grandfather used his mules to pull the car out. According to Popeye, there was a neatly dressed man who climbed down out of the car and introduced himself as President Woodrow Wilson. My grandfather thought he was a liar. So too were the two other men with him liars, men who had just introduced themselves as Henry Ford, the maker of the car, and Harvey Firestone, the manufacturer of the tires. My grandfather didn't read the newspapers—he couldn't read at all—so their faces were unfamiliar to him. He saw them as a group of rich men who got stuck in the mud and figured there ought to be at least a dollar in it for the man who pulled them out.

By the time the president shook his hand and there was no dollar in it, my grandfather had had enough. "You don't know who I am, do you?" President Wilson asked.

"No, I don't know who you are. But these other two fools are such darned big liars I wouldn't be surprised if you told me you were the President of the United States!"

It was a good story, a Popeye story, and it always brought laughter. Was it true? Who knows? That he told it was true enough for me. My mother acted as if she were hearing it for the first time. But she recovered her composure quickly. She was getting good at doing that.

It was a wonderful day for all of us, except, perhaps, for my mother. She stuck close to my father after I explained to her about the pig. In my father's shadow, she could deflect questions she couldn't answer and let him shield her from things she didn't know or people she failed to recognize or to know things about.

I'm sure she thought going with my father to Langley would shield her too. My father was her protector and she trusted him completely.

· ·

My parents' "accident" had taken place on the last leg of their trip back to Martinsburg from Langley.

My father had been upset by what he had been told at headquarters. He and my mother stopped for a few drinks to drown their sorrows at a local VFW outpost on the Sharpsburg Pike. When they got back into the car, they were both drunk. So drunk that my father had a terrible time getting the key into the ignition. But, unfortunately, he did get it into the ignition.

He started the car and the car somehow found the road. That my father was even remotely involved in the actual driving is probably debatable. My mother had immediately passed out, so she didn't know. Quite literally, the car ran off the road. It destroyed a woman's front porch. There was evidence of human agency here, albeit an intoxicated human agency.

According to the police report, my father was arrested and charged with driving while intoxicated. He spent two days in the Martinsburg jail, during which time my mother was in the hospital being treated for severe cuts and abrasions sustained when she was suddenly ejected from her passenger seat. She exited the car through the front windshield. She landed on the hood, or what was left of it.

Our ton-and-a-half red-and-white Ford Falcon removed a good portion of the screen porch from the frame of a house before coming to a rest. The car suffered extensive damage to its front end, including a broken front suspension unit and bent axle. Body damage was moderate, but repairable. The windshield was smashed from the inside by my mother's head and most of her body moving through it. She was unconscious when the authorities arrived and an ambulance was called.

My father was also unconscious, his body pinned between the steering wheel and the seat. All of the noise and motion of the wreck hadn't disturbed his sleep. Or, perhaps, he had been disturbed but was knocked out when his head hit the steering wheel. Either way, when the police officer on the scene revived him, he jerked up as if awakened from a nightmare.

The arresting officer placed him in handcuffs and charged him with driving under the influence of alcohol. There was no doubt about it. He couldn't stand upright, his speech was badly slurred. He apparently tried to claim diplomatic immunity. The arresting officer was not amused.

My father was taken to the Martinsburg City Jail and placed unceremoniously in the drunk tank. My mother was rushed to King's Daughter's Hospital, where an emergency room physician she had once worked with

UNITED STATES CIVIL SERVICE COMMISSION
BUREAU OF PERSONNEL INVESTIGATIONS
WASHINGTON 25, D. C.

DATE: 9-27-63

FILE: INO:ALC

Emergency Planning and Security Service
Veterans Administration Central Office
Washington, D. C.

TRANSMITTAL OF ARREST RECORD

NAME	POSITION, ORGANIZATION, AND LOCATION
Goodall, Harold Lloyd	Supervisory Contact Representative VA Center, Cheyenne, Wyoming

DATE OF BIRTH	FILE NO.
10-17-22	01 53658

Attached for your administrative consideration is a report of arrest record received from the Federal Bureau of Investigation. It bears a name which is the same as, or similar to, that of the person identified above. According to the Commission's records, the above-identified person is employed by your agency. *The Commission is conducting no investigation in this case.*

If this person has transferred, the arrest record should be forwarded to the gaining agency. If separated, the arrest record should be destroyed. It is not necessary to notify the Commission of action regarding the arrest except when such action is shown on Standard Form 50 and routinely reported to the Commission.

REMARKS:

☐ The Commission previously sent you a report of arrest record for the person identified above on _____

Kimbell Johnson, Director
Bureau of Personnel Investigations

RECEIVED

IN 206
DECEMBER 1961

FIGURE 15.1 FBI report of Lloyd's arrest, page 1.

CONTRIBUTOR OF FINGERPRINTS	NAME AND NUMBER	ARRESTED OR RECEIVED	CHARGE	DISPOSITION
CSC	Harold Lloyd Goodall #77-55-30866	4-14-55		
PD Cheyenne Wyo	Harold Lloyd Goodall #27212	11-14-61	DUI & CD	
SPol Martinsburg WVa	Harold Lloyd Goodall #CM-17399	7-9-63	driv under the influence of intoxicating liq	PG pd F of $50 & C sent 2 das in jail lic revoked for 6 mos

FIGURE 15.2 FBI report of Lloyd's arrest, page 2.

at Newton D. Baker stitched her up. She was admitted to a semiprivate room for observation.

My father was released from jail after two days and was fined $50. When he appeared before the magistrate, he was informed that his driver's license had been suspended for six months. This was his second offense, the first having taken place in Cheyenne in November of 1961. During that incident he had apparently beaten up the arresting officer and had been found guilty of civil disobedience in addition to driving while intoxicated.

The magistrate lectured him on the evils of drinking and driving. He appeared ashamed of himself and anxious to be out of the room.

He was worried about my mother. Visiting her in a hospital room had become too regular an occurrence. This time, he had been directly responsible for putting her there.

I wonder if he considered that maybe he had *always* been at least partially responsible for putting her there. I'm sure he did.

· ·

The arrest report and the magistrate's decision were forwarded to the Department of Justice in Washington. Under the personal signature of J. Edgar Hoover, my father's case was reviewed and a formal investigation approved.

Don't you find it the least bit odd that J. Edgar Hoover's personal attention would be required for this particular case of DUI? I do.

But then, I only have available to me what was contained in his dummy folder. In it, all of the paperwork concerning the arrest and subsequent letter of official reprimand are done on Civil Service or Veterans Administration stationery.

But why would the director of the FBI spend his valuable time reviewing something as relatively minor as that? Why would J. Edgar be interested in someone who was only a contact officer? Someone working for the VA in Wyoming?

It doesn't make sense. Officially.

Unofficially, or at least outside of the documents contained in the dummy folder, it makes quite a bit of sense. My father worked for the government. He knew secrets, top secrets. He was still being watched.

· ·

The letter of reprimand is a sad document for me to read. It includes both a review of the relevant facts in the case as well as verbiage about my father having brought "discredit to himself, his office, and to the Veterans Administration."

No doubt all of that is true. But it is still sad.

I wonder if a similar letter exists in his "covert file" in Langley? My bet is that it does. There, in a government Agency where men and women routinely plotted the overthrow of dictators and financed guerrilla groups and assassinated agents of their rivals at will, there is probably a letter of reprimand for my father for a DUI.

I'm not making light of the charge. Driving while intoxicated is a serious crime and it deserves to be severely punished. But it does strike me as ironic that this crime would be the one most damaging to his attempt to rebuild a career. Of course, there is no mention in it of what we ought to consider the contributing circumstances. Not that they would excuse the crime, but they would certainly help a judge understand his apparent psychological condition at the time he committed it.

But, of course, at his hearing he said nothing in his own defense. He admitted driving drunk and destroying private property. He accepted his fine and suspended sentence without objection. My guess is that he didn't then fully appreciate how the incident would affect his career. Nor might he have cared. He knew his career was stalled and that it was probably unlikely to ever be revived. Angleton hated him. Now that Philby had defected and Angleton had been shown to be fallible, he hated my father even more than he had before.

We would continue our exile in Wyoming.

· ·

As a matter of historical fact, J. Edgar Hoover was routinely brought in to investigate arrests involving FBI or CIA personnel. He was also brought in on cases involving government and military employees who held a top secret or secret clearance. Of all his investigations into the character and behavior of civil servants, J. Edgar Hoover was particularly fond of releasing his considerable federal dogs on the CIA employees' civil misdeeds. He still harbored a deep personal resentment that the Agency had been established in the first place. It was a resentment that grew into a generalized hatred of all Agency personnel. Any time Hoover could file an official report finding personal fault with them, he did so.

I could, I suppose, say some fairly damning things about J. Edgar Hoover. But what point would it serve? Those among us who still care

October 9, 1963

4042/00

TO: Assistant Administrator for Management
            and Evaluation (07)
         Veterans Administration Central Office
         Washington, D. C.   20420

ATTN: Director, Emergency Planning and
            Security Service (073)

SUBJ: Arrest Record – CSC Form IN-206 Re: Goodall, Harold Lloyd

1. We have reviewed, very carefully, your Personal-Official letter of
October 4, 1963 transmitting CSC Form IN-206 and the FBI Arrest Record
in the case of Mr. Harold L. Goodall presently employed at this Center
as Contact Officer, GS-11.

2. Prior to the receipt of your letter, the two arrests in question
had already been brought to the attention of the Center Director and
on September 17, 1963, a Personal-Official letter was sent to the Area
Field Director, Area 4 outlining the complete circumstances and recommended course of action concerning this case. Specifically, the Center
Director stated that Mr. Goodall has brought discredit both to himself,
to the Cheyenne VA Center, and to the VA as a whole and has lost effectiveness in his present position.

3. Mr. Goodall is highly qualified, technically, as a Contact Officer
and can contribute materially to the Contact Program of the VA. He has,
however, lost the respect of his associates and has rendered himself ineffective as a result of his drinking habits. The Center Director recommended that necessary action be initiated at the Central Office level to
remove him from his present assignment at the earliest practical date.
We are, at the present moment, awaiting word from Central Office on the
final action to be taken in this case.

4. The above facts are presented as requested by your letter of October 4,
1963. If further information is necessary, please advise.

                                DUDLEY S. DEAN
                                Acting Center Director

RFS   PERSONAL-OFFICIAL

cc: Director's Office (00)

about such things already know what a strange, strange man he was. We all have heard the stories about his alleged personal sexual preferences (despite his hatred of gays and lesbians), his clothing choices, and those clever little pink slippers he wore when he padded around his Georgetown digs. We know he conducted investigations into the lives of most of our American heroes—Elvis, JFK, RFK, Martin Luther King Jr.—as well as our most notorious villains. And we have been burdened with the historical knowledge that he often used his personal files to intimidate elected government officials, from modest civil servants to several presidents.

By all published accounts, J. Edgar Hoover was a brilliant, devious, difficult, prejudiced, pain-in-the-ass son of a bitch. He was a powerful man in an era of powerful men and he outlasted every one of them. He regularly defamed the people he didn't like and assassinated the characters of anyone who dared to challenge him. As he grew older and even more powerful, he flaunted his authority with unprecedented abandon, which is saying something in America.

He believed he was larger than America. He was larger than life.

. . . .

My mother drove us home to Wyoming. Before we left, her doctor in Martinsburg removed her facial bandages and the blood-caked Frankensteinian stitching. There were two small scars that made a ragged X on her head. My mother believed the scars marked her life in some tragic way. She clearly blamed my father for it, which I suppose I can understand even if her quiet complicity in agreeing to try to drive home was a contributing factor.

I could feel her blame as she drove us back to Cheyenne.

I could feel it after that, too. Like a ripple on water at night, her dark mood seemed to wash across the surface of her face and then disappear. But it did not really disappear. It was always there, deep as the ocean beneath the ripple and equally fathomless. Evidence, I guess, that as the scars on her head healed there were deeper internal psychological scars that never did. I used to blame the wreck but I have long since reconsidered that judgment.

It wasn't the wreck so much as it was *surviving* it that she held against my father. She was, at forty-five, a woman without much reserve left. She had lost her memory and her dreams, been stripped of her nursing career, and found herself, after madness, married to a man who was, by his own account, "all washed up." She had remarkable scars on her body that attested to having survived a horrific fire and now she had scars on her forehead to remind her that she had survived a nearly fatal car accident. She told me, without drama, that every time she looked at herself in a mirror she replayed her face crashing through windshield glass. If this woman had been *you*, what would you have to live for?

Me, perhaps. But that is so self-absorbed as to be off-putting even to myself. I have no doubt that my mother had once loved me, but since she had moved out of the straitjacket and back into our lives, she looked at me more as a confidant than as a son. She would learn to love me again, but that took time. Certainly during the summer of 1963 what she felt for me was unlikely to have approximated real love; it may at best have been a curious fondness born more of our shared secrets than our shared blood.

. . . .

My parents changed their will when they arrived home.

They pointedly informed me that in the event of their death, my uncle and aunt would have custody. Uncle Jim and Aunt Katherine were fine with me but I wondered then, as now, how different my life would have been had I been raised on a farm outside of Martinsburg. My parents insisted that the change had been made because of the wreck, a testament, I guess, to the fact that they realized full well they could have been killed and I would have been left, like Popeye before me, to fend for myself. But I doubt that was their reason. Or at least, that had not been entirely the reason.

I think they were *preparing* for their own death.

For my part, I had resolved during the silent ride home to develop my "being alone" skills. With my parents in such a depleted emotional condition—words I wouldn't learn to use until much later—my task was to survive them. I remember vividly the sadness of recognizing that plain fact. My parents seemed destined for self-destruction and if I couldn't help them avoid it, I at least wanted to find a way to avoid that fate myself.

. . . .

On the surface you couldn't tell my father had changed. He went to work in the morning and came home in the evening. He wore the same suits, starched white shirts, and conservative ties. His shoes were always highly polished. His fingernails were meticulously maintained. He still smelled of Old Spice and cigarettes.

The first clue to a fundamental change in him was that he didn't require us to go to church anymore. My father had been raised a strict Baptist.

His paternal grandfather—William Clinton Goodall—had built the First Baptist Church in Huntington. During the war, my father had regularly attended the nondenominational services offered by various chaplains and kept a paperback copy of the Holy Bible in his shirt pocket over his heart every time he flew.

After the war I think he lost at least a part of his earlier faith, and he became what he described to me once as a "pragmatic Christian." He was pragmatic in the sense that he attended church because government employees were expected to practice their respective faiths as a sign they hadn't gone over to the side of godless Communism. It was also pragmatic in the sense that church was a good place to meet people who could advance your career. So if my father was a practicing Christian, he was certainly a lesser one, a man who used prayer to advance his cause in this life rather than the afterlife.

Overseas, my father continued the habit of professing his faith publicly but keeping his private doubts to himself. And he had doubts. He told me later that he had doubted the existence of God or, if God did exist, how involved or concerned He may have been in the individual affairs of American intelligence officers. It was within that attitude that he found it within himself to name his agents in Rome after the Epistles. Nevertheless, he went to church and sat alongside other women and men, who, he believed, felt pretty much the same as he did. He avoided the true believers of all faiths, having figured out that fanatics of any stripe were best avoided.

In Rome we irregularly attended Catholic or Episcopal services and in London we irregularly attended the Church of England. I was too young to remember any of them. My mother later claimed to recall what people wore to services and that we all enjoyed our Sunday dinners in fine restaurants, but aside from those memories, neither one of us could say with any certainty that my father felt more or less disposed toward any one religion. He was a man who adapted his religious practices to the prevailing spiritual climate.

In Wyoming, we were Methodists. I don't know why. I do know that my father became adamant about going to church shortly after we moved there. By the autumn of 1963, I had been forced to attend Methodist Sunday school for over two years and thoroughly hated it. Church may have been a snore—people regularly snored in church—but Sunday school was torture. My Sunday-school teachers made us recite the names of the books of the Bible, both Old and New Testaments, and then commit entire passages to memory. No questions or comments were allowed.

I could clearly see where this practice was headed. The point of Methodist Sunday school in Cheyenne, Wyoming, seemed to be what my Thorndike and Barnhart *Student Dictionary* defined as "brainwashing." I was against it. God was fine with me, although I favored the New Testament version, but this whole religion thing was deeply suspicious. One grumpy Sunday morning I said so at the breakfast table and that was it. I didn't have to attend again.

And neither did my parents.

Did my father have a momentary loss of faith? Did my mother? I somehow doubt it.

I think my parents decided that attending services on Easter and at Christmas would be enough to keep up appearances for anyone still paying attention to what they did on Sunday. Besides, as my mother put it, "only heathens and Communists didn't go to church on Easter and Christmas." Given that my father's career was no longer likely to have much in common with his record of church attendance, my mother didn't remember the names of people she met there, and I had no use for Sunday school, the decision *not* to go was all right with each one of us.

What we did instead of getting up for church on Sundays was to remain in our beds longer than usual. Sleeping later in our family seemed like a really good idea. It was for me. I was a child. I still believed that while you were asleep nothing bad ever happened to you.

I doubt my father shared my belief. He still had nightmares from the war. He seldom slept well. Sleeping in for him was not about sleeping in. It was about not going anywhere. It may have been a metaphor for our current life.

And what about my mother? What did she think about sleeping in on Sunday mornings? I have no idea.

. . . .

Another thing that changed about my father was his attitude about going to work.

Prior to our return from West Virginia, he used to get up in the morning bright and early and be enthusiastic about getting to the office. Maybe he was excited about going somewhere, and doing something, but I doubt that what might have excited him was going on at the office. Out at the base, maybe. Or in the listening truck, perhaps. But after we returned, he slept in later and when he dressed to leave for work, he appeared resigned to it rather than happy about it.

I know now that saying "my father works for the government" and that "he moves paper from one side of his desk to the other" was a code used to cover the fact that he was a G-man. That's what all the G-men said about themselves, and what their children said about the work they did. It was a feature of popular television shows and movies of the era. It was in many of the novels and in the short stories about secret agents featured in popular magazines.

My father certainly looked the part of a G-man. He was a strong, silent type in a dark suit, white shirt, and tie. His shoes were polished and his nails meticulously manicured. He was clean-shaven and visited the barbershop every Saturday morning whether he needed a trim or not.

He seldom smiled.

He didn't invite people over to the house and rarely accepted invitations to theirs. He had work to do.

He *always* had work to do.

He was "gone" a lot.

· ·

The third sign of change after our return from that ill-fated trip had to do with furniture.

My father gradually moved most of our personal items from Europe down into the basement. By the time he had finished this rearrangement, our house was almost bare, at least compared to how it had looked. If we still didn't reflect the Wyoming wagon wheel–and–Indian blanket sense of style, nor did our home look so very different from anyone else's.

We fit in. We blended.

Our basement was where we now kept the past. Out of sight, out of mind, out of our conversations. Every piece of evidence that may have suggested who we were before Wyoming was removed from view, as if removing them from view would also remove the memory of our former selves.

· ·

But what bothered me the most about the changes in my father was his sudden transformation from a Friday-night fights kind of guy into a man who went bowling on Friday nights. And he took my mother with him.

My parents joined a bowling league that kept them out late on Friday nights. I was old enough to stay home alone, heat a frozen dinner, and watch my favorite television shows. Anyone who has ever been a kid in that situation might think that a little Friday-night independence would be perceived by the kid as a very good thing.

I was that kind of kid, but it wasn't me being left home that was the problem. It was that my parents couldn't be trusted to go bowling by themselves. They didn't go for the bowling. They went for the drinking. And then, somehow, each week again testing fate, they drove home.

I think my father got drunk after bowling and then drove home to prove he could. He drank straight vodka, any kind, so long as it was 100 proof. It made an otherwise reasonable man into a belligerent. He drank vodka because he believed you couldn't smell it on your breath. He drank vodka to excess to prove he was still man enough to drink and drive. That if he wanted to, he could get goddamn hammered and still make it home.

And he wanted to get *goddamned* hammered. Man oh man, did he ever want to. I don't know if he really wanted to make it home. I hope so but I don't know so. By then, my father was a burnt-out case.

My mother went along for the ride. That's what she said. I think she meant something quite different from what is usually intended by invoking that tired cliché.

She hoped for a death by car. If that sounds a little crazy, well, it *was* crazy. Nothing "little" about it. Let's look at the facts: my mother had been diagnosed as a schizophrenic during her nervous breakdown. She was, at the time, a recovering amphetamine addict and a practicing alcoholic. She had a good portion of her brains fried by shock treatments, and another part of her brain clobbered in a car crash. She had little memory of four or five years of her life and distrusted information she received about herself before that. That she wasn't in her right mind is an understatement.

That her brain functioning diminished when she drank to excess is a fact.

That she drank to excess after bowling is a fact.

That my parents made it home is a fact, too. But I prefer to call it a miracle.

· ·

I was only eleven years old but I already knew the expression "falling-down drunk" wasn't a single action but a *process*. It began when the back door flew open and smacked against the wall, and my father lurched through the kitchen searching for something to hold on to. It was followed by my mother admonishing him with the astonished (and, to my ears, astonishingly obvious) phrase, "Lloyd, you're *drunk*!"

"Yep," he replied, sometimes hiccuping and sometimes not. The hiccuping was not a good sign. It caused him to lose his balance, and was therefore immediately followed by a loud *clump*, which was his body slamming, often face-first, against the floor.

"Lloyd! You *are* drunk!" My mother would repeat as she made her own drunken, careful waddling way unsteadily through the kitchen and hallway, where his sprawled body now groped for a wall to steady his crawl down to their bedroom.

"Yep," he repeated. If he managed to stand and hiccuped again, he fell over again, and this Punch and Judy–like routine repeated itself until he banged from wall to wall and finally fell into bed.

If he didn't hiccup he tried to hide the fact that he *was* falling-down drunk, and would yell back at her in his belligerent voice "Am *not*," or—more likely—"Hell no, I need *another* drink."

In either form, this vodka-soaked taunt was delivered in a slurry sing-song voice, the voice I associated with somebody on the schoolyard saying "na-na-na-na-na" and pointing a finger at someone who just got caught being bad.

Clump. Trying to speak was always a mistake. I had learned by simply listening to this part of the process of being falling-down drunk that my father couldn't walk and talk at the same time while in this condition. I would have thought *he* would have learned that lesson as well, but apparently not. This was a process, and, as my Thorndike and Barnhart *Student Dictionary* defined it, "a characteristic of a process is that it is repeatable." The amazing thing was—and this was truly amazing to me then and is to me still—that he didn't hurt himself, nor even bruise his face, even after it had repeated hard contact with the wooden floor.

Drunks and fools have God watching out for them, right?

Nor did he suffer hangovers. Or if he did, he never showed it. Saturday mornings we would rise together at eight o'clock as if nothing had happened, eat breakfast, and drive to the barbershop for our weekly trim. If we talked about anything, it was sports.

I once asked him about his previous evening's bowling scores, but he couldn't remember them. I didn't ask again.

• •

"Naomi?" Usually after his second or third hallway collapse he would call for her help. By this time my mother, in her astonished fit of annoy-

ance at his admitted drunkenness, had already stepped or climbed over his sprawled body and bobbled or crawled her way to bed. Usually she remained fully clothed, passed out immediately, and proceeded without fail into a deep sleep. So she wouldn't—or couldn't—answer him.

"*Naomi?*" he would cry out again, this time a little more insistently. After a few more cries I would hear his final plaintive "*Help me.*"

This last plea signaled to me that he was truly in trouble. The sound of my father calling for help was pitiful. So I would get out of my bed and help him to his.

Wordlessly, I guided him to his feet and helped him use the wall to steady and move his body to the bedside, or, failing our ability to accomplish that, simply pushed and/or pulled his body into the bedroom. Because he was larger than I was, and more or less dead weight anyway, if I couldn't get him into bed I left him lying on the floor and put a pillow under his head and a blanket over him. He was generally out cold and snoring by then anyway.

Each time I helped him through his process of being falling-down drunk, which was at least once a week during bowling season, he grabbed my hand, put his index finger to his lips, and said, "Shhhhh. Don't tell your mother."

So I didn't.

But, in truth, I never thought I had to. After all, she had to know. It was just another part of our increasingly downhill-spiraling unspeakable life that remained hidden, that remained secret.

· ·

Wyoming's land mass is roughly equivalent to the total area of Pennsylvania, New York, and two-thirds of Connecticut. In 1963, Wyoming's total population was about one-tenth that of the city of Philadelphia.

In my unofficial estimate, at least three-quarters of the citizenry in the 1960s were hard drinkers, and probably at least half of the remaining quarter were themselves recovering alcoholics. This is a long way of saying that Wyoming was certainly not Utah. But it is also another way of saying that being drunk in Cheyenne in the 1960s was not that unusual.

Wyoming is the Ireland of the American West.

Why is that? Forget the purple mountains majesty and awesome snow-capped peaks that you see featured in Coors commercials, because that is Colorado, not Wyoming. There are Rockies in Wyoming but they are rougher, and if you discount Jackson Hole or Yellowstone Park there is very little reason to ever visit them.

When I think of Wyoming, I think instead of the bland reflective surfaces of the moon, bereft of just about any visible signs of life, punctuated by ghostly rock formations, sudden dirt devils, and a dryness so pure that fine leathers crack.

I think of gigantic oil and gas refineries.

I think of long, lonesome highways so numbingly straight and somnolent that people unaccustomed to driving on them are often reported to have fallen asleep and driven off the road.

I think of an area in the Unites States of America where most of the men and not an insignificant population of the women are armed and, therefore, by any reasonable person's definition, dangerous.

I think of long seasons for big-game hunting and trout fishing by women and men who think Hemingway is a small town in Idaho.

I think of an endless unpoetic prairie and a life that demands only to be endured.

• •

I didn't see my parents' drinking to be such a big deal. Drinking wasn't secret in this town. Nor was being drunk once in a while. People talked about it all the time, and they laughed at themselves and at each other about it, too. They had an elaborate language code for this intoxicated state of being, and when telling someone else about it, they said they got drunk, tied one on, went blotto, got stinkin' drunk, got shit-faced, got pissed, got a little too happy, got hammered, or were three sheets to the *fuckin'* wind. Metaphors for drunkenness were as ubiquitous in our homes as giant-sized bottles of aspirin. It was expected adult foolishness, no more sinful in those days before the surgeon general's warning than smoking cigarettes.

Everyone we knew smoked cigarettes.

People smoked cigarettes in every room of the house.

There were huge ashtrays on coffee tables, matches or lighters left out for convenience, and smaller ashtrays inviting a smoke while sitting on the toilet in a bathroom or fixing a quick ham sandwich in the kitchen. People drank when they smoked and smoked when they drank. Couples smoked in bed, before and after. Kids smoked at school, before and after. My teachers—with the sole exception of the athletic coaches—all smoked, although not in classrooms until high school. Mornings began all over town with that first cigarette, a couple of aspirins, and a cup of black coffee, and many people I observed smoked before they ate, while they ate, and after they ate, as if the cigarettes were part of the meal. People smoked in their cars, their homes, and their offices. On the street. In bars. In lines. Some stores banned it, but many didn't. It was as natural to smoke cigarettes in the sixties as it was to breathe, and often, in those smoke-filled days, there really wasn't a whole lot of difference.

So if people drank too much or smoked too much, nobody worried very much about it. It was a sign of weakness among men *not* to drink too much, or *not* to smoke too much. It certainly was a sign of weakness to complain about it.

Women smoked almost as much as men. They smoked to keep their weight down and because it calmed their nerves. Women who were housewives smoked because it passed the time and women who worked outside the home smoked because at break time it was what you did. A pack a day was just average. Two packs wasn't unheard of. Three packs was excessive but forgiven if the smoker had recently suffered a personal tragedy. When bad things happened, you were encouraged to smoke, and if you already smoked, you were encouraged to smoke even *more*. Come to think of it, the third leading cause of death in Wyoming was probably due to lung cancer.

My parents smoked. And they drank. I didn't complain about it.

I was deeply ashamed of my mother and my father when they came home drunk. When I had to put my father to bed. I worried about them driving in that condition, given what had once happened. I worried about other people on the same roads with them when they drove in that condition. I worried about myself when I had to go somewhere with them and, after too many drinks, my father tried to drive home. This combination of worry and shame led to an inward lessening of respect for them that I would learn to not outwardly reveal.

It was something I blamed them for, and eventually hated them for.

This was a secret I kept to myself, and *for* myself.

. . . .

On November 22, 1963, during our American history lesson, my fifth-grade class was informed that President John F. Kennedy had been assassinated in Dallas. At first, we waited for the punch line. This had to be a bad joke, right? Or maybe it was part of a new emergency drill. But the punch line never came and we were assured that this was no drill.

Everyone was suddenly shocked into an acceptance of it. At least to an acceptance of the *fact* of it. We didn't yet have a story. We were appalled.

This didn't happen in America. Girls cried and boys shouted. Teachers smoked and told us to remain calm although they were obviously not calm themselves.

The principal decided to act. We were marched single file into the hallway under the energetic direction of Mr. Finkelstein, who had been promoted that September to assistant principal and who firmly believed, as he told us, that this was the work of the Russians and we now should prepare for a nuclear attack.

He then produced his trusty baton and led us in a round of patriotic songs.

I don't think anyone really felt like singing, but we complied with his request because he was the responsible adult and the assistant principal, and because we didn't know what else to do. By the time we had finished "America the Beautiful" for the third or fourth or fifth time, our obedience and energy for song had waned. Mr. Finkelstein was the only person still singing. Even the other teachers had stopped.

We were dismissed and allowed to go home. I didn't have far to go. I ran across the street as if the missiles might fall at any moment. My plan was to get into the basement shelter as soon as possible.

My mother was perched in her living-room chair staring at the news. She had been crying, noticeable to me because I hadn't seen her cry in a long time. I asked her if we should go "downstairs"—meaning into the basement shelter—but she shook her head no. I sat down on the couch and mentioned that Mr. Finkelstein had told us that this was the work of the Russians and that we ought to prepare for nuclear war.

"Mr. Finkelstein is an idiot," my mother responded. "I wouldn't listen to him if he were the last man on earth. Listen to Walter Cronkite instead."

So I listened to Mr. Cronkite. I watched the screen, although there wasn't much to see. In later years, people all over America would associate the Kennedy assassination with the Zapruder film showing the shot and chaos that followed it. But that afternoon, we had precious little of a visual nature to go on. Without it, and without any coherent story to tell ourselves about what had happened, I remember that afternoon as a series of supposedly informed opinions being sought by newscasters and a lot of hypothesis making and surmise being the result. In fact, some people feared that the Russians *did* do it and that we might be—once again—on the verge of nuclear war.

"See?" I said, feeling at least partially vindicated.

She said, "I don't hear any sirens yet." We watched as Lyndon Baines Johnson took the oath of office. My mother ignored him and instead began expressing sorrow for the newly widowed Jacqueline Kennedy.

My father arrived home early and in a surprisingly good mood.

"Dad," I said, "didn't you hear? President Kennedy was assassinated."

He looked at me as if I had just said something remarkably dumb. "Of course I know that," he replied. "Where do you think I've been all day?"

He went out to the kitchen and poured a stiff drink. I followed him. "Mr. Finkelstein said we should prepare for nuclear war because the Russians are responsible."

He laughed. Really laughed. I hadn't heard my father laugh like that in a very long time.

"What's *funny* about that?" I asked, incredulously.

My father looked directly at me. "It wasn't the Russians," he said.

"How do *you* know?" I asked, a little mad at him. I mean, after all, he wasn't Walter Cronkite. He was a man who worked for the VA, who pushed paper from one side of his desk to the other all day. What could he know about it?

He took a deep breath and smiled. "I *don't* know," he said. "But it's what I think."

What he wasn't telling me then, and wouldn't reveal to me until much later, was that ever since the Bay of Pigs fiasco, there had been inside talk about the CIA holding a grudge of honor against the president and his brother Bobby. My father had his own theory about what actually happened.

But, as I say, I wouldn't know that until later.

When Lee Harvey Oswald's name was put forth with the single-man assassination theory, my father thought that was total bullshit and said so, in our living room. When Jack Ruby shot and killed Oswald at the Dallas jail, my father was convinced it was all part of the same plan. And when Allen Dulles was appointed to the Warren Commission he was convinced there would be a cover-up.

In my father's considered opinion, there were a number of groups—not individuals—who were in a position to carry off an assassination. He found it highly unlikely that Oswald could have pulled it off alone, although he was convinced that Oswald had been put in the Texas School Book Depository for the purpose of taking a pot shot and then was framed for the murder. That's why Jack Ruby was sent to kill him. Whoever was responsible had to shut him up. My father believed that the setup—complete with Ruby's supposed intrusion—had Agency written all over it.

When I suggested that the mafia had a hand in the assassination, my father dismissed it. "Bill Harvey was using Johnny Rosselli to try to get to *Castro*," he said. "He wasn't using him to get *Kennedy*."

But when he said these things to me, he was doing time as a resident in the Brook Lane Psychiatric Hospital. I was smoking cigarettes and shooting the breeze with him outside on a picnic table just to pass the time. I brought up the JFK topic because I had recently seen a copy of the Warren Commission Report in college and figured, correctly, he would have an opinion about it.

His opinion was that the Warren Commission Report was a whitewash job. "I knew Bill Harvey and Allen Dulles," he said, knowingly.

I didn't ask him for details. My father was a mental patient and always claimed to have known important people. He was probably suffering from delusions.

I had given up believing much of what he told me. I didn't know then that he had never once lied to me.

• •

My father's drinking reached a new low when I walked in on him in the bathroom one Saturday afternoon and he was swallowing what was left of a bottle of rubbing alcohol. He was so drunk by then that he didn't care if I stood there and watched him. He and my mother had been drinking steadily since they had gone bowling the night before.

I doubt he knew I was in the same room.

I slapped the bottle out of his hands. Trying to reach it, he slipped off the toilet seat and banged his head hard against the porcelain bathtub. He moaned once and was out cold.

I thought I had killed him.

I ran to get my mother, but she was drunk, too. Passed out in the bedroom with only her bra on and spread out across the double bed with a vodka bottle beneath her on the floor. I tried to wake her, but it was no good. I was persistent enough to bring her partially out of it, but she told me I was imagining things and said to go back to bed. It was only five o'clock in the afternoon and the sun was still clearly visible beyond the window. I covered her body with the sheet and decided to take matters into my own hands.

I called the police and explained what had happened.

Two police officers were dispatched to our home. Following their arrival an ambulance pulled into our driveway. The police got my father's dead drunk weight onto the stretcher and the ambulance attendants drove him up the hill to DePaul Hospital, where they did whatever they do to someone in his condition. I didn't ask and no one ever told me.

One of the police officers tried in vain to wake my mother, but he finally gave up and wrote a long note instead. He placed the note on the kitchen table and told me to give it to her when she sobered up. The note explained that her husband had been taken to DePaul but that attempts to wake her had failed. There was a phone number, which I suppose was the hospital switchboard. They had included their names.

One of the officers asked me if I would be all right.

I nodded. "So I didn't kill him?" I asked.

The policeman replied, "No, kid, you didn't kill him. He was trying to do that himself." He placed a hand on my shoulder and patted it. "Do you want one of us to stay here with you until your mother . . . ," he searched for a kind word, "*er*, wakes up?"

I was then twelve years old. I was a tall kid, strong, a junior high school football player. As long as my father was going to be all right, I could handle my mother. "No," I replied, "I'll be fine."

Our house was clean and well appointed. There were no signs of physical struggle, no record of domestic violence. My father's DUI records told the officers all they believed they needed to know.

My father had gone "a little crazy" after drinking too much. He "confused" the rubbing alcohol for more gin or perhaps vodka. That was their story and I didn't dispute it.

My father returned home the following afternoon sober but shaken. His throat was sore. He apologized to me and swore this would be the last time. It would not be the last time. My mother gave him a bath and put him to bed.

By Monday morning, she pretended the whole thing never happened. She told me I had acted rashly. My father wasn't drinking rubbing alcohol. What was I thinking? This kind of thing could be damaging to his career.

I pointed to the note that was still on the kitchen table. She picked it up, read it, and threw it in the trash can. Then she carried the trash can out to the incinerator, dumped it, and set the whole thing on fire.

Satisfied, I suppose, she came inside and returned the trash can to its place in the corner of the kitchen. "Don't tell me," she said, angrily. "Don't tell me you think you know what happened this weekend."

I stared at her. I had become accustomed to my mother not making sense. But "this weekend" as she euphemistically put it, *had* happened. It was not something she could wish away. Or forget about.

But I underestimated her. She would do exactly that.

Life as we knew it in Wyoming would only continue.

CHAPTER NO.	TITLE	Better Living Through Chemistry: Cheyenne
16	DATES	1965-1967

THINGS GOT BETTER. AT LEAST TEMPORARILY. I SUPPOSE THEY HAD TO. My father could no longer maintain his rate of deterioration and still do his job. My mother, if in deep denial about the toll drinking was taking on both of them, nevertheless resolved inwardly to make a change in her life.

Cans of beer replaced bottles of vodka. At least for a while, and at least most of the time. On a trip I made with my father to the liquor store, my father quipped to the proprietor that he had "been ordered by his doctor" to cut back, thus the changeover to beer. Obviously, they knew each other well enough for my father to feel he needed to offer an explanation.

"I'd get a second opinion" was the proprietor's response. He laughed and lit a Marlboro, only to see when he put it down that there was already one lit in the ashtray. "I can't drink too much beer," he went on, "fills me up."

My father nodded. "Me, too," he admitted.

· ·

According to his medical records, it was during this time that my father first sought professional psychiatric help. In addition to talking through at least some of his problems with a government-approved shrink, he began a regime of pharmacological remedies—biochemical technologies—designed to ease his chronic back and leg pain. Relief from chronic pain had been at the heart of his increased use of alcohol, although his stalled career, the boredom of life on the prairie, and a deep hatred of J. J. Angleton certainly fueled it.

Management of the chronic pain was the initial goal. The pharmaceutical solutions offered to my father in the mid- to late 1960s only added to his drinking problem a series of drug dependencies that seldom relieved his symptoms for very long. Chronic pain narcotics, like Percodan, were duly prescribed and warnings against ingesting alcohol while using them were given to him. But he drank alcohol because Percodan did nothing to relieve his nightmares and nothing outside of going blotto prevented them. The drug predictably interacted with the alcohol and he reported being confused, disoriented, occasionally manic, increasingly depressed, and sleepless.

Percodan was replaced with the harder narcotic lithium, which today is routinely used to treat bipolar disease of the manic-depressive variety. But lithium must be very carefully managed. Toxicity is easy to reach and often fatal. Once again, lithium cannot be ingested in combination with alcohol without risking serious side effects, including coma and death.

Lithium didn't work at all, probably because the diagnosis was flawed. My father was not bipolar. Nor was he manic-depressive. Other drugs, newer drugs, were introduced, each one promising to end his chronic pain or to erase depression or to allow for peaceful sleep. Some of them worked for a while, others didn't. On and on and on this revolving-door program of pharmacological experimentation continued.

One positive side effect of this "better living through chemistry" approach to my father's chronic pain was a decided decrease in the number of excessive drinking episodes. He followed the doctor's orders to a T because he wanted to believe that a chemical cure existed for his pain. Only when the pills proved ineffective did he return to what Ozzy Osbourne calls "the self-medication plan."

· ·

I should say, in my father's defense, that although he was an alcoholic, he was at least a functional one. He seldom missed a day of work. When he retired on full medical disability in 1969, he had accrued over a year and a half of sick pay and vacation leave.

He also managed to perform well in most social situations. In 1965 he was elected president of the Cheyenne Lions Club. Since 1961, he had attended their Wednesday luncheons, given speeches, led fund drives, and served as a member of one group or another. He attended my school's PTA meetings and many of my Little League games. Most of the time, particularly during the daylight hours, he was the veritable image of a responsible man, loving husband, and caring parent. People liked him.

He was a good guy.

He was my father. I loved him. I just hated his excessive *drinking*.

My mother, too, gradually improved. When she was doing well she could still be a lot of fun, just slightly off-center in a watched world where centering counted. She was, by nature as well professional inclination, a woman who cared for strays, whether it was a person in need or a mutt without a home. She loved to listen to popular music on the radio, watch *General Hospital*, and dance. She gave me what I needed, whether it was a baseball glove or money for a movie or new hiking boots for the Boy Scouts. She discovered from a friend of mine that I secretly wanted a dog and within a week she surprised me with a white toy fox terrier I named Yogi. Yogi was a female but I liked the name so it stuck.

I'm telling you these things because I don't want you to see my parents only through the haze of their occasional extreme intoxication. I want you to see them as incomplete and vulnerable persons, like all of us, made more so by the secrets they kept and by the lies they told, but good people nonetheless. They were a couple deeply, if dangerously and codependently, in love and they tried very hard to be good parents to me. In many ways, they were not too dissimilar from other kids' parents, particularly those kids whose parents worked at Francis E. Warren and had classified jobs they couldn't talk about.

. . . .

I knew those classified kids. We attended the same city schools, swam together on Tuesday and Thursday afternoons at the heavily chlorinated base pool, and played ball against each other in Little League. No matter where we were, we always knew *who* we were. We were held to a different—some might say higher—standard than other children. We recognized each other by our military haircuts, pressed clothes, and shined shoes.

By the way we rolled up our bathing suits inside white towels.

By the fact we always arrived on time.

We were the kids who had an easy, practiced adherence to politeness rituals, "yessir" and "no ma'am," always. There was a learned quietness about us, a certain way of being in the world predicated on the golden rule of classified childhoods: *we were to be seen, not heard*. We were a well-scrubbed, mostly white tribe of good students who were good sports. We mastered every task we were handed because we all knew that if we didn't, it might make the feared "black mark" against our mother or our father in their ominous-sounding "permanent file."

We were children of secrets. We learned to keep our feelings to ourselves and our mouths shut.

Christmas, 1964. We took the train back to West Virginia to visit Granny and Popeye and for my father's annual December trip to the place he called Washington that was not Washington but Langley. But never mind. We boarded a sleek Union Pacific Pullman in Cheyenne and rode it, gently rocking, across the wide American plains into Chicago, then transferred to a Baltimore and Ohio coach that had seen much better days. The B&O diesel groaned, hissed, squeaked, smoked, and rocked back and forth ungently all the way into the railway station in Martinsburg.

I hardly noticed. My father had given me a novel to pass the time while he and my mother entertained themselves in the lounge car. The novel was Ian Fleming's *From Russia with Love*. It not only helped me pass the time up there in the narrow railed top bunk on the gently rocking Pullman train, it captured my imagination in a way no other book had done since *The Kid Who Batted 1000*. I couldn't stop reading. I loved it!

James Bond became my new hero. My role model. I wanted to grow up to be just like him.

By the time we arrived in Chicago I was already asking my father for money to buy another one. He seemed amused by my request but gave me the money. This is exactly what he said: "It's not really like that, you know."

What did *he* know?

After all, I thought that he was just a regular guy who worked for the government. Looking back on it now, I realize it was the first time, and one of the only times, that my father gave me a clue about who he really was, or the life he led. But, unfortunately, I was too bullheaded to hear it. Maybe he was hoping I would do more with the words he was offering me than simply ignore them, take his money, and head off to the paperback rack in search of another James Bond novel.

I had always believed that my father hated to fly. Whenever possible, he arranged to take a train or to drive. When that didn't work out, he plied himself with alcohol and narcotic painkillers sufficient to ensure that even "if something bad happened"—as he put it—"I won't feel a goddamned thing."

My mother, on the other hand, *loved* to fly.

She loved the idea of it, the romance. I don't know for sure if she fully remembered the flights we took to and from Europe, but she said she did. She repeated exactly the same words every time she talked about them, and her apparent need to adhere to a script made me more than a little suspicious. Nevertheless, my mother claimed that flying was one of her very favorite things to do, second only to nursing. I knew she loved nursing. She had memories of nursing, and she didn't use the same words when she talked about them.

In the spring of 1965, my mother decided to create a new life for herself. She had concluded that if we were going to be "stuck out here on the prairie," she might as well make the best of it. It was a new life that included flying and nursing. Although my mother had excellent nursing credentials, she hadn't worked in almost twenty years. DePaul Hospital turned down her initial employment application, and, given her history of being treated for mental illness there, probably that was no real surprise. However, someone at the hospital told her there was an air ambulance service in immediate need of a flight nurse, "no questions asked."

This employment opportunity appealed to her on two levels. First, she could be a nurse again. Second, she could fly.

She joined Steve Stevenson's air ambulance service and told us what she had done at dinner. We were feasting on Betty Crocker's "award-winning chicken casserole," when she announced it. She said it casually, as if it meant nothing more than she would be away overnight once in a while.

I thought it was cool and said so. Boys in my Scout troop were talking about joining the Civil Air Patrol and getting pilot's licenses. I saw a rather direct line from my mother's new job to me sitting in a Cessna.

My father didn't say anything. Or if he did say anything, it was probably that she "could do whatever she wanted to," because that is something he did say when confronted with my mother's sometimes eccentric ideas.

· ·

In the light of day, my father was a quiet, soft-spoken man. When he did speak, he was careful and articulate, his gray-green eyes focused on listeners as if constantly searching for what we, or they, were *really* think-ing. He asked questions but seldom answered them. Instead, he would duck playfully behind a gentle smile, or respond only with an upturned eyebrow, or dismiss the question entirely with a slight wave of his right hand.

In the evening, when the drugs weren't working and when he began to drink more than a few beers, he changed into a different man. He became animated, quick to play the joker or comedian, and his gestures and voice rose to operatic proportions with the level of alcohol intake. Then, like a fallen operatic hero, he crashed. Gone was the fun, gone was the person, replaced by a vulnerable, moody, sullen enveloping darkness that was so very dangerous, if only to himself. For within that darkness was a self-recognized defeat, and, if not exactly an acceptance of defeat, then cer-tainly surrender to it.

I didn't think about it that way then. I didn't yet have the language.

I also wasn't privy to very much of this evolving dark side. My mother, who had quickly learned to read his narcotics-mixed-with-alcohol trajectories, would, at seeing the first turn in this nightly spiral, ship me off to my bed-room with a hug and kiss, where, with the door closed tight and my blanket drawn up, my job was to entertain myself. Usually, I read novels and imag-ined myself as James Bond or played records and imagined myself as Mick Jagger. I favored the Brits for some reason, maybe a remnant of my London days. For Christmas I was the only kid in my class who received his own television set, so when I tired of pretending to be famous and sought after, I simply watched whatever was on and thought about growing up to be a spy.

Eventually my mother would decide it was time for my father to go to bed. She led him down the hallway to their bedroom, making every effort to be as quiet as possible but rarely being able to pull it off.

Clump.

"Naomi!"

"Lloyd, be *quiet*! You'll wake him up."

Of course I was already awake. But I pretended not to be. I waited alone under the cover of darkness for the light to go out.

And so it would play out, until it no longer seemed unusual to me. How could it? It was not at all unusual. It was just what happened. It was how things *were*.

My mother the nurse had a new patient.

The next morning we would all rise, go about our lives, and pretend, again, that last night never happened.

My mother flew from Cheyenne to Seattle, Phoenix, Albuquerque, and San Francisco, tending the sick, the dying, and the injured. Each time she left home, she stood in front of us in her crisp white nurse's uniform and told my father to "be on his best behavior," by which she probably meant to limit his drinking.

He did.

Instead of performing his dark opera, he and I would pass the evenings pleasantly together, eating steaks we grilled, watching the news and comedy shows, and, on the weekends, whatever sport was on television. He filled me in on the announcers—the former Dodger Pee Wee Reese and the former St. Louis Cardinals pitcher Dizzy Dean—and the players, like Cleveland's "Sudden" Sam McDowell, who, I would later learn, was an alcoholic who often went to the mound drunk and then fired 100 mph fastballs; or the New York Yankees hard-partying threesome made up of Billy Martin, Mickey Mantle, and Whitey Ford. He filled me in about political leaders as well, including men he apparently had reason to dislike, like former Vice President Richard Nixon.

If my father had a warm place in his heart for hard-drinking ballplayers, he had a very cold place reserved for Richard Milhous Nixon. Defeated by the Kennedy money and Mayor Daley's Chicago power machine in his run for the presidency in 1960, and then by the citizens of California in his bid for the governor's mansion in 1962, Nixon was rumored to run again for the presidency in the next election. My father had been a Goldwater Republican in 1964—the first time I knew him to actively campaign for a political candidate—and I was surprised to hear him speak against a fellow Republican.

"Can't trust the son of a bitch any farther than you can throw him," he said about Nixon. "Bastard came to London to pin an award on me and I had to stand there and smile. I should have put a knife into him *then*."

My father rarely used foul language when we were together. That he had used two expletives in two consecutive sentences was memorable. That my father *disliked* Nixon was probably an understatement. I didn't know why and still haven't figured it out. Perhaps it was a severe difference of opinion or a personal matter. Or maybe my father was simply a good judge of character.

That my father was sitting in our living room in Cheyenne, Wyoming, talking about the former vice president of the United States and how he wanted to put a knife into him—well, that was just how it was in those days

growing up in my household. Hearing my father express personal knowledge of people we regularly saw on television was perfectly normal.

I used to have serious doubts about the stories he told about famous
people and celebrities. By then I knew he was "not well," which was a covering euphemism my mother applied to those times when he was confused
or disoriented from the dangerous biochemical combinations coursing
through his bloodstream. I knew where his pills were kept, as well as what
the prescribed dosages were, and my job was to monitor his intake of them
in relation to his intake of alcohol whenever she was out of town. For this
reason, I figured that some of what he talked about was part of the reason
he was "not well."

I had that exactly right. Just from the wrong perspective.

When my mother was away on an overnight, my bedtime tended to
correspond with my father's. Together we would empty his Benson &
Hedges–filled ashtrays, throw away empty Miller beer bottles and Coca-
Cola cans, lock the doors, tidy up, and turn out the lights. We brushed our
teeth in the bathroom and joked around like guys do. It felt good to be at
home with my dad.

At least until our bedroom lights went out.

It was at night when my mother was away—and maybe because I monitored his intake and he wasn't, therefore, as well anaesthetized—that my
father's hidden fears, his tucked-away secrets, his war memories and chronic
anxieties, surfaced into horrific nightmares. I awakened to gut-seizing
screams and ran into his room to witness my father out of bed, on the floor,
sweating profusely, the whole of his thin body shaking violently.

I would find him sitting with his knees drawn up to his chest, crying in
ragged heaving sobs, and trying desperately to slow down his rapid breathing.
His face bore the raw exploded look of an outward burst of pure terror.

"Dad?" I would say, quietly. "It's *okay*."

As his eyes focused on me, he seemed to come away from where he was
in his head and locate himself here in his room.

"Whoops," he whispered, automatically.

"Whoops" was the expression, nearly a comic one, of a man who had
slipped up. Or who was afraid he might have revealed something he
shouldn't have. He repeated it, a little louder. Having slipped up, he was
now vocally covering up.

I didn't buy it. I don't know what my face may have been saying to him
but I have little doubt that he read it accurately.

He always apologized for me finding him this way. "I'm *sorry*," he said. He was embarrassed.

I was embarrassed for him.

After his shaking subsided, I helped him back to bed. Part of me wanted to stay with him and part of me wanted to get the hell out of the house, out of Cheyenne, out of Wyoming.

But I didn't do that. Our life was what it was. There were some good times and there were bad times. My memories of that part of my childhood are filled with baseball games, school, friends, politicians, booze, flying ambulances, pills, and my father's awful nightmares. If there was a discernible pattern I still had no idea about its meaning.

So this is what I did: I waited for him to fall asleep, or at least pretend to. Then I backed out of his bedroom and turned off the light. I remained in the hallway for a minute or so, waiting. It was quiet and still in the house but as yet my night was not complete.

Finally, his inevitable request: "*Please* don't tell your mother."

I never did. I had been well trained not to. Secrets were sacred things and I knew better than to violate a sacred trust.

I remember the cold bitter day in March of 1976 when we buried him. The one clear thought I had the whole of that day was that my father in death was finally rid his damned nightmares. In death, my hope for him was that he had found peace in his final attempt at sleep.

. . . .

One sky-blue Saturday morning in 1966, Steve Stevenson invited our family out to the airfield for a day of fun in the air. Steve knew my father socially by then, or least that part of my father the Cheyenne social world knew and responded so well to, the part that defined him as a reliable government man and ex-World War II flyboy, the former president of the local Lions Club, husband to air ambulance nurse Naomi, and father of me.

My father hadn't wanted to go. Things had been going well for him on a new drug treatment and the idea of being around airplanes was probably not that attractive to him. But Steve had promised to take me up and my father probably thought he ought to go along, if for no other reason than because he was my father. My mother, by contrast, thought the experience of learning how to fly would be good for me. She had decided that I needed a new hobby, and given that I loved to build model airplanes, learning how to fly a real one seemed to her the next logical step.

My mother, bless her heart, sometimes made very large leaps in her reasoning.

Stevenson was an airplane aficionado and collector in addition to having an air ambulance service. He maintained a small fleet of old warships, including, as I recall, a German Fokker biplane from the First World War and a P-51 Mustang and P-47 Thunderbolt from the Second World War. He even had one of old Tooey Spaatz's mail service numbers. Things changed when my father actually saw the planes.

I mean *really* changed.

If it is possible to see a child emerge from deep within a grown man, then that is what I saw happen to my father. I was only fourteen and what I saw had no literary or philosophical referent. For me, he simply became *happy to be here.*

Steve walked us around his fleet and he and my father swapped bits of information about the makes, models, capacities, engines, cruising speeds, and pros and cons that went well over my head. Steve's inventory of aircraft included one North American AT-6 Texan trainer, and when we got to it my father became truly excited.

"I used to fly one of these," he beamed.

I didn't know that.

"I was in Anacostia in the Naval Aviation Cadet program and ours were SNJs, but it's basically the same ship."

I didn't know my father was ever in the navy.

One thing led to another and to my amazement, Steve offered to take my father up in it. "That's okay," my father declined. "I'd rather not."

"Why not?" Steve asked. They had been getting along famously and there was no reason not to go up for a free ride.

"I don't like to fly when *anyone* else is piloting," he replied. "No offense, Steve, but unless I have to fly on business, I don't leave the ground. I got shot up pretty badly in the war." He said it as if it was the most natural thing in the world. But what surprised me far more than these sudden revelations about my father's fear of flying was what happened next.

"Well, if you don't want to fly with me, why don't you just take her up by yourself, then?" Steve said, smiling.

My father paused. "You sure?"

"Hell, yes, I'm sure. If you trained on one, you can probably fly this old bird better than I can. These were relics by the time I came along."

I couldn't say, even today, if Steve's invitation was intended as a macho challenge or if it was simply the extension of a courtesy to the ex-flyboy husband of his flight nurse.

"Is it ready to go?" His eyes were on fire. I hadn't seen my father this excited since 1963.

"Yes. I was going to take your boy up in it, so I did the preflight check just before you got here."

My father looked squarely at me. "Are you ready?"

I don't remember what I said.

What I do remember is what I did, which was simply *go with it*. My father and I climbed into the cockpit and I followed Steve's instructions about buckling myself in. He pointed out the controls and gauges to me, but by then I had lost the capacity for anything less than wonder. From behind me I heard my father flip a switch and felt the mighty ignition of the 600-horsepower Pratt & Whitney. The little plane hummed and metal vibrated and my ears were awash in the engine's powerful roar.

The next thing I knew we were hurtling faster and faster down an increasingly shorter runway and then, with one smooth yawning upward motion, we were airborne. We were flying!

My father, my dad and I, were *flying*.

Flying with my father was pure aerial poetry. He was surprisingly good at it—surprising to me, given that I didn't know he could fly—and far more at home in the air than he ever was in our car on a highway. He was neither too reckless nor too tame, but instead balanced both inclinations in a way that seemed perfectly suited to flight.

He pulled the canopy back and let the cool winds tease our hair. Then he asked me if I wanted to take over.

This was my moment.

This feeling of taking over in the air was my own magical adolescent elixir, the original source of what became a lifelong quest for peak experiences. The feeling of overwhelming desire and the accompanying journey to a higher satisfaction became integral parts of my being, something that was first articulated for me that fine blue afternoon, enabled by my father, although I did not know it at the time.

I took control and flew. Guided by my father's encouraging voice I soared above Cheyenne. I was careful to follow his instructions. I turned smoothly twice, then three times, and headed back toward Stevenson's field.

I could have gone on that way forever. I never wanted us to land.

My father, of course, had no intention of *allowing* me to land. He took over the controls and brought us down smoothly. We climbed out of the cockpit together a pair of grinning boyish fools.

My mother was waiting for us. I don't know whom she was happier for, me or my father. There were tears in her eyes. Happy tears. We all hugged. "Did you like that?" she asked me.

"That was great!" I replied. "I didn't know Dad could fly."

They laughed as if I had just said the most outrageous thing. "You didn't know your father could *fly*?" my mother asked, incredulously.

I shook my head.

"There are a lot of things about your father that would surprise you," she said.

My father winked at me.

· ·

Unfortunately for me and my plans for flying lessons, my mother stopped working as a flight nurse for Steve Stevenson shortly after our great Saturday-afternoon adventure in the air. Due to a sudden nursing shortage, she had been hired at DePaul Hospital working in the emergency room. She wouldn't have to make any overnights.

Things *were* "better." If my father was occasionally driven by demons and my mother was occasionally a little off-center, we finally were at home with our lives in Cheyenne, Wyoming.

Or so I thought.

· ·

Senator Stuart Symington of Missouri visited us during the late summer of 1966. I believe it was late in August because I was already playing football. There was a photograph of us in the backyard and I was wearing pads and my Carey Junior High uniform.

He stayed at our house, slept in my bedroom (I took the couch), played a little catch with me, and stood by while my father grilled steaks in our backyard. He and my father got along like old pals, which led me to believe they knew each other pretty well. They drank beer from aluminum cans and argued about politics while the porterhouse steaks sizzled.

My mother was decked out in her best party dress and was positively dripping in charm as she regaled the senator with tales from the Stevenson air ambulance service and then from the emergency room. When I think back to that evening, to that in-house performance of her best self, it is obvious to me that my mother was trying very hard to prove something to Senator Symington. I didn't know what it was but I sensed, even then, that it had something to do with my father's career and our life in Wyoming.

She cleaned up the table after dinner, changed into her nurse's uniform, and went to work.

"She's one *hell* of a woman," the senator said.

"She's a saint," my father replied.

They drank a toast to her.

My father and Senator Symington spent the better part of the evening in the backyard, smoking cigarettes, talking, and drinking Scotch. I didn't go outside because my mother had told me they "wanted to be alone." I was a kid, so this wasn't surprising.

I didn't know it at the time, but my father had recently received a letter from the director of the VA center, Merle W. Allen, indicating that Lloyd had "rehabilitated himself" and that alcohol was no longer an issue in his work.

This letter appears in his dummy folder and I can only assume that a duplicate once existed in Langley. My guess is that my father was using the letter to full advantage to plead for a transfer. Symington was a senior senator and very influential within the intelligence community. If an overseas assignment was not in my father's future, then perhaps a domestic transfer might be. Anywhere, please, but *here*. If my parents had settled on being in Cheyenne, they still hoped it was only temporary. Senator Symington was their getaway ticket.

I heard the two men talking and then later arguing about something that was clearly very important to my father but hadn't seemed to convince Mr. Symington. Maybe it was about Richard Nixon, but I doubt it. Maybe it was about Angleton. I read what I would later learn to call Symington's "nonverbals" and found them all about not changing his mind. His arms were crossed over his chest. He avoided eye contact with my father. His face was a scowl. Eventually I gave up trying to figure it out and went to bed or, I should say, to the couch.

I prayed to the God who had freed me from church services to please not allow my father to get too drunk or take too many pills or have one of his full-blown nightmares. God, as usual, remained silent. But perhaps He or She answered my prayers. My father didn't get drunk, take too many pills, or have a nightmare.

July 13, 1966

4042/00

TO: Mr. T. V. Williams (201D)
       Field Director, Area 4
       Veterans Administration Central Office
       810 Vermont Avenue, N. W.
       Washington, D. C. 20420

SUBJ: Mr. Harold L. Goodall, Contact Officer

1. On November 4, 1963, I found it necessary to issue a letter of
reprimand to Harold L. Goodall, Contact Officer at this center because,
in my opinion, he had brought discredit to himself, this VA Center, and
the Veterans Administration, through his having been arrested and his
driver's license suspended for driving while under the influence of
intoxicating liquor, second offense.

2. After receipt of the above-mentioned reprimand, Mr. Goodall underwent a period of self incrimination and tended to draw into a self-
imposed shell. Later, however, he effectively evaluated his personal
situation, sought professional assistance, and entered into an extensive rehabilitation program.

3. I am pleased to be able to report to you at this time that
Mr. Goodall has successfully rehabilitated himself. I sincerely
believe that he is now more physically able and mentally alert than at
any time during his tenure of nearly six years under my supervision.
I have seen no evidence or had any reports of his using intoxicants to
excess for well over two years.

4. Mr. Goodall continues to perform the responsibilities of his position as Contact Officer in a very competent manner, and I sincerely
hope that the single deficiency of the past may now be erased from his
records. I feel confident he can fulfill positions of greater responsibility in a highly competent manner and that repetition of the
deficiency noted above is most remote.

M. W. ALLEN
Center Director

cc: Mr. Goodall (232)
    25 (2)

Copy forwarded to Dumm folder.
7/13/66 kk.

FIGURE 16.1 Letter attesting to full rehabilitation, July 13, 1966.

The next morning Senator Symington got up early, grabbed coffee with my father in the kitchen, and left to get back to Washington. Or maybe it was Langley. As chairman of the Select Committee on Intelligence, which he was at that time, he could have used the word "Washington" in much the same way my father used it. As he was leaving, I heard him tell my father, "I can't promise anything, but I'll see what I can do."

On his way out of the house he paused by the couch and ruffled my hair. "You're a good kid, Buddy," he said. "I really hope things work out well for you." The tone he used was sincere and slightly ominous, as if he had reason to believe that things might *not* work out so well for me after all.

Stuart Symington's connection to my father, to my family, and to Cheyenne, Wyoming, was never explained to me. I'm not sure I fully appreciated that he was a United States senator when he came to visit us. I surely didn't know he had been a presidential candidate for the Democrats in 1960, or chairman of the National Security Resources Board, or the first secretary of the Air Force when Francis E. Warren Air Force Base was recommissioned.

I would learn that the man who slept in my bedroom that night had been a staunch anti-Communist and fierce cold warrior. He was the man responsible for creating the false impression that the United States was suffering a missile gap in relation to the Soviet Union. He would also become one of the first politicians to speak out against the war in Vietnam.

I wonder what he was arguing with my father about. Russians? William Colby? Angleton? Maybe Vietnam? I have no idea.

What was he doing at our house? Visiting an old friend? Checking us out? Again, I have no idea.

And in what capacity had my father previously known him?

And once again, I have no idea. None at all.

. . . .

I loved the idea of James Bond. By the time we pulled out of the Union Pacific depot in Cheyenne for our annual Christmas trip to West Virginia in December of 1966, I had seen the movie versions of *Goldfinger*, *Thunderball*, and *Dr. No*, as well as a television special the previous year called *The Incredible World of James Bond*. I had read, and reread, *Thunderball*, *On Her Majesty's Secret Service*, *You Only Live Twice*, and *The Man with the Golden Gun,* in that order because my father said that was the order I should read them in.

I suppose that suggests rather strongly that my father had read them. If that is so, it's pretty funny. If not funny, at least amusingly ironic. My father the spy reading novels about spies?

Having been initiated by my father into the right way to read them—chronologically—I was now so addicted to Ian Fleming's fiction that I was reading them in whatever order I could find them. I took my new paperback copy of *Casino Royale* for the first leg of our trip—Cheyenne to Chicago—and figured I'd pick up another 007 novel during our stopover.

The world of James Bond, although fictional, always seemed very real to me. In my fourteen-year-old mind, I had no doubt there *was* a James Bond, an M, a Miss Moneypenny, and a Q, although I knew that in real life they probably didn't use these names. I knew a thing or two about spies, but I didn't know I was living with a real one.

"What is a *spy*?" Richard's question is once again good to reflect on. I'm not sure I knew what a spy "was" when I was fourteen. I only knew that spies were *necessary* because we were in a cold war and because the Russians were devious enemies. I had no doubt there probably was some terrorist organization out there, like Spectre. Nor, as I recall, did I believe that Americans could trust the East Germans, anyone behind the Iron Curtain, most Asians, and especially the Chinese.

Notice the omission from that list of any nation or organization in the Middle East. When I was growing up and learning what regions were important in the world from history books, television, movies, and fiction, the Middle East was not a part of my cognitive map. The only reference to our present danger I recall was a joke in the schoolyard. You asked some unsuspecting someone, using a serious quiz voice, to name two adjoining countries in the Middle East. The answer you usually got was "I don't know any countries in the Middle East," which pretty much summed up what my adolescent friends and I knew about the geography of the region in the 1960s. The punch line was "Iraq, and Iran." However, the point of the joke was a wordplay—"I rack" and "I ran"—that corresponded to hitting the unsuspecting boy in the nuts (I rack) and then getting away before he could retaliate (I ran). I'm not entirely sure that old bad joke hasn't worked its way into the faulty logic of our policies in those countries under the Bush Administration. Donald Rumsfeld reportedly believed it would take only ten days to conquer Iraq, thirty days to stabilize the country, and another thirty days to withdraw our troops. From Iraq we would move on to Iran. I rack, and I ran. Indeed.

But in 1966 I had no knowledge of the Middle East. My perspective on international terrorism by nonstate actors was entirely shaped not by histories or news reports but instead by reading Ian Fleming's fiction. I was convinced there was an evil genius plotting the ultimate domination of the world. If this was the world we lived in, this was a world that *needed* a James Bond.

I needed there to be a James Bond.

It was during the 1966 Christmas trip when I asked my father if he knew any real spies. We were railroading in our deluxe Pullman cabin along a cold, desolate stretch of Nebraska. My father tried to deflect my question in the usual manner, by laughing, raising one eyebrow, and giving me a dismissive hand gesture. "A spy?" he grinned. "And what is a *spy*?" Now you know why I had to smile when my friend Richard asked me the same question.

My mother quietly smiled.

I didn't answer his question. Instead, I pressed on. "No, *really*," I insisted. I pointed to the cover of my novel. "Is there a real James Bond? I mean *you* work for the government."

"Then maybe *I'm* a spy," he replied. His face was entirely ordinary. He could have been saying that he pushed paper from one side of his desk to the other.

"Yeah, *sure*." I turned sullenly back to my reading. The thought that my father was a spy was preposterous. *Why* would he *never* take anything I said *seriously*?

. . . .

We arrived in Chicago under dark gray skies and storm warnings. There were dirty, irregular intervals of packed snow along the gravel tracks, and the temperature hovered somewhere in the low twenties. An assembly of black crows sat close to each other on the humming telephone lines and I pretended to take aim at them and shot them with my index finger. The crows were Communist spies and I was the real James Bond.

I stood with my family by the exit door, rocking in time with the slow, gentle back-and-forth sway of the train as it pulled easily into the station, its giant air brakes loudly releasing a foul, used scent of burnt asbestos into the rich diesel- and soot-soaked air. The porter in his crisp white shirt and suspenders descended the stairs and placed the final step on the walk, and we all clicked down to the pavement, breathing in exotic Chicago aromas and taking in the architectural majesty of this old railway station.

Inside Chicago's huge Union Station there was a gorgeous bar, all brass polish and dark wood, and every year that is where we camped out until we boarded the Baltimore & Ohio's blue-and-gold Pullman. On the way to the bar I stopped by a station bookseller and purchased *For Your Eyes Only* and *Diamonds Are Forever*. I figured that two Bond books would keep me occupied for the rest of the trip and, if I spaced out my reading, might last me through the slow times during the holidays at Granny and Popeye's.

My father asked me if I needed to use the bathroom before we got on the train. I nodded. He and l left the bar and found a men's room. It was a large, tiled space with a row of urinals at the front and row of stalls toward the rear. It smelled of men's piss and disinfectant cleanser, in about equal proportions. There was bright sunlight streaming through the pebbled glass window at the end of the room.

I selected a stall and entered it, locking the door behind me. My father moved to a urinal. The door to the bathroom opened and a third man entered. He spoke to my father in a gruff voice, demanding money. My father said, "Hell no," and there was an immediate scuffle.

I froze, uncertain what to do. The fight—by then my brain knew it was a fight—continued. I exited the stall, my heart pounding against my chest, and caught the end of it. My father had the man by his hair in one hand and had twisted his arm behind him with the other. The stranger was cursing and screaming in agony. In one smooth motion my father smashed the man's face squarely into the bathroom wall.

Then he did it again.

And again, until this time the man's body slackened and he slid to the floor, blood streaming from his nose and mouth onto the polished tiles. My father seemed surprisingly calm. He looked at me and said, simply, "Find a policeman."

I ran out of the men's room and found a large man in a blue uniform and a badge by the shoeshine stand. I quickly explained what had happened and he returned with me to the scene of the crime.

My father was washing his hands, his victim still unconscious on the floor.

The policeman asked my father to see some identification. My father pulled out his wallet and handed over a plastic-coated card. I don't think it was his driver's license because the officer's manner became decidedly more respectful. He handed the card back to my father and made notes on a pad. "Do you know this man, sir?" he asked.

"Never seen him before in my life," my father replied.

"And what did he say to you, exactly?"

"He showed me a knife and told me to hand over my wallet."

"Then what happened?"

"I told him 'Not only no, but *hell* no' and removed the knife from his hand."

The officer paused. "How did you do that?"

My father shrugged. "Just my instincts," he replied. "Then I hit him in the throat, grabbed his hair, and . . . well, you see." He paused. "Maybe I got a little carried away." We all looked down at the bleeding heap of human refuse on the tiles. The would-be thief was coming to, slowly, groggily.

"Some instincts," the officer replied, eyeing my father with obvious respect. He took a handkerchief from his pocket and retrieved the knife. It was a thin steel blade, about six inches long. "You *stupid* piece of shit," the policeman snarled at the bloodied man as he snapped handcuffs on his wrists. "You sure picked on the *wrong* guy this time, pal."

I was intensely proud of my father and couldn't wait to tell my mother. I had no idea Dad could fight. Against a knife, too!

My father smiled and said quietly, "Will you need me for anything else, officer?"

The policeman was satisfied. He had my father's name, address, and phone number, so there was no reason to keep us. We left the men's room as an ambulance crew, two more cops, and a stretcher arrived.

"Wow," I said. "You were *incredible*." I was enthused. "You were like *James Bond*!"

My father winked at me, raised his eyebrow, and then dismissed it with his familiar hand gesture. "Let's go get your mother," he said. "We've got a train to catch."

. . . .

We arrived in Martinsburg and my father took his usual trip to the place he called Washington that was Langley. This time he returned with good news. We were moving to Philadelphia, Pennsylvania.

Maybe Senator Symington had intervened.

I had *very* mixed feelings about his announcement. I had by that time spent six years in Cheyenne and living there was all I really knew. I liked living there. My few remaining memories of Europe were like tiny flashpoints of illumination against a much larger emptiness.

NOTIFICATION OF PERSONNEL ACTION
(EMPLOYEE - See General Information on Reverse)

1. NAME, LAST - FIRST - MIDDLE		MR. - MISS - MRS.	2. STATION NO.	3. BIRTH DATE	4. SOCIAL SECURITY NO.
GOODALL,HAROLD LLOYD		MR.	321C	10-17-22	236-28-3794

5. VETERAN PREFERENCE				6. TENURE GROUP	7. SERVICE COMP. DATE	8. HANDICAP CODE
4	1. NO 2. 5-PT.	3. 10-PT. DISAB. 4. 10-PT. COMP.	5. 10-PT. OTHER	1	C5-27-43	52

9. FEGLI			10. RETIREMENT		11. (For CSC use)
1	1. COVERED 2. INELIGIBLE 3. WAIVED		1	1. CS 2. FICA 3. FS 4. NO 5. OTHER	

2. CODE	S.C.	NATURE OF ACTION		NTE DATE	13. EFF. DATE
702	A	PROMOTION-CAO			03-26-67

4. CODE	CIVIL SERVICE OR OTHER LEGAL AUTHORITY
H3	REG. 335.102

5. FROM - POSITION TITLE AND NO.	16. PAY PL. OCCUP. CODE	17. GRADE OR LEVEL	STEP RATE	18. SALARY
CONTACT OFFICER /VETERANS BENEFITS/ 02391000	CS 0962	11	8	PA $ 11,426

3. NAME AND LOCATION OF EMPLOYING OFFICE		
1C	CHEYENNE	WYO

3. TO - POSITION TITLE AND NO.	21. PAY PL. OCCUP. CODE	22. GRADE OR LEVEL	STEP RATE	23. SALARY
CONTACT OFFICER /VETERANS BENEFITS/ 01927000	GS 0962	12	4	PA $ 12,064

. NAME AND LOCATION OF EMPLOYING OFFICE		
1C CONTACT DIVISION	PHILADELPHIA	PA

. DUTY STATION (City - State)	26. LOCATION CODE
PHILADELPHIA PA	37-6540-1C1

. APPROPRIATION	28. POSITION OCCUPIED	29. APPORTIONED POSITION		
		FROM	TO	STATE
3230.0C00	1 1. COMPETITIVE SERVICE 2. EXCEPTED SERVICE	1-PROVED-1 2-WAIVED-2		

. REMARKS

. DATE OF APPOINTMENT AFFIDAVIT (Accessions only)	34. SIGNATURE (or other authentication) AND TITLE
OFFICE MAINTAINING PERSONNEL FOLDER (if different from employing office)	WILLIAM D. HAIG PERSONNEL OFFICER 1832
. CODE EMPLOYING DEPARTMENT OR AGENCY	35. DATE
A OO Veterans Administration	03-26-67

A FORM EP 1964	5 - 4650		PERSONNEL FOLDER COPY

FIGURE 16.2 Notification of Lloyd's transfer to Philadelphia, March 26, 1967.

In Cheyenne, I had good friends. I went to a school where I was well liked. My parents fit in, things were better at home. If my mother still occasionally complained about "this godforsaken prairie" or my father took out a road atlas to think about other places we could live, well, that was just how it was. I wasn't sure moving to a new city and starting our lives all over again sounded like a good idea.

I filed a mild family protest but to no avail.

My parents were ecstatic to be leaving. *Finally*. They put our house up for sale the day we returned to Cheyenne with our news. They sold it to the first bidder, for a copper penny more than they paid for it.

A moving van appeared one morning in late February and by later that afternoon we were well on our way out of Wyoming.

"I said 'Shit' when I came here and I'll say 'Shit' when I leave," my father announced on our way out of town. And he did say it. Shouted it, in fact.

So did my mother.

I don't remember saying anything at all.

· ·

For the official record: two known causes no doubt influenced my father's official transfer to Philadelphia. First, there was a winding down of the Minuteman I program at Warren Air Force Base. In the museum built in honor of the distinguished, if hidden, cold war history of this base, it is written that:

- In 1967 Francis E. Warren Air Force Base completed its conversion to Minuteman IIs. Minuteman IIIs would replace the IIs in 1975.
- In 1986, Warren Air Force Base became the sole domestic site for the Peacekeeper missile.
- In June 1992, the base itself became the official property of the Air Combat Command, headquartered at Langley, Virginia.
- In 1993, the Twentieth Air Force, headquarters for our country's ICBM wings, relocated to Warren, which makes it the most powerful combat unit in the world today.

Nowhere in the official history of the base is there any record of what my father did from 1960 to 1967. It does say that the missile operations required the support of a wide variety of specialists, officers, and support personnel. There is a tribute, albeit a small one, to the many families who were part of that overall national security effort.

The second reason we left Cheyenne was one I wouldn't learn about for a long time. In my father's diary next to the notation about Philadelphia was the single word "CHAOS."

· ·

What changed in my father's career?

Did it have anything to do with Angleton? I cannot say. Perhaps it did. I'll never know.

In 1967 Angleton was still serving as director of counterintelligence for the CIA, the same position he had held since 1953. He had never asked to be considered for promotion nor accepted any offer that would have changed his assignment. During this period, although he claimed he "had never once been wrong," he had in fact been wrong several times.

Once was in his protection of Kim Philby. In 1968, Philby published his memoirs under the title *My Silent War*. He depicted Angleton as a man who had been easy to dupe. Ben Bradlee, then the editor of the *Washington Post*, published a favorable review of the book, including its description of Angleton, and Angleton never again spoke to Bradlee, a man he had counted among his friends.

I doubt whether Angleton cared about my father's correct suspicions about Philby anymore. Philby had already defected and that defection was public knowledge. Having seen to my father's exile in Wyoming, and having had reports of his slow demise on the prairie, Angleton was probably done with him. After seven years and two DUIs, there was no point holding a grudge. My father would never again have diplomatic immunity. My father had been little more than a minor character in Angleton's larger aesthetic, a pawn who had become for a brief moment a knight and who was then reduced to a pawn again and sacrificed to save a bishop.

That Angleton had contributed to my family's troubles probably never crossed his mind. If it had, I doubt he would have graced it with a second thought. We were in a dirty war, a cold war, and personal sacrifices were required of all warriors and their families. Regrettable, perhaps, but required.

· ·

On my father's official request for a transfer, he lists as his reason "to be closer to my hometown." But we know that wasn't true. He never wanted to be anywhere *near* Huntington again.

His transfer carried with it a promotion and a little more money. Maybe it is as simple as that. But my father had never before been solely motivated by money or by rank. So I doubt that is entirely true. Philadelphia was no paradise for clandestine work, but neither was it so very bad. It was a major city. It was back East. It was not far from Baltimore, from Washington, from New York City, or even from Martinsburg.

But even so, the paperwork in his dummy folder can't make a dummy out of me. I have to consider this work-related move within the broader history of what was then happening in America. I have to see it as a logical extension of my father's intelligence-collecting abilities that he would be assigned to the City of Brotherly Love at the height of the Agency's domestic surveillance activities, while the city was in the throes of a civil war between the races. If he had skills as a domestic surveillance officer, and he did, this would have been an excellent place for him to practice his tradecraft.

There was plenty to learn about a lot of suspected agitators and trouble-makers then active in Philadelphia. Blacks who challenged the authority of the white city officials and police. Radicals and longhairs who were very likely threats to the government of the United States. Students and lefty faculty types who were stirring up trouble on college campuses with "free love" and antiwar protests. Priests who claimed we had no moral reason to be in Vietnam. Newly made veterans who filed their benefit claims in the contact office on the way to a protest rally or underground meeting.

In retrospect, there were probably two large reservations associated with these obvious career-advancing surveillance possibilities. The first was that what my father was asked to do was strictly illegal. Americans suppos-edly enjoyed the freedom of speech and freedom of association, as well as the right to deny unwarranted intrusions into their homes, their personal affairs, their political values, or their public lives.

The second reservation was a private one. A secret never openly dis-cussed in our household. But it was the unspoken concern over my father's self-medication. The new pills he acquired prior to leaving Cheyenne weren't doing the job. We all knew what that meant. Every evening in our apartment at 8200 Henry Avenue in Philadelphia, a newer mutant form of darkness emerged from within the man my mother and I knew and loved. It was a darkness that changed him into someone else. The man who had been my father was, despite his problems, a fearless cold warrior. The other man who replaced him in Philadelphia looked like my father but with a face and body that aged dramatically over the next two years. He was a person who became deathly afraid of his own mind, particularly where his mind went when the last bedroom light went out.

So the big "if" that would ultimately define our time in Philadelphia was "*if* my father could keep it together." If he could maintain control of himself. If he could once again be more like the man he was in Chicago than the man who moved us to Philadelphia. That man was one who went to work in the morning and came home from work at night, remembered to take his pills and shook when he didn't, poured a stiffer drink when he shook to "calm his nerves" and to swallow the damned pills, and then descended into a private merciless hell.

Philadelphia was not a step up in the world for our family. It was CHAOS, writ in the invisible ink of family secrecy.

17

Philadelphia and Operation CHAOS

1967–1969

MY FATHER'S NEW JOB, HIS LAST JOB AS IT TURNED OUT, WAS IN A LARGE brick-and-stone office building located at 5000 Wissahickon Boulevard in the Germantown section of Philadelphia. The building was a regional Veterans Administration center, and he was supposedly handling veterans benefits as an assistant contact representative.

It is hard to keep a straight face and say that.

It is particularly untrue in such obvious ways. On several occasions after he retired in 1969—by then I had my driver's license—I drove him over to the VA center on Wissahickon to file health claims. He didn't have a clue about how to complete the required paperwork. I asked him about it once. He seemed surprised by the question. He didn't answer me. Instead, he winked, made a gesture of dismissal with his hand, and looked away.

I read his response incorrectly. I thought he was being dismissive of my question, as if saying: "Look, you don't know about these adult things. Don't bother me about it. I know what I'm doing."

But he wasn't saying that. Not at all. He was saying that he couldn't answer my question *here*. That he couldn't answer it *now*. It would be too complicated to explain to me while we sat in the benefits office where other people could overhear us.

I was sixteen years old. Everything was either black or white and always personal. I interpreted his unwillingness to answer my question as a dismissal of *me*. I didn't bring it up again. Nor did my father volunteer any further information. By then, things had changed for the worse in our family. We were living in chaos. Everyday life in Philadelphia had created within our family an impenetrable distance between each one of us.

I had better explain Philadelphia.

. . . .

Philadelphia may have called itself the City of Brotherly Love but it was anything but that in the sixties.

In 1964, Philadelphia witnessed forty-eight hours of unprecedented violence and rioting in a white-owned retail area in a predominantly black neighborhood, a cultural precursor to the raging violence in Newark, the riots in Watts, and the burning of Detroit over the next three summers.

By 1967 the city was caught in the media's unforgiving gaze when three thousand black students showed up at a school-board meeting to protest the lack of African-American history and literature in the curriculum. They were met with extreme force captured all too clearly by the media cameras.

In 1967, Philadelphia was the fourth-largest city in the United States. It also boasted one of the largest and meanest police departments in the country. Its new police commissioner was the singular, soon to be legendary, Frank Lazzaro Rizzo.

Rizzo was the prize police product of an Italian neighborhood in south Philly, a high school dropout who would eventually become the city's first Italian-American mayor. But in 1967, he was still a colorful if brutal man fond of using his nightstick to create, and then to sustain, a "supercop" reputation. He had gained his reputation by using intimidation and physical violence against alleged criminals to rise rapidly through the ranks of what was then an Irish-dominated police force. He was a big man with big fists and a total fuck-you attitude, delivered with the appropriate Italian salute.

Rizzo was a staunch conservative whose hero was J. Edgar Hoover. Rizzo boasted that he hated anything or anyone who stood "anywhere to the left of J. Edgar," and that included criminals, perverts, beatniks, poets, musicians, college professors, Communists, Socialists, hippies, gays, lesbians, most blacks who weren't on his police force, most Irish because they were Irish, the Poles because they were Polacks, the Germans because they were

Krauts, the whole of France because of the *fuckin'* French, and anyone else, or any idea, daring to suggest that things should ever change, or that he, God, and J. Edgar Hoover had ever been wrong.

For all his bullshit, bang, big mouth, and bluster, he was also beloved in this city of inherent contradictions. He became the most powerful police commissioner ever in the history of Philadelphia, and would also become one of the most influential mayors since Boss Tweed indiscriminately ruled New York City. If he inspired fear and loathing among those who opposed him—and he certainly did that—he also inspired love and devotion among those whose values he reflected at police headquarters and, later, at City Hall.

Rizzo embraced his contradictions. He was, in so many ways, the right man for contradictory times. As a retrospective on his life produced by television station WHYY put it, he was also the man who "made Philadelphians question how they related to authority, to power, and to their families, city, and country."

Other women and men might question authority and power, or protest injustice or stand against the war in Vietnam, but not Frank Rizzo. He questioned nothing because he believed he had *always* been right. A few years later, while running for reelection as mayor in 1975, he said, unapologetically and openly to the media, "I'm gonna make Attila the Hun look like a faggot after this election is over." He never quit. He never backed down. He died of a heart attack while washing his hands in a men's room before lunch while running again for re-election to the office of mayor in 1991, at the age of seventy.

But in 1967 Frank Rizzo *was* Philadelphia. He was a rising political star. He embraced its contradictions as easily as he denied them. He embodied a version of the American dream—the common man who, by luck and pluck (although in Rizzo's case it was more like fist and nightstick)—made himself into an Emperor of the Streets. Little did I know then that Rizzo, the man who had just been named police commissioner, would figure rather directly into my future and into the history of my family.

* * *

Confession: At the time of my nuclear family's gradual implosion, during what would become the unhappy staging of our own Philadelphia story, I was no longer what my old Boy Scout troop leader back in Cheyenne would've called "a good boy." A good boy, a good Scout, would have stepped in and done something. Or at least I think a good boy would have behaved that way. I only know that I didn't.

I am ashamed by my lack of action.

Feeling ashamed doesn't make up for what I didn't do. Or didn't say. The fact is I was complicit; I allowed it to happen. It was easy to do because I didn't have to do anything at all. I just kept "it" to myself, our family secret of madness, secrecy, and demise. I never told anyone about it, not even my grandparents or uncle and aunt or any of my nice cousins. Certainly not any of my friends or girlfriends or any of our gang up on the corner of Ridge and Summit.

I learned how to balance the skill of remaining politely silent with the art of evasive maneuvers. If nothing else worked, I hedged around the truth. The funny thing about hedging around the truth is that after I successfully hedged a couple of times, it became easier, almost natural. My silence was an even more refined form of discreet ambiguity. It was an absence of real talk, of curative talk, something I chose not to do for almost medicinal purposes, and as such my silences about my life quarantined most of what was important and meaningful to me. But silence, too, has an emotional cost. After a while, not speaking the truth about my family to others at school, and about my experiences at school with my family, established within my narrative identity a hidden and a very much clandestine self.

My sense of keeping silent and therefore constructing my own clandestine self had been cultivated over the years in the family. It was the product of keeping secrets and of finding ways to skillfully deflect the conversation to another topic and, preferably, to another person. It got easier as I got older. And the older I got and the easier it was, the less I noticed I was doing it. My friends in Philadelphia thought I was cool because I was a "quiet one," and because I could stay out at night, and because I didn't ask permission or forgiveness. I did what I wanted to do. Or so they thought.

The truth was quite a different story beneath all appearances to the contrary. I was quiet only when my friends brought up what was happening in their homes. I didn't have anything warm and fuzzy to offer to the conversation. I wasn't about to relate what was going on in my family. So, instead, I kept my silence. I listened to them, envied my friends their fun stories, and empathized with them when the stories were occasionally sad. But overall I didn't add to the mix my own tales of home.

I stayed out at night because staying in meant finding myself in what I would later learn to call "a double-bind conversation." We repeated the same spirals of unhealthy engagements, the same old accusations and denials, the same arguments that ended in the same ways, with nothing resolved and our hearts in ruin. Besides, my nights were reserved for the development of my clandestine self, the self that explored what teenagers everywhere wanted to explore: the romance and intrigue of love, the powerful pull of lust, the meaning of music and the philosophies of popular songs, and, in our time and in our own ways, various means of achieving an altered state of consciousness. Out on the corner I was somebody new, somebody I liked and other people liked. At home I was neither.

There was one additional language bit that figured into my clandestine public performances. If I was asked a direct question, such as "How are things at home?" my answer was always "Fine." "Fine" was a code word for keeping secret how I really felt. It was at the very least a cover-up of something that could not otherwise be fashioned into a good story, or even a pleasant one. It is a word that exists for a lot of us at the end of things, particularly at the end of bad relationships. Every time in my adult life that I hear the word "fine" used as a response to a relationship issue or question, I tense up. I know better. Fine usually means *not* fine at all. "Fine" is the easy answer given by those of us who have settled for something less, or who have given up any hope of getting anything better.

· ·

One year after our move to Philadelphia, my father's "work"—whatever it was—was not going well. Viewed in retrospect, the easy answer is that his unease was due to a final confluence of personal, familial, pharmaceutical, and organizational ills. But I also believe that he was engaging in illegal counterintelligence activities that no longer seemed justifiable to him. He did not believe in the war in Vietnam. He did not subscribe to the domino theory. He never liked the policies of Lyndon Johnson and he hated Richard Nixon. He had been waging the cold war since it began and he had learned to question the so-called wisdom, as well as the motives, of his superiors.

My father was caught in a Faustian bargain: in exchange for a transfer out of Wyoming, he had sold his soul once more. He agreed to use his considerable skills to do work he no longer believed in. I didn't then have the benefit of this elaborate language of explanation with which to parse and measure the messiness of his life. I only knew things for him, and for us, were "bad."

How bad it was for him I would not fully comprehend until more than thirty years later, when his detailed medical records were released to me under the Freedom of Information Act. In them was clear evidence of a painful physical, emotional, and mental collapse. On June 21, 1968, fifteen months after we moved to Philadelphia, a physical examination indicated "sciatic neuritis, right leg; multiple gunshot wounds, both legs; nervous condition; loss of hearing, left ear; pulmonary emphysema; enlarged heart; hypertension; eye condition, bilateral; diabetes mellitus."

The psychiatric report requested by the attending physician is perhaps more revealing. In the words of Dr. I. Kotzin, a staff neuropsychiatrist:

> Mr. Goodall complains of being sick all of the time—extreme nervous condition . . . he has crying spells, even at work, but hopes that no one sees him. He also describes some migraine headaches . . . lasting 2–3 days during which time his eyes become hazy and he feels sick to his stomach. . . .
>
> He is 45 years of age, tall, of asthenic habitus [sic], is neatly dressed, tidy, polite, cooperative and attention is easily gained and held. He has excessive wrinkling for a man of his age and generally he looks about 5 years older. . . . At no time does he smile and general facial expression is one of preoccupation. He has a mottled flush on his face . . . indicating some vasomotor instability. Digital tremors of the extended hands are noted. . . .
>
> DIAGNOSIS: Psychoneurosis Anxiety Reaction, moderately severe with depressive features.

However much my father was suffering at work, he didn't talk about it at home. At least not to me, or with me around. How much my mother was privy to the hard details of his deteriorated condition is difficult to know because she, too, was kept at least partially in the dark, and because she, too, was hardly what anyone would call stable.

What I remember from those two years at 8200 Henry Avenue, apartment A-15, was my father's increasingly noticeable absence from my life. Or, viewed differently, perhaps it was *my* absence from *his* life. The difference is likely to be moot. I don't know. Maybe he expected more from me and I didn't offer it. Maybe if I had demanded to know what was wrong with him I would have felt more compassion than fear or alienation.

But, on the other hand, it is possible I am being unduly harsh, judging my actions as a teenager as if I were an adult. Not just any adult, but one with knowledge of psychology and communication and medicine. At the very least a trained therapist, capable of prescribing a course of action designed to lead to a lessening, if not erasure, of his problems. I don't know. It's a dialogue I have within myself often enough to know these are questions that cannot be answered. I believe the questions are important, though.

I only know in my heart that I would have saved him, saved all of us, if I could.

• •

What details do I remember about my father's two years in Philadelphia? Not much. I remember his increasing surrender to his chronic pain earlier and earlier in the day, complaints that increasingly powerful narcotics could not quell. I remember the trembling, uncontrollable nervousness noted in the doctor's summary. And I remember the final year when he retreated entirely from the world, announced his early retirement, and went to bed. There, in a closed-door retreat into an all-consuming darkness, he bore his pain and suffered his nervousness, he worried about my mother's nocturnal weirdness and no doubt about my life out in the streets.

I remember that against doctor's orders or even good sense he still had a couple or three drinks a day, but that he seemed not at all motivated by them to begin his old operatic habits. At night, after work, he took his medications, drank steadily and quietly and stared at the television screen until the combination of alcohol and narcotics killed any consciousness capable of keeping his eyes open and his body erect.

He didn't sleep, exactly. I don't think I can call it sleep, even though his eyes were closed and he was in a prone position on the bed or the couch. It was more like a drug-induced pause, a near-death stupor between two narcotic ellipses that still arrived fully armed with those recurrent nightmares.

In the daylight, when he left the apartment, he wore dark Ray-Ban sunglasses. He was hiding, more than shading, his darkened, bloodshot, sunken eyes. When he removed them at home, he looked like a broken and washed-up prizefighter, a lanky lightweight due to weight loss who should have been a light heavyweight given his height and original build. He had once been a contender.

I remember also his constant agitated state, the ever-present bodily shakiness that prevented him from driving. The shaking only lessened with drinking and drugs, not because they did his nerves any good, but because the combination numbed his senses at their source, silencing whatever terrible historical noise that vibrated through his overloaded synapses, endlessly repeating—what? His past? Yes, I believe it was his past that was endlessly being repeated inside his head.

By the date of his application for early retirement on May 10, 1968, his body weight was down to 125 pounds. He was six foot one.

He didn't eat very much. He claimed he couldn't chew properly and suffered from bleeding duodenal ulcers. He had multiple pairs of dentures and claimed none of them fit; he had all of his teeth pulled at the age of forty because, as he put it "the crowns were flat." They were flat because in those days he ground his teeth at night. Until they weren't teeth anymore.

If he managed to eat much of anything it caused extreme stomach discomfort. I remember he never went anywhere without a milky bottle of Maalox. This combination of physical deterioration and digestive woes meant that he increasingly relied on vitamins and vodka for nutrition. When we gathered around the family dinner table, more often than not he smoked Benson & Hedges 100s, nervously dripping long gray ashes into whatever food remained on his dinner plate.

Despite his depressed mental and physical condition, my father was unceasingly kind and encouraging to me. I do remember that. Sometimes I cling to it. He seldom raised his voice. He was, as the doctor's report succinctly put it, "preoccupied." Although he rarely asked about my schoolwork, he did encourage me to believe that I should go to college, because, as he often put it, "education is the one thing the government can't take away from you."

I had no idea what he meant. How could I? I didn't then understand what "the government" had taken away from *him*. Or what the government still had *left* to take away from all of us. I had no idea that his poor mental health was partially the result of the work he did, the accumulation of a lifetime of doing what the government asked of him and not being able to talk about it.

My father raised me to be a proud American, but also a questioning one. It wasn't until much later, toward the end of his days, that he leveled with me about how much he distrusted the government. But that was after Watergate, after Nixon, and after Vietnam. Everyone talked like that.

He never went deeper into it. Not with me.

I think he saw my long hair, beard, and liberal, Democratic Party point of view as already evidence enough of my own distrust of the government. I wonder what he thought when I was elected president of the Young Democrats at my college in 1972? When I told him that I rode on a bus around the state of West Virginia in the company of Hubert H. Humphrey, Jay Rockefeller, and then later with the Democratic candidate for the presidency of the United States of America, George McGovern?

Had he, by then, turned away from his lifelong Republicanism?

The last political thing he said to me had to be a joke. When I asked him who he liked in the upcoming '76 election he proclaimed loudly, "I'm an anarchist!" Bullshit. Bull*shit*. He was never an anarchist. I cannot believe that about him. He was all about order, even when order failed him. Even when his party, the Agency, and his beloved country failed him.

I remember that moment as if it were only moments ago. We were in the backyard in Hagerstown. It was after Watergate broke and Nixon went on television to say, "I am not a crook." Nixon was lying and everyone in the country knew it. Certainly my father knew it. He had told me in Wyoming that Nixon couldn't be trusted.

I had just accepted my first full-time teaching job, as an instructor of speech and a debate coach at Clemson University. I was to receive my master's degree that August from Chapel Hill. I had survived Paul Dickerson Brandes—my tyrannical thesis advisor—and thought I knew everything. They say *sophomore* means "wise fool," but in my experience it is far more likely to be a young person with a master's degree. *Armed* with a master's degree may be more accurate. It can be a license for intellectual arrogance as well as a license to bore.

I went on and on about the deviousness, the outright lies, the secrets kept, and the lives lost due to the singular failure of Republicans. I presented my arguments as if they were a debater's first affirmative case. I expected my father to provide a rebuttal. But he didn't rebut. Instead, he laughed loudly at my little backyard speech and told me that he was an anarchist. He said he didn't care anymore. He told me he was going to vote for whoever was having a good time.

He pretended to be having a good time himself. Whatever new regimen of drugs he was on had produced a mild euphoria that would last for a few hours every day. He asked me who I thought was having the most fun.

I had come armed for an argument and got none. Instead, I got what I perceived to be another opera. A dark, comic, ironic one. What was he trying to tell me? I have to believe he was trying to tell me something.

An anarchist. Jesus *Christ*.

I mean, *really*.

. . . .

Our move to Philadelphia corresponded with the startup for Operation CHAOS. CHAOS was a major part of the CIA's domestic surveillance and spying program and it had been unleashed on American citizens, and Vietnam antiwar protestors in particular, in 1967. It grew out of a much longer-standing program of domestic surveillance carried out by various special operations groups organized by the CIA and dating back to—well, *officially* dating back to the Eisenhower administration.

CHAOS was created in response to White House pressure to investigate the possible influence of foreign governments and their agents (read: Pinkos and Reds and spies) on American dissent. Specifically, the charge given to the CIA was to collect and correlate information with the FBI on dissenters of every stripe, political rabble-rousers, and even college and high school students who might be susceptible to foreign influence. CHAOS was particularly interested in those persons associated with anti-war protests, racial movements, and civil disobedience or antigovernment writing, speaking, organizing, or other possible activities that could be perceived as threats to the current administration, its conduct of foreign policy, or the government's ability to maintain law and order.

Sounds positively anti-constitutional because it is.

Nevertheless, CHAOS was responsible for the collection of information on over thirteen thousand Americans. It made full use of a wide variety of government intelligence-collecting technologies and agencies, including the use of photographs from high-flying spy planes and information gleaned from illegal bugging devices and FBI-sponsored wiretaps. It also had deep enough pockets to pay informants and infiltrators in protest groups, and to hire and train new undercover agents. CHAOS supplied disinformation to protest leaders to lessen their credibility, much as the CIA had provided disinformation to Communist and Socialist organizers to negatively impact their standing with supporters. It provided a central clearinghouse for propaganda and employed thousands of journalists to report on the activities of groups they were familiar with as well as to write stories that had little basis in fact.

CHAOS *was* Big Brother. Just because the radicals were paranoid didn't mean the government wasn't out to get them. They were. It was that simple. But CHAOS wasn't limited to radicals. It had a reach that extended into college groups, such as the notoriously radical Young Democrats, as well as into the suspicious antigovernment activities regularly sponsored by fraternity and sorority houses called parties. Chances are good that if an individual belonged to an organized social group or political organization on a college campus during the late 1960s or early 1970s, CHAOS knew about it. They may have been watching. If an individual became the least bit interesting politically on campus, or if someone made antiwar speeches or stirred up trouble over racial or gender issues, chances are very good that CHAOS opened a file. They were listening, too.

CHAOS, true to its name, did not limit its illegal domestic surveillance activities to watching and listening. CHAOS sponsored disorder, disruption, and mayhem. It may have had a hand in the seventeen minutes from hell caught on camera that antiwar protestors experienced at the hands of Mayor Daley in Chicago during the 1968 Democratic National Convention. It certainly had a history of contributing to protest activities in order to tip off the local police. It arranged for reporters to cover the story, to see the protest in a radical way, without bothering to tell them of their role in creating or fueling it.

CHAOS was evil. It worked all sides of every street. It was the embodiment of an American satan, state-sponsored and well funded. Its officers and agents operated thoroughly and without principle, except the overarching principle of "national security." CHAOS was the official government definition of what national security meant.

It would prove a hard definition to defend on national television. The program unraveled in the public confessions of Nixon-era administration officials trying to cover their asses after Watergate, and former CIA officers and hoodlums who remained unapologetic and unrepentant all the way into their prison uniforms. CHAOS, it turns out, made use of illegal break-ins to the homes, offices, hotel rooms, and apartments of suspected government enemies.

One of their capers was unsuccessfully carried out at the Watergate complex. Nixon was pissed about the release of the Pentagon Papers. He was convinced that the Democrats were behind it. The break-in at party headquarters in the Watergate was a CHAOS operation ostensibly run out of the White House by the president's lawyer, John Dean. It was Dean's testimony before Senator Sam Ervin's Watergate Committee that brought an end to CHAOS during the waning days of the Nixon presidency. Colby ordered it terminated. That official termination and the reasons for it were part of the family jewels. Along with the attempted assassinations of political leaders, the domestic spying activities of the CIA and FBI would prove to be the most damaging aspects of Colby's document. They led directly to the opening of the Church hearings.

For the record, I should say that CHAOS was reactivated under President Gerald Ford and was expanded considerably under President Ronald Reagan. Democratic Presidents Carter and Clinton neither supported nor approved of it or of any other domestic surveillance activities.

Following 9/11, and with then–Attorney General John Ashcroft's campaign of domestic surveillance, as well as President George W. Bush's public statements in full support of them to fight an everlasting war on terrorism, it is probably safe to say that the new offspring from the illegal loins of CHAOS are alive and well in America. Certainly all the earmarks are in place: widespread surveillance and use of wiretaps, as well as sophisticated tracking and analysis software used for e-mail, cell phone communication, and the Internet; infiltration of organizations, particularly those with any ties to Muslims or the Middle East; phony "news" broadcasts created and produced by the government and fed to the networks; phony "news reporters" planted in White House briefings and press conferences to ask scripted questions favorable to the administration's point of view; op-ed pieces written by former and current administration officials supporting the government's war on terror; massive funding for newly created attack groups, such as Swift Boat Veterans for Truth; and so on.

CHAOS, by this or some other name, no doubt still operates in our country.

Then as now, collecting secret intelligence on American citizens is illegal, anti-American, and undemocratic. It is dirty work of the first political order. Back in 1967, everyone in charge of the operation, from the president on down to my father, knew that. But their defense for everything they did was that they were engaged in fighting a cold war. This was an issue of national security. Vietnam was burning proof that fighting Communism *over there* is preferable to fighting it *over here*. The domino theory was in play. If Vietnam fell, who would be next? How long would it take for them Russians, them Russians, them Chinamen, and them Russians to be at our front doors?

The CIA had been actively engaged in precisely such illegal activity for the same exact political reasons since its inception in 1947. My father, who once believed that collecting this information was his part in the fight against Communism, may have been recruited for the 1967 cause because of his background, his experience, and his success in doing precisely that. But the man who was recruited to conduct these operations in Philadelphia had become, in the interim, a very different man.

I cannot say with any degree of certainty that CHAOS is what finally broke him. I know only that he came to Philadelphia in pretty good shape and that within fifteen months he applied for early retirement from a combination of mental, emotional, and physical collapse. I can only offer evidence from his medical records of his condition. I can only recall the lives we led at home during this time.

. . . .

My mother was distraught over my father's deteriorating condition. She was also angered by his intention to pursue an early retirement. She believed that without work, he would have nothing to do. My father had no hobbies, no interests outside of his job. She rightly imagined that if he retired early he would become terminally bored and even more preoccupied with wherever his mind took him when the pills wore off and the pain kicked back in.

She tried several nursing strategies to see if she could motivate him, heal him, or just encourage him to regain his self-confidence, if not his health. She planned them like a ward nurse plans a weekly work schedule.

I know she did because I helped her.

When he first announced his intention to retire, my mother, playing the role of a bad nurse, cruelly berated him for being a quitter. It was designed to make him mad enough to get back into shape.

My father sat there trembling in his chair and took it, took every false word of it, his eyes retreating further and further from her, from me, from us. He was against the ropes. She hit him with one verbal jab after another designed to wear him down, make him give up the retirement. Give up and go back to work.

It didn't happen. Nor did I step in and stop it. I wish I had. But I had given her my promise not to intervene. She knew best, she said. She was a nurse. She had a history of dealing with sick patients. She was his wife and she loved him. So I sat on the couch and watched and heard. And *saw*. I saw my poor father refuse to fight back. I saw my mother continue to jab away, her face becoming more and more angry. She said terrible things to him and I sat there and let her do it. I allowed it go on. I know I should have said something, but I didn't. Finally, I left the apartment and headed up to the Ridge, the intersection of Ridge and Summit avenues where my friends hung out.

Mornings during our bad-nurse period we all woke up and pretended nothing bad had ever been said the night before. That was our way. When my mother finally admitted that her bad-nurse strategy wasn't working, she took me aside and said she had a better idea.

She was a nurse. She had treated sick people before.

She told me not to worry.

∙ ∙

Her next strategy was to treat my father as a kind of human stray and win him over to her way of thinking with unusual displays of kindness. She played the good nurse, the one all of us hope for when we feel bad, the one who fluffs our pillows and holds our hand and tells us everything will be all right. My mother soothed and forgave and nurtured him. She hoped to convince my father that he was still worth saving, still worth the world to her and to me. I suspect this new approach was partially the result of hearing him tell both of us he didn't want to live anymore.

A son doesn't forget something like that. I'm sure a wife doesn't either.

It was as if he was perfectly willing to check out of this life and leave the wreckage of us behind. He looked at us and said, "I want to die." He was not so much stating a fact as pleading with us to go along with his decision.

We couldn't do that.

∙ ∙

My mother closely monitored his daily intake of prescription drugs. There were quite a lot of them. They all carried strong warning labels. You were not supposed to mix any of them with alcohol.

I was instructed to pour down the sink any booze I might find hiding behind a can of shaving cream in the bathroom or china in the kitchen or that I would find covered by a blanket in the trunk of the car. She watched my father's every move, much as a psychiatric-ward nurse watches a mental patient thought to be suicidal.

That second strategy, nurturing and caring and loving and all that other happy horseshit, didn't work either, so my mother augmented the good-nurse strategy with pure professionalism. She was a nurse again on home duty in our personal emergency ward, 24/7.

After my father said he wanted to die, my mother and I went through a long period playing out scenarios of "Things He Could Swallow to Hurt Himself." We hid or emptied bottles of rubbing alcohol, witch hazel, mouthwash, cough syrup. Even aspirin was off-limits to my father without my mother's approval.

I remember getting a bad cold that winter. I couldn't find the Nyquil because my mother had poured what was left of it down the sink. For backup and because my cold came fully equipped with a headache, I asked for some aspirin only to be told she couldn't remember where she had hidden it. She offered me some prescription medication she had under lock and key instead, but I declined. The next morning I bought my own aspirin and Nyquil and kept them tucked under my mattress.

. . . .

Thus began the escalation silently known as "Guess what we can hide from each other?" It was a kind of perverse game. We selected randomly from the categories of physical items, emotional states, and mental conditions. The objective was to keep secret the selected item or items. No clues were given nor was any relevant information exchanged. The winner, if you could call it that, was the family member who could name what one of the other family members was hiding.

It was twisted but we engaged in this nightly melodrama as if our lives depended on it. Again, I found my way out of the drama by making my way up the street to the corner of Ridge and Summit.

Finally, after the bad strategy of hate had turned into a good strategy of love, and our love went unrequited and my father kept finding places to hide things and feelings from us, my mother declared the nuclear option: she threatened to leave him. We knew she would never actually do that, so we didn't take her seriously.

I think our denial of this possibility offended her. But by then, it didn't matter. I left the apartment, my father retreated to the bedroom, and my mother fretted on the couch watching television. We all knew she would wake up the next morning as if nothing had happened.

I knew my parents were hopelessly entangled—their married lives, their stories of the past, their scars—and I believed they always would be thus entangled. Some things I just *knew* weren't going to happen in that story. There was an inner pattern that held steady even when every outer sign was going crazy.

. . . .

After my mother's failed attempts to motivate my father back to work by threatening divorce, she gave up talking about it. Both of them wore blank expressions that I read as resignation. It seemed to me that they had given up the struggle, the hard family work, of pretending that things could be good for us again.

My father stopped talking about taking early retirement, and then he stopped going to work entirely. He just woke up one morning and decided not to go in. Then he made the same decision the next day. And the next. And he continued calling in sick for—what was it?—about two months? I remember only that he spent most days propped up in bed reading the *Philadelphia Inquirer*. My mother fretted. I went out.

I've tried to focus on the day he gave up. I've searched my memory for a precipitating factor, an incident he talked about, or anything that can clarify for me what triggered retirement. I remember only that he was mad as hell about something that happened at work.

It wasn't a large, extraordinary thing, but something small and ordinary.

I think it was something he had been asked to do. He said, "I'll be damned if I'll ever do *that* again."

This family event occurred late in 1968. The Tet Offensive had begun at the end of January, and bad news about Vietnam was on television every night. More troops were committed with no end to the war in sight. Then Martin Luther King Jr. was murdered by a Mississippi racist while standing on the balcony of a Memphis motel on April 4, and for a few days people in America feared a race war. This was not to be the only politically motivated shooting: on June 5, three bullets found the body of Robert F. Kennedy. At Columbia University, the first major student takeover of administration buildings produced the closing down of the campus. Rumors circulated of a student rebellion in our country to rival the one in France that had effectively shut down Paris. President Johnson appeared on television and declared that he "was not seeking, and would not accept," the nomination of his party for reelection. He was taking early retirement too. The world had changed too much, too fast, for LBJ and for my father.

There was the first large march on Washington by Vietnam war protestors and students and anyone else who believed the media coverage would give them an audience for their grievances. There were rumors of machine guns placed on the roof of both the White House and Capitol. Apparently the government was fully prepared to shoot its own citizens to prevent a coup.

Then came the campaigns, Hubert Humphrey against "Tricky Dick" Nixon. In the same summer it was first Miami, then bloody Chicago. Nixon, the "peace with honor" candidate, won with Spiro Agnew as his running mate. Remember Agnew? Remember him saying the words "nattering nabobs of negativism" and leading the charge of the "silent majority" against the Left? He was the Dick Cheney of 1968.

Nineteen sixty-eight. Those were the days, my friend. That was the year, following close on the heels of the rotten election of Richard Nixon, that my father decided to retire.

What was the line he used to quote? "The world is too much with us, late and soon."

. . . .

Now to my mother. That line is taken from Hamlet and for good reason: at the time of my father's retreat to the bedroom, I increasingly felt like I was trapped in a Shakespearean tragedy. In 1968 my mother acquired her own King Claudius in chemical form: her own "nerve pills." Her need for them had nothing to do with what was on television or in the newspapers or going on out in the streets. I'm not sure it had very much to do with my father's deteriorating psychological and physical condition, except as a systemic contributing factor. It had to do with a pot roast.

It began the morning my father found the first frozen pot roast beneath the cushion in his chair.

Now, of course, I can look back on it and see the metaphor at work. Or at least I think I can. We were a family who hid things from each other. We hid intangible things such as how we felt or what we thought, and then progressed to hiding tangible objects. My father's stash of vodka. The mouthwash. The witch hazel. An entire clandestine life. I, too, was hiding things: that I wasn't much attending high school, that I preferred to ride the bus down to Center City, walk over to Rittenhouse Square, play guitar and smoke dope and hang out with the hippies until it was time to ride the bus back home. But when my mother began hiding frozen meat in the furniture, well, that was quite a surprise to all of us.

Communication in any family is a complex of systemic language loops and feedback information. One word or phrase becomes intricately connected to another word or phrase in the systemic family psyche. Every family has a codebook to decipher the deeper meanings of those words. So it was that this sudden appearance of obvious insanity was simply connected to our ongoing habit of hiding things and keeping secrets from each other.

"Sleep" was, in our family, one of those code words. Sleep was an altered state of consciousness as much as a term we used to describe rest. "Going

to bed" was an excuse my parents used to cover up an inability or unwillingness to deal with each other or their own lives in the daylight. When they
slept, they were invulnerable and unaccountable. Properly narcotized or
blotto, sleep was as close to death as they could get.

I have no doubt my mother acquired the so-called nerve pills for a variety
of good reasons. Her husband refused to go to work, her son was increasingly alien to her, and her life was not the life she wanted. However, the
reason she gave the doctor for needing them probably had little to do with
it. She claimed she couldn't sleep and needed something that would knock
her out. She used her former status as a nurse to bully a younger physician with problems of his own into prescribing the powerful narcotic she
claimed would help her sleep. She undoubtedly needed her sleep, but she
was trying to go to bed to cover up a new illness, an uncontrollable mani-
festation of insanity that truly frightened her.

My mother was suffering from a sleeping sickness her doctor didn't have
a name for, much less a treatment. These days the medical community does
have a word—parasomnia—to provide an official label for it. Still, there are
few effective treatments available and, as yet, no known cures.

In my mother's case, her symptoms began with sleepwalking. Because
my father was already in a pharmacologically induced comatose state by
the time I arrived home at night, after my mother began sleepwalking
it became my job to lock the front door to prevent her from leaving the
apartment.

With the only way out of our apartment thusly secured, her early nocturnal
roaming was just that: she roamed from room to room, sometimes turning on
lights (which she never turned off), and sometimes rearranging magazines or
knickknacks—these were the telltale signs of her nighttime movements. She
didn't open drawers but she would open closets. On one occasion she walked
into my bedroom, turned on the light, opened the closet door, squatted, and
peed on my tennis shoes. My father had warned me not to try to wake her,
but pissing on my shoes was intolerable to me, so I spoke to her as gently as
I could: "Mom, wake up, *you are peeing on my shoes*."

Her eyes were suddenly wide open. "Am *not*," she replied, offended.

She finished her business, pulled up her panties, pulled down her dress-
ing gown, and exited my room in a huff, leaving the closet door open and
the overhead light on.

The next morning I brought up the incident and she denied it. She
laughed, saying that I must have been dreaming. My shoes were still wet

but I knew proving it was so wouldn't solve anything. I cleaned the floor in my closet and threw away the tennis shoes.

A few nights later she hid the first of her frozen pot roasts in my father's chair.

After that she started taking nerve pills. Mostly, they knocked her out. I believe she thought that by tranquilizing herself into a near-death state, she would avoid sleepwalking and hiding meat in the furniture. It didn't quite work out that way.

Her nighttime actions became decidedly stranger, more surreal than harmful: she would rise, get fully dressed, and then sit in the living room upright in her chair. Or she would take out every pot and pan in the kitchen and place them on top of each other, from the floor as high up as she could reach. Or she would remove from the refrigerator only white items—milk, cream, sour cream, even turnips—and line them up along the countertop.

These were laughable faux pas. She denied having done it, of course. But by then we didn't believe each other's denials. The denial was a lie. But we were all liars here.

Then one of us would again discover a pot roast or pork chops under the pillow in a chair. A package of chicken would be found under a sofa pillow, or a package of hamburger would turn up beneath an armchair.

"Naooooo-mah!" My father said her name like Fred Flintstone used to yell for Wilma. I say this because our family pattern of denial, avoidance, and secrecy was evidence of something like Bedrock learning. I'm not being funny. Maybe a little ironic, but not *funny*.

"Naooooo-mah," he would croak, "there's a goddamn pack of pork chops in my seat again!"

My mother hated to get caught because she steadfastly denied doing it. She marched into the living room like a nurse called into a patient's room to remove a bedpan. She gave my father a bright diplomatic smile that became, as she turned away from him and I could see her face, an astonished expression shot through with a kind of terror. She discarded the offending package of frozen meat. Her throwing it away was probably a symbolic act that spoke more to her need to get rid of something embarrassing. In our family's code for secrets, this was a signal that we were not supposed to discuss it.

What we were learning from each other—because that is what families do, learn communication patterns and coping strategies from each other— was Bedrock primitive and cold war modern simultaneously. Ours was a family pattern of covering up, of hiding things, of keeping secrets, that was so impenetrable as to render anything we might say about finding food in the furniture ineffable. It was *unspeakable*. So we didn't discuss it.

For my part, I had accepted that my parents were both hopeless, burnt-out cases. Not even doctors could help them. My father's official retirement on January 9, 1969, on full medical disability with a psychiatric recommendation, confirmed it. My mother's increasing daytime depression and nighttime food weirdness settled it.

I spent less and less time in our apartment. I just wanted to get away from my family.

• •

When I went to school I lived my weekday life after school up on the corner of Ridge and Summit, or worked longer hours for my after-school boss, J. Gross & Bros. When I didn't go to school, I went downtown. Weekends I played my red Hagstrom electric twelve-string guitar with my friends on their parents' back porch or down in their parents' basement or out in their father's garage. At night on the weekends, or whenever else I could manage it, I wrapped myself into the welcoming arms of a series of girlfriends.

Believe it or not, in our own crazy way, I thought we were a normal family and that I was living a normal teenage existence. I had grown up believing we *were* normal. I didn't know anything else. It was "normal" what we did and how we acted. My parents told me so.

Which is why, from Philadelphia forward, I *never* wanted to be normal. "Normal" was where the truly weird was—for me—originally, thoroughly, and finally located. "Normal" is where secrets ran so deep they drained a family's strength and sucked every drop of lifeblood right out of arteries and veins. "Normal" was the name we gave when people kept things to themselves and hid important truths from each other.

"Normal" was also a family appearing absolutely ordinary, not standing out in any way. Never drawing attention to one's self. Fitting in and measuring up and doing well enough to get by. "Normal" was formal, at least out of doors, where people could see and evaluate you. "Normal" was neatly trimmed and pressed and polished. It was button-down shirts and proper trousers and loafers with bright pennies in them. "Normal" was insanely boring, in clothing, attitude, and mind. "Normal" was a state of consciousness that needed, in my humble opinion, to be altered.

For all these reasons, to be "normal" was to live with a long, slow, irreversible death sentence. It meant life as it was and things as they were, because remember: I thought *we* were ordinary average normal people.

We were normal people. Ours was a normal family.

By the age of sixteen, all I wanted in life was to be *free* of what was normal.

. . . .

Then I made a big mistake. We left Philadelphia because I was thrown out of high school. In truth, I was asked to leave the state of Pennsylvania. My father brokered a deal with Frank Rizzo to keep me out of jail. In return, he agreed to move our family out of the state.

I was thrown out of high school because I "incited a riot." Saying it that way makes it much larger than it was. The truth is, I gave a speech against the new school dress code. It was my first public speech. I had no idea it would change my life.

In retrospect I see it now as part of a larger pattern. It was a personal wake-up call to the power of language. It was a clue. At the time, I thought it was an accident and the whole incident at Roxborough High was just an assembly that got out of hand. At the time, I didn't attribute any further significance to it. I felt as if I had been blamed for events that were beyond my control.

But was it that way? Or was it part of a pattern of language usage in the emerging story that would become my destiny?

Here is how I remember it: There I was in a crowded high school auditorium during an assembly. My presence on the stage was decided at the last minute by a fellow student, a high school organizer for the radical antiwar group Students for a Democratic Society, or so he claimed to be at the time. Years later, when SDS was routinely associated with terrorist activities, I scanned television and newspaper accounts for images of him but never found one. Who was he? I don't even remember his name. Frank, maybe. For all I know, "Frank" could have been working for my father.

What I do remember is that he was an outspoken guy, an "idealist," as some teachers had labeled him. He asked me if it was true I had been suspended from school for wearing Beatle boots.

I had, I told him. It was a three-day suspension and I was still pissed off about it. I felt the whole dress code was a bad idea. Girls had to wear skirts that touched their knees; boys couldn't wear leather or muscle shirts or boots of any kind. Hair length was regulated. I said that I thought there were a lot more pressing problems in the world. Vietnam. Hunger. Race riots. Equal rights for women.

"Good," he replied. "Then you need to say that during assembly."

As the student assembly began, I stood backstage and listened to a series of short speeches by fellow students on various school problems. Each speech garnered applause and two or three of them were punctuated by shouts of "Right on!"

When my name was called and I appeared on the stage, the audience was ready for something to break. The momentum was building. I was seized by panic, mostly because I suddenly realized that I didn't have the slightest idea what I would say. I remember the floodlights were directly on my face. I remember the overly warm auditorium was filled with vaguely unfamiliar faces, and that the guy who had asked me to speak was urging me to "say something, *now.*"

What I said surprised even me.

I began with the fact that I had been suspended from school for the crime of wearing black Beatle boots. I then linked that suspension rhetorically, if illogically, to larger issues of the day, including the failure of city fathers to address bad schools and teachers, inner-city crime, poverty, and the Vietnam War. My argument, if that is what you could call it, was that the vice principal, and by extension all authority figures, would rather suspend kids for what we chose to wear to school than solve real problems. I apparently became passionate about it and raised my fist into the air, which prompted the already pumped-up in the audience to cheer. So I repeated the gesture and they continued to cheer, several times, each time our collective noise notching me further up toward something new. When it came out of my mouth what I said seemed not only just and right, but *inevitable.* I shouted it, but I only became aware of the words when I heard their echo: "So we need, right now, to walk out of here!"

Which we did.

The explosive effect of hundreds of Roxborough High students storming suddenly out of school and into the streets during morning rush hour was akin to setting fire to an explosives arsenal. Fights broke out along Ridge Avenue among members of rival gangs and their fighting stopped traffic; automobile and truck horns joined the general noise and shouting, and the wail of police sirens added tension to an already dramatic event. Teachers, curious to see what the interruption was about, abandoned classrooms and behind them came their unsupervised students, whose collective mass then multiplied the problems on the streets and further fueled the collective sense of chaos. Within minutes the scene was out of control.

I had incited a riot.

That evening my parents and I watched a local news report of the violent outbreak that was now labeled a "school protest of the Vietnam War." The cause of the disruption and violence was an end-of-the-school-year speech at a junior-class assembly. The assembly had been called by school administrators to allow students to voice concerns about perceived problems in the school, problems the administrators said they had planned to resolve over the summer.

I was never mentioned by name. I almost escaped notice. But someone at a local news station interviewed "Frank." He said, "It's about time that students got actively involved in bringing this unjust war to an end." A reporter then said Frank Rizzo had vowed to intervene, and that "reckless disregard for the law by war protestors and student agitators would not be tolerated in his city."

I had never heard of Operation CHAOS. I had no idea that my father had been one of the government men charged with the responsibility for infiltrating antiwar and protest groups. I wonder, now, if he had been watching me all along. I doubt it. But I am less convinced that my father didn't know about "Frank." One of the tricks used in CHAOS was to put young men into student groups, such as the SDS, and use them to stir up trouble.

. . . .

Nothing happened to me directly as a result of my speech, but our lives changed. My parents "decided" to leave Philadelphia, a decision I would later learn my father had negotiated with school officials and with Frank Rizzo.

I was officially labeled a "school agitator." This label was recorded in my permanent student file, where it was also noted that I was a "potentially dangerous person." I had given a public speech that caused a city riot. I was deemed a threat to peace in the Keystone State.

That is why and how we left Philadelphia. From my point of view, it is how we ended up in Hagerstown, Maryland.

But we could as easily have ended up moving to Rome. Or to London. Or to Paris. But no. My parents chose to move to Hagerstown. Why Hagerstown?

Hagerstown was a more anonymous place than even Cheyenne. A city of seventy thousand, it was known for nothing much and was distinguished by nothing at all. City boosters talked up the Mack truck assembly plant and bragged about the town being at the intersection of I-85 and I-70, which made it a prime business location. The Moller Pipe Organ Company was touted as the finest pipe organ manufacturer in the world, but sales had fallen off and the company faced a series of cash-flow problems that led to its eventual demise. The main street in the downtown used to be a place where elected officials in Washington kept their mistresses and fancy boys in fine mansions. These fine mansions had clearly seen better days and now housed lawyer's offices or served as rental space for apartment dwellers. The first radio station in Maryland—WJEJ—still broadcast live out of its original building downtown, and had a dwindling, if loyal, listenership. It was a local joke that the call letters stood for "Jesus Entering Jerusalem" because the original owner feared, in 1932, that radio was probably a fad.

In 1969, Hagerstown was on its way down. Or at least it seemed so to me. After Philadelphia, it was a major disappointment. I couldn't imagine living there, even after we moved in. We lived once again in a garden-style apartment, this time on the edge of the less prosperous south side of town. We were a stone's throw away from nowhere. I was not happy about finishing high school in Hagerstown.

I couldn't complain to my parents because it was my fault we were living here. Of course, that fault was kept secret from any new people we met. But it was nevertheless a black mark in my permanent file. That fact would be spelled out for me in the very near future.

On the first day of school I was coolly greeted and unambiguously escorted into South Hagerstown High School by an athletic vice principal sporting a crew cut. His office walls were lined with sports trophies and awards for citizenship. There was a framed photograph of him standing with Spiro Agnew and several other photos of him in a military uniform posing with his unit in a combat location that I later learned was Korea. He told me that he had gone over my records from Roxborough very carefully and would be keeping a close eye on me. "We don't approve of agitators and war protestors here," he said. He rapped a wooden ruler hard against his desk.

He repeated the rap for added effect.

I didn't recognize myself in his sentence. It was clear to me that how I felt about it didn't matter. It was a warning and the ruler was implied reinforcement. I was a prisoner here and there was no Bill of Rights to protect me. Mr. Vice Principal went on to say that if I got out of line, which he hoped I would, my punishment would be swift and righteous. It wouldn't be a three-day suspension or even banishment from the city. He would personally and happily beat the hell out of me.

I had no doubt that he would.

"Then," he concluded, "I would be only too pleased to escort you to the Armed Forces Induction Center and ship your antiwar peacenik ass off to Vietnam." He smiled in an unfriendly and unencouraging patriotic way and showed me the door. "That is your final warning," he said. He smacked the ruler hard against the desk one more time. It broke. If I hadn't gotten the message by now, I never would.

It wasn't fair. I had once given an impromptu speech against a dress code and things had gotten out of hand. But now I was an agitator and war protestor and enemy of all right-thinking citizens of Hagerstown. I was considered a threat to peaceful society. I was here to complete high school in Hagerstown but it felt like I was trapped in some kind of Arlo Guthrie song.

. . . .

In retrospect I see an emotional parallel between my clandestine cover being blown in Philadelphia and my father's *persona non grata* status that swept us away from London and into exile in Wyoming.

We had both been betrayed by the truth. Our futures were mutually determined by powerful men who never once believed they had been wrong. We had both been labeled as troublemakers.

My father never reprimanded me for my speech. Maybe in my speaking out for something I believed in he saw in his son a quality—albeit a reckless one—that reminded him of himself. Or maybe not.

We didn't talk about it.

I graduated from South Hagerstown High School in June of 1970, got a draft deferment, and went off to college to create new life for myself away from my parents. During the last conversation we had, on the eve of my leaving, my father only requested one thing from me: that I promise *not* to become a Communist.

18

Decline, Denouement, and Death

1970–1976

"GATSBY TURNS OUT ALL RIGHT IN THE END." WHAT DID MY FATHER MEAN by that? When I think about how to tell his story, I find myself returning to this statement for a clue. For so much of my father's saga I have been guided by it. I must return to it now.

After Gatsby is murdered, what happens?

Nick Carraway provides the denouement. He offers us the interpretive key to the whole mystery. If he didn't, *Gatsby* wouldn't be a great novel, or perhaps not even a very good one. We would be left hanging in post mortem midsentence, with a dead hero in a swimming pool. We would know scant more about the mystery of Gatsby than his party guests knew. Unanswered—and unanswerable—questions would remain, and the questions would forever define our relationship to him as unresolved. Who was he? Where did he come from? What made him tick?

But with the denouement, Nick gives voice and perspective to the story and Gatsby is redeemed.

It all begins when Nick surveys Gatsby's life following his murder and begins to reveal Gatsby's secrets. Myrtle's husband, Wilson, killed him and then committed suicide. The police believe only what they are told, so Wilson is labeled a madman and the explanation everyone seems content with is that he murdered Gatsby out of grief. Nick could have walked away from the story at this point and it would have been enough. But instead, he takes control of the story by arranging Gatsby's funeral. So it is that we learn Gatsby's real name—James Gatz—and meet his humble Minnesota father. We are shown a book Jimmy Gatz kept as a child, a diary with a plan for self-improvement. Through this artifact of an ordinary childhood, we grasp the conflicting patterns that defined Gatsby's character, his motivations, his ideals, and his pluck. We glimpse who he wanted to be. We are privy to his favorite book and reading habits. These clues are codes for a well-examined life that was kept secret from the world.

The funeral is organized by absences. We watch as one by one Gatsby's so-called friends, party hangers-on, and business associates all back out of attending it. In the end, not even Daisy, his beloved illusive dream girl, attends his funeral. Nor, as Nick observes, does she bother to send a message of condolence or sorrow.

The denouement continues as Nick rounds off the questions surrounding the lesser characters.

The book could have ended there. It would have been enough. We have achieved a finality of understanding about the people who surrounded Gatsby and who populated the story of his last summer. The novel would have made money and maybe earned a place on a best-seller list. It would have been remembered as the tale of careless people, of fickle friendships and spent summer love affairs. It might have been considered a good beach read for 1924. In truth the novel sold a little over twenty-three thousand copies that summer. Although Fitzgerald was disappointed with sales, he attributed the lack of them to the absence of a strong enough female lead character. He believed women controlled the fiction market.

But Fitzgerald was wrong about his masterpiece needing anything. And he had no idea that it would become the high icon of twentieth-century American literature.

When Fitzgerald died, in 1940 at the age of forty-four, none of his books were in print and he thought of himself as a literary failure. He didn't suspect that *The Great Gatsby* would be reborn a classic, that it would be used as a codebook in the cold war, or that its story line would shape the lives of anyone like me. Or you. Or any of the millions of readers who annually purchase more copies of the novel than it sold in his lifetime.

I think *denouement* is key to understanding what earned this popular novel its rightful place among great books. But the denouement wouldn't have been complete without the final turn, literally, into the prose poem of the novel's last page. It is the ultimate denouement, wherein the meaning of a singular life in a bygone era is revealed to have been driven by the same dreams as our own, where love—even unrequited love—is the grand story we are all here to live, and the words of that story erase the lines of history and replace them with a poetry of destiny.

Nick creates the American meaning of Gatsby's life standing one last time on his fabled lawn. Nick explains to us he has made plans to move back to the Midwest, packed his trunk, and sold his car. He considers "the huge incoherent failure" of Gatsby's house. Then Nick sits down and, in three short paragraphs, Jay Gatsby is forever inscribed in our hearts. Nick says:

> And as I sat there, brooding on the old unknown world, I thought of Gatsby's wonder as he picked out the green light at the end of Daisy's dock. He had come a long way to this blue lawn and his dream must have seemed so close that he could hardly fail to grasp it. He did not know that it was already behind him, somewhere back in that vast obscurity beyond the city, where the dark fields of the republic rolled on under the night.
>
> Gatsby believed in the green light, the orgiastic future that year by year recedes before us. It eluded us then, but that's no matter—tomorrow we will run faster, stretch out our arms farther. . . . And one fine morning—
>
> So we beat on, boats against the current, borne back ceaselessly into the past.

. . . .

The trouble is figuring out what Gatsby's "turning out all right in the end" means in terms of my father's decline and death. I must find where our true denouement begins.

In my life, I have too often been premature in my judgment of my father's life. Following his death, I rushed to judgment as a child rushes toward certainty, believing that the meanings I had so partially understood summed the total of how it was, who we were as a family, what it was all about, and so on, believing, falsely, that what I thought at twenty-three would be true for all eternity. But I have learned I was wrong.

Like Nick Carraway, I find myself at the end of a long season of studied observation, enveloping mystery, intriguing possibilities, circles, arrows, and evidential surmise. My father's mysterious death seems long ago, and yet not so far away. The cold war has morphed into an enduring war on terror. There are circles within the circles and the arrows all share a common trajectory. I will try to put it straight.

. . . .

My family settled and, to borrow a term from Herbert Simon, "satisficed" in Hagerstown, finding artificial satisfaction in our lives there.

My parents bought a little house after I left for college. They lived together in what I believed was a state of perpetual decline. It depressed me to visit, so I didn't visit very often. When I did, I was highly self-medicated.

It didn't matter. So were they.

I found hidden bottles of vodka stashed here and there and just ignored them. What was the point? My father was in and out of Brook Lane so often that I thought he would stop cutting off the blue plastic wrist wrap with his name printed on it. If they couldn't cure him, how was I to fare any better?

My mother, amazingly, returned to nursing. She got a job in the emergency room at the hospital downtown and worked the 3 p.m to 11 p.m. shift that nobody else wanted. She loved it. It got her out of the house and reconnected her to life outside of our imploded family.

I think she had given up on us but couldn't let go.

It is strange that one characteristic of the Goodall clan is how well we functioned at work and how poorly at home. I never understood it. It was as if my mother became a different person entirely when she put on that white uniform. She ceased to walk stoop-shouldered and slow. She held her head high and walked with a bounce in her step. She smiled and cracked jokes about doctors, other nurses, and patients.

I was glad to see her return to the fun person I remembered from so long ago. As Nurse Naomi, she came back to life. I also thought that because she was a nurse she would notice when I was self-medicated. But apparently not.

Maybe she thought it was our secret. Like father, like son.

Once, when she came home in her uniform and I had already carried my father to bed, I asked her why she put up with it. She looked at me with her dark, fathomless eyes and said nothing for a while. Not, I don't think, because she was searching her soul for the answer, so much as she was considering how to tell me the truth in her heart without breaking mine. She said, finally, "You will never be half the man your father was." Her voice was not cruel, but compassionate.

I was a disappointment. I had gone astray from the expectations my parents had for my life and while she would always love me as her son, she didn't respect the choices I had made. I had remained in school and become a teacher. I didn't earn much money and probably never would. Nor was I a real patriot, nor had I been a soldier, nor had I volunteered to work for my government and gone proudly into the State Department or the clandestine services. She knew I had been offered the chance and declined it. "You could have inherited your father's points," she said. "You have no right to judge him."

I never asked her again.

If my mother was distraught over my father's repeated visits to Brook Lane, she didn't show her distress to me. When I was at school, she telephoned with the news. She made it seem natural, as if my father's visits there were no more unusual than summer thunderstorms or snowfall in January. Her voice was matter-of-fact. I tried to keep the judgment out of mine.

. . . .

Kim Philby received his nickname from his father. He said it was taken from Rudyard Kipling's novel of that name. The novel tells the story of a British boy raised in India who becomes a spy. Well, that is one way to tell what *Kim* is about. It just happens to be *my* way.

Nevertheless, it is interesting to me that St. John Philby called his son by the name of a spy and that his son turned out to be one. Not just *any* spy, either, but perhaps the most important Soviet spy in history.

"What is a *spy*?"

In interviews conducted with ex-CIA officers I am always interested to know if what "they" say is true: that you never really leave the clandestine service. So I asked them.

More often than not I get another question in reply. The question differs depending on the person I ask, but it is as if I had tapped into a truth that only appears on the surface to be an evasion. Here are some of the ways my question has been answered:

"Do you ever stop being a philosopher?"

"Do you ever stop being a poet?"

"Do you ever stop being a scientist?"

"Do you ever stop being a thief?"

"Do you ever stop being a lover?"

"Do you ever stop being a friend?"

"Do you ever stop being a traitor?"

"Do you ever stop being a patriot?"

They volley my question back at me. Playfully. Seriously. With wit. Even humor. At first, I took their refusal to answer in a simple declarative sentence to mean no. I still do. No, of course you don't ever really retire from the stage. You simply play a different role. You are no more capable of being an "ex-spy" than you are an "ex-information exchanger." If you traffic in the business of knowing secrets about persons, places, murders, and politics, you don't suddenly stop knowing about them. Or wondering about them. Or turning events over again in your sleep, trying to figure out what went right, or, more likely, given the ambiguities of this uncertain business, what may have gone all wrong.

Nor do you stop phoning your old friends. Talking about this and that. Inquiring about a book you've just read, or a play you've seen, or a movie you want to attend. Recalling old times and *lang syne*. Asking about old what's-his-name? What's he up to these days? What was she up to *then*?

You do not leave behind who you have become, even if you want to.

It is the stuff of your life. It is the *story* you have been part of and it's the character you played. We are shaped by our memories and circumstances, and each and every morning we awake to carry ourselves and who we are into the world and see what happens. We make all of it up as we go along.

For those who have lived among, and have themselves spun, the intricate webs of secrecy and legend, role-playing ceases to be a second nature. Instead, it becomes one's *only* nature. It is no more unnatural for an old spook to live in so-called retirement from the Veterans Administration in the Maryland suburbs than it is for an old CIA analyst to live in a gated community in California and pretend he had nothing to do with spying. All he or she did, after all, was push paper from one side of their desk to the other side.

Do you ever stop being a _____? I don't think so.

When I was a young academic living in Huntsville, Alabama, I interviewed the surviving members of Wernher von Braun's original German rocket team. I was a researcher for an oral history project. The idea was to capture the memories and record the experiences of these scientists before they died. One of them, I won't name him because he's dead and I can't see that it would serve any purpose now, was a kindly old gentleman who had received numerous civic awards. He spoke with a mild German accent that made him seem like the very model of a fine old European, which, in many ways, he was. He loved his wife, his children, and his grandchildren.

He was a scientist of the first order. His research led directly from the early Redstone rocket to the powerful Atlas that launched Neil Armstrong and his crew to the moon. Every morning this fine old European gentleman raised an American flag in front of his ranch-style house, and every evening he lowered it. He appeared to all the world to be a proud American.

Yes, he told me, after I got to know him and he accepted that I wasn't out to expose him, he once had been a Nazi. He had believed in Adolf Hitler, although he had misrepresented that belief when he met with the Americans who arranged for his transport out of Peenemünde. "We all did," he said quietly. "We feared the Russians more than the Americans."

He had wanted Germany to be victorious in the Second World War. He had worked on the V-1 and the V-2 programs and knew exactly what the buzz bombs were being used for in the war. Toward the end of things, the German scientists were reduced to distilling rocket fuel from Polish potatoes. "You know," he mused warmly, "I often wonder what things would be like if we had only had a *few more potatoes*. . . ." He glanced at me and smiled. "But you won't want to put that in your report, will you?"

And so we beat on, boats against the current, borne back ceaselessly into the past.

Identity carries us there.

. . . .

Brook Lane Psychiatric Hospital.

It was a good place for spies with mental problems. The doctors were former government-service types who had supposedly gone into private practice for larger sums of money, but I've often wondered if that was true. It wasn't a fancy place, just a converted farm in rural Maryland, complete with a white barn used for a cafeteria and two outbuildings used to house the patients. The consulting offices were located in the main house, a white clapboard affair with modest furnishings and soft lighting. Wire mesh fences surrounded the grounds, which consisted of about ten acres or so of sparsely wooded grasslands, and through which ran a rock-filled brook. As you sat on a bench next to it, or walked by it, this brook actually *babbled*. So, too, did the patients.

I met several of them over the years.

There was a curious uniformity about them. They were all men, for one thing. I don't believe I ever saw a female patient, although there were women in white uniforms who may or may not have been nurses. At Brook Lane, it was hard to say for sure. Some of the doctors seemed to have no more medical understanding of addiction or dependency than the babbling brook did. Often, they didn't remember what drugs they had prescribed, and more than once I had the distinct impression that one of them had been detained by a lunch otherwise known as Russian vodka. By then, I knew the supposedly invisible scent of vodka so well it was impossible to make a mistake. There is no other liquor as likely to make the breath foul in quite that way, particularly when accompanied by a cigarette or four or ten.

But nothing was exactly as it appeared to be at Brook Lane. It was as if we entered a world inside the gates more than slightly askew and everyone in residence there refused to admit it. Personal idiosyncrasies were ignored. Clothing was a matter of personal taste. There was one pathetic guy, always flirty and ready to curtsy for me, who insisted on wearing a sundress and being addressed as "Missy." No one said anything about it. We called him "Missy."

There was another fellow who dressed in a three-piece suit and counted each step he took aloud. "One, two, three, four, five . . ." By the time I knew him he was up to "one million five hundred and sixty-five thousand, two hundred and eighty," which he followed with "one million five hundred and sixty-five thousand, two hundred and eighty-one." His number had grown so large as to cause an exaggerated pause in his step, so that as he called out where he was in his infinite numerical progression, his leg rose to a holding position that only relaxed as he reached the end of his recital. He looked like a mechanical man.

I learned that with "Mr. Bernoulli," as he preferred to be called, the best thing to do was ask him to sit down. Once seated, he conversed normally. Or, *more* normally, I suppose. If a simple statistic or—God forbid—a binomial distribution entered the conversation, he became strangely agitated. "No, no, no!" he said. "That's all wrong. It's like this." He rose and continued his numerical progression as he walked away.

"Some nut that worked for the NSA" was the response I received when I asked my father about him. I thought NSA stood for National Science Association and that Mr. Bernoulli was a crazed mathematician. His affliction, some form of obsessive-compulsive disorder, seemed reason enough to avoid any form of higher math.

Or maybe he was speaking in codes. As I say, at Brook Lane, anything was possible. What was considered ordinary included the extraordinary so regularly that I began to think of Brook Lane behavior as an example not of things gone wrong, but of how things may be contextually organized for analogical meanings, wherein there were two distinct levels of talk. The first level I'll call "digital," because there is a one-to-one relationship between the words used and their dictionary or common-sense usage definitions. The other level is "analogic," which refers to the other world that the words may be used to reference. In that other world, for example, a numerical progression conjured up other associations, events, persons, and secret histories. In that other world a copy of a novel called *The Great Gatsby* was a codebook. "Gatsby turns out all right in the end" becomes a digital statement with an analogic referent. Only back then, I didn't know the analogue.

There, *I* was the odd one. Boring, even. I had no noticeable tics or quirks. I didn't talk to birds or speak Hindi. I hadn't misplaced some essential part of the self or committed murder or attempted suicide. I had no in-depth knowledge of Ezra Pound's *Cantos*, nor did I recognize the papal mystery in Leonardo da Vinci's paintings. I never belonged to a secret society that had its own handshake or went back centuries. Nor had I ridden a red camel through the shifting sands of the Arabian Desert or hiked Mount Ararat in a lightning storm or gone diving for pearl-laden oysters off the coast of Thailand with three naked women. I couldn't name the seven natural wonders of the world, much less claim to have seen them. I hadn't kept a mistress of either sex, smoked opium in Turkey, or gotten drunk on the local grappa. I had never been arrested or been detained as a subversive or been tried for crimes against the state.

At Brook Lane, when asked to speak, I found I had little to say. Little to offer. Nothing much of conversational value.

My world, the world of the so-called sane, seemed pale and ordinary and entirely uninteresting by comparison. I didn't mind my visits to Brook Lane because the stories I heard there, the behavior I witnessed, and even the mysterious babbling brook we used to sit by, intrigued me. The only thing I didn't enjoy was my father being there.

I didn't enjoy the fact that my father, despite appearances to the contrary, was certified as insane. He didn't behave oddly. He was still nervous and his hands shook. He blinked furiously when agitated. He was thin and pale. He chain-smoked and wished aloud he had a drink. But he didn't say outlandish things nor did he display any of the eccentric behaviors of some of the other patients. He spoke in much the same way he always had spoken to me.

I had serious doubts about the accuracy of his diagnosis. Or I should say diagnoses, because they varied. Once he was admitted as manic-depressive, and another time as having delusions. Six times—or was it seven?—he was admitted as an alcoholic, and at least that many times for taking too many pills, or the wrong ones, or the right ones but with too much alcohol. After that he was labeled paranoid with schizophrenic tendencies.

The oddest statement he made was that someone wanted to kill him. On the last visit I made to Brook Lane, his doctor told me that my father "suffers from intense nightmares of increasing frequency, symptomatic of guilt and depression, and exhibits unreasonable fears of political assassination."

Assassination? I had by that time graduated from college and a master's program. I doubted these doctors at Brook Lane were doing my father much good. Nothing they tried to do worked. If there was a kind of fucked-up that someone on the staff hadn't called him, I didn't know the name of it. I lobbied my mother to change hospitals. She told me that "the government" said Brook Lane was the best place for him. Despite all the chaos "the government" had wreaked on my family, my mother still believed what they told her. She still followed their orders. So he remained in and out and in again at Brook Lane.

My father always said that "they" were out to get him.

I didn't listen to him well enough. I mistook pure reason for nonsense.

I got it all wrong.

. . . .

My father planned his funeral the year before his actual death. I don't think it was a premonition. It was decidedly more substantive than that. He had returned from what would prove to be his last visit to Brook Lane. He laughed about it. He told me on the phone, "The crap bastards will *never break me.*"

I laughed, too. I thought he was just talking tough. I wanted to encourage him. Tough was a good sign. "Crap bastards" was a fun turn of phrase he used when he talked about the doctors at Brook Lane.

He said the doctors at Brook Lane tried to talk him out of remembering things, of saying things, things he knew were true. He didn't tell me what those things were. Not then. Not in so many words. He said only that these crap bastards tried to fill his head with a bunch of shit; thus, his nickname for them. But it was after his final return from Brook Lane that Frank Church opened Senate hearings on the subject of the CIA and clandestine operations. At the time, I failed to make the connection.

Crap bastards, indeed.

He knew then that he was destined for death. The crap bastards wouldn't let it go and they couldn't let it go on. If they couldn't break him, they'd "resolve" his case in some other way.

Crap bastards.

• •

Samples Manor is a pleasant-enough-sounding name for what is a small country cemetery on a hill overlooking the rural Maryland village of Dargan. Dargan was the place of my mother's true birth and it was the place she never claimed to be from. Yet it was the place she and my father returned to in death.

Samples Manor cemetery stands just behind and above the solemn white clapboard Methodist church. The choice of this burial site was no surprise to me, although this funeral was the first time I had actually been here. I had heard the name "Samples Manor" for years, and for years had ignored it. Death had just become part of my life.

I wondered at the time why my father agreed to be buried here.

He made it clear to us that he was *not* to be buried at Arlington. He had earned that right several times over, by virtue of his service in the war, his official status as a United States vice consul, and his wounds—physical, emotional, and psychological. But he said, "Arlington is for heroes, not for patriots. Not for me." At the time, that sentence made no sense to me, but I think I understand it now.

My father told my mother that he wanted a soldier's grave. Just a simple white cross, nothing fancier, nothing more revealing of the details of his life. He remembered the tens of thousands of white crosses marking soldiers' graves in cemeteries throughout Europe, some of them with the memorable inscription for soldiers whose names were known only to God. He had given speeches to veterans' groups on such hallowed ground. He identified most closely with the unknown soldiers and for a long time I didn't know why.

I do now.

I didn't think about Brook Lane, or what he said about having been there, on that winter's day in the cemetery. I thought about his grave, the complete simplicity of it. I witnessed his official legacy for the first time, this plain white serviceman's cross and the words carved onto it: his name, his staff sergeant rank during the war, and the dates of his birth and death.

Is that how he wanted to be remembered?

I think it was. A patriot. Not a hero.

I have worried about his grave. I wanted to spend my inheritance on a grander tombstone, something larger and more befitting the man, even if it was the grave of a man who thought himself "only" an American patriot.

But my mother said no. She said he wanted only what was already there. He wanted, in death, the anonymity of a named but nevertheless unknown soldier.

We waited for the minister. I tried to focus on a nearby tree.

It was an oak, I think, and it stood alone over the gravesite. It was winter and its thick limbs were bare because it was winter, but I imagined that it would indeed be a grand and beautiful tree by early summer. I thought my father would like that. Not that he was inclined to appreciate nature—he wasn't particular about nature—but because it would provide shade for the grave. He liked shade. He always preferred to stand in the shade, just as he preferred to walk in the shadows. Darkness was his constant friend.

· ·

A black Ford sedan arrived. It stopped directly across the road from the entrance to the cemetery, in full sight of us and the suspended coffin and the lone oak tree. Finally, the driver's door swung open and a tall, dark, exceedingly thin man wearing a black overcoat, dark glasses, and a hat stood up. He didn't move toward us. He remained by the side of the road, stark still and upright next to his sedan, apparently content to simply watch.

The cold rain fell on him and he didn't retreat.

I wondered why he was wearing sunglasses on such an overcast day. Before we had much time to think about who this man was, or why he was wearing sunglasses, or what he might be doing in the middle of the afternoon here in rural Maryland on a rainy gray winter's day, the minister finally arrived.

The thin anonymous man removed his hat for the twenty-one-gun military salute. Once the shots had been duly fired, he replaced his hat and disappeared back into his car. He started the engine and slowly pulled away.

I believe that man to have been James Jesus Angleton.

I cannot confirm it but I doubt it can be denied. He came to pay his respects, such as they were. I imagine he thought himself a victor. Not only had he outlasted my father, he had finally bested him. He had won my father's eternal silence. My father would not testify.

Angleton would later show up for the funerals of the others. The men the crap bastards couldn't break. In June, he attended the funeral of Bill Harvey. Harvey, in particular, had taken the Church hearings badly. He was one of the few to have been so named, and that only in conjunction with the failed attempts on Castro. His long, slow decline into alcohol and official madness was similar to my father's, although the madness was less about losing his mind than keeping it intact. Bill Harvey died of a heart attack in his wife's arms. He, like my father, left a diary and papers. His wife burned them, but Agency goons broke into their house anyway and carried away what was left.

It was a pattern.

· ·

The gravediggers from Brown's Funeral Home began the mechanical process of lowering my father's coffin into the ground. Rather rapidly, I thought. On a nicer day it would have seemed rude. But it was truly miserable on this slick, damp, and darkening hillside. With each turn of the great wheel the coffin moved lower and the air grew heavier with rain and sleet and particles of snow. We were sad, and the cold crosswind on our faces was a whiplash on our skin.

I said, aloud, "Goodbye." It was all I could say. I was totally fucked up inside.

My mother wept all the way down the hill and continued to weep all the way home. She didn't stop weeping until I gave her a narcotic.

Within minutes, she was asleep. I worried if perhaps I hadn't given her too much.

Her breathing was widely spaced and shallow, as if her spirit was moving between worlds, and her body only thinly remained in this one. I stayed with her for a while, holding her hand, in that exact darkness that is partially made out of the material of night and partially made out of the ineffable meaning of darkness itself that can never be denied its place on this earth, or in our hearts.

I then knew that her life was over.

I don't think I allowed myself to wish her dead, but I may have. She had been distraught and had told me she wanted to die. She said that her life was over. If I agreed with her in my heart, even for a second, I'm sure my guilt made me take it back. We were alone together in that death room, in that bedroom of enveloping darkness. Neither one of us had a clue about what was supposed to come next.

I remember thinking that my mother and I had become friends. She had once been my mother, but she and I had become friends and had behaved toward each other as friends for a long time. It was within this context of friendship that I recognized what family ties often deny or at least obscure. It is a relational truth that teaches us we are here not for a reason, not for a *purpose*, but for a *person*. We exist *for* them. We exist *with* them. We do not exist without them, although our bodies may continue to march on.

My father was the purpose my mother had decided would define her life. Everyone who knew the two of them knew that. My father was now dead and yet, cruelly, my mother was still alive. Left behind. She was barely breathing. Barely here at all.

Though deeply asleep, she started suddenly. She whispered, "Lloyd?" For a few brief seconds she opened her eyes widely and searched the available darkness for my father's face but could not find him.

The lost look on her face broke my heart.

The drugs once again kicked in and I calmed her and she was asleep again as soon as her head fell back against the pillow. But I had seen the truth. There would never be Lloyd in her life again. She was left with me. I could be her friend, even a son again to her if that is what she asked of me. But it wouldn't be enough. I could not remember my father the way she did. I was Harold Lloyd Goodall Jr. in name only.

To her, I would always be Buddy. It was a good name, a perfect name, for a friend.

I finally tried to sleep but found I could not. I was unable to move, unable to speak, and unable to cry. Not for my mother, not for my father.

Not even for myself.

. . . .

My mother requested an autopsy. She later told me she wanted to know what caused his death, because she didn't believe he died of a bad cold or the flu. She was a nurse and knew about death. No part of the official story rang true to her.

The official story didn't add up. My father's death sentence didn't follow from the sentences that said he only had a bad cold or maybe the flu.

Here's what I think happened.

My father felt bad, visited the VA. Why he visited the VA in a town thirty miles away, in another state even, is something I'll never know. Maybe he didn't trust his local doctor. Maybe he was in Martinsburg for some other reason and decided to stop by the VA. I don't know. He was alone.

His fatal error may have been in talking to a doctor at Newton D. Baker. Maybe it wasn't even a doctor, because I could never find a record of his having been seen by one. But he spoke to *someone*. And then someone— maybe someone there or maybe someone somewhere else—decided that here was the perfect opportunity to "resolve" his case once and for all. My father was ill and not in good general health. It wouldn't take much to send him over. It wouldn't even have to look suspicious.

He got "a shot of something." Those were my mother's words, not mine.

Someone could have killed him in a number of ways. There is no point in speculating about that. But my belief is that they used an injection. It is possible that someone at the VA had access to the virus that causes Legionnaires' disease and used it on him. But Legionnaires' disease is only a probable construction made out of two words on a piece of paper that showed up a year after my father's death. So it didn't have to be *that* virus. It could have been pneumonia. It could have been that simple.

Pneumonia is a ubiquitous cause of death.

He was in a hospital. A veterans' hospital. They had a lab. They treated cases of pneumonia all the time. It's a common disease among veterans, particularly among veterans who smoke heavily and who are not in good general health.

It wouldn't be hard.

He could have been "resolved" pretty easily. "Resolved" is a good old-fashioned Agency word. For the historical record, it was borrowed from senior members of the old British intelligence service known as the SOE. They had a wide variety of euphemisms for doing in one of their own, or someone else's, who knew too much and who was likely to put themselves into a compromising situation. In addition to "resolve," the British used "discover the truth about" and "bring a case to its logical conclusion."

But "resolved" is the word the government—our government—used for my father's death. It appeared in the letter sent to my mother and she was the one who repeated it to me. "Resolved," she told me. "They finally *resolved* your father's death." She didn't know that "resolved" was a code word. She thought it meant that the government had revealed a mystery. But it meant the exact opposite of that. There was no mystery to reveal, only an official case to "resolve."

My father got "a shot of something." Maybe when he got the shot, he knew. Or at least suspected. Maybe he didn't. No matter. He drove himself home and went immediately to bed. He was following doctor's orders. So far, so true.

My mother went to bed later under the influence of sleeping pills. She often used them to get to sleep. She slept very soundly. She didn't hear anything, or feel anything, for a good ten or twelve or perhaps fourteen hours.

But how long she slept is not the point. It is just another fact of the night of my father's death that doesn't entirely make sense. What I am more concerned about is the claim she made that my father died "peacefully" in his sleep. It would have had to be peaceful given that she didn't hear anything. No noise. No gasping for air. No scream.

Nothing.

Of course, we all wanted to believe he died peacefully. We all want to die peacefully ourselves, and in our own beds at night. Because my father had lived with so much pain it only seemed fitting. As my cousin-in-law Shirley put it, "It's as if the good Lord reached down and placed his hand over your daddy's heart." You cannot dislike the sound of that. Nor disagree with it.

The autopsy revealed multiple bleeding abscesses on both lungs. The cause of death listed on the report is pneumonia. Pardon me, but that doesn't add up. Pneumonia requires *fluid* in the lungs. The autopsy doesn't say anything about fluid in the lungs.

A year later the government sent my mother a letter saying the death had finally been resolved. But who requested it? What was there to resolve? The autopsy clearly indicates that my father died of pneumonia. So why is it that a review of his case indicated that he died of Legionnaires' disease? Why review it at all?

Resolved. Did that mean re-solved? Did it mean that someone "in the government"—as my mother put it—had looked again into the circumstances surrounding his death? Why would anyone have done that? There was no mystery left to resolve. He died of multiple bleeding abscesses on both lungs. He was in poor overall health and had very little resistance left to ward off any virus or, for that matter, any disease. He died, supposedly, of pneumonia.

Yet his case had been reopened. Then it was resolved.

All of those words, even if some of them are code words, are, on the surface, true. But they don't tell or contain the *whole* truth. I think the whole truth requires placing the facts under a historical and political, not biological, lens. My father was a man who kept secrets but he had been ready to speak.

I think he was finally *silenced*.

· ·

The Final Report of the Senate Select Committee was released on April 23, 1976, just forty-five days after my father's death. His not coming forward to testify didn't seem to matter. Not naming names did little to forestall the collateral damage.

Internationally, the prestige and trust our allies had in the Department of State, the United States Information Agency, overseas military personnel, and anyone who had contact with an American embassy or organization or who did business in a foreign country became suspect. Some people had been suspect before, but the Church Committee hearings served to underscore and capitalize what had been only parenthetically contained or lightly italicized in the international world.

The immediate effect of the Church Committee hearings on foreign intelligence gathering was devastating—however elliptical or forgetful those who provided testimony were or might have been. Networks and resources dried up. Contacts disappeared, one way or the other. Career officers resigned. Agents were arrested on suspicion and grilled unmercifully by local authorities as well as by members of other intelligence organizations. People died.

Certain truths were sacrificed. Certain cases were resolved.

There were other collateral victims as well. Bill Harvey, in June. Richard Helms, the following year. James Jesus Angleton. Even William Colby, eventually. There were countless other women and men whose careers ended when they responded to these hearings and their various revelations with their own resignations. But the real collateral victim was the Agency itself and, by extension, our country.

The sudden decline of reliable human intelligence on the ground overseas attained velocity speed, and the intelligence services—sold already on their collective high-tech future—increasingly relied on satellite technology and electronic eavesdropping to collect information. Intelligence agencies had used telephone monitoring since the late 1940s and satellite surveillance since the early 1960s, and by the mid-1970s they were skilled in tracking bank accounts using large mainframe computers. New advances in information technologies, orbiting and fixed-position satellites, spy planes like the SR-70, and advanced listening devices promised a future for intelligence that was a veritable systems analyst's wet dream. It was applied information science as conceived of by a committee of George Jetsons: it was fast, image-oriented, expensive, distanced, objective, unemotional, robotic, quantitative, and nerdy. It was a left-brain intelligence run amok at the synapses on an artificially intelligent right-brain high.

The problem of central intelligence relying so heavily on technology was that it omitted what was *human* from what was considered intelligent. Without reliable information generated *in vivo*, the language of the local people was lost. And within that loss of language was also a much greater loss—the loss of a robust historical appreciation of customs, habits, politics, religions, and the subtleties and nuances of cultures. The *quality* of information used by American intelligence organizations entered a sustained period of decline.

The decline became glaringly obvious in the wake of 9/11, when we realized we had no idea what was really going on in al-Qaeda, or where Osama bin Laden was, or who could be trusted on the ground in Afghanistan or Iraq or Iran or Turkey or Saudi Arabia or Kuwait or—well, I've made my point. After 9/11, intelligence organizations posted an open call for new officers familiar with Arab languages and cultures on their recruitment websites and turned to long-retired field officers who had served in those regions, often pleading and offering bonuses to women and men now in their seventies and eighties to come back to work.

It became painfully apparent that there were definite limits to what technology could provide in the way of real intelligence. It had been a large mistake to assume that James Bond was a cold war relic whose best plays were now reserved for the big screen. It was a huge error to think that the day of the field officer was at best a fond memory.

· ·

The family jewels and the Church Committee hearings and the *Final Report* also told us a different story about the business of intelligence. If the CIA was founded on the assumption that the cold war would be a clandestine one whose essential weapon was intelligence, then it was a war that was only winnable through an accumulation of knowledge used to deploy deceit. Deceit, and by association deceitful knowledge, was intelligence derived from an economic calculus. The cold war was simply to be the triumph of capitalism by other means. But following the hearings and the release of the *Final Report*, intelligence was largely seen as the cause of widespread collateral damage to what it meant to be an American.

Our national security was revealed to be sinister. The CIA had more in common with organized crime than it did with the Constitution and laws of our land. This was unfortunate because America's interests have been used in the service of freedom, of liberation, and of doing good in the world. But what Colby and the Church Committee revealed was the dark side of national security. It was a side so sinister, so illegal, so immoral, and so corrupt, that it obscured our nation's worthy ideal.

It cheapened it. It cheapened *us*.

The cheapness of domestic surveillance, the funding of criminals and illegal activities, the attempted overthrows of governments, the attempted assassinations of leaders, and the everyday dirty tricks of America's intelligence network contained a deeper thesis about the potential harm of building a foundation for national security out of the material of diplomatic secrets, political half-truths, paid assassins, domestic surveillance, and lies.

It reduced the greatness of our American story about democracy, freedom, and a government only as good as its people into a scandalous international tell-all that revealed none of those things to be true. It was a tawdry, titillating story of the organized deception of none other than the American people. It played best on television because it was news that could be spoken in sound bites accompanied by images—the named faces of barefaced liars and the ignoble apprehension of leaders who proved themselves to be criminals. In America in the 1970s, these revelations about the CIA had yet to be fully understood within the context of our culture. They were not simply the story of an intelligence service gone mad or politics gone wrong; they were the story that defined a crisis of identity we had yet to embrace. For what America was to Americans was who America was in the world.

Our government was not something removed from the stuff of our selves. It was part and parcel of it. We believed in what we stood for. We had to be fully accountable for our actions as well as for the actions of our leaders. We had lost the war in Vietnam. Our former president *was* a crook. We couldn't trust the CIA or the FBI or even our local police. The soul of America was damaged. On July 4, 1976, our country would turn two hundred years old.

It was time for a reckoning of our present selves against the measure of American history. American idealism. The very soul of what it means to be a free, democratic society.

· ·

My mother lived for seven more years. During that time she tried to pick up the shattered pieces of her life. She returned to nursing and remained a nurse until she retired at the age of sixty-five. She reunited with Jerry Terlingo. I'd like to believe that she fully enjoyed those seven years, but I know better. She told me she had accepted Jerry back into her life because she wanted to free me from the responsibility for caring for her.

I never questioned that my mother loved me with all her heart. I hadn't turned out as she had expected, but by then she had accepted who I was. I had never become even half the man my father was to her, but I understood and accepted it. I was happy with who I was, and she was happy enough about that.

I am quite sure that Jerry loved my mother with all of his heart. When she developed stomach cancer that advanced into her lymphatic system, he remained with her in her hospital room until the staff required him to leave. When I was called in to make the final decision about life support, he refused to come with me. "She'll be fine," he said. "I can't live without her."

Nor did he. Within a few months of her death he succumbed to what was described by his doctor as "a broken heart." According to her wishes, he was not buried in Samples Manor Cemetery.

Before she died, she told me all she knew, all she remembered, about my father. Most of what she said is contained within these pages. We shared the final conversations that rounded off what had been ambiguous and unsaid for so very long between us. That last afternoon, her body bloated from morphine, I asked her one last time if she was ready to go.

She looked me hard in the eyes and blinked twice.

It was our agreed sign. I nodded immediately to the attending physician, took hold of my mother's hand, watched her eyes close, and held on to her hand as she died. She had held on valiantly to December 21, 1983.

It was important to her to die on that date and in the late afternoon. It marked the date and time of her thirty-sixth wedding anniversary. As she wished, I buried her next to my father's grave with a stone that bears only her married name: Naomi Saylor Goodall.

. . . .

James Jesus Angleton died on May 12, 1987. He was sixty-nine years old and, not unexpectedly for a man who could have been the poster boy for his beloved Virginia Slims, the cause of his death was lung cancer. His obituary made the front page of the *New York Times* under the heading "James Jesus Angleton, Counterintelligence Figure, Dies." The known aspects of his long and distinguished career were detailed in an account that highlighted his successes and the length of his tenure at the CIA.

By the time of his death, Angleton had been heralded as a genius and derided as a paranoid who became obsessed with his own myth. His legendary file on Kim Philby had long since disappeared.

. . . .

The cold war ended, not with a big nuclear bang, but a long historical whimper.

I remember the day the Berlin Wall came down and speaking those "bang and whimper" lines from T. S. Eliot aloud as I walked across campus. I remember thinking about my father. I doubt he would have believed it was true.

I am sorry he had to miss it. The final collapse of the Soviet Union occurred on Christmas Day, 1991, the date Mikhail Gorbachev resigned as president.

. . . .

My father and my mother both earned a better narrative ending than the one I had previously given to them. When I thought I had finally put away their lives, when I thought I had freed myself from their story, I did not acknowledge the great gift they left to me, a gift of understanding history in a very human way. When I left Hovermale's office with a key to a safe-deposit box, I opened that history. It overwhelmed me. When my son began asking his questions, I felt I owed it to him to try to find a better answer. I also knew in my heart I owed *them* a better answer.

If nothing else I have now brought their story here, where this story of love, country, secrecy, and family should have come long ago. It is the final narrative resting place of our cold war, the symbolic date in Moscow we too easily associate with the great triumph of capitalism and the great fall of Communism. I think my father would understand it differently: *Gatsby turns out all right in the end*. For him, Gatsby was less a character than an idea of America that he willingly sacrificed his life to support and that my mother, the saint, understood.

I'd like to be able to offer a fine prose poem that makes something larger out of their lives. But I am not a poet. I'm not F. Scott Fitzgerald either, and this isn't a novel. I'd like to say that their hopes for America in the post–cold war era have been realized, and that Gatsby indeed turned out all right in the end. But those hopes have not been realized.

The cold war that so divided the world also held it together. Without the intrusive power of the Soviet Union to fear, old nationalist antagonisms, assertions of revenge for perceived historical wrongs, tribal warfare, and religious intolerance rose up throughout the new independent states and satellite nations. Atrocities occurred. The siege of Sarajevo pitted neighbors against neighbors in an open civil war and ethnic cleansing from 1992 to 1995, claimed tens of thousands of lives, maybe hundreds of thousands of lives, and destroyed a once-beautiful city that had been the site of the 1984 Olympic Games.

New politicians everywhere in the newly formed states promised democratic reform and, in most cases, made a hash of democratic governance and in several cases have been exposed as being just as corrupt, if not more so, than their former Soviet-controlled leaders. Just holding elections doesn't make you into a democracy. Citizens of former Soviet republics discovered that their mental imprisonment and lack of technological expertise rendered them the economic fodder of the new global order. It will require a generation or two to produce the appropriately educated and skilled societies that can compete fairly in world markets. Elsewhere rebellion, warfare, and jihad in the name of ethnic pride, freedom, or the will of Allah continue to be waged daily. Millions more in Africa and South Asia have died from malnutrition, disease, and universal neglect. Trafficking in humans has become the newest method of financing terrorism.

Since the slow death of the Soviet Bear, the United States of America has enjoyed an unprecedented period of post–cold war affluence and unparalleled power throughout the world. We take pride in defeating Communism, and we take pride in reigning as the world's only superpower. We have become a militarized nation as well as the largest producer and storehouse of weapons of mass destruction. Like every other militarized nation advancing its economic interests and values before us—most recently, Imperial Japan and Nazi Germany before World War II come to mind—we feel the need to expand our influence backed by the shock and awe of our military machine.

The cold war begat the war on terror. Our careless affluence; our deep ignorance of other cultures, languages, and religions; our dominance on the world's mediated stage; and our undifferentiated and militarist pride in spreading the values of freedom, capitalism, and democracy in order to make the world safer for our salesmanship coalesce to become the new enemy for those in the world whose impoverished backward ways of life, whose unwarranted fundamentalist interpretations of sacred texts, and whose abject disregard for the rights of women are further threatened by the appeal of our democratic and tolerant ideals.

There can be no doubt that we should ask hard questions about our "right" to change the world in our own image. But there also should be no mistake about the awful fact that no matter how strong our persuasion, there will always be a global social movement of terrorists we must always defeat. There may have been a time in our recent past when there was hope for a different outcome, but that option no longer exists. Our invasion of Iraq made it so. We have succeeded in producing a fragile democracy and a new, well-armed and well-financed generation of fanatical opposition to it. To *us*. To you, regardless of how open-minded, tolerant, and liberal you are. And to me. Readers of this book are the "apostate intellectuals" a new generation has been reared not only to hate but moreover to destroy as their sacred duty in this world.

We are in this fight whether or not we like it, or approve of it, or voted for it. There is no way to win it, and no easy way out of it. To find a way out of it—to find what Richard Nixon once called "peace with honor"—requires a better and more honest appraisal of the relationship of the cold war to this new one in the story we tell ourselves about it.

It is *because* we won the cold war and history's bragging rights that we framed the war on terror as yet another enduring struggle. It is *because* we bracket the end of our cold war story around the collapse of the Soviet Union that President Bush and his neoconservative administration foolishly rushed in and readily brought down the sorry regime of Saddam Hussein. He, too, had a narrative inheritance to complete. It is *because* our mediated world watched and applauded the tearing down of the Berlin Wall that our leaders staged the toppling of Saddam's statue in Baghdad; it was an iconic moment that was supposed to remind those watching it of the end of the cold war. If Iraq fell in a fortnight, could peace in the Middle East be far behind? That national narrative inheritance allowed our president to declare a very premature victory without a clear plan for winning, or even keeping, the peace.

As I completed this book there was a movement afoot among officials in the current administration to stop calling this enduring struggle against the terrorists a "war." Focus groups were assembled, surveys analyzed, and reports on the projected failure of this particular public-relations spin circulated in and around Washington. I know, I have read them. The Pentagon was alerted of a likely forthcoming strategic change in our deployment of language. I know because I was asked for my input. Because even our president admits this is a war we cannot "win," Americans may be pleased to hear that terrorism is being strategically redefined as "violent extremism," although there is some doubt that President Bush will go along with it. It may well have been a bad idea to call the post-9/11 retaliation a "war on terror," but we have a president who doesn't admit mistakes and, if possible, doesn't ever change his mind.

Call it what you will. As Kurt Vonnegut Jr.'s unstuck-in-time hero, Billy Pilgrim, put it: *So it goes.* From my perspective, we, too, have become unstuck in time. Fighting the war on terror, or the "global struggle against violent extremism," or even This Damn Mess as if it were the cold war— hey, it's still déjà vu all over again.

A strategy of redefinition, however it plays out, is only the beginning of another chapter in this enduring story. It is a chapter whose form has yet to be determined and whose narratives have yet to be written. It will no doubt be all about what those of us who have inherited this narrative, this global situation, and this legacy of enduring violent extremism must do to reclaim our national honor as well as any real sense of national security. Too many of us have forgotten the hard lessons of what truly brought down the Soviet Union and allowed us to declare victory in the cold war. We have forgotten that America is most powerful as a grand idea whose most cherished constitutional principles must not be cheapened by political expediency, and whose image abroad must not be diminished by either a confused message, unwise intrusions in the civil wars of other nations, or brute militarism.

We must, as a nation, lead by example rather than by force. We must show the world's mediated citizens that living in a free and open society with a democratic form of government yields a culture of happiness and prosperity, not a culture of fear and unparalleled national debt. If we cannot fold these values into our campaign for public diplomacy, we will fail to win the hearts and minds of those still open to persuasion.

My father told me that *Gatsby* turns out all right in the end.

That is hopeful. But I think that ending has yet to be written.

Rest in peace, my father. Rest in peace, my mother.

What I have inherited from your narrative tells me there is still a lot of work to do.

AT THE ONSET OF THIS PROJECT I BELIEVED THAT WRITING ABOUT MY father and mother would bring me closer to them. I believe it has. I also thought that researching their lives and trying to answer the confounding questions of my childhood and adolescence would clear up my lifelong confusion about them. I believe it has partially done that, although now there are newer questions and deeper mysteries that remain unresolved. And, at the beginning of this project, I thought that by the time I reached the end of it, I would have finally learned something profound about the truth of my parents' experiences. If not the whole truth and nothing but, then at least something wise enough to serve as the final resting place for their story and their contributions to our understanding of the legacy of the cold war.

Having reached that ending place, I find myself once again with the story that my father passed on to me when he left me that worn copy of *The Great Gatsby* thirty years ago. I find myself at the beginning again, only differently this time. When I consider the story in that great novel against the life of my father and mother, I realize I was the one who wanted there to be a connection. I was the one who read into my father's diary entry about his use of the novel as a codebook a larger meaning about the place of that fine story in his own well-examined, if troubled, life. I was, as Umberto Eco says, *completing* the story by reading it this way.

Now I read that connection differently.

I think there were times when I was guilty of substituting or maybe just confusing the characters in a story with the real life of the author. In the novel, Gatsby turns out all right in the end because Nick Carraway says he does, but F. Scott Fitzgerald had no such luck in his own lifetime. His was a sad, ragged, alcoholic exit and he was only to achieve the fame he sought in life a decade after his death. Similarly, we are led to believe that Daisy continued her charmed, flawed existence as a character in a larger story while we know that the model for that character, Zelda Fitzgerald, never attained the artistic success she so desperately sought, ended her days in a mental hospital, and died tragically in a fire.

I don't know why my father passed along *The Great Gatsby* to me. It was the book beneath his diary. *Were* they connected? Was he, as I supposed at the beginning of my quest, giving me permission to research his clandestine life and to use the novel as a codebook for interpreting it? Or was he simply giving me his favorite novel? Or was it something else, perhaps, bequeath-ing to me a mythic American story about love and friendship to aspire to, or a higher morality tale to live by?

What was I supposed to do with *The Great Gatsby*?

I doubt I will ever truly know.

I only know what I have done with it. I have used it to craft my own life story. I have lived through the lens of its story line as a way of knowing about the past, as a way of thinking about the meanings of persons and ideas and events, and, at times, as a way of doing the work I call a career. But those are the things *I* have done with the book. They may or may not ultimately have anything to do with my father's intentions. Or his life. Or my mother's. Perhaps in my desire to use the novel as a codebook for my father's life, I have confused fictional characters with the lives of real people who meant, and who still mean, the world to me.

But I don't think so.

The lesson I've learned, the wisdom I've acquired (if I can be so bold as to call it wisdom), is better framed as a personal interpretation of that series of words first authored by Fitzgerald then repeated by my father: Gatsby turns out all right in the end. I read those words now as a puzzle given to me to solve.

I think I have figured it out.

I understand those words as a reference not only for the larger meaning of the novel, but also for the ongoing larger aesthetic, the mythic struggle between Good and Evil that consumed my father's life and finally destroyed him. I had always heard these words as a moral conclusion about character, a summing up of the meaning of Jay Gatsby's life. But because I have now added something of my own life to figuring out this story line in relation to my father's clandestine career, I hear the words echoing, lingering, even challenging me in the form of an ongoing question. That question is: *does* Gatsby turn out all right in the end?

· ·

To answer that question I have to come full circle in my story, back to the questions Nic asks that Sandra and I can now better—if never fully—answer. What was my father's work? What was my childhood like? What was it like to suddenly move from London to Cheyenne, and why did we do it? How did I like high school? Why did my father retire so early in his career? What was my mother's life all about? How did my father turn out in the end? How did it feel to grow up during the cold war? What was it like having a father who was a spy?

My answers now are personal ones, but their implications cast longer shadows. The answers do connect my family to cold war history, and to the effects of the code of secrecy to what happened in our homes and in our lives. They establish the basic pattern of communication that defines how we turn out in the end. In this way, there is an intricate relationship between how we choose to live and how our nation turns out.

Every aspect of our national character lives in every act of character in our homes and families. If our nation keeps secrets, so too do we learn to justify the secrets *we* keep. If it isn't for national security, it's for personal security. If it's not civil defense, it's a defense of our selves. If our leaders say one thing and do quite another, well, is it any real surprise that we use the excuse of their faults to cover up our own?

An open society, a democratic society, doesn't need to behave this way. Not telling the truth diminishes our stature on the world's stage and sets in place the conditions for abuses of power. So, too, did engendering a culture of fear and heightened anxiety about nuclear war create fallout in nuclear families. We cannot afford *not* to learn from cold war history, or else Santayana's dictum will once again prove true. We cannot lie to other nations and then expect them to believe in us. We cannot enter into wars without a plan for winning the peace. We cannot fuel an already politically divided country with fear of imminent terrorism without paying a much larger cultural, economic, and social price later.

America is an idea—a beautiful one. Democracy is an experiment—an ongoing one. Both ideals require telling the truth so that justice at home and abroad isn't blind. Both require reliable information disseminated widely, so that our passionate engagement and active, intelligent participation in the political process aren't rendered victims of power, privilege, and the silent protection of those who have abused their power and flaunted their privilege. Even then, there are no easy guarantees.

I know there are those who actively plot against us. They must be dealt with as enemies who have attempted to destroy us in the past have always been dealt with. But we must not use the fact of them, and of 9/11, to dishonor the higher principles we must continue to defend. By doing so we only discredit our national character in ways that further embolden our enemies and expand their ability to recruit new volunteers against us. We must work every day for truth, for justice, and for an American way of life that shines as brightly as the green light on Daisy Buchanan's shore.

With that light we can offer the world hope, as my father before me did and as I do, that Gatsby *does* turn out all right in the end.

PREFACE

I locate the present study within a broader tradition of scholarship that goes under the general heading of new narratives and history or cultural studies of the cold war era. There are excellent treatments of a variety of topics related to my particular interest that have informed and shaped this book. They are: Boyer (1985), Curtin (1995), Gaddis (1998), Gallagher and Greenblatt (2001), Grossman (2001), Kuznick and Gilbert (2001), May (1999), McEnaney (2000), Parry-Giles (2002), Saunders (1999), White (1998), Whitfield (1996), and Winkler (1993).

Interest in recovering the narratives of cold war families is beginning to generate some new histories as well. I especially recommend Field and Field (1999), Kolb (2005), and Richardson (2005).

Gregory Bateson was a pioneer narrative anthropologist and scholar of communication whose thought influences work in a variety of fields. I recommend reading him chronologically, beginning with his classic ethnography *Naven* (1936) and then forward to Bateson and Ruesch (1951), Bateson (1980, 1991, 2000).

The Yogi Berra quote was "loaned" to me by my friend and fellow cold war and communication scholar Bryan Taylor, whose long-term project is directed at the aftermath of Los Alamos and the rise of nuclear culture and families. In this book, I have drawn from Taylor and Harnet (2000), Taylor (2002), and Taylor, Kinsella, Depoe, and Metzler (2005).

My own ethnographic interest in government agencies and intelligence organizations reaches back to my first autoethnographic account of the Star Wars command in Huntsville, Alabama, in the mid-1980s; that account is contained in Goodall (1989). This work anchors my continuing interest in the cultural relationships between the cold war and the current war on terror (or global struggle against violent extremists). For details, see Goodall (2002, 2005, 2006). For my first treatment of communication patterns in F. Scott Fitzgerald's *The Great Gatsby*, see Goodall (1983).

CHAPTER 1

Parts of this chapter originally appeared as Goodall (2005).

For additional reading on the rhetorical, historical, and familial resources George W. Bush drew on in response to 9/11, see Goodall (2006). See also Bostdorff (2003), Giroux (2004), Gunn (2004), and Ivie (2003).

CHAPTER 2

The genealogical and familial information contained in this chapter is the result of records and photographs provided by Betty Ann Adkins, Ruanna Hess, Shirley Collis, and Earl Goodall, and a subsequent e-mail exchange with the master genealogist of the Goodall clan, Dr. David Goodall. Recollections of the Goodall family and my father in particular were obtained through interviews conducted with Warren Bills, Bill Hastings, Ansel Miller, Sara Levin, and Betty Ann Adkins. The idea of *homo narrans* is one I originally found in Fisher (1984). The quote by Georges Gusdorf comes from Gusdorf (1979).

CHAPTER 3

Roland Barthes' concept of the "presence of an absence" in reference to photographs can be found in Barthes (1977). My understanding of the histories of the OSS and early days of the CIA can be traced to yeoman work by Hersh (1992). See also Trento (2005), Winks (1987), Wise and Ross (1964). A detailed biography of Allen Dulles by Peter Grose (1994) was very helpful. Materials on the history of the Veterans Administration and Newton D. Baker General Hospital are available in the archives of the Martinsburg, West Virginia, public library.

CHAPTER 4
Material about the life of Edna Marie Caslin Goodall was obtained through interviews with her granddaughter, Sara Levin.

CHAPTER 5
Material in this chapter was drawn from conversations with the principals.

CHAPTER 6
For an explanation of the close relationship between organized labor and the Communist Party in West Virginia, see Perry (2005). West Virginia had long been a contested state for labor organizers, dating back to the early 1920s. It was a struggle that only gained momentum as organized labor became more closely affiliated (in word, if not in deed) with the American Communist Party. It is a matter of historical record that Wisconsin Senator Joseph McCarthy strategically launched his anti-Communist crusade in the Colonnade room of the McLure House Hotel before the Ohio County Republican Women's Club in Wheeling, West Virginia, on February 9, 1950, when he held up a piece of paper and announced he had the names of 205 Communists then working (he claimed) in the State Department.

Material on Clare Boothe Luce during the time she served as ambassador to Italy is drawn from a variety of sources, including the aforementioned Hersh (1992), biographical details from Lyons (1989), Martin (1991), Shadegg (1970), and Sheed (1982). I found it interesting to read Ambassador Luce's views on diplomacy, found in Luce (1955). I have also used background material from Divine (1981), Dulles (1965), and McKee (1962). The recollections of how Ambassador Luce treated my mother are taken from conversations with my mother over a number of years.

Much of the material describing William and Barbara Colby is drawn from his memoir, Colby and Forbath (1978).

CHAPTER 7
This chapter benefits from the many published accounts of the life of James Jesus Angleton (a.k.a. KU/MOTHER and Hugh Ashmead). Those I consulted include Hood (1994), Mangold (1991), Martin (1980), Powers (2002), Rositzke (1977), Trento (2005), Wise (1992), and Wright (1987). An interesting fictional account of Angleton's CIA world is contained in Buck-

ley (2000), Littell (2003), as well as in Norman Mailer's 1991 novel, *Harlot's Ghost* (New York: Random House).

William Colby was a far less colorful figure than Angleton. As a result there is far less written about him. In addition to historic treatments of the CIA that cover his work in Italy, Vietnam, and Washington, I consulted his own words, found in Colby and Forbath (1978) and Colby and McCargar (1989).

For a concise scholarly introduction to the history of modern Italy, I relied on Smith (1997). In addition to Cold War histories about the CIA's involvement, I am indebted to Bull (1997), Del Pero (2001, 2002), and Drake (2004). For a more general history of Communism in Italy written from a sympathetic critical and cultural perspective, see Shore (1990).

CHAPTER 8

Wives of diplomats and spies have received sparse treatment in the scholarly or popular literature beyond the often richly imagined descriptions of their lives provided in novels. However, one useful primary source is the account given by Kim Philby's wife. See E. Philby (1968). For an account drawn from interviews, see Corson, Trento, and Trento (1989). For an intriguing account of the unsolved murder of Mary Meyer, an ex-CIA wife (and the role Angleton played in trying to locate her diary), see Burleigh (1999).

Abbe Lane (1992) composed a lively, if thinly disguised autobiographical novel. Much of the biographical information I have used can be found on various celebrity websites; quotations from her interview with Frank Thistle for *Adam* magazine was taken from one located at http://www.discomuseum.com/AbbeLane.html (accessed September 28, 2005). Biographical material concerning Leonard Creo is drawn from the Art in Context website (www.artincontext.org) and an exchange of personal e-mail. It was Mr. Creo who alerted me to the use of the *Rome Daily American* (1945–1984) as a primary vehicle of communication for Americans living in the city and the fact that 40 percent of the newspaper was owned by the CIA. Family recollections of Ms. Lane and Mr. Creo are presented throughout this chapter as they were represented to me. The story I create is conjecture based on the fact of my portrait, done by Mr. Creo, and, at least according to my mother, commissioned by Ms. Lane. Neither Ms. Lane nor Mr. Creo remember who provided the commission, although Mr. Creo believes it may have been either the *Sunset Boulevard* actress Gloria Swanson or Canon Shrieve from St. Paul's, the American Episcopalian church.

There has long been a close association of the CIA to popular culture. For an excellent recent treatment, see Kolb (2005). In this account, he chronicles his life as an agent for Muhammad Ali and a CIA spy. Additional testimonies of the close relationship between the arts, popular culture, and spying can be found in the excellent volume by Saunders (1999).

The *International Herald Tribune* was purchased by John Hay Whitney, then ambassador to Great Britain, in 1959. The relationship of the CIA to articles appearing in it during the Cold War is a matter of historical record; see Hersh (1992). However, it must be said that the CIA used a wide variety of newspapers, magazines, and publishers to encourage points of view or promote particular policies. I have no doubt it still does.

CHAPTER 9

The complex life and times of Harold Adrian Russell "Kim" Philby have generated much investigative reporting, scholarship, speculation, and imagination. I have read quite a bit of it, but given that my interest in him is limited to his predefection years and specifically to his relationship to my father, I have called on a few reliable sources rather than a plethora of them. I have drawn biographical details from Knightley (1986); I have also formed a perspective on the man based on additional material found in Page, Leitch, and Knightley (1968), E. Philby (1968), and K. Philby (1968). Two wonderfully rich studies of the British Secret Intelligence Service rounded out my view of the attempt to link Philby with the Soviets: West (1983, 1989).

For my description of the Suez crises, I have relied on published accounts, most notably Neff (1981). For a military perspective, I used Varble (2003). For a British diplomatic perspective I relied on Kelly and Gorst, eds. (2000) For a perspective on the border wars and the relationship of the Suez to them, see Morris (1997).

The story about my father's first (and perhaps only) encounter with Philby originally emerged during a group psychotherapy session at Brook Lane in 1971. As I recall, he was directed to act out a conversation that altered or changed his professional life. The audience was made up of other former (and perhaps some current) government types, some of whom were introduced to me as belonging to one or another of the intelligence services. Later, I asked my father who Philby was. He told me that he was a man who betrayed his friends and his country, and who had defected to the Soviet Union in 1963. I was curious why meeting Philby had changed his professional life, so I pressed on. "That's a very long story," he replied, dismissing it with his characteristic hand gesture and smile. So the account I present here is obviously a historical reconstruction based on the words of a man who was then hospitalized for a mental condition. However, I maintain that evidence of his illness seldom, if ever, appeared in personal recollections. I am also very much convinced that his hospitalization was our government's preferred way of dealing with him, as well as with other people who had veered away from the prescribed path but could be "rehabilitated"—in this case, medicated and talked back into it.

Brook Lane (www.brooklane.org) still functions as a private, not-for-profit mental hospital (and "wellness center") outside of Hagerstown, Maryland. According to its own history, it was founded after World War II and operated by the Mennonite Church until 1958, when a new board of directors was named. The history page of Brook Lane's website also says that during the Vietnam War, "the Center became a haven not only for those with emotional challenges, but for those who conscientiously objected to the war. The Center became a melting pot of individuals who sought a nonviolent means of service to their country in lieu of military service."

There is no way I know of to establish a formal link between Brook Lane and the intelligence community. Nor is that my primary interest here. Many mental hospitals were used to treat intelligence officers and analysts over the years; Hersh (1992) reports that during the late 1940s and throughout the 1950s, one entire wing of St. Elizabeth's was reserved for members of the clandestine services. So whether Brook Lane was a secret facility for treating spies or whether there were physicians there who were used by the government because they knew how to deal with people like my father doesn't matter. What does matter is that he was a patient there, that his diagnoses and treatments varied considerably, and that not only did he participate in group therapy but also he believed that the "crap bastards" working there were trying to discredit him and that when he was last released from there he believed that someone was trying to kill him. I don't recall a "conscientious objector," but perhaps that is another way of saying that the physicians and therapists treated those who found a conscientious reason not to follow orders, or who had, in some way, objected to current government political and/or military policies.

That would be one way to define "emotional challenges," and would also have provided a common gathering place for dissidents. Today Brook Lane maintains its connection to the Mennonite Church but has broadened its reach to include other denominations.

CHAPTER 10

The idea of using codes and codebooks enjoys a long and well-documented history. I relied on Bamford (2001), Kahn (1967), and Martin (1980). For a classic treatment of cryptography, I gain much from Smith (1944). I have also relied on my studies of the symbolic uses of language as they are informed by the literary critic Kenneth Burke. For an introduction to his thought, see Burke (1989).

Blenheim Palace enjoys a fascinating history, which I was introduced to while taking the tour of the palace and grounds during my sabbatical in 2004. For additional historical information, I used Green (1982).

For the description of practical espionage, I drew from Kolb (2005), who in turn credits Copeland (1969).

St. Dunstan's Church of England Primary School is still located on Ann Boleyns Walk in Surrey. My dark memories of the education I received there are no doubt not a fair representation of it today. The speech used here was quoted to me by Dr. Pete Kellett, who was also exposed to these sentiments.

The American School of London has been located at One Waverley Place in St. John's Wood for over forty years and continues to provide high-quality education for an international student body, albeit at an increasingly premium fare. When I attended the ASL, it had not yet relocated to its new campus.

CHAPTER 11

The idea that the CIA, the State Department, the military, and other government agencies kept tabs on their employees through active surveillance is well known. I am particularly grateful to the detailed research and analysis provided in Newman (1989).

The high level of tension in Berlin during the cold war is well documented. I have benefited from the description provided by Wyden (1989). The mood of the time in our government is captured in Divine (1981); the rhetoric of the era's contributions are carefully analzyed in Medhurst (1997).

The legendary Bill Harvey suffers a tarnished reputation due to his alleged failures to kill Fidel Castro and his alleged links to the assassination of President John F. Kennedy. But this tarnish is unfair, in my humble opinion. I draw on accounts of Harvey's Hole presented in Martin (1980) and Murphy, Kondrashev, and Bailey (1997). I also benefited from visiting the International Spy Museum in Washington, D.C., where a replica of the tunnel is housed, complete with an audio diorama. The newer revisionist interpretation of the significance of the tunnel and whether or not the KGB knew about it can be found in Evans (1996).

The Allen Ginsberg line is drawn from his poem "America" (Ginsberg 1988).

Jacques Ellul's theories (and fears) about living in an advanced technological society are found in Ellul (1955).

My analysis of Angleton's paranoid, brilliant, and power-driven organizational personality is the result of a reading list too extensive to cover here. A synopsis of my view of communication in the formation of identity in organizations can be found in Eisenberg and Goodall (2004). I am intrigued as well by the notion that bureaucrats are not "evil" but that the organizations that induce them to act are often evil workplaces; for an extensive account of this idea, see Shorris (1982). I also believe there is an analogy between the "violent, dangerous criminal" described so eloquently in the work of sociologist Lonnie Athens and the likely organizational counterpart who uses "symbolic killing" as a motive to reinforce his or her power and identity. For a synopsis of Athens's work, see Rhodes (2000). Athens in the original may be located in two essential readings: Athens (1992, 1994). The article on the employment interview as a "symbolic killing" is found in Goodall, Wilson, and Waagen (1986).

CHAPTER 12

A brief history of Francis E. Warren may be found on the Wyoming Governor's website. I am also indebted to Gould (1967, 1968), Schulp (1982), and the *Dictionary of American Biography*.

Francis E. Warren Air Force Base's own history cite can be found at http://www.warren.af.mil/history/index.shtml (accessed September 28, 2005).

An admirable biography of General John J. Pershing is available through the Arlington National Cemetery website: http://www.arlingtoncemetery.net/johnjose.htm (accessed September 28, 2005); see also his obituary published in the *New York Times*, July 16, 1948.

As a boy I studied Wyoming history in school, but for this undertaking I consulted Riegel (1964) and Marquis (1973).

CHAPTER 13

As a person who actively participated in the construction of a basement nuclear shelter in my own home, the concept of civil defense has clear memories for me. I have also benefited from some excellent scholarship on the subject, namely Altheide (2002), Bernhard (1999), Grossman (2001), McEnaney (2000), Tobin (2002), and Tuttle (2001).

The Cuban missile crisis scenes are taken from a variety of sources, including Fursenko and Naftali (1998), Kennedy (1999), and May and Zelikow (1997).

CHAPTER 14

The long-term effects of growing up in a culture of fear under a nuclear (or biological, or chemical) cloud is just beginning to attract the interests of cold war scholars. I have been influenced in my thinking by the theoretical convergence of two lines of academic thought: George Gerbner's cultivation theory (see Gerbner and Morgan 2002) and the "rethinking" of cold war culture characterized by Tuttle (2001). In my view, these theoretical orientations can benefit from recent memoirs, personal narratives, and interviews that ask new questions about the links between history, culture, psychology, and media.

CHAPTER 15

The life and work of J. Edgar Hoover has been exhaustively chronicled and critiqued. I have benefited from Gentry (1991) and Summers (1993).

The JFK assassination has spawned a vast investigative, film, novel, and analytical legacy. I don't pretend to represent any particular part of it in the account given in this chapter, but I do—for the record—concur with the conclusion provided by the House of Representatives Special Committee on Assassinations in 1979: the JFK assassination, based on the evidence available, was probably the result of a conspiracy. I am interested in the longer-term influences of that assassination—the images of it, the controversies surrounding it—on our culture, our views of our government, and our personal lives. One excellent example is found in Trujillo (1993).

CHAPTER 16

Senator Stuart Symington's visit to our house became part of our family story and we relived it over the years. I still have no clear notion of what the visit was about. I gained additional information about the senator from Olson (2003) and Wellman (1960).

CHAPTER 17

My understanding of the politics and the role of student movements in Philadelphia during the 1960s has benefited recently from Lyons (2003). See also Paolantonio (1994), which presents a fascinating study of personality and its influence on political life.

The history and operations of CHAOS are described in the "Supplementary Detailed Staff Reports on Intelligence Activities and the Rights of Americans, Book III" in the Final Report of the Select Committee to Study Governmental Operations with Respect to Intelligence Activities (April 23, 1976). The Rockefeller Report (U.S. Commission on CIA Activities Within the United States 1975) offers the best footnote on domestic surveillance conducted by the CIA under orders from the White House. That footnote is dedicated to Operation CHAOS. The Church Committee report (April 1976) is also essential reading, and the relevant section devoted to Operation CHAOS is conveniently available online at http://www.icdc.com/~paulwolf/cointelpro/churchfinalreportIIIi.htm (accessed September 28, 2005).

A decidedly more acidic interpretation of Operation CHAOS is available on Verne Lyons's website (http://www.serendipity.li/cia/lyon.html; accessed September 28, 2005). Lyons is a former CIA officer and the essay "Domestic Surveillance: The History of Operation CHAOS" is reprinted there. For a broader view of the CIA's covert operations strategies during this period, see Agee (1975). For an understanding of the role of Richard Helms in it, see Powers (1979).

CHAPTER 18

As I was editing this chapter the news broke that W. Mark Felt, the number-two man at the FBI during the Nixon Watergate scandal, admitted to being "Deep Throat." Felt was pissed at being passed over by Nixon for director of the FBI after J. Edgar Hoover died, on May 2, 1972. He also had a friendly information-exchange relationship with Bob Woodward of the *Washington Post*. And he claimed to know enough about what the White House was covering up to provide tips to Woodward and his investigative partner Carl Bernstein. For many of us, Deep Throat—whatever his personal motivation—was a hero because he led the reporters to the cover-up, which in turn led to the scandalous resignation of Richard Nixon. Today, in our post-9/11 culture, with large questions being asked about the constitutional protections afforded to reporters to keep secret their sources, I have to wonder whether another W. Mark Felt would step forward to tell reporters what he knew about a cover-up in the current Bush administration. I have to wonder whether a pair of investigative reporters would risk jail sentences to protect their sources. I doubt it. Finding out that Deep Throat was Felt is a resolution of a thirty-year mystery, but his coming forward now provides only an imperfect denouement. Felt, who for years has been named in the press as a leading suspect, is finally revealed to be the man after all. As a June 1, 2005, editorial in the *New York Times* put it, the announcement by Felt was a little like finding out that Superman was, in fact, Clark Kent. Furthermore, his reasons for doing it are not quite as grand as we collectively imagined. And, in the end, there are still doubts about the authenticity of his claim. John Dean, an indicted co-conspirator and one of Nixon's White House lawyers, said that Felt didn't have the access to the White House or the time to rearrange flowerpots on window ledges, and perhaps there were other people, still unnamed, who were involved. Not all endings are ultimately satisfying.

REFERENCES CITED

Agee, Phillip. 1975. *Inside the Company: CIA Diary.* New York: Stonehill.

Altheide, David L. 2002. *Creating Fear: News and the Construction of Crisis.* New York: Aldine De Gruyter.

Ambrose, Stephen E. 1981. *Ike's Spies: Eisenhower and the Espionage Establishment.* Garden City, NY: Doubleday & Company.

Andrew, Christopher. 1995. *For the President's Eyes Only: Secret Intelligence and the American Presidency from Washington to Bush.* New York: HarperCollins.

Athens, Lonnie. 1992. *The Creation of Dangerous Violent Criminals.* Urbana: University of Illinois Press.

———— 1994. "The Self as a Soliloquy." *Sociological Quarterly* 35:521–532.

Bamford, James. 2001. *Body of Secrets: Anatomy of the Ultra-Secret National Security Agency—From the Cold War Through the Dawn of a New Century.* New York: Doubleday.

Barthes, Roland. 1977. *Image, Music, Text.* New York: Hill and Wang.

Bateson, Gregory. 1936. *Naven.* Repr., Palo Alto, CA: Stanford University Press, 1958.

———. 1980. *Mind and Nature: A Necessary Unity.* New York: Bantam Books.

———. 1991. *A Sacred Unity: Further Steps to an Ecology of Mind.* New York: HarperCollins.

————. 2000. *Steps to An Ecology of Mind: Collected Essays in Anthropology, Psychiatry, Evolution, and Epistemology*. Chicago: University of Chicago Press.

Bateson, Gregory, and Jurgen Ruesch. 1951. *Communication: The Social Matrix of Psychiatry*. New York: W. W. Norton.

Bayer, Robert. 2002. *See No Evil: The True Story of a Ground Soldier in the CIA's War on Terrorism*. New York: Three Rivers Press.

Bernhard, Nancy E. 1999. *U.S. Television News and Cold War Propaganda, 1947–1960*. Cambridge: Cambridge University Press.

Bostdorff, Denise M. 2003. "George W. Bush's Post-September 11 Rhetoric of Covenant Renewal: Upholding the Faith of the Greatest Generation." *The Quarterly Journal of Speech* 89:293–319.

Boyer, Paul. 1985. *By the Bomb's Early Light: American Thought and Culture at the Dawn of the Atomic Age*. New York: Pantheon.

Buckley Jr., William F. 2000. *Spytime: The Undoing of James Jesus Angleton*. New York: Harcourt.

Bull, Anna. 1997. "Italy and the Legacy of the Cold War." *Occasional Paper No. 8*, European Research Institute, University of Birmingham (UK).

Burke, Kenneth. 1989. *Symbols and Society*. Chicago: University of Chicago Press.

Burleigh, Nina. 1999. *A Very Private Woman: The Life and Unsolved Murder of Presidential Mistress Mary Meyer*. New York: Bantam Books.

Bush, George W. Address before a joint session of Congress, September 20, 2001.

Colby, William, and Peter Forbath. 1978. *Honorable Men: My Life in the CIA*. New York: Simon & Schuster.

Colby, William, and James McCargar. 1989. *Lost Victory: A Firsthand Account of America's Sixteen-Year Involvement in Vietnam*. Chicago: Contemporary Books.

Copeland, Miles. 1969. *The Game of Nations: The Immorality of Power Politics*. New York: Simon & Schuster.

Corson, William R., Susan J. Trento, and Joseph. J. Trento. 1989. *Widows: Three Spies and the Wives They Left Behind*. New York: Crown.

Curtin, Michael. 1995. *Redeeming the Wasteland: Television Documentary and Cold War Politics*. New Brunswick, NJ: Rutgers University Press.

Del Pero, Mario. 2001. "The United States and 'Psychological Warfare' in Italy, 1948–1955." *The Journal of American History* 87:1–31.

————. 2002. "Containing Containment: Rethinking Italy's Experience during the Cold War." Working Paper #2, The Cold War as Global Conflict, International Center for Advanced Studies, New York University.

Denzin, Norman K. 2002. "Cultural Studies in America after September 11, 2001." *Cultural Studies—Critical Methodologies* 2:5–9.

———. 2004. "The War on Culture, the War on Truth." *Cultural Studies—Critical Methodologies* 4:137–143.

Divine, Robert. 1981. *Eisenhower and the Cold War*. New York: Oxford University Press.

Dorril, Stephen. 2000. *MI6: Fifty Years of Special Operations*. London: Fourth Estate.

Drake, Richard. 2004. "Italian Communism and Soviet Terror." *Journal of Cold War Studies* 6:57–63.

Dulles, Allen. 1965. *The Craft of Intelligence*. New York: Signet Books.

Eisenberg, E., and H. L. Goodall. 2004. *Organizational Communication: Balancing Creativity and Constraint*. 4th ed. New York: Bedford/St. Martin's.

Ellul, Jacques. 1955. *The Technological Society*. Repr., New York: Vintage, 1967.

Evans, Joseph C. 1996. "Berlin Tunnel Intelligence: A Bumbling KGB." *International Journal of Intelligence and Counterintelligence* 9:43–50.

Field, Hermann, and Kate Field. 1999. *Trapped in the Cold War: The Ordeal of an American Family*. Stanford, CA: Stanford University Press.

Fiedler, Leslie. 1965. "When You Comin' Back to the Boat, Huck Honey?" In *Love and Death in the American Novel*. Repr., New York: Anchor Press, 1998.

Fisher, Walter R. 1984. "Narration as Human Communication Paradigm: The Case of Public Moral Argument." *Communication Monographs* 51:1–22.

Fitzgerald, Francis Scott. 1924. *The Great Gatsby*. Repr., New York: Scribner, 2004.

Foucault, Michel. 1972. *The Archaeology of Knowledge*. Trans. A. Sheridan Smith. New York: Harper and Row.

Fursenko, Aleksandr, and Timothy Naftali. 1998. *One Hell of a Gamble: Khrushchev, Castro and Kennedy 1958–1964*. New York: W. W. Norton.

Gaddis, John Lewis. 1998. *We Now Know: Rethinking Cold War History*. New York: Oxford University Press.

Gallagher, Catherine, and Stephen Greenblatt. 2001. *Practicing the New Historicism*. Chicago: University of Chicago Press.

Gentry, Curt. 1991. *J. Edgar Hoover: The Man and the Secrets*. New York: Plume.

Gerbner, George, and Michael Morgan. 2002. *Against the Mainstream: The Selected Works of George Gerbner*. New York: Peter Lang.

Ginsberg, Allen. 1988. *Collected Poems, 1947–1980*. New York: Harper Perennial.

Giroux, Henry A. 2002. "Democracy and the Politics of Terrorism: Community, Fear, and the Suppression of Dissent." *Cultural Studies—Critical Methodologies* 2:334–348.

———. 2004. "Beyond Belief: Religious Fundamentalism and Cultural Politics in the Age of George W. Bush." *Cultural Studies—Critical Methodologies* 4:415–426.

Goodall, H.L. 1983. "The Nature of Analogic Discourse." *The Quarterly Journal of Speech* 69:171–179.

———. 1989. *Casing a Promised Land: The Autobiography of an Organizational Detective as Cultural Ethnographer*. Carbondale: Southern Illinois University Press.

———. 1991. *Living in the Rock n Roll Mystery*. Carbondale: Southern Illinois University Press.

———. 1994. "Living in the Rock n Roll Campaign, Or: Mystery, Media, and the American Public Imagination." In *Bill Clinton on Stump, State, and Stage: The Rhetorical Road to the White House*, ed. Steven A. Smith, 365–415. Fayetteville: University of Arkansas Press.

———. 1996. *Divine Signs: Connecting Spirit to Community*. Carbondale: Southern Illinois University Press.

———. 2000. *Writing the New Ethnography*. Walnut Creek, CA: AltaMira Press.

———. 2002. "Fieldnotes from Our War Zone: Living in America During the Aftermath of September Eleventh." *Qualitative Inquiry* 8:74–89.

———. 2004a. "Deep Play in a Poker Rally: A Sunday Among the Ferraristi of Long Island." *Qualitative Inquiry* 10:731–766.

———. 2004b. "Narrative Ethnography and Applied Communication Research." *Journal of Applied Communication Research* 32:185–194.

———. 2005. "Narrative Inheritance: A Nuclear Family with Toxic Secrets." *Qualitative Inquiry* 11:492–513.

———. 2006. "Why We Must Win the War on Terror: Communication, Narrative, and the Future of National Security." *Qualitative Inquiry* 12 (in press).

Goodall, H. L., Gerald L. Wilson, and Christopher L. Waagen. 1986. "The Performance Appraisal Interview: An Interpretive Reassessment." *The Quarterly Journal of Speech* 72:74–87.

Green, David. 1982. *Blenheim Palace*. Oxford: Alden Press.

Grose, Peter. 1994. *Gentleman Spy: The Life of Allen Dulles*. Boston: Houghton Mifflin.

Grossman, Andrew D. 2001. *Neither Dead nor Red: Civilian Defense and American Political Development During the Early Cold War*. New York: Routledge.

Gunn, Joshua. 2004. "The Rhetoric of Exorcism: George W. Bush and the Return of Political Demonology." *Western Journal of Communication* 68:1–23.

Gusdorf, Georges. 1979. *Speaking (La Parole)*. Evanston, IL: Northwestern University Press.

Hartnett, Stephen J., and Laura A. Stengrim. 2004. "'The Whole Operation of Deception': Reconstructing President Bush's Rhetoric of Weapons of Mass Destruction." *Cultural Studies—Critical Methodologies* 4:152–198.

Hersh, Burton. 1992. *The Old Boys: The American Elite and the Origins of the CIA*. New York: Scribner.

Hersh, Seymour. 1974. "Huge CIA Operations Reported in U.S. Against Anti-War Forces, Other Dissidents in Nixon Years." *New York Times*, December 22.

Hitz, Frederick P. 2004. *The Great Game: The Myth and Reality of Espionage*. New York: Alfred A. Knopf.

Holstein, James A., and Jaber F. Gubrium. 2000. *The Self We Live By: Narrative Identity in a Postmodern World*. New York: Oxford University Press.

Hood, William. 1994. *Myths Surrounding James Angleton: Lessons for American Counterintelligence*. Washington, DC: Consortium for the Study of Intelligence.

Howard, Russell D., and Reid L. Sawyer. 2004. *Terrorism and Counterterrorism: Understanding the New Security Environment*. New York: McGraw-Hill.

Imber-Black, Evan. 1998. *The Secret Life of Families: Truth-Telling, Privacy, and Reconciliation in a Tell-All Society*. New York: Bantam.

Ivie, Robert L. 2003. "Evil Enemy Versus Agonistic Other: Rhetorical Constructions of Terrorism." *The Review of Education, Pedagogy, and Cultural Studies* 25:181–200.

Johnson, Loch K. 1986. *A Season of Inquiry: The Senate Intelligence Investigation*. Lexington: University of Kentucky Press.

———. 1989. *America's Secret Power: The CIA in a Democratic Society*. New York: Oxford University Press.

Kahn, David. 1967. *The Codebreakers: The Story of Secret Writing*. New York: Macmillan.

Kelly, Saul, and Anthony Gorst, eds. 2000. *Whitehall and the Suez Crisis*. London: Routledge.

Kennedy, Robert F. 1999. *Thirteen Days: A Memoir of the Cuban Missile Crisis*. New York: W. W. Norton

Kessler, Ron. 1994. *Inside the CIA*. New York: Pocket Books.

Knightley, Phillip. 1986. *The Second Oldest Profession: Spies and Spying in the Twentieth Century*. New York: W. W. Norton.

———. 1988. *The Master Spy: The Story of Kim Philby*. New York: Alfred A. Knopf.

Kolb, Larry. 2005. *Overworld: The Life and Times of a Reluctant Spy*. New York: Riverhead Books.

Kuznick, Peter J., and James Gilbert, eds. 2001. *Rethinking Cold War Culture*. Washington, DC: Smithsonian Institute Press.

Lane, Abbe. 1992. *But Where Is the Love?* New York: Warner Books.

Littell, Robert. 2003. *The Company: A Novel of the CIA*. New York: Penguin.

Lucas, Scott. 1999. *Freedom's War: The US Crusade Against the Soviet Union, 1945–56*. Manchester, UK: Manchester University Press.

Luce, Clare Boothe. 1955. "American Diplomacy at Work: An Address, by The Honorable Clare Boothe Luce," Severance Hall, Cleveland, Ohio, March 23.

Lutz, Catherine. 2002. "The Wars Less Known." *South Atlantic Quarterly* 101:285–296.

Lyons, Joseph. 1989. *Clare Boothe Luce*. New York: Chelsea House.

———. 2003. *The People of This Generation: The Rise and Fall of the New Left in Philadelphia*. Philadelphia: University of Pennsylvania Press.

Mangold, Tom. 1991. *Cold Warrior James Jesus Angleton: The CIA's Master Spy Hunter*. New York: Simon & Schuster.

Marchetti, Victor. 1974. *The CIA and the Cult of Intelligence*. New York: Alfred A. Knopf.

Marquis, Thomas B. 1973. *Cheyenne and Sioux*. Stockton, CA: University of the Pacific Press.

Martin, David C. 1980. *Wilderness of Mirrors*. New York: Harper & Row.

Martin, Ralph G. 1991. *Henry and Clare: An Intimate Portrait of the Luces*. New York: Putnam.

May, Elaine Tyler. 1999. *Homeward Bound: American Families in the Cold War Era*. New York: Basic Books.

May, Ernest R., and Philip Zelikow. 1997. *The Kennedy Tapes: Inside the White House During the Cuban Missile Crisis*. Cambridge, MA: Harvard University Press.

McEnaney, Laura. 2000. *Civil Defense Begins at Home: Militarization Meets Everyday Life in the Fifties*. Princeton, NJ: Princeton University Press.

McIntosh, Elizabeth P. 1998. *Sisterhood of Spies: The Women of the OSS.* Annapolis, MD: The Naval Institute Press.

McKee, Mary J. 1962. "Congresswoman Clare Boothe Luce: Her Rhetoric Against Communism." PhD diss., University of Illinois, Urbana-Champaign.

McLaren, Peter. 2003. "The Dialectics of Terrorism: A Marxist Reponse to September 11." In *9/11 in American Culture*, ed. by Norman K. Denzin and Yvonna S. Lincoln. Walnut Creek, CA: AltaMira Press.

Medhurst, Martin. 1997. *Cold War Rhetoric: Strategy, Metaphor, Ideology.* East Lansing: Michigan State University Press.

Medhurst, Martin, and Herbert W. Brands, eds. 2000. *Critical Reflections on the Cold War: Linking Rhetoric and History.* College Station: Texas A&M University Press.

Morris, Benny. 1997. *Israel's Border Wars, 1949–1956: Arab Infiltration, Israeli Retaliation, and the Countdown to the Suez War.* Oxford: Clarendon Press.

Moseley, Leonard. 1978. *Dulles: A Biography of Eleanor, Allen, and John Foster Dulles and Their Family Network.* New York: The Dial Press.

Murphy, David E., Sergei A. Kondrashev, and George Bailey. 1997. *Battleground Berlin: CIA vs. KGB in the Cold War.* New Haven, CT: Yale University Press.

Murphy, James M. 2003. "Our Mission and Our Moment: George W. Bush and September 11th." *Rhetoric & Public Affairs* 6:607–632.

Murphy, Robert. 1964. *Diplomat among Warriors.* Garden City, NY: Doubleday & Company.

National Commission on Terrorist Attacks. 2004. *The 9/11 Commission Report.* New York: W. W. Norton.

Neff, Donald. 1981. *Warriors at Suez: Eisenhower Takes America into the Middle East.* New York: The Linden Press/Simon & Schuster.

Newman, Robert P. 1989. *The Cold War Romance of Lillian Hellman and John Melby.* Chapel Hill: University of North Carolina Press.

Olson, James C. 2003. *Stuart Symington: A Life.* Columbia: University of Missouri Press.

Page, Bruce, David Leitch, and Phillip Knightley. 1968. *The Philby Conspiracy.* Garden City, NY: Doubleday & Company.

Paoloantonio, S. A. 1994. *Frank Rizzo: The Last Big Man in Big City America.* Philadelphia: Camino Books.

Parry-Giles, Sean. 2002. *The Rhetorical Presidency, Propaganda, and the Cold War, 1945–1955.* New York: Praeger.

Pechatnov, Vladamir. 2001. "Exercise in Frustration: Soviet Foreign Propaganda in the Early Cold War, 1945–47." *Cold War History* 1:1–27.

Perry, Roland. 2005. *Last of the Cold War Spies: The Life of Michael Straight—the Only American in Britain's Cambridge Spy Ring.* Cambridge, MA: Da Capo Press.

Philby, Eleanor. 1968. *The Spy I Married.* New York: Ballantine Books.

Philby, Kim. 1968. *My Silent War.* New York: Ballantine Books.

Powers, Thomas. 1979. *The Man Who Kept Secrets: Richard Helms and the CIA.* New York: Alfred A. Knopf.

———. 2002. *The Intelligence Wars: American Secret History from Hitler to Al-Qaeda.* New York: New York Review of Books.

Radu, Michael. 2002. "Terrorism After the Cold War: Trends and Challenges." *Orbis* (spring):275–287.

Rhodes, Richard. 2000. *Why They Kill: The Discoveries of a Maverick Criminologist.* New York: Vintage Books.

Richardson, John H. 2005. *My Father the Spy.* New York: HarperCollins.

Riegel, Robert. 1964. *The Story of the Western Railroads: From 1852 Through the Reign of the Giants.* Lincoln: University of Nebraska Press.

Rositzke, Harry. 1977. *The CIA Secret Operations.* Boulder, CO: Westview Press.

Ryan, D. 2004. "Framing September 11: Rhetorical Device and the Photographic Opinion." *European Journal of American Culture* 23:5–20.

Saunders, Frances Stonor. 1999. *The Cultural Cold War: The CIA and the World of Arts and Letters.* New York: The New Press.

Shadegg, Stephen C. 1970. *Clare Booth Luce: A Biography.* New York: Simon & Schuster.

Sheed, Wilfred. 1982. *Clare Boothe Luce.* New York: E. P. Dutton.

Shore, Cris. 1990. *Italian Communism: The Escape From Leninism.* London: Pluto Press.

Shorris, Earl. 1982. *Scenes from Corporate Life.* New York: Penguin.

Smith, Denis Mack. 1997. *Modern Italy: A Political History.* Ann Arbor: University of Michigan Press.

Smith, Laurence D. 1944. *Cryptography.* London: George Allen and Unwin.

Summers, Anthony. 1993. *Official and Confidential: The Secret Life of J. Edgar Hoover.* New York: Putnam,

Taylor, Bryan. 2002. "Organizing the 'Unknown Subject': Los Alamos, Espionage, and the Politics of Biography." *Quarterly Journal of Speech* 88:33–49.

Taylor, Bryan, and Stephen J. Harnet. 2000. "National Security, and All that It Implies . . . : Communication and (Post) Cold War Culture." *Quarterly Journal of Speech* 86:465–487.

Taylor, Bryan, William J. Kinsella, Stephen P. Depoe, and Mary S. Metzler. 2005. "Nuclear Legacies: Communication, Controversy, and the U.S. Nuclear Weapons Production Complex." *Communication Yearbook* 29:363–409.

Tobin, Kathleen A. 2002. "The Reduction of Urban Vulnerability: Revisiting 1950s American Suburbanization as Civil Defense." *Cold War History* 2:1–32.

Trento, Joseph J. 2005. *The Secret History of the CIA*. New York: Carroll & Graf.

Trujillo, Nick. 1993. "Interpreting November 22: A Critical Ethnography of an Assassination Site." *Quarterly Journal of Speech* 79:447–466.

Tuttle, William M. Jr. 2001. "America's Children in an Era of War, Hot and Cold: The Holocaust, the Bomb, and Child Rearing in the 1940's." In *Rethinking Cold War Culture*, ed. by Peter J. Kuznick and James Gilbert. Washington, DC: Smithsonian Institution Press.

U.S. Commission on CIA Activities Within the United States (Rockefeller Commission). 1975. *Report to the President* (June). Washington, DC: U.S. Government Printing Office.

U.S. Senate Select Committee to Study Government Operations with Respect to Intelligence Activities (Church Committee). 1975–76. Final Report, Books I–VI. Washington, DC: U.S. Government Printing Office.

Varble, Derek. 2003. *The Suez Crisis 1956 (Essential Histories)*. Oxford: Osprey Publishing.

Weick, Karl. 1995. *Sensemaking in Organizations*. Thousand Oaks, CA: Sage.

Wellman, Paul. 1960. *Stuart Symington: Portrait of a Man With a Mission*. Garden City, NY: Doubleday.

West, Nigel. 1983. *The Circus: MI5 Operations 1945–72*. New York: Stein & Day.

———. 1989. *Molehunt: Searching for Soviet Spies in MI5*. New York: William Morrow.

White, John K. 1998. "Seeing Red: The Cold War and American Public Opinion." Conference on the Power of Free Inquiry and Cold War International History, September 26, U.S. National Archives and Records Administration at College Park, MD.

Whitfield, Stephen J. 1996. *The Culture of the Cold War*. 2nd ed. Baltimore: Johns Hopkins University Press.

Winkler, Allan W. 1993. *Life Under a Cloud: American Anxiety About the Atom*. New York: Oxford University Press.

Winks, Robin W. 1987. *Cloak and Gown: Scholars in the Secret War 1939–1961*. New York: William Morrow.

Wise, David. 1992. *Molehunt: The Secret Search for Traitors that Shattered the CIA*. New York: Random House.

Wise, David, and Thomas B. Ross. 1964. *The Invisible Government*. New York: Random House.

Wright, Peter, with Paul Greengrass. 1987. *Spycatcher: The Candid Autobiography of a Senior Intelligence Officer*. New York: Viking.

Wyden, Peter. 1989. *The Inside Story of a Divided Berlin*. New York: Simon & Schuster.

ARCHIVAL SOURCES

Cold War Project. Harvard University.

Allen Dulles Papers. Seeley G. Mudd Manuscript Library. Princeton University.

John Foster Dulles Papers. Seeley G. Mudd Manuscript Library. Princeton University.

Frances E. Warren Air Force Base archives. Cheyenne, Wyoming.

National Archives and Records Administration. College Park, Maryland.

National Military Archives. St. Louis, Missouri.

National Civilian Archives. St. Louis, Missouri.

Naval Air Corps Naval Air Museum. Pensacola, Florida.

Army Air Corps Museum. Fort Rucker, Alabama.